One Day in December

One Day in December

Celia Sánchez and the Cuban Revolution

NANCY STOUT

MONTHLY REVIEW PRESS

New York

Library of Congress Cataloging-in-Publication Data
—
Stout, Nancy.
  One day in December : Celia Sanchez and the Cuban Revolution / Nancy Stout
; foreword by Alice Walker.
      pages cm
  Includes bibliographical references and index.
  ISBN 978-1-58367-317-1 (cloth : alk. paper) 1. Sanchez Manduley, Celia,
1920–1980. 2. Women revolutionaries—Cuba—Biography. 3.
Revolutionaries—Cuba—Biography. 4. Cuba—History—Revolution,
1959—Biography. 5. Castro, Fidel, 1926—Friends and associates. I.
Title.
  F1788.22.S26S76 2013
  972.9106′4092—dc23
  [B]
                                    2012045594

Monthly Review Press
146 West 29th Street, Suite 6W
New York, New York 10001

www.monthlyreview.org

5 4 3 2 1

Contents

Foreword
by Alice Walker

NOTHING MAKES ME MORE HOPEFUL than discovering another human being to admire. My wonder at the life of Celia Sánchez, a revolutionary Cuban woman virtually unknown to Americans, has left me almost speechless. In hindsight, loving and admiring her was bound to happen, once I knew her story. Like Frida Kahlo, Zora Neale Hurston, Rosa Luxemburg, Agnes Smedley, Fannie Lou Hamer, Josephine Baker, Harriet Tubman, or Aung San Suu Kyi, Celia Sánchez was that extraordinary expression of life that can, every so often, give humanity a very good name.

A third of a century ago I saw a photograph of Celia taken twenty years before, just after she and her fellow revolutionaries became the official Cuban government. She was in the uniform of the Cuban rebel army, thin as a rail, her dark hair cut very short. Her face was gray and drawn, and she was (I believe) smoking a cigarette. Knowing her life story now more fully, I realize that lung cancer would contribute to her early death, which came close to the time I saw that picture.

I SAT DOWN TO READ *One Day in December* with little notion that it would affect me so deeply. I read it through, then immediately turned to the first page and read the entire more than four-hundred-page manuscript again. I had the sensation I experienced the first time I saw a Frida Kahlo painting, probably the self-portrait of

Frida wearing the necklace of thorns with a dead hummingbird attached: I knew life for women, and for a certain kind of creative rebel, whether female or male, a suffering, creative, and utterly devoted-to-life rebel, would never be the same. This book about Celia Sánchez produces a sensation like that. Filled with amazing revelations and documentations of a revolutionary woman whose life seems to me exactly the *medicina* our desperately flailing societies and countries are crying for. A clear vision of what balanced female leadership can be; and, even more to the point, what a truly egalitarian revolutionary leadership of female and male partners might look like.

Yes, the male we're talking about here is *el Jefe*, Fidel Castro. Revealed in this book to be brave and conscientious, also at times almost comically naïve, but unfaltering in his devotion and service to the people of Cuba. The most telling aspect of this was his adoption, along with Celia, of numerous Cuban children, many of whom had lost their parents during the Revolution. Not only did the two adopt these children but, during long years of assassination attempts and other social and political dramas of the most hair-raising sort, they managed to raise them.

Amazingly, Fidel and Celia worked together long before they ever met (sending each other covert messages detailing the work to be done); when they did meet they remained for the most part inseparable until the day of her death. But were they lovers? This is the question that, while Celia lived, obsessed Cubans and non-Cubans alike. Reading this book one sees something so fascinating, so precious, so good for us, that the question loses all meaning. We, in most of our relationships with one another, are headed somewhere else (other, for instance, than conventional marriage—very good news in my opinion) and these two offer a model of a revolutionary partnership that *thrived*. What they did in moments of privacy is, as this biography sees things, chiefly their own affair. But the question, in subtler forms, is considered. Whether, or to what extent, they were lovers, they were *beloveds*. Soul mates, *compañeros*, buddies, who reveled in each other and, together, devoted their lives to the cause of freeing the Cuban people from a brutal dictatorship and its legacy; while envisioning and working toward the creation of The New Person (sometimes referred to as "The New Man") and The New Society.

For much of the world Cuba already represents the future, if in fact there's one to be had. It has taught the world, especially the poor and First World–dominated countries, what it means to bear, over decades, the brunt of implacable, unrelenting and lethal hatred. Coming unfortunately, in Cuba's case, from its nearest neighbor, the United States. And shown how, even so, to move steadily forward guided by one's own understanding of one's needs.

The people in this book who were tortured, assassinated, disappeared, left me yearning for and missing them. For instance, Frank País—a young schoolteacher of twenty who was the other *comandante*, Fidel's partner in guiding the overthrow of the dictator, and Celia's primary contact in the early days of the Revolution—was murdered by Batista's police a month after his younger brother, Josué, had been killed by them. Their mother, Rosário, who claimed their bodies, is now gone too, yet I am still able, as I experience their story, to feel some of her agony. And that of two indomitable rebel women, Clodomira and Lydia, tortured sadistically before they died in the custody of the police. Much of the world continues to grieve the loss to humanity of Ché Guevara, assassinated so young and with so much still to offer, but he is far from the only astonishing person who is missing, and played a role in Celia's Revolution and her story.

Cuba has suffered so much I sometimes think of it as the country whose greatest wealth is the people's collective experience of deeply shared emotion. All those who struggled so bravely and died, sometimes horribly, were passionately loved and appreciated by the revolutionaries they left behind, and strengthened. I believe it is the glue of this mutually lived history, and the hope of creating a free and healthy Cuba that, even today, holds the country together. In this book we see some of the cost of seeking to live one's own way, charting and being drawn by one's own destiny. These fallen heroes, women and men, young and old, many of them revealed for the first time in this book, are cause to mourn.

But just as much, and also as revealed in this book, cause to celebrate, or simply to admire.

Reading this story we see precisely why Fidel Castro adored Celia Sánchez and why Ché and Celia were good friends. All three of these revolutionaries were persons of the highest moral character and integrity; deeply human also in their transgressions and imperfections, they were equals of the fiercest sort. There was also a price on all their heads.

We see something else as well: That the women of Cuba were full participants in the Revolution, combatants, covert operatives, and even co-instigators. It was in fact Celia and Haydée Santamaría who, early on and with other women, took up arms to fight the dictatorship. Celia, the daughter of a doctor, who frequently helped her father in his attendance on the poor, a society girl and high-school beauty queen, this woman who wore red lipstick, wide skirts, high heels (and would wear high heels with her rebel army uniform when she felt like it) took to the mountains of eastern Cuba with Fidel, Ché and other revolutionaries no less brave but far less known, and placed her life against the killing machine of wealth, corruption, and depravity that so insulted and wounded her beloved country.

I love this book. Biographer Nancy Stout is to be congratulated for her insightful, mature, and sometimes droll exploration of a profoundly liberated, adventuresome and driven personality. I love the life of Celia Sánchez, a life that was singular, *sui generis*, and true to its time of revolution and change in Cuban society, but also archetypal in its impact and relevance to all times of social struggle and revolt, including this one, in which Cuba's arch-enemy, the government of the United States of America, is also experiencing transformation. To fight the demons that have overtaken us, and to lead the world back to its senses, such an intrepid woman warrior would have to exist: a Durga, a Kali. A Celia.

Knowing her as well as I now believe I do, I ask myself, Did we meet? I remember visiting Cuba for the first time in 1978. Celia would have been very ill by then; she died in 1980. I do recall a visit to the Federation of Cuban Women and if I'm not mistaken I met Vilma Espín, another remarkable revolutionary, and perhaps Haydée Santamaria, whom I surely had "met" in the story of the torture and murder of her brother Abel, one of those captured after the attack on the Moncada garrison in 1953. I remember Haydée especially for her reply to the guard who brought her one of her brother's eyes: *If he would not talk, nor can I.*

I longed to learn the story of these women, so beloved of each other, so trusted and so true. Now I've learned part of it. This story will no doubt be another medicine for our time: how to be completely trustworthy in times of battle; how to set out together, as women, to change the world, with men (happily) beside us or without them.

I wrote the poem below during the Arab Spring, when the people of Egypt rose up to begin the necessary change of their own corrupt society. It is dedicated to the Egyptian people. It seeks to speak to Cubans as well, and their country rich in martyrs.

Our Martyrs

When the people
have won a victory
whether small
or large
do you ever wonder
at that moment
where the martyrs
might be?
They who sacrificed
themselves
to bring to life
something unknown
though nonetheless more precious
than their blood.
I like to think of them
hovering over us
wherever we have gathered
to weep and to rejoice;
smiling and laughing,
actually slapping each other's palms
in glee.
Their blood has dried
and become rose petals.
What you feel brushing your cheek
is not only your tears
but these.
Martyrs never regret
what they have done

having done it.
Amazing too
they never frown.
It is all so mysterious
the way they remain
above us
beside us
within us;
how they beam
a human sunrise
and are so proud.

CELIA, TOO, WAS A MARTYR, though she lived nearly sixty years and died of natural causes, if cancer can be called natural. I believe, though, that the deeply harrowing and stressful work she did as a revolutionary, including protecting Fidel, whom she loved, and whom she understood to be Cuba's rightful and destined leader, a leader always under attack, consumed her. Weighing on her also was the grief she had to repress when personal losses and tragedies intervened, in order to fulfill her duties to the Revolution and the country.

She always recalled their life up in the mountains. There, despite all kinds of hardship, they'd joined with families and clergy to witness marriages and baptisms, planted flowers, and conveyed battle news via radio broadcasts of music. In the steamiest days of August, they'd celebrated their leader's birthday party and their confidence of imminent victory with a party and ice cream cake.

May the example of Celia Sánchez's extraordinary life strengthen and encourage us. She kept records of virtually everything those around her did during the Revolution. In a way it is through this selfless wisdom, her caring about future rebels she saw coming to the place Cuba pioneered, that we most clearly see her.

Preface

BEFORE I KNEW that she was a designated hero, I became interested in the projects she created.

Celia Sánchez's name came up during my first trips to Cuba, in 1992 and 1993, when my assignment was to photograph architecture. And during my second series of trips, in 1995 and 1996, to research and document, through photography, Havana's famous cigar industry, her name continued popping up. I was surprised to learn that Celia had been the power behind Cuba's most profitable export cigar, the famous Cohiba, and to see a large portrait of her hanging in the factory that produces it. Her importance, the palpable essence of her power, impressed itself on me, but I had yet to learn about her association with Fidel and her role in the Revolution.

Those were especially bleak years, during the "special period," and a friend, photographer Raul Corrales, confronted by food shortages, remarked sharply, "If Celia were alive, things wouldn't be like this." I had no reason to doubt him but little grasp of what he meant. "She was a big player in this chess game, the Cuban Revolution, which exists, whether you North Americans like it or not. It exists."

LIKE MOST BIOGRAPHERS, I researched my subject's childhood, starting with her relationship to her mother, who died when Celia was six. Celia's father was a country doctor, a bit glamorous, with a taste for history and a library of fine books. I learned that Dr. Sánchez was a political activist who believed in social justice, a man who believed in a better future for all Cubans. I traveled to Manzanillo, and met the city's historian, Delio Orozco. We traveled down the coast, visiting the historian of Campechuela, who told me how Celia had escaped from the military police by hiding in a thicket of thorns. We went to the place where she was arrested. There, I began to sense that her greatness might reside not so much in the buildings she'd produced as in her willingness to risk everything to rid Cuba of false leaders who relied on backing from both the United States and the Mob. I sensed that she was something of an avenging angel. Considering what I knew of her father, that seemed very much in Celia's DNA.

I RETURNED TO CUBA in 2000 having made a decision to write a book, though not yet this book. The plan then was a study, in text and photos, of her architectural and design projects in Havana: the Coppelia Ice Cream Park, the Convention Center, Lenin Park, and the many workshops she opened to furnish these. These three flagship projects could constitute a huge accomplishment for any woman. I'd supplement my own photographs with archival selections provided by the Ministry of Construction.

I started, comfortably enough, by contacting the architect she hired for the Coppelia project, Mario Girona, whose family and hers were related. I widened my contacts to include the rest of the Girona clan. They all had known Celia since childhood, and her father and theirs were best friends. Highly educated, one with a career in the diplomatic service, one a painter, all had spent time in the United States, and all spoke English. They were longtime leftists, communists from the old Partido Socialista Popular (PSP), and Celia had spent the better part of 1948 with them in Brooklyn. One, who'd mostly stayed in Cuba, had run money to Castro in Mexico. They were all stylish and comfortable and lived in an award-winning building, on the 18th, 20th, and 21st floors. The seven months of that year I lived in Havana saw many regularly scheduled brownouts, or blackouts, and I had to walk up all those flights. Once up there, you tend to stay.

I spent many hours with the family. At some point, the diplomat, Celia Girona, said that they'd feel more at ease if I met Flavia. So she took me to see Celia's sister. From the start, my sources were intimate, and having participated in one way or another in the Revolution, were politically comfortable. The Gironas' only regret, seemingly, was not having fought in the Spanish Civil War.

QUITE A LOT HAD been written about Celia over the years, as my bibliography reflects, but there was, curiously, no biography, no single-source reference on her life. Which was a great piece of luck. Detective work, hunting things down, following leads, finding people, asking them questions, and visiting the sites of events is what I love. The necessity of doing that made my project inexhaustibly engaging, and gave this book a personality I hope befits its subject.

Another bit of good luck was an introduction to Argelia Fernandez, translator-interpreter at a series of art, design, and architecture lectures at the Ludwig Foundation. Argelia and Celia had met, when Argelia and her ambassador husband had been posted in Paris and Beirut. Whatever qualms the Cubans may have had about me as biographer of their national hero were laid to rest when they saw that I was in Argelia's hands. We developed a foolproof technique. Not just recording all interviews to transcribe later, I began to type "live" into my laptop as well. Each evening I'd go over the day's interview. If something didn't make sense, or had been a little shocking, Argelia and I would call our interviewee up and clarify: Is this what you said? Are you comfortable saying that? Argelia and I would discuss the meaning of a word, or we'd call in one of the old revolutionaries to verify what certain words, when used in the 1950s, in Oriente Province, meant. Or we'd contact members of the underground. We'd ask ourselves, Who else can tell us? And that could lead to another interview, another call. While we were nailing down the best translation and interpretation, we were, as it turned out, building confidence around town that the North Americana was trying to get it right.

Together, we talked to soldiers from the rebel army, then moved on to Celia's friends and neighbors, hailing from the eastern end of the island, people who had known her before and during the war. Gradually, I met other members of the Sánchez family, nieces and nephews, and people who worked for Celia, in her household. These were normal people who, like it or not, had ended up with a guerrilla fighter in the family. I found out what I could, and took an interest in everything they were willing to tell me. Ernestina Gonzalez, Celia's cook going back to her years running her father's house, drew a line at what she would discuss; she still worked for Fidel, and was reticent, as anyone would be, at discussing her employer. So we spoke about food, and I wrote down Celia's winning recipes for stuffed turkey and mango upside-down cake.

SINCE NO ONE had undertaken a biography, I found all these people who rightly considered themselves experts about the Celia they knew and loved. They had been waiting for someone to come hear their stories. My lead question was designed to put everyone on the same footing, and I hoped at ease. "Describe the first time you saw her," I began. "Tell me, too, where it was and an approximate time or date. What she wore, and how you recall her voice." I would add that I asked everyone I spoke with to do the same. People who were worried about saying the wrong thing soon relaxed. Later, I'd find out that people who'd spoken with me urged the more reluctant to go ahead. "She's interested in details," was the way they described me. Details became the sustaining element of my search and told me more about her and Fidel than anyone was ready to say.

It was only after hundreds of such conversations that I was granted access to documents held in the Archives of the Council of State, a collection of primary material from the Revolution, collected and organized by Celia herself. Each day, Argelia and I would go to the capital's Linea Street, to a building once a bank, now a vault of history. We sat in an alcove where a banker once sat, behind a glass door, and read the letters written in the Sierra Maestra. Celia's letters to her family and comrades, and theirs to her, informed and enriched what I'd learned in my many interviews and chats over coffee, juice and, occasionally, rum or beer. I went home, back to New York, to mull, digest, and organize Celia's story. I've never tired of reliving it. My book does include those building projects that were my starting point, but only at the very end.

I traveled to Cuba on every vacation, wrote on weekends and mornings before going to work. I am glad that it took ten years to complete because so much, for the reader, has changed. At the beginning, I was assured the American reader's ear—and eye, I suppose—could not possibly cope with Spanish names. But the world's more global now, and of course our ears can hear names in other languages. And the grittiness, maybe we should say the prevarication or paradoxes of guerrilla warfare, that once horrified some of my friends, even made others indignant, have become understandable in light of the Arab Spring.

MY VERSION OF CELIA'S STORY introduces many new characters to the history of the Cuban Revolution. Revolutionaries don't act alone. Celia was supported and saved, more than once, by her family and friends. I have always been aware that if I didn't include their parts of the story, too, maybe they wouldn't be told. Many times in our conversations they prompted me to ask myself: What does it mean to have a friend, a daughter, or a sister who is a revolutionary?

NANCY STOUT
New York City
November 2012

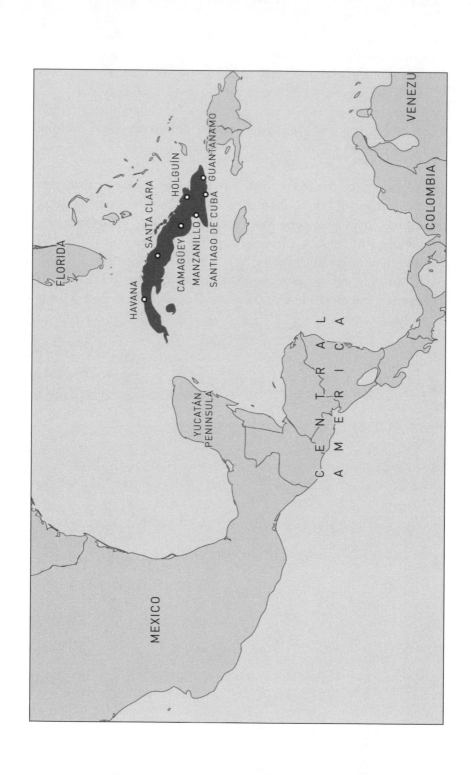

MAP OF CUBA (detail)

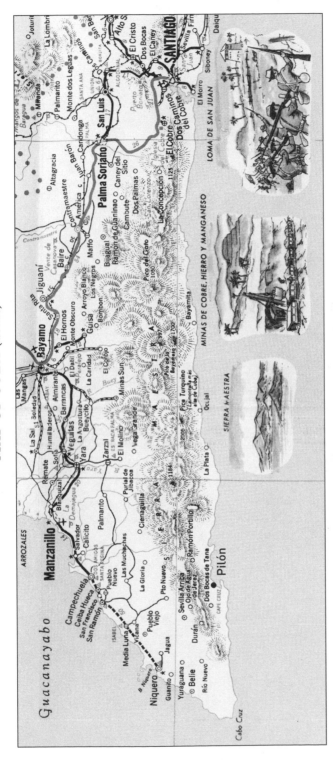

The seat of the Cuban Revolution was located in the southwestern region of Orient Province, seen here in a detail of an Esso road map, Mapa de las carreteras de la Republica de Cuba, published in 1956.
(*Courtesy of the Newberry Library.*)

Part I

PILÓN

A Tap on the Shoulder

IT IS A DAY IN PILÓN much like any other, except that it's late in the year, so it's cooler and there is more traffic in town. Here on the island's Caribbean coast, it is the start of the *zafra*. Sugarcane, bright green in the fields, arrives from the surrounding plantations on wagons that roll along the streets leading to the sugar mill. This is a factory town, but more reminiscent of the Wild West, with noise and bustle and farmers traveling the unpaved streets on horseback.

Celia, as always, wakes up early. Her bedroom sits to the back of the house, overlooking the patio and part of her garden. A door from her room leads directly onto a wide verandah. At its end, on a corner post, a radio occupies a shelf. She turns on the morning news, broadcast from Havana. The house is clapboard, L-shaped, single-storied, with verandahs on three sides, and stands elevated about three feet above humid ground. It is simple enough, but— and everyone agrees—it is the prettiest house in town. The furniture, mostly antique, includes Cuban pieces shaped from palm trees, woven from willow branches, or of pine clad in cowhide. The rest is imported: rattan from the Philippines, with slipcovered cushions, or her parents' wedding furniture, made in Italy, carved and upholstered, and purchased from her Spanish grandfather's department store in Manzanillo.

The Cabo Cruz sugar mill in Pilón, Oriente Province, Cuba. *(Courtesy of Oficina de Asuntos Históricos)*

Celia and her father live in one of the "yellow houses" inhabited mostly by mill management—called this not because they are painted that color but because they alone get a few hours' electricity each day, and glow at night. Pilón is company-owned.

At the end of the year the southeast coast enjoys a breeze off the Caribbean and the air is fresh; it is the best time of year for growing flowers. Standing on the verandah, she can admire the gardens wrapping the house on three sides. As she walks along the side porch, she says a few affectionate words to the birds in cages hung at intervals along this outdoor living space: the glider, hanging swing, and rocking chairs are all empty at this early hour. What sets the house apart, besides Celia's flair for decoration, are her father's collections of books, artifacts, and nineteenth-century Chinese porcelain pieces, their colors predominantly vibrant shades of rouge, with black, green, and gold leaf accents.

She takes beauty seriously: her hands are carefully manicured; she always wears makeup, paints her lips bright red. She dresses well, copying clothing shown in *Harper's Bazaar* and *Vogue*. She is extremely slender, but there is nothing flat about Celia. Errol Flynn later summed her up for the *L.A. Examiner*: "36-24-35." The full-skirted dresses she favors, the look of the 1950s, show off her bust and narrow waist.

She pulls her thick black hair into a ponytail. Her look is pretty, but doesn't stop there, surging over into another category suggesting, or revealing, maybe warning, that she is smart as well. Most telling is the way she shapes her eyebrows into thin, high arches with a line upward—like the accent marks over the final letters of José Martí.

In rope-soled *alpargatos*, with long multicolored ribbons tied securely around her ankles, she walks almost silently along the side porch to the front of the house where the porch gives onto the small front garden and the street. This section serves as the waiting room for patients. Coming in from surrounding plantations as well as the town, they await the doctor, who is still asleep. In this season, when the mill runs around the clock, patients begin to arrive at dawn or even wait through the night. Celia looks at the narrow strip of garden that separates the house from the street.

When I first visited Pilón in 1999, this little garden had dark red and bright green plants spelling CELIA on one side of the walk leading to the front door, FIDEL on the other.

CELIA'S LIFE FOLLOWS A CHARMING, even genteel pattern: each day she goes into the kitchen to greet Ernestina, the cook, and

The house and medical office of Dr. Manuel Sánchez. He and Celia moved to this house, in Pilón, in 1940. *(Courtesy of Oficina de Asuntos Históricos)*

they talk about various things: food and children, since Ernestina was expecting a child, and any bits of information Ernestina might have gleaned from neighbors on her walk to work. It is a conversation they have carried on for fifteen years.

Ernestina brews coffee, and Celia pours a cup and carries it to her father's room, at the back of the house next to her own. In the bathroom with its smooth floor, walls, and ceiling finished in wood, she fills the porcelain tub, mixing the water carefully to temperature, and opens the window looking out on the inner garden. The window sill is so low that a person could leap straight from the tub onto the patio, paved in stone and shaded by a gigantic mango tree.

As the bath fills, Celia lays out towels, hangs a freshly laundered medical jacket on a hook on the wall, placing her father's trousers, underwear, socks, and shoes nearby. Manuel Sánchez prefers lightweight Florsheims, American-made, but any attachment to the United States ends there, with those shoes.

In the kitchen, she'll have cocoa and toast as she goes over the day's menus. Celia has given Ernestina the menus for the week, loaded the pantry with provisions for the month—this is the tropics, even butter comes in a tin—and makes sure the vegetables and meat have been brought down from the family's farm in the foothills of the Sierra Maestra. Even though Ernestina must know every recipe by heart, it is important that each dish be prepared the way Dr. Sánchez likes it. While he bathes, dresses, and has breakfast, Celia readies his three medical rooms. In the *consultorio*, she'll file papers, straighten his desk, shelve books; in his surgery she'll lay out instruments; and finally she will check the medical bag he'll carry for afternoon house calls. She'll keep an eye out for Cleever, the gardener, and, if the need arises, have him saddle horses and help load them into a launch, so she and her father can travel along the coast, disembark, and ride up into the mountains to make remote house calls. She also will make sure that their Ford has a full tank.

It is now 7:00 a.m. The office is about to open and Celia is ready to schedule. She will talk to all the patients waiting on the porch and learn why they have come. Not all visits to Dr. Sánchez are medical. Pilón, despite the greater area's roughly 12,000 inhabitants, has no priest, and the nearest Catholic church with a priest in residence is in Niquero, about 25 miles away on roads

Celia (standing, left) was the middle child of eight children, preceded by Chela (Graciela), Silvia, the oldest, and Manuel Enrique. She was followed by Flávia (seated, front left), Orlando, in the middle, and Grisela. This studio photograph was taken in 1925 or 1926, before the birth of the baby Acacia and the death of Celia's mother, Acacia Manduley. *(Courtesy of Oficina de Asuntos Históricos)*

marked on a 1945 map as seasonal with long impassable periods. Few people go to Niquero from Pilón unless they own a car—and few people do—and coastal ferries do not go there and return on the same day. So the doctor is consulted about family matters, abuse, disputes, confessions, ambitions; he sometimes acts as a marriage broker. Such consultations go hand in hand with diagnosis and treatment of malaria, water-borne diseases, tuberculosis, malnutrition, gunshot and knife wounds, and alcoholism, as well as the more natural adjuncts of a rural doctor, dentistry and delivering children. Everybody comes to Dr. Sánchez; he does not insist or even expect that all his patients pay.

Celia has been following this daily pattern for fifteen years, and soon will begin the sixteenth. Or so things appear. She isn't stuck here in Pilón; she likes it and has a small side business selling accessories, for which she travels fairly often to Miami. She is her father's assistant; people call her "the doctor's daughter."

He delivered her on May 9, 1920, at 1:00 p.m. at home, in Media Luna, a town farther up the coast. He and his wife, Acacia, took her to the civil registry on October 16, 1920, and registered her as Celia Esther de los Desamparados Sánchez Manduley. Celia, after her grandfather Juan Sánchez y Barro's first wife, Celia Ros; they chose her middle name from the liturgical calendar, Nuestra Señora de los Desamparados, our lady of abandoned ones. She was a middle child of eight children, preceded by Silvia, Chela, and Manuel Enrique, and followed by Flávia, Griselda, Orlando, and the baby Acacia, named after their mother. Celia's mother died when she was six, and Celia had needed special attention following this separation because she had suffered mild anxiety neurosis, begun to cry frequently, developed a fever. Her father had kept her out of school, although she was nearly seven, to enter later with Flávia, who was a year and nine months younger. He taught her himself, and continued to do this even after she entered school, and hired special tutors for her.

Celia will work with her father until ten, or until he leaves the house for his small clinic in the sugar mill; then she is free to supervise the house or work on one of her many projects. She is an avid gardener, likes any activity that takes place outdoors, and she has a personality that is more cowgirl than housewife in this regard. Deep-sea fishing is her favorite sport, picnics her favorite

Celia and Flávia in a photographer's studio in Manzanillo, c. 1926. *(Courtesy of Oficina de Asuntos Históricos)*

pastime, and flowers—especially orchids—are her passion. Her main collaborator and sidekick, Cleever, is Jamaican, and lives with his wife at the edge of the garden. He keeps the shrubbery under control and implements her landscaping projects. The most recent are beds planted in patches of single colors to form designs. To make pocket money, she bakes and ices cupcakes, particularly during the harvest season, and Cleever takes them around town on a tray, knocking on back doors.

ON THIS PARTICULAR DAY, she sits at the big worktable in the kitchen, reading the paper while she makes telephone calls: simultaneously talking, reading, planning, eating lunch, raising money for Epiphany, or *Día de Reyes*, on January 6, when members of her Catholic charity would be giving out toys to Pilón's children. She had launched this activity in 1940, when she was twenty and new in town, setting a bit of a trend because the Catholic Church had never been active there, and not all that many of the area's residents were Catholics. Pentecostalists and Spiritualists thrived in Pilón and in the surrounding hills.

As 1956 approaches, it is again time to sell raffle tickets and prepare for the church supper on New Year's Eve. She'll go, before that, to Santiago and buy toys in bulk. This year, because the sugar workers have been on strike, there is little money around. Calling merchants, Celia reminds them to donate items for the raffle, or make pledges of food, pointing out that parents with little or no work are counting on these gifts.

Sometime on this day, she gets a message. If it comes by telephone, it is almost certainly coded. More likely it is spoken, by one of those who wait on the porch, who otherwise appear as patients to see the doctor. Fidel Castro sends word that his right-hand man, Pedro Miret, is coming to Pilón. He will be accompanied by the 26th of July Movement's national director of action, Frank País. Castro wants her to show them locations along the coast where he and his guerrilla fighters, returning from exile in Mexico, can land.

However it reaches her, the message is a tap on her shoulder, an invitation to become one of the instigators of the revolution that Castro had put in motion last July. Clearly Celia is not solely what she appears to be: a father's daughter, a civic-minded and house-proud woman, a member in good standing of the provincial gentry. Although, she is those things as well. It might be tempting to say she is unique in her place and time.

She was, in fact, fairly representative: a thirty-five-year-old woman in 1950s Cuba, looking for a person (it could have been nearly anyone), or political party, or any movement whose objective was to remove Fulgencio Batista from power.

Since Batista seized the presidency by a *coup d'état* in 1952, Fidel Castro had emerged in the minds of many as the person most likely to end the dictator's reign. He fearlessly, even rashly, had led an attack against the Moncada garrison, the national army's command headquarters in Santiago. The army reacted with extreme force, summarily executing most of the participants, but Fidel escaped the massacre, aided, in part, by the Archbishop of Santiago, Monseigneur Enrique Pérez Serrantes, Spanish, sent to Cuba in 1922, who had personally tried to protect the few survivors of the 26th of July attack. The Archbishop even went so far as to search for the young revolutionaries hiding in the hills, dressed in his cassock, carrying a cross, and (some say) using a megaphone. Fidel argued his own defense at trial, was imprisoned for a time, and released in May 1955. Less than two months later, he went into exile. Between his release from jail and his exile in Mexico City, he founded his revolutionary 26th of July Movement, named for the day in 1953 when the Moncada was attacked, and took on one goal: removing Batista. Celia had decided to join Fidel and his movement.

After the 1952 coup, she, along with everyone suspected of opposing the dictatorship, was put on the list of organizations considered dangerous. This wide range included her fellow members of the Orthodox Party, formed legitimately in the late 1940s and led by the popular Eduardo Chibás. Not intimidated by being listed, she became an activist. She joined two clandestine anti-Batista groups, headed by men in the coastal towns of Campechuela and Manzanillo.

Even before the attack on the Moncada or the formation of these groups, she and her father had carried out a personal project that had its own seditious element. On May 21, 1953, along with a small group of Martí scholars, they erected a statue of Martí on the top of Cuba's highest mountain, Turquino Peak in the Sierra Maestra.

This range extends along the southern coast. They approached from a small wharf on the Caribbean, from the southern side, where the land dips below sea level then soars to an elevation of 6,560 feet. The military had been intent on the packing case the group hauled up, imagining it held guns, so had kept up surveillance as it was transported to the mountain. But Manuel Sánchez's resistance project was conceptual: to place José Martí on the highest plane so he could reign over Cuba. The feat's oddity, as much as its symbolism, made an impression on military officials, who deemed all the participants suspicious. Later—during the Revolutionary War—Fidel would favor the lofty heights of Turquino's western companion, a peak called Caracas, and make his command post there, just above the La Plata River.

Those who became activists in response to Batista's seizure of power had already been struggling over more than a decade to reform Cuban politics. Ramón Grau had become president in 1944 through fraudulent elections. In 1947, a new political party was formed, officially named the Cuban People's Party but generally called the Orthodox, and Manuel Sánchez established a branch in Pilón. The party leader, Eduardo Chibás, even stayed in the doctor's house in 1948. He began his presidential campaign in Oriente Province, and there is a photograph of Celia wearing a hat, quite properly, sitting among the bigwigs on the platform. The new party showed its strength in the 1948 elections, increasing its power. Still, Carlos Prio Socarras, who succeeded Grau that year, was not appreciably better. It became obvious to Batista, who had ruled Cuba in the 1930s and was living in retirement in the United States, that even if he returned he would be unable to win the 1952 fall elections. It was that year he staged his coup. By the next year, police arrests and station house beatings were common. The police were out of control whenever and wherever they chose. Torture by police agents was so widespread, writes British historian Hugh Thomas, that Batista was compelled to give his "personal assurance" that it would be investigated.

The process by which Celia became a political person is not an unusual one. It is the story of how revolutionary and national liberation movements begin. It is precisely those without power— teachers, nurses, housewives, secretaries, telephone operators, cane workers, bus drivers—but with intelligence and self-esteem who quite legitimately make the decision to fight for their cause. The language of these movements addresses loss of freedom (this means free press, free speech, religious freedom, adequate incomes, adequate health care, access to a stable system of justice), and without access to those rights or freedoms, the participants come to the conclusion they have nothing to lose. So, they take chances. They organize. They become members of movements that are as passionate as they are imperfect.

HER VARIANT OF THAT STORY began in 1940, when Celia arrived in Pilón and embarked upon a rarely mentioned period of mourning. At fifteen, she had fallen in love with a young Spaniard, a Catalonian named Salvador Sadurní. He had arrived in Manzanillo after attending a U.S. business college, paid for by his uncle who planned to leave Sadurní his profitable hardware store in that city. Both Celia and her sister Flávia had left their father's house after outgrowing the local school in Media Lunato to attend the Institute, a private school for girls, in Manzanillo. There Celia started a club she called *Los Pavitos*, whose members were mostly her sisters, cousins, and their friends. They went to their favorite park, walking in groups of three or four, and when they saw someone they wanted to get to know, they would invite him to a beach party or picnic, which they then organized with elaborate care.

Salvador Sadurní, from Barcelona, was older (nineteen to Celia's fifteen), with a well-defined future. From friends, cousins, and a few photographs I've been able to piece together this relationship. Celia's friend Berta Llópiz has no doubt he was "crazy, crazy for her," and her Girona cousins added the telling detail that he and Celia, along with their friends, avidly followed the news of the Spanish Civil War, discussing whatever they'd read or heard on the radio. This was a cord that bound them all together, tightly; no matter where they were, these young friends—spunky, attractive, confident—would whip out a donation can that each carried along with school books, picnic baskets, and all their other paraphernalia, to collect money to support the Republican cause. I found out a bit more by probing Celia's brother-in-law, Pedro Álvarez, husband of her sister Chela. He affirmed that Sadurní was a great guy, "one of the best," but said that Salvador and Celia were each too independent to be a good couple. I pressed for a reason, and we

Celia with Salvador Sadurní in Media Luna, 1937. *(Courtesy of Oficina de Asuntos Históricos)*

agreed that Celia was still pretty young, only fifteen when she met Salvador, but they had stayed together and created an affectionate and devoted friendship. Pedro added that Sadurní spent his nights "singing to other women," and at this point Chela broke into the conversation to remind her husband that Salvador had performed several pieces of music written and dedicated to Celia on a local radio station. Slowly, another image of the young man began to emerge: he had been a businessman-musician who spent his free time writing and performing songs. He played the guitar, would hire and rehearse musicians, then take them with him like troubadours, to serenade under people's windows and perform the music he'd written. His group played at houses all over town. The families would send somebody down to the street with money and to thank the leader of these musical bands for including their household. He was flirting with tradition, strictly speaking; a man only serenades the girl he is in love with, and he had extended his serenades to an alarming number of women. Even at the age of eighty, Pedro still allowed a certain jealousy to creep to the surface when he spoke of Sadurní. But I could almost feel Chela's pride as she spoke of the midday or lunchtime radio programs

Cousin Olga Sánchez and her boyfriend, León Moreno, spent many weekends with Celia and her boyfriend, Salvador Sadurní, at the Sanchez farm in San Miguel del Chino, where this picture was taken in 1937. *(Courtesy of Oficina de Asuntos Históricos)*

when Salvador performed. At least two pieces of Sadurní's music had been for her sister: a tango called "Celia" and "Los Pavitos," named for her group of girlfriends, "those illusive queens who dance one day, swim the next, and that's the way they enjoy life." It was a good description of how the singer was charmed by this vibrant young girl who had a life of her own, championed her friends, and was, above all, busy and independent. In a world where a woman was supposed to be in tune with "the man who might be her future husband" and learn very early to be quietly available—"there for him"—she had at fifteen already turned the tables. She, and everyone else, seemed to be happy with Salvador. The couple was often seen together, and Celia was pleased with all this recognition in Manzanillo, at the time the third-largest city in Oriente Province.

She went home on weekends to work for her father in Media Luna, and Salvador Sadurní would come down the coast to visit her on Sunday, the day when both the hardware store and doctor's office were closed. Sometimes he came with his friends—bronzed, muscled, smartly dressed in bathing suits, on a yacht he had rented; a less glamorous boyfriend would have taken the coastal ferry— and they often went to the Sánchez family farm in the highlands of San Miguel del Chino. Celia's friends say she took it for granted that life was going to be wonderful.

SALVADOR DIED ON JUNE 9, 1937, when he was twenty-one and Celia had just turned seventeen. He injured his knee in a sports accident, and it ballooned up and required surgery. The swelling turned out to conceal an undetected aneurysm, and he bled to death on the operating table. As she watched him die through a window in the operating room door, he called out her name.

"Celia was horribly affected by his death," her cousin Nene states flatly. "She was in love with him, but only realized she was in love with him after he died." Others have said the same, but less succinctly. She lived in the moment; and that moment ended almost before she was fully aware it had arrived.

There were various suitors in the ten years after Salvador Sadurní's death, and, inevitably, some were boring and one or two were heartbreakers. Chela, who has lived in Miami forty years, is confident she would have married Sadurní "for sure, for sure." Flávia, in Havana, who was able to view the complete spectrum of Celia's life including her long friendship with Fidel, said that no one had been able to touch Celia's heart after Sadurní, that his ability to show his love for her became the gold standard. Flávia, who thinks carefully before speaking, added an astonishing comment: "I am under the impression that she really fell in love with Sadurní, and when he died, she was inoculated against love."

Celia became something of a widow. Outwardly, she developed a rash, a skin ailment that lingered. People felt sorry for her; they already viewed Manuel's children tragically, as their mother had died young. The year after Sadurní died, when the town held its festival, the Feast of St. James, she was sponsored as festival queen by *Los Pavitos*, *Alianza Feminista*, the Women's Club, and several of the top social clubs: the Yacht and Fishing Club of Guacanayabo, the Spanish Colony, and the Manzanillo Circle. She won hands down amid all her tragedy and pathos.

She performed the ancient Spanish rite of looking for a mate by going to Cespedes Park, just as her father and mother had done— although Flávia remarked that it seems impossible that in 1938 women still kept to the segregated paths walking in one direction while men (to view their faces) walked in the other. That summer she dated a young man who disappeared in the fall, off to study at the University of Havana.

The next man literally arrived on her doorstep as a full-blown infatuation in August, Manzanillo's hottest month, when being indoors was so unbearable that the Sánchez women placed chairs outside on the narrow sidewalk. Someone noticed a young man passing the house again and again and finally brought out a chair for him. They recognized Pepín Artime, the son of a local hotel owner (Celia's aunt Amanda Manduley's husband was the proprietor of the Hotel Casablanca). It didn't take long to discover that Pepin was interested in Celia. She was surprised at the sudden interest, tried to ignore him, but Artime continued to arrive daily. At parties he'd only dance with Celia. Her friends began to tease her about this budding romance until Pedro Álvarez, then Chela's boyfriend, stepped in because he knew that Artime was engaged to the daughter of a rice grower. He invited Chela and Celia for a drive in the country to test a new car (his father owned the local Ford dealership); in enforcement of the strict social rules, he drove them past the house where the Fluriach sisters lived when he knew Pepin Artime would be sitting on the porch with his fiancée. Celia did not ride by silently, or wave at him, or simply stare, which probably would have been enough to make him squirm, but called out loudly: "Hello, Pepin. Good-bye, Pepin," furious she'd been drawn in. The next morning he was in the street in front of her house, but Celia refused to see him; in the days to come, he was there, asking to speak with her. Her sisters were astounded at the depth of her anger, since they knew she really didn't care for him. They may have missed what she was saying: I will not be played around with.

She exhibited this shift to an iron will in other aspects of her life as well. During their last year at the Institute, in the late spring of 1939, Celia and Nene took a final exam and the teacher, Rodríguez Mojena, also the superintendent of the school, returned everyone's bluebooks except for theirs. He pronounced them unreadable. "We had difficult handwriting," Nene concedes. I obtained a sample of Celia's handwriting as it was then: girlish, filled with loops and floating circles, but quite readable. "I was so embarrassed," Nene said, "that I gave my school uniform to someone else." A few days later, the director sent a summons. They were to come in separately and take an oral exam, but by that time Celia had stopped going to school. "I took the exam, but it was two months later," Nene says. "My father made me do it."

As long as she refused to take this exam, Celia could not graduate. The most influential person in her life, her father, was very unhappy at her stubbornness and tried to explain to her what was at stake. "Let Rodríguez Mojena be who he is," he had argued, "you are only hurting yourself." Her aunt, Amanda Manduley, a teacher and upholder of the glorious profession, thought the world had come to an end. Even Uncle Miguel, who had frequently demonstrated, by word and gesture, that Celia could do no wrong, became disgusted with her behavior. Nobody came out well; withholding the diploma from a daughter of one of the leading families in town wasn't in the Institute's best interest. Nene says that a private joke in their social circles was that Celia couldn't graduate because her professor couldn't read and she couldn't write. When Nene finally took her exam, Mojena told her this kind of writing might be acceptable in high school, but not at university.

Celia had been an uneven student, excelling only in what she liked (history), and maybe she was afraid of going to university. "We all assumed we were going to university," Nene confirms. "If someone studied baccalaureate, they were going to go to university." Weeks passed, and Celia did not go back to school. The crisis at home mounted but she never relented. Her real diploma, one might say, had been questioning authority, and this huge rebellion is the badge that symbolized her education. Her family was highly educated; by skipping college, Celia was taking her first big step toward nonconformity.

THE DIPLOMA DEBACLE is so uncharacteristic and implausible that Pedro Álvarez Tabío, while director of the Council of State's Office of Historical Affairs, investigated the Institute's records to see if they actually did let Celia Sánchez graduate retroactively, but he did not find her name on the list of alumnae. In other words, Mojena did not reconsider at the time (this would have required opening the bluebook and reading her answers), nor were the records changed later, after Celia became one of the country's leaders.

She had fallen from grace, gone from top to bottom, from sweetheart (*novia*) to beauty queen (*reina*) to black sheep in rapid succession. She, so self-assured, had been used to getting what she wanted, so coming up against the Institute must have shocked her. It was her first big confrontation with both authority and the fact that she wasn't perfect.

It was in the aftermath of all this that she arrived in Pilón. There, having convinced herself that she could achieve what she longed for by just being herself, by doing her own thing (for which a university degree isn't a requirement), she became a doer. In this new location she came into her own. This was manifested in caring for her father, decorating his house, developing the garden, working with her charity, the Servants of Mary, teaching herself to drive, exploring every inch of the region, making friends, showing those friends what she'd discovered, accompanying her father on horseback into the Sierra Maestra, and finding all the great places to go fishing. Leaving behind her adolescence and Manzanillo allowed her to quietly mourn Sadurní. She was able to get away from the ghosts of her on-again, off-again Romeos. In Pilón, she could make a fresh start.

2. JANUARY 6, 1956

Planning the Landing

ON ONE OF THE LAST DAYS OF 1955, following Fidel's orders, four men drove south from Manzanillo to meet Celia and have her show them landing points along the coast. They followed the old coastal highway from Manzanillo to Campechuela, then continued south on a road branching inland and across the southwestern peninsula to Pilón. This last section was not a highway, it was more like a network of farm roads for trucks and equipment, chiefly connecting sugar mills but also used by the public. Over considerable stretches the road was too narrow for vehicles to pass, so drivers would stop at each plantation and phone the plantation ahead to see whether the road was clear, and wait if it wasn't. The sixty miles would have taken three or four hours; had it been hurricane season the road would have been even slower, or simply impassable. The only other way to get from Manzanillo to Pilón was by a coastal ferry that ran just a couple times a week—too long a wait between arrival and departure on the south coast, and the police took note of the passengers. Celia's new associates were in the government's "armed and dangerous" category.

Pedro Miret had been in Fidel's original military movement. He had recruited soldiers for the 1953 attack on the Moncada and was caught by Batista's army, tortured, and became one of the few to survive and face imprisonment on the Isle of Pines. Now he was moving back and forth between Cuba and Mexico, selecting soldiers, getting ready for Fidel's return.

Frank País, from Santiago, was known as an agitator, an accurate if mild characterization. He had begun his career as a student leader and had organized a militant group. Recently, between Fidel's release from prison and travel into exile, Frank had been appointed the 26th of July Movement's "national director of action," a euphemistic title for the job of planning military strikes, sabotage, urban guerrilla warfare, and reprisals. He was Celia's new boss. They knew of each other but had not yet met. Manuel Echevarria and Andres Lujan were also Fidel's men. They were with the 26th of July Movement in Manzanillo. Echevarria had been sent to Pilón earlier to meet and, in a sense, vet Celia. She had passed all the tests.

They came to Celia for her knowledge of the region. She knew the coast; they didn't. In the period leading up to this meeting, her organizational skills had been noticed and admired by one of Fidel's most-trusted followers, Antonio "Nico" Lopez, who had traveled to Bayamo and Manzanillo during the first days of November, visiting all the 26th of July organizations. He had met with the clandestine leaders from all the towns in the region: San Ramón, Campechuela, and others, but by November 1955, he knew that Celia's zone was so well organized that it wasn't necessary to check in there. Frank knew another thing that Fidel's four delegates coming to Pilón did not: Celia Sánchez was the one person seemingly acquainted with practically everyone in this end of Cuba.

The party arrived in Pilón around one o'clock, on a sunny day. She showed them coves, inlets, and beaches. But first, right after giving the visitors lunch, she spoke privately with Frank under the canopy of the big mango tree over the patio. It was the first time they had met face to face, and this meeting only enhanced the esteem in which they held each other.

The group left the house around three o'clock and boarded a motorboat Celia had arranged to borrow from the sugar mill. They traveled close to shore, first going east to El Macho, Celia's primary recommendation for a landing point. It was secluded, a secret cove that she knew well from years of fishing; from here, the guerrillas could land on the beach, follow the Macio River inland, and move straight into the mountains to the west of Turquino. Then she showed them Marea del Portillo, between El Macho and Pilón. Less wild, it even had a road away from the beach. Loaded into trucks, Fidel and his men could be in secluded mountain areas in a matter of minutes. This part of the coast was miles from the Rural Guard in either direction, as well as close to the mountains. As they traveled westward, she showed them other good landing spots, past Pilón in the general direction of the large port, Niquero, close to the tip of the peninsula that was Oriente Province's western extreme.

They got back at dark, wet from a storm that had blown up, and her guests changed into dry clothing from a stock of vacation clothes left behind by Celia's brother-in-law, brother, and father. Celia served dinner that night in the Mango Bar, as they called their stone-paved dining terrace under the giant tree. She had selected a traditional but special Cuban meal: *puerco ahogado* (piglet, deep fried), *congri* (black beans cooked with tomato sauce and spices added to rice, which came to Cuba from the Congo via Haiti), *tostones* (green plantains cut into rounds, then crushed and deep fried), and salad, followed by *guayaba con queso crema* (a dessert of local white cheese accompanied by guava paste), and coffee. Her visitors slept in the mill's guest house and had breakfast the next morning at the Sánchez house before setting off for Manzanillo. From there, Frank headed east to Santiago, while the others drove Miret west to Havana.

Celia's life was never the same again. Soon after that meeting, Fidel gave her the go-ahead to develop the plan for the landing, and ordered all directors of 26th of July groups in the coastal region to help her.

After the meeting, Celia walked across the street to get her younger second cousin, Elbia Fernández, to help tidy up the mill guest house. As they were stripping off the sheets, Celia casually mentioned that Frank País had spent the night there. "No, Celia!" the younger woman told me she exclaimed. Elbia describes being covered by goose bumps: "I knew he was important and that the whole thing Celia was involved in was dangerous." Because Celia's house had been full of Christmas guests, family members, she had gone some days earlier to the mill manager's house and, as Elbia recalled, "told him that she was expecting some visitors soon from

Santiago and her house was full of family. She asked if she could put them in the guest house. He said, 'Yes, of course, Celia. But you'll have to find the Jamaican who takes care of the guest house to be sure it's clean.' Celia never once mentioned who those visitors were." She and Elbia had cleaned the place themselves, brought sheets to make up the beds. I asked Elbia what she had thought of Frank País, and she replied, "He was just divine."

SOON AFTER THIS, Celia went to the mill and removed a set of nautical charts from the office. The mill was an easy walk from her house, and she was on friendly terms with most of the people who worked there. If they noticed her poking through the files, I get the impression that nobody thought it suspicious. At any rate, no one chose to mention it.

The mill office would have been in something of an uproar. The harvest started sometime in early December, with cane arriving at the mill even before the machinery was in working order. After that, the Cabo Cruz mill was running day and night, from mid- or late December through February. This was the start of the season, and when a handful of executives, plus one or two chemists, would arrive from Havana. The owner of the mill, Júlio Lobo, widely referred to in Cuba as the *Czar de Azúcar* (Sugar Czar), showed up at the beginning of the harvest as the mill's machinery was put in place to negotiate the sale of last season's sugar in order to make room in the warehouses for the new crop. This little mill, the Cape Cruz, always produced more than its quota of sugar and he could sell the surplus at pure profit.

Lobo's executive staff circulated among his various mills throughout Cuba, and one of them, an economist named Ramiro Ortíz—described as second in command after the manager—was Celia's boyfriend. He was a little older. They had a good relationship, and she would sometimes stay with his mother and brother when she visited Havana. Berta Llópiz, one of Celia's closest friends, explains that Ortíz was a man she might have married (Berta called him "her last chance at a normal life"), but that Celia wasn't in love with him, or not in love enough to put Ortíz through the double life she was starting. Yet he knew what she was up to, was supportive, and for that reason, Berta had urged her to get married. "I would tell Celia, it is because you are in the M-26 that Ramiro Ortíz can help you," which I took to mean "*protect* you."

We don't know whether the charts were stored in Ramiro's office; they probably weren't, but Celia knew the office staff and left with the charts she wanted. Maybe she gave a plausible reason; in any case, she took the charts straightforwardly and signed them out, leaving her signature in the file. The mill didn't have everything she needed, so she went aboard a Portuguese ship anchored in the harbor to get more. The ship came regularly to pick up sugar, and she had been on it several times with her father. She found the charts she wanted in the ship's collection. When the officers of the Portuguese ship discovered that some of their charts were missing, they filed a report with the Cuban Coast Guard.

The Servants of Mary took advantage of the extra harvest prosperity, and handing out toys on January 6, the Feast of Epiphany, was a tradition, so Celia was not the only one to officiate in such an event in Cuba—Mrs. Batista gave out toys in Havana. But it is safe to say that no one interpreted the custom in quite the way Celia did. She brought intensity, commitment, and a degree of detail to this project that no one had imagined. She initiated the toys project a few years after she moved to Pilón, at Christmastime in 1941 or 1942. In the beginning, her friends say, she gave children numbered tickets and told them to collect a gift at her house, but it became clear that small, poor rural children couldn't come into town to pick up a present. Their parents were working virtually around the clock in the harvest (most for the first time in nine months) and were too busy, too exhausted, or too drunk to accompany their children to town. So she began taking a "census." She drove to every plantation in her father's old Ford convertible, would stop and take out her notebook, write down each child's name, age, where he or she lived, and clothing sizes.

This census and those toys are keys to comprehending Celia's part in the early stages of the Revolution. Every year she raised money with exceptional dedication to purchase toys that, people point out, were of the same quality she received as a child, and purchased from the same vendors. Many in Pilón loved her for this. By 1955, Celia, with her annually updated census (which by now consisted of several hundred children's names, addresses, sexes, ages, and sizes), was buying toys for a second generation.

Celia's charity, the Servants of Mary, raised money on New Year's Eve. Traditionally, she'd go to Havana one or two days later to purchase toys to distribute on January 6, Epiphany. This photograph, showing her in Havana with a friend in 1941, may document such a trip. *(Courtesy of Oficina de Asuntos Históricos)*

This means that when she walked into the mill, as several people mentioned to me, the workers "would go crazy over her," because they recalled receiving toys themselves, and were now relying on her to give a similar gift to their children. When she went to filch the charts, it would have been no different, the workers being thrilled to see her.

Until she could take the maps to Miret in Havana or consult with Frank in Santiago, she had to behave normally: participate in the church supper, dance, and raffle held each New Year's Eve. To withdraw from these duties after so many years would have drawn attention.

Several weeks prior to the annual fiesta, Celia divided the Servants of Mary committee women into teams; each visited different stores and asked the owner to donate a bag of beans, rice, vegetables, or whatever they could give. Local families also participated; they would cook, serve the food, collect money, and as Elbia said, "supervise discipline." The beer and rum companies were donors, so everything they made that night would go to the Servants of Mary's efforts. Men paid for dances, and, Elbia remembers, "Celia would tell us to eat a lot and dance a lot so that our partners would have to spend money." Celia had tapped a new demographic: the people who came to the supper weren't townspeople as much as farmers and ranchers from outside town. The event gave country people an excuse to celebrate New Year's Eve with their friends rather than stay at home, isolated. They were landowners and had money, thus bought raffle tickets generously. A young cattle buyer with a good eye, Guillermo García, had given Celia a calf to be raffled off, and farmers were happy to purchase tickets with the dream of adding a fine piece of livestock to their herd.

The event was always a success, and for over a decade people had admired Celia for spearheading it. The New Year's Eve party to ring in 1956 gave perfect cover to all the subversive things she was doing.

Traditionally, money now in hand, Celia would go to Havana or Santiago the day after the raffle to pay for her purchases, and it was then, I think, that she took the nautical charts to Miret in Havana. The bulk of the toys had been selected months in advance, so these last-minute trips were made to pay for prior orders, and most of the toys were purchased in Santiago. In Havana, she usually headed for the Hotel San Luis on Belascoain, on the block between Animas and Lagunas; it was a familiar place (her father liked its atmosphere and had taken his children there when they were young), affordable, and appropriate to her mission. The owner, Cruz Alonso, was a Spanish refugee who had created a hangout for Latin American revolutionaries and political activists living in exile.

This year, she probably returned to Pilón, then took the bus to Santiago, and after she paid for her purchases at two or three factories, arranged to have the toys shipped to Pilón on a boat that took cargo along the coast. Arriving a day or two after New Year's Day, Celia would likely have stayed the night with her sister Silvia in the fancy Alta Vista neighborhood. When she got home to Pilón, the Servants of Mary wrapped the toys. Elbia recalls, "I remember being on the porch of her house where the gifts were separated and wrapped, each with the name and address of the child. Many times we started this work at night and ended at dawn, tired and satisfied."

Once back in Pilón, she set her sights completely on January 6, when the toys were distributed. Truck drivers who worked for the mill would load all the gift-wrapped packages and distribute them to the various settlements that dotted the landscape and edged the sugar plantations. That year, due to the union-organized strike that had involved the cane-cutters, many families had no income, so Celia had purchased wholesale hundreds of pairs of shoes to give out as well—and because her census was so up to date, she could match recipients to sizes. Her colleagues grumbled. Berta Llópiz says she protested when Celia announced that they were going to be giving out shoes to the cane-cutters' children in addition to the toys. Celia simply replied that there was "no comparison" between the plantation children and the town children, "because the town ones have shoes. The others don't. The others use *alpargatos*." When Berta told me this, we laughed at the irony, since the rope-soled shoes were what Celia herself mostly wore.

Berta estimates that they gave out about a thousand gifts in January of 1956. She didn't know it then, but Celia was making a special appeal to the striking cane-cutters. The trip to Santiago (to pay for and collect the toys she'd put aside) presented a perfect cover to talk with Frank and find out if Fidel had given the go-ahead to plan the landing that would kick off the revolution. Her boss, a teacher of fourth-graders, told her how she should go about it.

A GLIMPSE OF THE TOUGHNESS in Celia—which common sense told me had to be there for her to have done what she did in the Revolutionary War—was revealed by Elbia Fernández, the younger second cousin. At times, Celia's father was away overnight. When this happened, Celia often asked Elbia if she would stay with her. On one such night, the two cousins were talking in a bedroom at the back of the house, across the hall from the bathroom, which had a big window overlooking the patio. Suddenly, Elbia noticed a man looking in the bathroom window. She quietly let her cousin know. Celia, no change in her voice or calm demeanor, suggested that they go to the kitchen and get some coffee. As they passed the door that led to the patio, Celia said, "Open it. I am going to shoot him." Elbia opened the door and Celia fired a pistol into the

Pilón, 1952. Celia is surrounded by friends and is seated with José Larramendi in front of his house. Behind her, in the white dress, is her young second cousin, Elbia Fernandez, whom Celia affectionately called "The Teacher." *(Courtesy of Oficina de Asuntos Históricos)*

night. The peeping tom disappeared, but Celia wasn't content. She turned to Elbia and said, "Let's search the patio." But the young woman refused, frightened, so Celia went out alone to search the dark and shadowy space. When she came back inside, Elbia told her that if she wanted someone for protection, she had picked the wrong person.

I asked Elbia whether Celia had appeared to take aim, but she answered that she had been too frightened to notice. How much of this was bravado or a bluff? I got the impression that Celia was invigorated by the encounter; she certainly didn't fall to pieces, and drank her late-night coffee with gusto, happy that she'd followed her instincts and sent a clear warning. Evidently she kept a small pistol under her pillow, or at least Elbia thinks she must have, since it was at the ready. This seems surprisingly dangerous, and therefore uncharacteristic of Celia, but it's clear she did keep a weapon someplace close at hand.

Like Elbia, people around Celia were unaware of what might be going on in her mind. She was secretive to the extreme, and of course, that was part of what made her brilliant as a member of the underground.

3. JANUARY 1956
Frank País

ONE OF THE THINGS you're sure to notice on a hillside as you arrive in Santiago is the Frank País Teachers College. The Revolution — which is what the older generation calls the Cuban government — constructed this school almost immediately after victory in January 1959. And the word "victory" is rarely used today, nearly always substituted by something else: "the triumph over the regime of the tyranny," referring to Batista's years in power, or simply "the triumph." In Santiago, the most prominent symbols of that triumph are the memory and the name of Frank País. He was too busy opposing the regime to get in much teaching while getting ready to rewrite the history of the nation.

The País house, now a museum, is the first place I went in Santiago de Cuba, the name given by the Spanish conquerors. Columbus landed on the eastern end of the island in 1492; a few years later Hernán Cortés built a house on a *balcón*, a ledge, on one of the steep hills above Santiago's port. He conquered Mexico while his colleagues remained in Cuba to build homes and a church, creating a city. The oldest part of Santiago has been constructed on the foundations of these ancient buildings, and the present-day cathedral sits on a foundation tracing back to 1520, the year after Cortés sailed for Mexico and the year African slaves were first imported to the island.

Portrait of Celia's boss, Frank País. There were two military components of the 26th of July Movement: combat activities, weapons training, and logistics (*acciones de guerra*) were under the direction of Fidel, but the underground (clandestino) unit was commanded by Frank País. *(Courtesy of Oficina de Asuntos Históricos)*

Frank's parents' house lies close to the oldest part of the city in a neighborhood developed in the late eighteenth and early nineteenth century. It is modest, pretty, and only a few blocks from the house where Mariana Grajales lived with her militant sons, António and Josué Maceo, commanders of Cuba's rebel army in the Second War of Independence (1895–98). When my guide found out that I was writing about Celia Sánchez, she quickly adapted her tour of the house and led me to Frank's room, where he and Celia carried on their discussions. His white linen jacket hangs in a glass case, as it might have hung the day of their first private meeting, placed over the back of his chair. The guide stretched her arms, lifted a ceiling panel, and pushed it back to show me where Frank hid papers, and moved to another room where he stored guns.

A halo hangs over Frank País. Outside Cuba, Che Guevara is the most-loved hero of the Cuban Revolution, but inside the country that place goes to Frank. At least that is the sentiment of the older generation, who often remark that if Frank were alive, he would be leading the government at Fidel's or Raúl's side. There were two military components of the 26th of July Movement: *acciones de guerra* (combat activities, weapons training, and logistics) carried out under the direction of Fidel; and the *clandestino* (underground) unit, commanded by Frank País. (Administration was based in Havana and under the supervision of Armando Hart and Haydée Santamaria.) Two retired *comandantes*, Delio Gómez Ochoa and Dermidio Escalona, made a point of mentioning that the two-part military organization had been copied directly from the Second War of Independence, in which military strategies had been left up to the generals in the field, but clandestine activities were planned by Martí. In this regard, then, Frank País was Martí's successor. On the day in early 1956 that he received Celia in Santiago he was twenty-one years old.

Frank had been born of old parents. When people describe Frank, they nearly always mention this. Rosario García, his mother, was about forty at his birth and her husband, Francisco País Pesquerira, much older. His father was a Baptist minister, and thus a man who delivered weekly sermons. I assume he did this in the usual way: using quotes of the church fathers well mixed with biblical texts to shape a message. Frank's middle name, Isaac, is from Genesis, and it stands to reason his parents named him for the son of Abraham. Frank's father died when he and his two brothers were still quite young, and Rosario raised them on a small church pension she supplemented by doing washing and ironing.

Frank entered Teachers College of Oriente Province (*Escuela Normal para Maestros de Oriente*) at the same time Batista took over Cuba. In high school, he had been a student leader, led demonstrations, organized protests, and after the 1952 coup put together an armed secret organization called Eastern Revolutionary Action. But as soon as Fidel and his men were out of prison, he transferred all his energy to Fidel. When he became Celia's boss, he was in charge of all the subversive activities for the movement on a national level, from sabotage to uprisings, yet he still lived with his widowed mother and two brothers, Agustín and Josué, at 266 General Bandera. This is where Celia went in early January 1956 to receive orders. She entered the single-story house with white plaster walls, just like all the others in this old neighborhood above the port, where doors and windows open directly onto narrow streets, and Frank steered her to his room. Neither was a scruffy revolutionary, by any stretch of the imagination. She wore dresses, mostly, sunglasses, sandals; or maybe she had on high heels that day, and was carrying a pocketbook, and no doubt flashed her big smile, a spectacular *sonrisa* showing both rows of teeth. Frank had an oval face, broadest at the cheeks, eyes set wide over a straight nose, white skin with a rosy hue where it was slightly toasted by the sun. He had brown hair, although in some photographs it is almost blond. Che Guevara commented that Frank was one of the few people who in person look like their photographs, and these show that he had a beautifully shaped mouth, wide, full, and sensuous (like the lips painted by Man Ray, floating in a blue sky above the little observatory). But the look in his eyes is what people remember. Che thought it cold, and others agree.

As I've mentioned, it doesn't take long to pick up on the love and reverence Cubans, especially the old guard, have for Frank. To find out more, I conducted an interview with Carlos Iglesias, called "Nicaragua," at the Council of State's Office of Historical Affairs on Linea. Iglesias is one of the old revolutionaries who describe themselves as having been "there at the beginning," small, wiry, and bald with a beautifully shaped head. He had prepared for the interview and began to speak immediately, before I had time to pose questions. "I have been thinking about Frank. To begin with, so that you can understand him, I thought of something to bring you," and he handed me a piece of transparent plastic tubing with a very small aperture, an IV line from a nearby clinic. He watched my face and lack of comprehension. "It is soft, but something you couldn't possibly break," he explained, speaking quietly while he wrapped the soft plastic around his knuckles, then stretched it taut, all the while speaking just above a whisper. "He never cursed; he usually was smiling; when he wasn't talking about war, his conversations were about music, *zarzuelas*, and women. . . . He was good-looking—not athletic. His shoulders were narrower than his hips. And he liked to dress well. And there were lots of girls after him. He was always dreaming of a great and sublime love. There was one girl he preferred, and he went steady with her. She was tall, blond. She looked something like you. Her name was America [Domitro]. She was from a Romanian family, but the family had lived in Santiago a long time. Their name originally was Domistrov. Her brother was Frank's bodyguard."

Nicaragua had been in school with Fidel and Raúl; he later met Frank at the Teachers College. "By this time, I had been fairly well educated at the Jesuit high school, so we would talk about things that most people didn't understand at the time." Before long, Frank, then twenty, became the mentor to Nicaragua, who was twenty-four. "I had never put my hands on a gun. He threw a gun on my bed and said, 'There, take it apart!'—and I was afraid to touch it. But Frank was a good teacher. . . . We were living in a very dangerous period and what he wanted was dangerous."

ON THE DAY HE MET WITH CELIA, Frank probably wore slacks and a well-pressed shirt with tails loose, Cuban style (there are some of these in the museum as well). He was 5' 7", taller than Celia by a couple of inches.

There, in his bedroom, he explained how she must go about planning Fidel's return to Cuba. He told her to create a completely new network made up of persons of her own choosing, and to select individuals for her action cells. He suggested former Orthodox Party members, and people she was familiar with from other organizations, from every town along the coast. He advised against the old or fainthearted, because one of his plans for assisting Fidel's landing called for capturing some of the army's guard posts. These were manned by the *Guardia Rural* (which for the most part guarded the big landowners). And her people had to be militant enough to attack army garrisons and quickly knock them out, in order to impede or slow the Rural Guard's arrival at the landing area. Frank explained that he would assist her by ordering 26th of July Movement sabotage units to create havoc. They would cut telephone and telegraph wires, making it difficult for the Rural Guard to notify army headquarters in Manzanillo and small garrisons elsewhere. Frank also told her that he would direct the entire clandestine apparatus of the movement under his command in the area—and this meant not only Pilón, along the southern coast, but all the coastal cities of Niquero, Media Luna, Campechuela, and Manzanillo, roughly a 50-mile radius in western Oriente Province—to help her out. Choosing the right people and developing a strategy for attacking the posts was her affair, with Manzanillo as her special base of operations.

Frank went on to the next point: he was also putting her in charge of transport. This meant getting Fidel's men out of the region after they landed. She had to figure out how to get them away from the coast and into the mountains. The guerrillas would be bringing enough military supplies from Mexico to arm and

uniform her militants; and when Fidel and his men landed, there
had to be two groups (Fidel's guerrillas and Celia's militants)
ready and capable of attacking the nearest army post, capturing
their weapons, and then rapidly move the guerrillas into the
Sierra Maestra.

In clandestine work, you must make an unwritten contract with
your boss, your handler, and Frank—from here on out—became
the largest part of Celia's universe. He set the rules; she had to
abide by them. He would send her into danger and she would
go there. But he would also be her protector. She (who was so
independent) would be like a child with its mother, entering a
state of dependence most of us could not tolerate. From that day
forward, she would be restricted, even within the 26th of July
Movement, in whom she could talk to about this project. For
the moment any discussion would be limited to issues of where
the landing was going to take place. Everything else, such as the
creation of the new network of militants, was something she could
only discuss—at least for the time being—with Frank. With no
one to talk to near her base in Pilón, she was entering something
a bit like a secret engagement with a long-distance fiancé, only
the most limited telephone conversations allowed. Frank probably
included a pep talk that day, since it was a daunting assignment
he was handing her. Not that there was any doubt she could do it.
She'd been preparing for the part, for years. Still, it required much
more than anything she'd undertaken in the past. She didn't know
it then, but over eighty men would be arriving in a boat along her
section of the coast.

FRANK'S PORTABLE RECORD PLAYER is in the museum, and a
bunch of albums. He may have put on a record for Celia, that
was something he often did, or he may have played the piano.
Music would have been a good camouflage to their conversation
in a neighborhood where all windows were open, all houses
were attached, and no one knew who was in the pay of the
police. Music, as a mask, was equally a way of protecting others.
Neighbors innocent of revolutionary intentions, maybe someone
cleaning the floor of a house next door, or washing dishes, might
overhear them; if questioned, that person could truthfully say,
"I heard music." Every account given by people who went to see

Frank mentions that he played the piano during their secretive conversations, and a couple of these visitors were disconcerted, not in a negative way, of course, and not by the discussions, which concerned guns, ammunition, and violence, but because he was so much more accomplished than they were. Further, playing piano seemed to help him think, analyze.

Celia would have spoken briefly to Frank's mother, Rosario, had she been present in the house. Frank did what he did with his mother's knowledge, her full blessing, and encouragement; Celia would have known this. The Lord told Abraham to sacrifice Isaac, his favorite child, and Abraham accepted this, although it was the worst thing imaginable. Such things are an act of faith. That was the surest way Rosario García could have accepted her son's militant lifestyle.

Once outside Celia reentered Santiago's busy streets, lit by shatteringly bright sun. She probably went to her sister's house. If so, Frank would have sent his regards to Silvia, but only if he permitted Celia to confide that she had seen him.

4. FEBRUARY–JUNE 1956

A Change of Strategy

WHEN SHE GOT HOME TO PILÓN, Celia spent a period of time—
perhaps as much as a month—thinking through her assignment.
That in itself is interesting since she was such a woman of action.
She studied the situation, mapped the area, thought her tasks
through, and mulled over how best to assist Fidel and his soldiers.
She always came back to the same thing: a large group of men was
going to land in a place they did not know. Nor did the people in
the area know them. Her analysis: she needed to create not one
group but two: her militants plus a shadow group to recognize and
help the rebel fighters. Who? She came to the conclusion that only
the country people, farmers and ranchers who sparsely populated
this coastal area, were dependable. She needed a group to protect
the guerrillas, beyond the Orthodox Party members proposed by
Frank, and decided that it should be composed of farmers willing
to participate directly, even if just by letting Fidel's soldiers camp
on their property. She made a trip to Santiago to lay this out to
Frank, arguing that the farmers were best suited to this aspect
of the operation and could provide her with sound intelligence.
Frank agreed.

The first farmer she contacted was Guillermo García, who had
donated the calf for the New Year's Eve raffle, and ranched on a
section of the southern coast where the mountains rise straight

up from the sea. García's was one of a string of ranches running through the Platano River Valley, perfect, in her opinion, because this location sat halfway between Pilón and Cabo Cruz, the western most point of the peninsula, whose lighthouse would be the first beacon the guerrillas would see when they approached Cuba. García was famous for knowing his region intimately, or, as Cubans described it, "from palm tree to palm tree." His region included Boca del Toro, a place where the Toro River flowed into the Caribbean. In Celia's opinion, this could be another good place on the coast for guerrillas to land, for the simple reason that it was away from other south coast garrisons.

Guillermo García and Celia had met around 1930, when they were children and he accompanied his father to deliver sides of beef to Dr. Sánchez's house in Media Luna. Once Celia and her father moved to Pilón, ten years later, Guillermo helped her with the New Year's Eve church suppers. Since he was a cattle buyer, it was customary for him to do business with all kinds of people and constantly travel through the countryside, visiting farmers and looking at their livestock. He was not only acquainted with farm people across the whole outer end of the peninsula, from Pilón to Niquero, but knew—or at least had a good idea of—what they thought about Batista's government. Even before Batista's coup, this region had known a particular history of oppression. Its farmers had been exploited by the state in various ways since the time of Machado's government in the 1930s, by graft in various forms, but also by the Rural Guard.

As it turned out, Guillermo was more of a militant than Celia anticipated: he informed her that he was already taking part in a few resistance activities involving the December 2 strike by cane-cutters, and readily agreed to help her. In the end, she relied on him to gather his own network of people between his home in Bocadel Toro and Pilón. (According to Pedro Álvarez Tabío, Guillermo García solicited support and established a network of people in El Platano, La Manteca, Duran, Ojo de Toro, Las Puercas, and any other settlement he thought was necessary to line up sympathizers.) Even to wait for Fidel was treasonous in the government's eyes, and active preparation only increased risk. Did Guillermo inform his recruits of this? It probably wasn't necessary. This population had no love for the Rural Guard and had been defying them, whenever possible, for decades. In the minds of the locals, anti-government activities rumbling beneath the surface were directed, first and foremost, at the *Guardia Rural*, because it represented a semipermanent, yet never-ending, occupation of their area.

CELIA TOOK TO DRIVING AROUND in a jeep, purchased a boat (both financed by the Movement), and traveled all over the region while putting together the pieces of her revolutionary jigsaw puzzle, and recruiting new people. There are many stories of how she might have done this, and they only became understandable after Elbia Fernández explained to me how Celia had hidden (she called it "buried") a method of recruitment in social events. Celia used her customary projects and her long-established activities as cover for carrying out Frank's assignments. She had been a social organizer since her teenage years in Manzanillo and had never really changed. Since arriving on the south coast in 1940, she'd hosted social events—fishing trips, picnics, trail rides—now she loved deep-sea fishing, and frequently she and her friends would go out fishing at night. They'd load onto a boat, and voyage into the deep parts of the beautiful Caribbean, arriving home in the morning in time to go to work. Or, on a weekend, she'd get together a party to fish all day in one of her favorite coves; they would cook their catch over a fire built on the beach and come back at dusk. She would also organize trips with friends to go tromping in the mountains, and buy beeswax and honey from someone she'd heard about, or maybe they'd go on horseback to collect orchids for her garden.

In the summer of 1956, Celia did as she always had, and so did not attract unusual attention. She'd hire a truck, put benches on its open back, and invite her friends for an excursion. Celia brought a picnic basket, and the other women brought covered dishes. They'd drive to a remote spot—this year more often in the mountains rather than on the coast—and, as Elbia explains, if the place had a river or a waterfall, or any attraction, it provided an object for their outing. If not, then the group would improvise a baseball diamond in a field, and their game made an excellent cover for an entire afternoon. The residents of these little settlements wouldn't be able to take their eyes off all the stylish, town-bred men and women having such a good time in their cow pasture, and nobody noticed how, by the end of the day, Celia had spent several innings in conversation with one of their neighbors. Nor had the group of friends that accompanied her, because it was only later that Elbia and Elbia's sister-in-law, Berta Llópiz, figured it out. "At the time, I couldn't imagine that [these trips] served as decoys to her revolutionary activity," Elbia commented. She pointed out that the residents who lived in these places they visited—"so far away from the ports"—rarely saw visitors and noticed if anyone from the village left for the day (so Celia couldn't summon them), and would be extremely suspicious if just one or two outsiders arrived. Any small change in the natural course of events would have been discussed endlessly, so Celia's way around the problem was quintessential Celia: go to a village, overwhelm the locals with numbers, bring along food; once there more or less keep to her role as hostess, busy talking to everyone and no one in particular. In that way, with everyone having a good time, she could just disappear.

She told these people, plainly, what she wanted. In some cases a "yes" may have come immediately. But most people don't want to volunteer for anything, let alone anything dangerous. After all, this wasn't about pledging a bushel of sweet potatoes at the end of the harvest season for the Servants of Mary supper—although that is the sort of conversation she probably was having with them, too. Agreement to become an activist comes in many cases after a cataclysmic event. That had certainly happened when the army, rather than take prisoners in the attack on the Moncada in 1953, killed most of the young men involved and the Catholic Church had intervened.

Yet not everybody in the mountains even knew about the Moncada, let alone had heard of Fidel Castro. So Celia approached them in another way: as herself. Convincing them would have taken time, and meant discussing pros and cons. She no doubt used every variety of persuasion, never taking no for an answer.

If Celia heard about a disaster, she would pay a visit. María Antonia Figueroa, the director of a school in Santiago who turned into a revolutionary and 26th of July member, told me that if Celia heard that a young woman had been raped by one of Batista's soldiers—and Figueroa emphasized that "young woman" meant someone's daughter, sister, or wife—Celia would visit that woman and inquire if there was anything she could do to help. The mention of rape, in any discussion about pre-Revolution Cuba, always carries with it the implication of the army or Rural Guard, although, for all we know, these women could have been raped by a drunken relative. But rape was common, and carried with it a stigma, a feeling of helplessness and shame, and Celia, as the doctor's daughter and also his nurse, could offer much welcome help. Moreover, victims and their families believed that she was discreet. Figueroa says that Celia would offer to take the woman to see Dr. Sánchez (although I think it seems very likely that she would do the examination herself). If a farmer's wife or daughter or sister had been raped by the Guard, Celia's offer of help was another way to build her small but growing army and advance her cause.

CELIA'S FIRST DIRECTIVE FROM FRANK had been to put together a network of militants from towns along the coast. So one of her first activities was to set up a surveillance system, which she called "vigils," to log the movement of the military garrisons. She recruited various people to accomplish this activity, drawing them as Frank had suggested from Orthodox Party faithful and 26th of July Movement members in the newly formed chapters in Pilón, Niquero, and Media Luna, where the garrisons were located. After a month or two Celia knew the names of the garrison personnel, their schedules, guard changes, patrol routes, the type of weapons they carried, the effectiveness of those weapons. Over time, her people became acquainted with every one of the enemy's weaknesses, for example, whether a soldier on sentry duty routinely catnapped. This information helped her to plan a surprise attack as ordered by Frank. Over the first half of 1956, she carefully selected people she considered best qualified to carry out such attacks.

We need to bear in mind that Celia was setting up a regional, clandestine military operation: she was selecting her own army; picking people to train that army; and, in some cases, she would also be supplying it with uniforms and weapons. Although Frank assured her that Fidel would be bringing uniforms from Mexico, she also acquired them because she needed Cuban army uniforms for her assault teams, so they would look like a small company from

Batista's army. Arriving in the back of a truck, rolling up to the garrison, to jump out and offer assistance, and to help those poor members of the army (out of their guns and ammunition). The garrison's personnel would move to put in a call to headquarters in Manzanillo or Santiago, requesting reinforcement, but the electric, telephone, and telegraph wires would have been cut. So, when the attack came, it would be dark inside the garrisons, and the soldiers would have to defend themselves without the usual comfort of being able to find their arms and ammunition easily. Celia's army would be there to offer assistance by stealing Batista's soldiers' guns and ammunition at gunpoint, and encourage them to hand everything over, without any fuss, because it was easier that way. Then back in the truck, and onto streets and along main roads, to be waved through by 26th of July sabotage units that would already have set up official-looking road blocks. This is how Celia planned for her troops to carry out their attack.

IN SELECTING HER FORCES, Frank had asked for "proven militants" from various organizations Celia had worked with over the years. All her recruits lived along the coast. She needed to induct enough personnel to storm a guard post, yet use discretion in her choices, picking the younger and more independent over the older and more experienced. Young people were also closer to the age of army recruits, and it was hoped that young faces would all look alike to old soldiers, and therefore be indistinguishable. It is thought that Frank encouraged her to select her militants not only from a variety of groups, but put together individuals who did not know each other, since he tried to keep the members of his own action groups separate, unaware of each other, and their functions compartmentalized.

Later that summer, Celia's recruits were given basic military training by the Movement. She directed some of this instruction herself, in the hills outside Pilón. She taught her troops to crawl along the ground and gave firing-range demonstrations. Why she elected to do this, when all those Movement men were available, is anybody's guess, but in trying to understand Celia's behavior we have the peeping-tom incident as a reference point. When that prowler looked in the bathroom window, she hadn't called Cleever from his small house across the garden, or gone across the street to summon Elbia's father: she got her pistol, which she evidently kept loaded, and fired it at him. Celia consistently favored a hands-on approach. After all, she was a local, able to blend in; she probably also had to see for herself her troops' offensive capabilities.

These military workshops took place outside the towns on property that was often "borrowed" to the surprise of the owners if they discovered it. It required chameleon-like behavior on her part, since Pilón was under the control of Sergeant Matos of the Rural Guard, who kept watch over every activity. For her, he was the enemy, but we can assume that as far as Matos was concerned she was pretty much someone he respected, a woman who ran a successful local charity, the doctor's daughter whose maverick ways called for some accommodation on his part. Why? Because her father treated everybody equally, as doctors do: the *batistianos,* the paramilitaries, the 26th of Julyers, cane-cutters, mill executives, everybody in the town.

She was aware of Sergeant Matos's respect. His style of vaguely tangible deference would have been good enough for most people, but not for her. Celia befriended his son. A newspaper article from that time shows a photo of Celia and Wilfredo Fernández, Elbia's brother, a pole resting on their shoulders to hold up two huge fish. Celia had caught a 75-pound sierra (everybody in the boat had helped her haul it in). In a second photo, the entire fishing party of nine is assembled. Showing this clipping to me, Elbia pointed out herself, then Celia's friend Carmen Vásquez, and, moving her finger across the yellowed paper, came to a young man in the back row: Sergeant Matos's son. She explained that Celia had invited "Matito" to this particular fishing party so as to render all her fishing trips, in the eyes of his father, harmless. If the sergeant wondered what these people were up to out there on the water, his son could reassure him that they had gone out to catch fish.

Eventually, Celia had people everywhere: some studied all movement along the coast, including traffic on the highways, and reported directly to her; others drew up assault strategies. She lined up vehicles to accomplish Frank's additional mandate: transporting the arriving guerrillas into the mountains. She considered her best bet the truckers who regularly drove cane to the mills in Niquero and Pilón. They'd be picking up the guerrillas near their place of

Crescencio Pérez was a local patriarch with family spread throughout the Sierra Maestra. Celia recruited him in 1956 to help the guerrillas when they returned to Cuba at the start of the Revolution. *(Courtesy of Oficina de Asuntos Históricos)*

landing. Who among the truckers, in the Pilón area at least, had not received a toy or transported toys for her on Kings Day and could say no to Celia and foist the new responsibility on others less reliable than themselves? She also recruited men who worked in the administrative offices of the sugar mills and regularly drove jeeps into the coastal cane plantations. They wouldn't seem out of place if they were seen behind the wheel of one of the mill trucks. She obviously chose well. When Fidel and his men landed, there was a fairly large fleet of trucks waiting along the coast. None was detected by the government's forces or agents.

AFTER GUILLERMO GARCÍA, the next major figure Celia recruited was Crescencio Pérez, whom she had not previously known. It is likely that his name came up on weekend outings—at a ball game or picnic near some waterfall. People would have told her that she needed Crescencio Pérez not only because he was a local *don*, a patriarch, but because he hated the Rural Guard. To back it up, they told her tales of Pérez's arrest and escape during Machado's presidency. She listened closely to the region's folklore.

Crescencio lived in Ojo de Agua de Jerez, a settlement of five or six houses located on the main road between Manzanillo and Pilón, a road she often traveled; but she lived on the coast and he in the upper foothills, in another world. Crescencio was the man for her, they explained, because the Rural Guard gave him a wide berth. He had a great number of children spread throughout those hills, and over the years his family and neighbors, in formidable numbers, had protected him. He'd earned his reputation as a person to be respected. She wanted to know more about him and his family, and found out that Crescencio was a famous womanizer—a good many of his children were by women other than his wife. In his case, the story had a promising twist: he recognized the children as his own and had them baptized with his name. Here was a regional patriarch whose sexual prowess had earned him a certain dignity, since he not only openly recognized all his children but held the sway to do so. But not all his neighbors, especially those men whose wives he'd seduced, harbored benign feelings toward Crescencio. So, while he might be a good person to work for Celia's cause, she was aware that she might be venturing onto thin ice here.

She made an appointment to meet him through Juan León, a relative of Crescencio's. In the first quarter of 1956, he came to Pilón. The patriarch was sixty-one years old, with a square jaw, gray hair, blue eyes, with head reared back in his photographs, somewhat rooster-like because his head presided over such a solidly built, poker-straight body. He immediately promised to help her in every way possible. Álvarez Tabío thinks this happened so readily because Pérez liked rebellious causes, and Celia, by nature, was persuasive.

She must have been curious to meet this man; and, though she always dressed meticulously, she would have taken special care of what she wore that day, so as not to disappoint him. He may have felt the same about her; Juan León would have filled him in on her background: that she was the daughter of the doctor, of a man who had spoken out against Machado, and would have told him about her political background, her support of the Orthodox Party, of Eduardo Chibás and Emilio Ochoa. León might have described what he knew, or had heard, about the men in her life, her love affairs. Celia found out from Crescencio that Ignácio Pérez, his favorite son, was already eagerly conspiring with the union-organized cane-cutters in their strike against mill owners, and she could see that this worked to her advantage, that the old man was eager to be dealt in, handed a role. Several things jelled, and Crescencio needed little encouragement to act.

Guillermo García and Crescencio Pérez, in a completely natural way, began traveling in their own regions, saving Celia from exposing herself unnecessarily. This was helpful, since the Rural Guard watched everyone's movements, especially those named on the government's lists—Cubans say "marked"—as Celia was for her previous Orthodox Party activities. García, as he went about purchasing livestock, now rallied like-minded farmers near the coast. Pérez's recruitment extended throughout his fiefdom: his children and their neighbors and relatives who lived in the central highlands from west to east in the Sierra Maestra range. The enlistment of these two men expanded Celia's network to cover an immense territory; it soon had representatives in Belic, Ojo de Agua, Alegria de Pio, Rio Nuevo, Las Palmonas, Santa Maria, Guaimaral, Ceibabo, Convenencia, El Mamey, Palmarito, Sevilla, Las Cajas—all possible routes that Fidel's men might take if they had to travel on foot from their landing point and into the mountains. Crescencio and Ignacio devoted themselves to Celia's project, and by the middle of 1956, they had made useful contacts with people almost all the way east to Pico Turquino. Álvarez Tabío wrote that Crescencio and Ignacio passed through Purial de Vicana, El Cilantro, El Aje, La Caridad de Mota, La Habanita, El Lomon, Caracas, El Coco, El Jigue, and La Plata, laying the groundwork along a route the guerilla columns followed later. In other words, Crescencio and Ignacio Pérez had pledges from farmers and ranchers that paid off two years later, in early 1958, when the rebel army was being aggressively pursued by Batista's army during the war.

Celia could not let her field commanders know about each other. For one thing, Crescencio had, at some point in the past, compromised a woman in Guillermo's family, and in the 1930s had treated Guillermo's father so badly that feelings against him remained strong in the García family, enough that the antipathy would have outweighed even the most ardent anti-Batista sentiments. She no doubt evaded questions and lied flat-out when she thought it was appropriate to ensure her network's survival until her first two great missions were accomplished.

When Crescencio and his son Ignacio traveled from farm to farm, and house to house, they were recruiting clan members who were anti-Batista and anti-Rural Guard. People in this region had been exploited at every opportunity, for decades, and in an especially brutal manner, so it wasn't all that hard to get them to come aboard—to say, in effect, "Sure, when these guys arrive, we'll do our part." Every generation had the desire to rid the place of government soldiers—dubbed *casquitos* or "little helmets"—who usually took the job to receive extra pay. If posted in the mountains, they received a per diem they never had to spend, living as they did by extortion, so it became the equivalent of bonus pay. Blatant expropriation of goods was the Guard's standard behavior. Another factor worked in Crescencio's favor: most of the Pérez clan had heard about Fidel and the Moncada when they agreed to join Crescencio's cause, but it's generally agreed that their decision was less a matter of supporting Fidel than of the pleasure of involvement: It was an opportunity for one more fight. In this instance, the fight was especially sweet because of the endorsement of their patriarch. Before long, Crescencio had secured the Pérez family's collective pledge, and Celia's network had real security in numbers.

In Guillermo García's region near the coast, members of the Rural Guard regularly helped themselves to the ranchers' cattle and horses. Logistically, the area was somewhat more important since it was closer to where the guerrillas might land: Boca del Toro, the cove called "mouth of the Toro River," in Guillermo's zone, was one of landing spots under consideration. The ranchers who agreed to go along with García surely took some time to think over the consequences: if they were caught, they would be jailed, and they didn't have the safety in numbers that protected the Pérez family. If they were suspected of assisting the guerrillas, their buildings would likely be burned down. Each enlisted farmer and his wife made a decision to take a chance, based on others who were willing to do the same, and with a sense of community. It is my impression that García told them about an upcoming rebel invasion and mentioned the doctor's daughter, which would have given them pause. If she was involved, she would be exposing her father, and if she was ready to take risks, they had better help her. When Guillermo showed up to ask if they had made a decision, they joined his team. By May, the job was done and Guillermo described all this to Frank and Celia at a meeting in her house.

BY THE MIDDLE OF 1956, Celia had signed up another member of the Pérez family, Ramon Pérez Montane (called Mongo), Crescencio's brother, who owned a house, store, coffee farm, and granary near Purial de Vicana in the Sierra Maestra. His place could be approached from Niquero by going directly east via several farm and seasonal roads to the region of the Vicana River. This put him about ten miles north of Pilón as the crow flies. From her viewpoint, Mongo was ideally situated. She liked his place because its location, just inside the Sierra Maestra,provided a natural protective barrier. Plus, it was a place of business and therefore a legitimate destination. Anyone stopped by the Rural Guards had a reason to be there and could say they were purchasing coffee from Mongo's warehouse. Mongo's coffee trees provided a place where Fidel's men could camp out undetected. And finally, she trusted Mongo. Celia recommended his farm as the place for Fidel's guerrillas to assemble after they'd landed, and designated it the "point of departure" for the mountains. Mongo's farm was called *Cinco Palmas,* five palm trees. For the revolutionary forces, it would become a landmark.

Celia had a particular respect for country life. The Sánchez family owned three farms covering about 40,000 acres—in the foothills above Campechuela, known as San Miguel del Chino, named after a Chinese man who owned the first store in the region. This was mostly a cattle ranch, but also planted heavily in fruit orchards. Júlio Girona, her cousin, spent a summer there in the 1930s and described how all the Sánchezes convened on the weekends with their guests, around eighteen people of all ages. After-dark entertainment lit by kerosene lamps consisted of storytelling while the very young caught fireflies, and during harvest season, they watched cane fields set on fire (a method used to facilitate the harvest) in the valley. The house was two stories with a palm-thatched roof—two houses, actually, the front house had bedrooms and a second building, of the same height, was a kitchen and dining room. All the furniture, of pine, had been made on the farm by the cowhands—beds, tables, and dressers, chairs covered in cowhide. A tin tub filled by buckets of hot water (up until then, he'd only seen this in American westerns) was used for bathing in one's room, but the younger generation always washed en masse in the river, though the sexes were separated by a clump of apple trees—"with only the blossoms between us," Girona notes. Mongo knew Celia's appreciation for country furnishing and country places, and when she asked him to jeopardize his house, coffee plantation, pasture lands, and warehouses, he surely realized that she did so fully respecting his property, his livelihood, his way of life.

BY APRIL, CELIA WAS INVOLVED in something that, even after numerous conversations with her sisters and study of the liturgical calendar, I cannot fully explain. Over two days (it could have been April 2 and 3, or April 3 and 4), the Archbishop of Santiago came to Pilón on an unprecedented Holy Week visit. He served Mass, officiated at marriages and first communions, events organized in advance by the Servants of Mary. It was more than unusual that during such a busy part of the year an archbishop would elect to go to a complete backwater. True, Pilón was within his archdiocese, but its church wasn't even operating, and no regular Mass was held. Moreover, this trip bypassed large cities like Bayamo, Manzanillo, and Holguín that were clamoring for his attention. The question thus naturally arises what prompted him to come to Pilón.

What makes the situation even stranger is that during the week of the Archbishop's visit, huge cracks began to appear in the armor of Batista's regime. On Tuesday, April 3, some of Batista's professional officers who had not taken part in his coup, and who therefore questioned his means of authority, mutinied. They called themselves "*Los Puros*" (the Pure Ones). Their uprising was squelched immediately. If the Archbishop knew about it in advance (and I have no evidence of this, but heard of other instances where secrets were passed via the confessional), he may have been happy to get as far away as possible from Santiago and its garrison, the second-largest military installation in the country.

Whatever his motives, the Archbishop was in Pilón at the moment *Los Puros* tried unsuccessfully to take over. A great deal of planning had gone into the mutiny, as it had into Celia's two-day event: 115 of Pilón's children received their First Communion and 58 couples got married. According to several of Celia's friends, in particular Carmen Vásquez Ocaña, whose parents were married at one of these mass ceremonies, Celia simply provided the opportunity; she telephoned local people, gave the date and place of the event, and asked whether they wanted their names on the list. Carmen, who was about fifteen when her parents got married, explained that due to the shortage of priests in the vicinity, very few couples were married. Priests came from Spain, and when they retired they went home and were not replaced. Celia adamantly thought that the Catholic Church wasn't doing its job, and promoted these ceremonies because, as Carmen put it, people felt better about themselves if they could be married in the Church. Celia not only put people's names on her list, she took care of the details, using her own money to purchase marriage licenses ($2 each, a significant investment for most rural couples). Ernestina had just had her baby and Celia was the cook. She wrote to Flávia's daughters, Alicia and Elena: "I was out all day in the streets performing marriages and baptisms and in the afternoon preparing the children for First Communion and every five minutes I would come in and look at the pot on the stove."

The Archbishop's trip to Pilón may have had multiple motivations, but was surely more than just a coincidence. Did he want to get out of Santiago in advance of the mutiny by *Los Puros*? Did he come to Pilón to vet Celia? Within two weeks, the military had restructured itself. Batista's closest supporters arrested over two hundred officers, leaving the army "cleansed" of its moderate members. The new, hard-line army presented itself in Santiago, when a group of students mounted a protest, lining the sidewalks around the courthouse during the noon break of a trial involving two students, Eduardo Sorribes and Andres Feliu. One or two cars passed, carrying members of the military who fired shots directly on the protestors; two students were killed and others wounded. The date of this attack was April 19, 1956, and marks the moment, to some people's way of thinking, that the 26th of July Movement became a real army. It was then that Frank País decided the military had gone too far, and it was time for the movement to retaliate, as told in a stringent account by a 26th of July member who was with Frank on that day.

On April 19, students were on trial in Santiago, and, as Carlos "Nicaragua" Iglesias describes it, a few army cars drove slowly by the courthouse and fired into the crowd of protesters during a recess. In addition to the two young men killed, Carlitos Diaz Fontaine and Orlando Colas Carvajal, several were wounded and hundreds were arrested. Lawyers, court police, and the press were present and saw it all; this didn't faze the army. Frank, seeing that the 26th of July Movement had to show fortitude, went through the city that afternoon, contacting twelve members. Nicaragua worked as a bank teller. Frank had gone to his bank, waited in line at his window, then handed Nicaragua a deposit slip with a handwritten message: "Tonight we are going out."

They stole cars "because we didn't own cars," Nicaragua says, and, with four members in each, and carrying M-1 machine guns, they divided up the city so one car would meet up with another. "And we started shooting anything in uniform." They killed three soldiers that night; Nicaragua pointed out that Frank's decisiveness had been reassuring because, until then, Frank looked soft, talked quietly, was very smart but seemed to be a dreamer. In responding to the April 19 attack on the demonstration, he comported himself "militarily . . . and this behavior *allowed* older people to accept him."

Also at about this time, Frank put Lester Rodríguez in charge of administration of Santiago's 26th of July Movement organization, to free himself to concentrate on the coming landing. Lester was Fidel's age, thirty, but many in the Santiago organization were older, at least in their forties: head of propaganda Gloria Cuadras, legal adviser Baulilo Castellanos, a trial lawyer who defended Fidel after Moncada, and treasurer María Antonia Figueroa. All were professionals and well known in Santiago. Figueroa describes herself as "a very prominent person in the community and the director of a school." She had no trouble raising funds after Frank's bold retaliation ("I was raising thousands of dollars") and claims she had too much money to keep in her house or to justify easily in her bank account. She flew to Mexico and asked Fidel to appoint a new treasurer to take over her work.

While these events had been taking place, Celia, at work in Pilón, added a sophisticated intelligence source to their operations. She recruited Randol Cossío, the brother of her favorite grade-school history teacher, but also the personal pilot of Colonel Alberto del Rio Chaviano. In charge of the first regiment of Santiago, Chaviano was one of Batista's most trusted men; he had participated in the 1952 coup and was the commanding officer behind the Moncada massacre. In June, she sent Cossío to see Frank and, starting in that month, Cossío began to keep a diary annotating all shipping activity that took place in Santiago's harbor. He paid special attention to Coast Guard activity, as she and Frank requested, and was able to provide surveillance reports for the entire southern coastal region, from Santiago to Niquero. Months later, as the landing approached, Celia and Frank would be increasingly equipped with statistics, thanks to the seven months' intelligence from Cossío; they were able to project the best time of day, day of the week, and even the optimum day for Fidel to return to Cuba.

5. JUNE AND OCTOBER 1956

Final Plans

ON JUNE 24 A NUMBER OF FIDEL'S MEN were arrested in Mexico. They had been there for a year, training under Alberto Bayo, a veteran of the Spanish Civil War, when the Mexican police arrested them on charges of preparing to attack another country. Fidel got most of his men released on July 3 by negotiation and by making a large payment. But he was alarmed, and rushed the purchase of the *Granma,* a twenty-year-old 64-foot diesel-powered cabin cruiser built to accommodate no more than twenty.

By now, Randol Cossío's surveillance showed that navy planes' reconnaissance was confined to a corridor about 13 miles wide, along the southern coastline between Santiago and Cabo Cruz, never flying farther off shore than this narrow route. It became clear that if Celia and Frank switched locations to a spot around the point of Cabo Cruz, between the peninsula's tip and the active shipping lanes at Niquero, the *Granma* could land outside the navy's circumscribed reconnaissance. Celia, however, saw the problem with that right away. Her region along the southern coast was still a better candidate because it had many hidden coves and shipping canals, and, most important, greater proximity to the foothills of the Sierra Maestra, leading to the heights around Turquino. The coast between Cabo Cruz and Niquero was appealingly remote as a place to land, but also far removed from the final destination. Landing where Celia recommended would permit them to make a quick flight to safety in the surrounding highlands. Her preference—the coves east of Pilón, El Macho (closest to Turquino), and Marea del Portillo—would ensure that the rebels could get into the Sierra on foot. Even from Pilón itself, with its web of shipping canals, she could load the guerrillas into a few trucks and get them into the Sierra Maestra's foggy forests in a matter of minutes. But in Pilón, they would have the Rural Guard garrison to contend with, whereas El Macho and Marea del Portillo were far safer. The next-best place was Boca del Toro, also free of the Rural Guard's observation, located west of Pilón. Guillermo García lived there, and his network of sympathizers could get the rebels under cover in their sheds and pastures until trucks could move them farther into the upper foothills and to Mongo's farm.

She had a point, but Las Coloradas Beach was chosen, a very small port on Oriente's western coast. The light at Cabo Cruz would be their landmark; then they'd travel very briefly north and land just below the powerful beam that came from the Niquero lighthouse. There was some logic to this; but rather than the twenty miles from a more eastward landing point to Mongo's *Cinco Palmas*, Las Coloradas made the trek to the rebels' first waystation a good deal longer.

Cubans traditionally compare their huge island to an alligator facing southeast, its back toward Florida, and its head and forefeet oriented toward Haiti, Jamaica, and the open Caribbean. Celia had advocated a landing on the alligator's chest, within striking distance of the Sierra Maestra range at the shoulder and collarbones. Now the landing was to take place on the top of the alligator's right front toes. The boat would come through the Yucatán Channel, pass south of Cuba at some distance, traveling in open waters, and reapproach the island at Cabo Cruz; sighting the beacon there, the rebels would travel up the coast only a short way, land, be met on the beaches by Celia's operatives, and be moved out of the area in waiting trucks. Under the new plan, Celia saw that her truck drivers were going to be even more important—the greater distance from the landing point to the mountains made the transport leg a much more crucial part of the operation.

In a perfect scenario, some of the rebels would join Celia's militants (who would don uniforms and assume weapons brought on the *Granma*); together, they would knock out the small military garrison at Niquero, capture more weapons, and then travel straight for the mountains through the plantation roads to Mongo's *Cinco Palmas*.

Having fished off these coasts for twenty years, mostly at night, she could think through and plan for every contingency. The southwestern point of the peninsula, where they would be landing, was a triangle. It was almost uninhabited. South of Las Coloradas, the best land was planted in cane and there were some woodlots owned by rich Cubans and North Americans. When these lands ran out, the vegetation gave way to cactus and sea grapes as the terrain elevated in terraces forming the western ridges of the Sierra Maestra.

East of Las Coloradas and north to Belic were some small, poor settlements of woodcutters and colliers. They transported their goods on horseback and foot to Las Coloradas and from there ferried in motorboats up the coast to Niquero or down to Cabo Cruz. Celia went there to look around and was faced with a new group of very humble people to enlist. Little seems to be known about how she handled this. Aside from the meager income they had from their wood and charcoal sales, they subsisted on small parcels of land and by fishing. Guillermo García would not likely have visited these farmers on his trips to purchase cattle, so he was not in a position to help her, and Crescencio Pérez had no relatives in this area. She was almost certainly on her own. She went fishing, probably before the end of August, made sketches of the coastline, and had conversations with fishermen. Celia took into account the possibility that the *Granma* might overshoot its goal and land north of Niquero, at Media Luna or even Campechuela.

In August 1956, Frank tried to dissuade Fidel from his plan to return to Cuba within the year. He flew to Mexico to lay out his case. In his view the 26th of July Movement wasn't ready, not in Santiago nor in the other cities where he wanted to stage uprisings. And he would surely have conveyed Celia's misgivings about the new landing spot. The imminent return of the guerrillas was no secret in Cuba, especially for those who took Fidel's promise literally: by the end 1956, he had vowed, he would begin the liberation of the country, or would die trying—"We will be free or we will be martyrs."

CELIA, ALONG WITH FRANK, understood that Fidel was not going to be dissuaded or long delayed. She was confronting the difficulty her involvement in the coming fight could mean to her family—in particular for her father.

Her father had brought her up. The way she thought was instilled by him, and she admired him immensely. In 1911, having earned both his M.D. and a degree in dental surgery, he elected not to stay in Havana, although that would have been the normal choice for a young doctor with two medical degrees. He returned to Oriente Province and took his first job in Niquero, considered an outpost at the time, got married in 1913, and moved to Media Luna to assume a position as doctor for the sugar mill. From his arrival, he set himself apart from the others, ignoring the advice of Media Luna's "smart set" and buying a house in the working-class neighborhood of New Town, on the main highway, and only a few blocks from the sugar mill. Nobody could understand why he'd do such a thing: the mill owners certainly couldn't fathom why he wanted to live near the workers. Although his bosses admired him, Dr. Sánchez continued to have run-ins with them for nearly three decades.

He educated Celia the way men educate a son: taught her to hunt and fish, let his heroes be her heroes, and instilled in her a love of Cuban history, which essentially is colonial and military history. She learned about Cuba's struggle against Spain; against the United States; that Cuba had always been occupied by foreign powers; that theirs was a country where the poor and the dispossessed had been at the mercy of imperial powers. He hired tutors. When, as a small child, she produced what must have been very dusty meringues (baked on the patio, in a mud oven over ashes), he ate them, declared them fabulous. He carefully cultivated her awareness of art and literature, and personally enhanced this through his own friendships with a leading painter of the time, Carlos Enríques, and the poet Agustín Guerra. The most affirming aspect of this singular father-daughter relationship had been her work in his medical office. He had taken her into his world and began preparing her for the future, the way a more conventional father trains a son. It does not seem he gave the same opportunity to his oldest son, Manuel Enrique, possibly due to the fact that he was at school in Santiago, along with Silvia and

Chela, and later went to the United States; in other words, Manuel Enrique was not around, and the youngest son, Orlando, simply did not have his sister's aptitude. When the family discovered Celia's interest in sewing, her father hired a woman to teach her how to make patterns.

Dr. Sánchez couldn't manage his accounts, and left this to the women of the family. Celia graduated into the job of money manager in 1939 when her grandmother died, making him dependent on her in this way. She soon organized his life completely, including planning his occasional vacations abroad down to the last detail, writing letters to shipping lines, corresponding with hotel managers, sending telegrams to alert or confirm her father's arrival. She even packed his suitcase, suggested what to wear in each city based on weather or some other criteria that she, sitting there in Pilón, had carefully researched, read, or heard about. She would write out notes suggesting where to go, what to see, what to shop for. While he was away, she stayed at home to run his office, advise his substitute, another doctor who took care of his patients, often a member of the Girona/Fernández family. These substitute doctors, however, weren't also dentists, and Celia is known to have extracted a tooth on more than one occasion. Meanwhile, she had to keep the house filled with flowers, tend her garden, and, as Carmen Vásquez Ocaña remembers, did these things with absolute pleasure.

"Celia had real passion for her father," Carmen reflected, and described how Celia shooed everyone from the house after lunch each day so nothing could disturb her father's nap ("not one crack of a screen door or of a window being opened"). She'd load them into the car—Carmen, much younger, seems to have spent most days with Celia—and drive to a woman's house where they drank coffee in little cups made from condensed milk tins in a room with walls papered in newspapers. Celia dubbed this house *Estrada,* after Fellini's *La Strada*, echoing her interest in the cinema, and when it was time to wake Dr. Sánchez, they'd go home again.

I heard this observation about Celia's passion for taking care of her father from the Gironas as well. Only they took it a bit further, saying that when the time came she transferred that passionate care to Fidel.

But now, in the summer of 1956, Dr. Sánchez was nearing seventy and she had taken care of him for nearly two decades.

Dr. Manuel Sánchez, seated with a friend on the porch of his house in Pilón. Dr. Sanchez educated Celia the way men educate a son. And she, in turn, had real passion for her father. *(Courtesy of Oficina de Asuntos Históricos)*

Every day, with her increasing immersion in clandestine activities, she had to yield control a bit more, passing the baton to Acacia, her youngest sister. Aware that after the landing this part of Cuba would likely become a war zone, Celia decided to send her father on vacation to Europe.

On August 21, Celia mailed her father a letter, mostly about the drought they'd been having, her garden, and news that some American geologists were looking for oil near Manzanillo. She wrote again September 5, saying that his reply had taken only three days from Amsterdam, faster than most letters from Havana. She assured him that the whole family loved hearing about his health and the good time he was having, and that they expected him home soon. She includes the Bronx address of Orlando, who is "waiting for you," and a joking postscript: "Your sisters have purchased a television set but they don't touch it. They don't turn it on unless someone comes who can tune in a program."

With their father away, and Acacia taking over the medical office, Celia made straight for Manzanillo and began raising money. Her partner was the 26th of July Movement's treasurer in the city, Micaela Riera, a good-looking, well-dressed young woman who flouted the police and always kept (as nearly all these people did) an open-date, first-class airplane ticket out of the country.

(The first-class fare was not an indulgence. If you appeared to be from a rich or prominent family, Catholic, and white, the police and army would turn a blind eye for about twenty-four hours.) Celia and Micaela were selling 26th of July bonds—contributions, really, since people reasonably feared getting caught with these documents—handmade showy certificates, with "26th of July" heraldry at the top, drawn in black and red ink—and destroyed them. Celia was assisted by Enrique Escalona, a young man who worked in a Manzanillo bank and organized a network of sympathizers among his fellow workers.

She also enlisted a longtime friend, Dr. Rene Vallejo, who operated a surgical clinic in Manzanillo, to begin soliciting the cooperation of doctors in training field medics. As the time for the landing approached, this training was given in all the coastal areas where she'd done her recruiting. Volunteer doctors taught farmers and ranchers first-aid: how to make splints, crutches and stretchers out of tree limbs, how to give injections, to craft bandages using gauze wrapped over cotton. They were preparing for lightning attacks, skirmishes, and inevitable injuries. The doctors collected medicine and supplies, and Celia shipped them down to the coast, where the packages were buried in fields or placed in cisterns in preparation for the arrival of the rebels. Also under her direction, women in Manzanillo sewed uniforms, made or adapted knapsacks and cartridge belts. Merchants, usually relatives of 26th of July members, donated clothing and footwear. Elsa Castro, a young movement member, offered the pickup and delivery system of her father's stationery store (without her father's knowledge). Elsa explains how Dr. Vallejo would, say, drop off a fountain pen for repair, but in reality hand her vials of medicine. In the shop, Elsa and Celia would make packages (wrapped in plastic then covered in burlap), and the next day the mailman would pick them up and get them on their way to the southern coast where recipients hid them in holes and caves.

BY MID-SEPTEMBER, Celia was back in Pilón, where she gave dinner parties and raised money with the Servants of Mary. Her friend Berta Llópiz reports that she made trips to select toys for the coming New Year's celebration. She kept up her small business selling accessories because it provided continuity, and good cover in case she needed to travel outside the country. Celia's life had become extremely stressful, Berta Llópiz told me, and Celia was afraid of being discovered. Even with Acacia acting as nurse and receptionist when her father returned from his vacation, she still lived in the house, which had become her headquarters. She was in something of a bind: when she wasn't around patients noticed, and made a big issue of her absence. Berta says that if Celia didn't recognize a patient, she'd tell everyone in the house to say that she wasn't home. By this time, the army had grown openly suspicious of her. According to the two Larramendi sisters from Pilón, then in high school, she sometimes arrived at their house with a thermos of coffee and a pack of cigarettes, and would wrap her head in a scarf and sleep all day while they watched over her. Most people I interviewed think that her father knew what she was up to, but I am not so sure of that. She told Acacia to be careful and say she wasn't in. But Berta says that when patients arrived in the night— since Pilón, a port town, was prone to bar fights and shootings people came to the door at all hours—the "old doctor" would forget that Acacia was there, and shout, "Celia, get up. I need you to help me." (If he'd really known what she was up to, I don't think he would have exposed her so casually.)

María Antonia Figueroa remembers seeing Celia during the later months of 1956, when she was working around the clock, and I asked her to describe Celia on these occasions. Figueroa took a few moments, and began with Celia's voice and how softly she spoke, that she didn't allow tension to distort it (people often mention this when talking of Celia). Figueroa described her makeup (eyebrows drawn in black pencil, red lipstick), and her hair, jet-black and shiny. On the particular day recollected, the two women had met in Manzanillo and Celia had been wearing sandals and a floral-print dress—Figueroa shaped her hands to indicate a pattern of oversized blossoms. Pinned on the neckline was a bunch of fresh flowers. Figueroa called it "flowers on flowers."

The Last Five Days of November

In October Frank flew once again to Mexico. He told Fidel, apparently quite flatly, to forget about making the landing at the end of the year—they couldn't pull it off. But Mexico was getting increasingly difficult. Batista had placed agents there, and Fidel was uneasy. Unsuccessful in his bid, Frank returned to Santiago and intensified his work preparing uprisings to divert the government forces from the landing. Celia, learning of Fidel's determination to come within the year, made a quick trip to Havana to ask Armando Hart and Haydée Santamaria for permission to fly to Mexico and return on the *Granma*, accompanying Fidel and his soldiers in the landing. She pointed out that she knew the coast better than any others who would be onboard, could guide the crew into any of the harbors, and could then be there to coordinate the truck drivers. Haydée was supportive; Armando talked the idea over with Frank. Fidel was consulted, and was ambivalent about the dynamics of having a woman on the trip. It was Frank who made the decision: Celia was in command of the landing, and should be there, on the coast, directing the preparations for it, not on the vessel en route from Mexico.

In mid-November Mexican police arrested Pedro Miret and seized the rebels' arsenal (hidden in a Mexico City residence). On the 21st, Mexican authorities gave Castro three days to get out of the country. He and his men traveled to the Gulf city of Vera Cruz, then up the coast to Tuxpan; there, as many men as the *Granma* would hold crowded aboard. Some had to stay behind, but eighty-two set out for Cuba at 2:00 a.m. on Sunday, November 25, determined to change history or die.

It was another two days before Arturo Duque de Estrada, in Santiago, received a telegram from Mexico: "*Obra pedida agotada*" (Work ordered out of print), signed "Editorial Divulgacio." This was the code to confirm the *Granma*'s embarkation. During Frank's visit in October, he and Fidel had calculated the time to complete the Gulf of Mexico crossing, but they hadn't taken into consideration that the boat would be overloaded both with men and cargo. Instead their calculation, of four days, was based on a crossing under normal conditions and with a reasonable cargo. Frank estimated the landing would take place sometime on November 29.

As soon as the Editorial Divulgacio telegram reached Santiago, the planning phase, in which Celia and Frank and their many lieutenants had been immersed all year, shifted to implementation.

Frank traveled all over Santiago, making contact with the leaders of his action groups, going over arrangements for the uprisings throughout the city and the province, to take place more or less simultaneously with the rebels' arrival. Lester Rodríguez (now directing the 26th of July Movement in the city so Frank could concentrate on the landing) sent coded instructions to all the major players, to take their battle positions.

That month Santiago had been filled with city police, armed forces, the military secret intelligence service (SIM), and customs police. Perhaps hedging its bets, the government was also backing at least one paramilitary group, the *Tigres,* directed by Rolando Masferrer, age thirty-eight, a senator and publisher who sought to protect Batista militarily. All of these forces were looking for Frank, whose idea of making himself invisible—in such marked contrast with Celia's methods of blending into her various surroundings—was to drive around in a new car purchased by the movement, a fire-engine-red Dodge. Those who recognized him and had some sense of what he was involved in could hardly believe their eyes: it was Frank País behind the wheel of that attention-grabbing automobile.

By the end of the month, the man in the street, in addition to all the police and military agencies in Santiago, expected Fidel to arrive before the year was out. Oscar Asensio Duque de Heredia, who had been the editor of the high school newspaper and was now president of the student body at the Teachers' Institute—a position Frank had formerly held—as well as a member of 26th of July Movement, left an account of what Santiago was like at the time. Rumors were everywhere, in open talk of invasion; insiders announced that they knew the exact date for Fidel's arrival; that hundreds or even thousands of men were coming with him; that cargos of weapons had already arrived; that millionaire former president Prio, exiled in Florida, was funding Fidel and that tanks and planes had been provided. Such gossip was augmented by the military, which issued its own disinformation, fueling the fire to inspire the government forces to greater vigilance. The higher-ups knew from their informers in Mexico that something was in the offing. Even then, Duque de Heredia remembers, "We would see Frank in the red automobile, bought with movement funds, carrying out his grand activity, along with Pepito Tey and other well known revolutionaries. This car, which many of us called the Red Threat, would drive about under their noses."

Rodríguez also contacted Celia. She alerted her people in Manzanillo. "Celia came to my house, the house where I lived with my mother," Elsa Castro recalls. "Ours was one of the [eighteenth-century] wooden houses. Celia had given me a jacket to keep for her, black with long sleeves and zippers on the pockets." Celia came by that day to collect the jacket.

On the 28th, Frank ordered Lalo Vásquez (using a coded phone call) to take up his position in Niquero, to coordinate the on-the-ground activities of Celia's militants as they attacked the garrison in that key city, so close to the action just north of Las Coloradas beach. In Niquero, the militants would disguise themselves as members of Batista's army, ascend the hill above the port, and attack the garrison there. Lalo would give the order to initiate this component of the region-wide uprisings; then the 26th of July sabotage teams would cut electrical wires and telephone lines, ruining the communication systems and bringing about general chaos.

That same evening, Celia left Manzanillo at the wheel of a black car, taking the old coastal road from Manzanillo south to Media

Luna. Headed for a dinner party, she was dressed in a chocolate-colored skirt, and had on the black jacket. She parked her car in front of a house ablaze with lights, going inside to join the jubilant dinner guests. There was food on the table; they all ate and drank as people came and went, receiving instructions. The dinner party was stage one for the reception of Fidel's landing.

Lalo Vásquez also left Manzanillo that night, taking the same road Celia had, but he stopped in Campechuela, the first town, a little over twenty miles south, to see a man from the 26th of July Movement, Segucha, in charge of local ground operations. Lalo told him to alert his militants and have them await orders.

It was after midnight when Celia left the dinner party; she was accompanied by two men, Adalberto Pesant (called Beto) and Cesar Suarez. The three got into a jeep and went south on the main road, a dirt-and-gravel highway, threading their way past one sugar mill after another—the Teresa, the San Ramon, and the Isabel—as they made their way down the coast. Choosing to ride in these early hours when no one was about, they reached Ojo de Agua de Jerez at dawn on the day the *Granma* was expected, the 29th. They were now a good distance inland. Celia knocked on Crescencio Pérez's door and when he opened it, proclaimed, "Fidel is coming."

Segucha's orders went out on that morning. His urban militants left their houses and fanned out over the countryside. Vásquez had driven farther south, to Niquero, where before dawn he had quietly let himself into an abandoned building formerly used for ice making. The second member of his team was already there waiting. Lalo greeted a young farmer and friend of Guillermo García's, Manuel Fajardo, a burly country boy with a completely round face, a sharp contrast with Lalo, who was urban and nerdish, with a wiry build.

Receiving Celia, Crescencio promptly excused himself to get dressed. She became impatient, and to spur him on called out, "You'd better get going," and he came out in his fanciest clothes: white *guayabera*, white pants, and a black lariat fastened around his neck. She noticed that he'd even put on black leather street shoes. "Where do you think you're going dressed up like that?" she asked. Standing before her, he added the finishing touches: a black felt hat on his head and a revolver tucked into his belt, concealed under the tails of the *guayabera*. He explained that he would be going from house to house all day, all over the region, and should the Rural Guard stop him, he could convincingly tell them a family wedding was going to take place and he was there to invite all his friends. Celia laughed. Given the number of Crescencio's children, spread throughout the mountains, the alibi was perfectly plausible.

Crescencio went out into the highlands to start his rounds—later to hold a place in Cuban lore comparable to Paul Revere's Ride. Celia stayed at his house, the Revolution's temporary headquarters until Fidel could arrive. She had made this choice in part because the house sat close to three roads: one that connected her to Lalo and Fajardo in the Niquero icehouse, and beyond that, Las Coloradas; a second that went south to Guillermo García's territory, branching inland, and continuing on to Pilón; the third, the one she'd just taken, linked her with Media Luna and Campechuela. If the boat overshot Las Coloradas, she'd assured the rebels, they would still find many good landing spots north of Niquero, abandoned wharves where they could quickly and easily tie up. Segucha had reception teams all along that stretch of coast, operating out of Campechuela, and already out and waiting.

Crescencio Pérez and his son Ignacio made their visits, knocking on doors throughout the mountains. At *Cinco Palmas*, Mongo did not move—he was Fidel's point of contact. The same went for Guillermo García. Having been informed that the boat was arriving, he waited at his house in Boca del Toro, east of Pilón; in the event Fidel came ashore along the southern coast, instead of at Las Coloradas, Guillermo would be there to meet him.

Throughout that day Crescencio's little army of farmers fanned out over the mountain regions in southwestern Oriente, spreading the word to be on the lookout for "The Ones Who Are Coming" (as the story is sometimes called). Parallel groups of urban militants monitored streets or spread out in fields, there to watch the police station, any travel on the highway, or activity on the coast. The transport drivers, who mostly worked for the sugar mills, filled their tanks and took up their positions, driving slowly along the coast, over back roads, scanning the horizon. Not all these teams were told Fidel was arriving. To some, this was just another drill. They were accustomed to drills; Segucha's people had been practicing these maneuvers for months, going to their places, to be prepared for the actual moment. But everyone knew that 1957 was fast approaching, and Fidel had made a solemn promise to return before it arrived.

That afternoon in Santiago, Frank—driving his red Dodge—picked up Oscar Asensio Duque de Heredia in front of the Renaissance Bookstore on Enramades. As soon as Oscar got in, Frank handed him a fancy little revolver with "4º de Septiembre" decorating the handle in colored enamel. This was a gift Batista liked to hand out to commemorate the day he'd first taken over Cuba, in 1933. Frank passed Oscar two boxes of bullets, warning him that the gun was loaded. A year before, Oscar had interviewed Frank for his school paper after Frank had been charged with killing a policeman in the town of Caney; the charges had been dropped for lack of evidence, and Frank had denied having any part of it. Now, as Oscar held the pistol in his palm, he wasn't so sure of Frank's claim he did not kill that policeman a year earlier. Frank's enigmatic, almost playful way of handing him the gun that day seemed to confirm it.

Frank drove into the red-light district (what Cubans call a "tolerance zone") and stopped in front of a warehouse. He got out, took out a batch of keys, and tried several before opening the wide door. He signaled Oscar to stay in the car and went inside. A couple of minutes later, Frank emerged carrying a large bundle so badly wrapped that Oscar could see it held rifles and machine guns. Frank put it in the trunk, but it was too large for the trunk to close properly. They drove to Drucha where he stopped in front of a house, honked the horn for someone to come out, and when he did, Frank told him to stay inside and wait for further orders. That was the pattern for the rest of the afternoon, driving from street to street, zigzagging through the city in the Red Threat crammed with weapons, telling people to stay home, wait, stay on alert. They passed several policemen with shortwave radios, and army units, yet nobody took notice of the bright red car with its trunk flapping open. Oscar at some point looked over his shoulder and was horrified to see the trunk had actually opened completely. He told Frank, who casually pulled over in front of a laundry, got out, and rearranged the weapons. When he caught the "unbelieving eyes of the curious," to quote Oscar, a little smile appeared on Frank's face.

It was late afternoon when Frank and Oscar picked up several people on San Geronimo, and then drove around the bay to a remote neighborhood called Punta Gorda, where they stopped in front of a lovely modern house. The place was vacant, and inside Frank led Oscar to a room holding a modest arsenal: rifles, pistols, and more than a hundred hand grenades still in parts on the floor. He told Oscar and a few other young men to assemble them. He warned they had to do this before nightfall because under no circumstances were they to turn on lights. It was after six on a late fall evening, and darkness was closing in.

AS DUSK DESCENDED OUTSIDE THE ICEHOUSE in Niquero, Lalo Vásquez and Manuel Fajardo asked themselves what to do next. Fidel's estimated arrival time had almost passed. What if he did not appear that night? Lalo must have gotten word that Frank's uprising was getting under way, and wanted to ask Celia what she had in mind. He was thinking about their militants who, by the next morning, would have been out for 24 hours. Manuel agreed that if the landing did not happen that night, Lalo should leave and find Celia, ask her for further orders. Lalo did not know where she was, but Celia had told him that in an emergency he was to go to her father's house and speak to her sister Acacia.

IN SANTIAGO, AT THE PUNTA GORDA HOUSE, Oscar noticed that Frank kept coming and going throughout the evening with different groups of people. Oscar stopped Frank on one of these trips and asked if it would be possible to bring him a coat and something to eat, as it had gotten cold. Frank gazed at the younger man and said he'd send Oscar home in a car immediately. When Oscar got there, he found his mother worried by his prolonged absence; some of his friends from the Institute had come by to ask where he was. After eating and getting a coat, he tried to fool her with the pretext that he was going on a fishing trip. Knowing better, she hugged him tightly, and Oscar saw tears in her eyes.

Taras Domitro, Frank's bodyguard, picked Oscar up on a street corner, as arranged, and they drove to Vilma Espin's house to wait for Frank. When Frank arrived, he lingered on the porch, leaning on the railing, talking to Vilma, a very pretty young woman. Frank insisted on making jokes, Oscar says, "so no one would suspect the enormous responsibility weighing on him at that moment." Vilma gave Frank packages that he put in the car, and then he, Taras, and Oscar went to a small grocery store to buy bags of crackers and other snacks. They got back to the Punta Gorda house after midnight and it was full of people, some asleep on the floor. Oscar recognized Baulilo Castellanos, the famous lawyer who had defended Fidel and his men after the Moncada, who was burning, on Frank's orders, all the written plans for the uprisings. The lawyer kept saying, "It is a shame to have to destroy these. They are documents for history." All the doors and windows of the house were closed, and Oscar watched the lawyer hold his jacket over the mouth of the fireplace, shaking his head regretfully as maps and lists and drawings crumbled to ash. (Had Celia been in that room, she would have snatched all those artifacts and figured out a way to preserve them.) For Oscar, still in the dark as to what was taking place, the flames in the fireplace demonstrated that Frank's staff was afraid the plans would fall into the army's hands, and that the 26th of July's desperate action was about to begin. Earlier in the evening, Oscar had suggested to Taras that their action had all the marks of a suicide mission. Frank's bodyguard thought about it a bit, and said, "There is a possibility that part of the army will unite with us." He was hopeful: at this point anything was possible.

IF LALO AND FAJARDO WERE NERVOUS waiting in the icehouse, Celia by comparison was in turmoil as she paced the floors of Crescencio's house. She was the type of person who liked to settle things right away: jump in the car, drive somewhere, talk things over, investigate what was happening, sniff things out, make a decision. Now she could not. She had to wait. She was in the vexing position of the general in his headquarters, in command but remote from the officers in the field on whom she was depending. They were to bring Fidel to her. So she brewed coffee and smoked cigarettes.

WELL BEFORE DAWN ON THE 30TH, while it was still dark, Lalo left the icehouse and drove to Pilón. He had to pick his way across farm roads edging the cane fields, and probably, on this drive flick off the headlights as he rolled past houses. Arriving at the doctor's bungalow, he knocked on the door and Acacia let him in. Following her directions to Celia's location, he retraced his route, driving north through the sugar plantations, following the contour of the hills, and, by my calculation, arrived at Crescencio's shortly after daybreak.

THAT SAME HOUR Frank was starting his uprising in Santiago.

At the house in Punta Gorda, somebody woke Oscar at 5:00 a.m. He went downstairs and met Frank, who pointed to him and then to the red Dodge. Oscar got in the back with Taras, who had a machine gun on his lap, prompting Oscar to pat the little "4th of September" pistol in his pants pocket and check his breast pocket for the box of bullets. Armando Hart and Haydée Santamaria (in Oscar's eye, glamorous revolutionaries because they had fought at the Moncada), got into the front seat next to Frank. It was still somewhat dark, but the bay was emerging into visibility, revealing the outlines of the mountains behind.

Several such carloads of revolutionaries began to drive slowly toward the city, following the road along the bay as the sun was coming up over the water. They pulled up in front of an old two-family house on San Felix. A few cars had arrived ahead of Frank's and were unloading their passengers. Waiting on the sidewalk for him, María Antonia Figueroa, Gloria Cuadras, Ramon Alvarez, Luis Clerge, and Enzo Infante bore rifles and revolvers. Somebody pounded on the gate leading to the upstairs apartment. A tall man, heavy with a reddish complexion, came out and asked what they wanted at this hour. Somebody answered, "Open up in the name of the Revolution." The man stood there, astonished, then asked, "What do I have to do with the Revolution?" At which point Frank stepped forward and said that his house had been selected as their headquarters. "Not my house. Why my house?" the man shouted, and went back inside. The revolutionaries recognized him as the owner of the Cuba Theater; they all went to movies there. Two servants crept out to see what the fuss was about, and Frank softly ordered them to call the lady of the house.

AT CELIA'S HEADQUARTERS, either Beto Pesant or Cesar Suarez was watching the road when Lalo drove in. Although Crescencio's house sits in a clearing near the road, it was protected by three other houses shadowed on three sides by trees. Lalo went into the house, greeted Celia, and he told her of the start of Frank's Santiago uprising. Underlying this conversation was a single question: What if the *Granma* didn't arrive soon? What would be their course of action? What should Lalo tell the militants and 26th of July sabotage units to do? How long should they stay out? Should he pull them in, abandon the campaign before it even started?

The *Granma* had been due the day before, and the uprising in Santiago would create a point of no return. This widespread action was intended to distract the military; and if they were lucky, distract them until Fidel's forces were not only on land but able to join other 26th of July forces and attack a coastal garrison, steal their guns, and escape into the mountains. So, she reasoned, if Frank was now beginning the uprising, he must have word that Fidel had arrived. So Fidel would be brought to her soon.

Yet she had no confirmation of this. Nor, for that matter, even a rumor. She had to make a decision, and make it immediately. This dilemma was probably the most significant, and wrenching, of Celia's life.

She and Frank had always been prepared to see all hell break loose once the uprising began, particularly since it was going to put an end to any lingering impression that the 26th of July Movement was a ragtag bunch of kids, rogues, and cowboys: it was going to emerge as an army, with soldiers dressed in green uniforms. In response to what was taking place in Santiago, or about to, the vengeance of Batista's army would be unleashed all over Oriente, likely all over Cuba. In Frank's plan, the militant groups were meant to take action as soon as the *Granma* arrived, and then quietly slip back into their normal lives. That is what she'd rehearsed with them, and what they were prepared to do. But it was essential that this happen on a very tight timetable. Delay and uncertainty were creating a new dynamic, throwing a wrench into the works. Her militants were being required to stay out longer than planned, and soon would be connected, in people's minds, with the resistance they would hear about in Santiago. Celia weighed the consequences of their staying out longer. Who were the most vulnerable? Was she being asked to put the lives of Fidel and his men first, before the lives of her men and women in the field? Protecting the arriving rebels was what all the planning had been for. She had done everything she could think of, so far, to protect Fidel; neither Frank nor she thought their revolution could go ahead without him. Frank's plan had always been to stage an uprising *concurrent* with the *Granma*'s arrival. So, assuming the cabin cruiser had come ashore, though she didn't know where, the question was what orders should Lalo give to the people spread out along the coast, waiting for the boat that probably had already landed?

The decision she had to make was ruthless either way. Send her people back to safety, and risk the rebels' landing without help, exposed and unprotected? Or keep her people out there, in increasing danger of detection, and hope the boat they were waiting for came soon, and somewhere near Las Coloradas?

IN SANTIAGO, WHEN THE LADY of the house chosen as headquarters, Susette Bueno Rousseau, saw Frank, she was not enthusiastic. Still, she opened the gate, asking him, "Is it time?" As the 26th of July members filed into her apartment (Oscar described it as "their beautiful home"), Susette, a heavyset woman of about thirty, launched into an argument with her red-faced husband. Frank simply ignored them, wasting no time in setting up a machine gun, as Oscar noticed a nursery. Frank posted lookouts at windows, telling them to avoid being seen by neighbors or passersby. Susette finally convinced her husband they should "just leave." She quickly packed a suitcase with the things they needed, mostly for the baby. Somebody—not Frank—advised her to take all her jewelry and money: "We trust our comrades, but if we have to withdraw, these things could be in danger from the other side." The couple left, carrying their baby who slept through it all, as more revolutionaries quietly arrived. A three-story building stood directly across from the apartment; Frank sent four people to occupy it. Someone arrived with a sack of uniforms and emptied the contents on the floor in one of the rooms. Frank was the first to put his on. Others followed. Then it was Oscar's turn to get dressed in green gabardine. There were very few uniforms left, but he found one that fit. Haydée Santamaria helped him slip on the armband with its radical-looking red and black bands and 26th of July insignia in white stitching.

CELIA SET TO WORKING OUT all the scenarios of what might have happened to the *Granma*. Had they been intercepted by the Coast Guard? Had they been delayed by weather—at this time of year it was changeable, and the Caribbean often rough. Or had they come ashore outside the designated area? As of that morning, they hadn't shown up near Niquero or Pilón. Nor, she suspected, in the area including Media Luna and Campechuela. She kept returning to the issue that baffled her: Frank's plan was an uprising concurrent with the landing. So did his having moved forward mean Fidel had landed? That uprising was understood as crossing the Rubicon. Not only would the police, the army, the *Guardia Rural*, and the paramilitaries be on alert, the government in Havana would be rudely awakened from its dreamy belief that the ragtag dissidents in the eastern provinces posed no serious threat. From now on, anyone who was young and looked even vaguely like a supporter of the 26th of July Movement would be fodder for the police and military intelligence. That description fit every one of her militants, on alert, waiting to go forward with attacks. Her people in the underground had been away from their jobs the day before, all of Thursday the 29th. Her truck drivers would be less suspicious—unless they were stopped and their trucks found to carry arms. Still, how many more hours could they cruise around and remain inconspicuous? These questions turned over and over in her mind. Her mission had been clear: they were there to assist the landing by camouflaging it; to make lightning attacks, then disappear, resume their lives. Each hour without word that the *Granma* had landed made this mission less possible to carry out.

The moment was crucial. If her choice was to protect her militants, she would need to call off the operation right away, to bring them in while there was still time for them to assert a presence at home, or even—since Lalo had come early—show up at their jobs. Being late or absent on this particular Friday, the 30th, would quickly become very dangerous. An epidemic of late-coming would surely catch the attention of some of the wrong people. Managers and coworkers would already have noticed who had been absent the previous day. The truck drivers had somewhat better cover, since they operated on their own, out on the roads, but still, they were accountable to their bosses.

The situation was agonizing. The lack of communications only made things worse. It is quite likely, by the way, that the memory of this terrible morning guided Celia later, once the war was underway, in pulling out all stops to build a system for keeping the Revolution's commanders in contact with each other.

IN SANTIAGO, IN THE ROUSSEAU HOUSE, shouts were heard from the street: "*Viva Cuba Libre! Viva Fidel Castro! Viva la revolución! Abajo Batista!*" Everybody knew that the time had come, and that Pepito Tey and his group had started the uprising when, at 7:00 a.m. exactly, the occupants of the Rousseau house heard gunfire. Tey and his men were attacking National Police Headquarters. The telephone began ringing off the hook. Frank was getting information and giving orders to the heads of the various action groups around the city. Some of the calls were from the Rousseaus' neighbors, who were alarmed but nonetheless curious about the activities going on in the apartment. Gloria Cuadras and Ramon Alvarez monitored the radio, expecting to hear an alert, and discovered that all the stations continued to play music and run commercials.

WHILE CELIA STARED DOWN HER PREDICAMENT, Lalo took a nap. When he awoke, she informed him of her decision: to call the operation off only if the *Granma* did not arrive by the next morning. Meaning she would try to maintain protection for the landing guerrillas for another full 24 hours. She ordered Lalo to go back to Niquero and stay put. As Lalo made the drive south to Niquero, he knew that they had entered new, even more dangerous territory. Celia had been specific in her orders: he and Manuel Fajardo were to wait out the day and night; he would, if it came to it, call the rescue operation off the following morning. Were she to learn that the landing had taken place, she would come to Niquero and inform him. If she hadn't knocked on the icehouse door by nine the next morning, Saturday, December 1st, he was to leave and cancel all operations along the coast. She was stretching the operation as long as was conceivable.

She surely hoped Mongo would arrive soon to tell her that Fidel was at Cinco Palmas, that the rebels had all arrived in the night, into El Macho perhaps, and someone had brought Fidel to his house, as was the plan, instead of to her, in Ojo de Agua. If so, she would be able to reduce almost certain losses. It is doubtful she went outside Crescencio's house to walk around or visit any of the other houses in Ojo de Agua de Jerez; she would have shielded Crescencio's neighbors from knowing she was there. Restless even in normal circumstances, she was now confined yet longer by the decision she had made. Her mind moved to the others, picked for their youth and willingness to take risks, hoping, as the day developed and Batista's military got word of the uprising, that they wouldn't get caught. She had to think beyond the possibility that Fidel would arrive that day. If by nine the next morning she had to call off her operation, she would need to assess the costs of the delay.

She had not yet met Fidel Castro, so her thoughts about him would not have been firsthand or personal. She must have had thoughts, too, about other men she had backed, starting with Eduardo Chibás: how her father had been a founder of Chibás's Orthodox Party, Chibás's visit to Pilón in 1948 on the campaign circuit, when she had sat on the podium, the only woman in a line of men. After Chibás, she had supported another politician who had turned out to be a flop, Emilio Ochoa—he had flown into the country unprepared, ignoring so much of the help waiting for him, and failed. What had come out of it? She had met and worked with various militant groups in nearly every city, and in every small town in all the coastal areas for years now, and for this reason the local people trusted her. Would Fidel Castro be just another letdown? The stakes were higher this time around, which would have made her feel even more desperate, and cooped up, after 48 hours, very little sleep, hundreds of cigarettes, and a million tiny cups of coffee, all leading to disappointment.

She may have put Fidel out of her mind, her heart with her people, and with Frank.

IN SANTIAGO, FRANK'S BATTLE was well under way, and he was outnumbered and vulnerable. Some of the assaults he'd planned were successful, some fizzled, but they were widespread enough to dilute the military's response. The most dramatic conflicts took place in the oldest part of town, where 26th of July soldiers led by Jorge Sotus threw grenades and incendiary bombs (Molotov cocktails, in fact) through open windows and doorways and against the façade of the Customs Police Maritime Headquarters.

This operation was a particular success: they were able to enter, acquire guns, and leave.

The Cuban army, ensconced in the Moncada Garrison, moved cautiously that day. The biggest attack was against the National Police Garrison, led by Pepito Tey, who with his 26th of July soldiers was able to enter the building. Otto Parellada's group came down Padre Pico, entered the School of Visual Arts, crossed the courtyard, and got onto a roof overlooking the police station. They shot at the police running into the station's courtyard. From there, they engaged the police in battle, with the advantage of firing from above, and were able to maintain that stronghold for most of the day. When the besieged police surrendered, the 26th of July soldiers freed prisoners from their cells and set fire to the building. This was a relatively successful operation, since they had held the police garrison until the afternoon and damaged the iconic building. Beyond that, they could go no further. Tey had been gunned down outside, and his body lay there, and was photographed, his blood splashed against the side of the building and running into the gutter.

Several of the 26th of July attackers arrived at Frank's headquarters to tell him the news about Tey, as others told him news of the deaths of his friends Antonio Aloma and Otto Parellada. Frank and Jorge Sotus argued about what to do next. Lots of ad hoc attack plans were being put forth, and Frank vetoed them all. He was against taking off into the mountains, even though it had been one of the plans; he thought the trucks weren't up to the trip. Somebody telephoned with news that the army had left the Moncada and was heading northeast on the Central Highway, to El Cobre, as well as to other points nearby. Frank decided that he would unilaterally declare a truce. They had accomplished their goals: any more action would cause a useless loss of lives and weapons. And it would no doubt surprise and confound the government forces to have the successful uprising suddenly go quiet. He told everyone to leave the headquarters, a few at a time; to leave all weapons behind; to hide in houses throughout Santiago, and stay there until further notice.

"Since there was no other alternative, I thought of various places to hide out," Oscar remembers, but he settled on the home of an old guitarist, Emilio Carbonella, and his wife, Targila Planas.

A friend of Oscar's, a young woman at the Institute, often visited the couple at 57 Reloj. "So there I went, sure they would not fail me," although he could still hear gunshots and machine-gun fire in the streets as the old musician opened his door and took him in.

The army retook the city around 3:00 p.m., although details as to the hour conflict. After that, Santiago would descend more deeply than ever into corruption and sadistic and ruthless police tactics. When you consider the magnitude of the insult that the 26th of July Movement delivered, it is amazing there were so few casualties that day. Historians often call the uprising a bloodbath, but it was not. The greater number of losses was taken by the *batistianos* (eight), but the 26th of July's three deaths were of enormous significance to the movement: Tey, Aloma, and Parellada were leaders, Frank's partners from the beginning.

Frank had set out to distract the army, if only for a few hours, and he dumbfounded it. The army was holed up in the Moncada for eight hours. In over fifty years since the event, very little new information has surfaced, but it seems that Taras Domitro (and therefore Frank) actually did have inside information: some of Batista's soldiers had refused to fight against the revolutionaries. This is corroborated by the fact that soon after as many as 67 soldiers were arrested and court-martialed. More cracks were appearing in Batista's army. In Cuba, nobody has forgotten that Frank's new army emerged that day, disciplined and real. Middle-class parents understood that their children had been the soldiers on an urban battlefield. And nobody was foolish enough to think that things would be the same afterward.

In reaction, many in Santiago with money left Cuba, moving away to Spain, Puerto Rico, Mexico, the United States. A few went to France. Citizens without that kind of income sent their children to stay with relatives in places they thought were less violent, like Cienfuegos or Camaguey. But these cities soon became hotbeds, too, since the Battle of Santiago marked the beginning of an all-out war against the government.

CELIA, MEANWHILE, CONTINUED HER WAIT, as did Guillermo García and Mongo Pérez, also anxious, also trapped in houses. Lalo and Fajardo began their final shift in the icehouse, while the clandestine forces desperately improvised. The hours passed.

Saturday, December 1, after 72 hours, it was all over for the clandestine network. Celia did not make a 9:00 a.m. appearance at the icehouse. As she had instructed, Lalo called off all activities in Niquero, then drove north, seeing the directors in the other towns, having them call in their teams. Also per her instructions, he found out what damage had already been done, and made sure it was known by everyone that she, personally, would guarantee their protection. He told the directors that she would be following him up the coast and would visit some of them, on her way back to Manzanillo.

INFORMERS IN MEXICO HAD ALERTED the army to the *Granma*'s departure. army intelligence predicted that Fidel would head for Oriente Province, knew the identities of some of his supporters, and concluded that one person in particular could lead them straight to Fidel. Saturday morning, orders were issued to capture Celia Sánchez Manduley, dead or alive.

CELIA REMAINED AT HER HEADQUARTERS throughout the day, in keeping with her plan to extend protection, albeit reduced, for the *Granma*, and hoping to hear from Crescencio or Guillermo. She probably thought about the previous decade. It was as if she'd been training for this moment, maybe subconsciously, before Frank or Fidel. In 1948, she'd helped her father organize a rally for the Orthodox Party's presidential candidate, Eduardo Chibás. He and his party became the center of her social and intellectual life. She'd gone to every party meeting in these coastal towns, had invited people—by tens and dozens and hundreds—to listen to Chibás's hour-long radio show on Sunday evenings in her garden, the radio fastened to a corner post. Farmers and ranchers—some now waiting, like her, for Fidel to arrive—had planned their market day to include the broadcast. She'd liked "Eddy" Chibás and went to visit him in Havana at Party headquarters, across from the Capitol in the old boxing gym formerly used by Kid Chocolate. Chibás was then forty-two years old, with a wife and young child, but not exactly a family man or glamorous politician: short, balding, and myopic, recognized by his thick, hexagon-lensed, gold-rimmed glasses. He drove his Packard convertible through stop signs and traffic lights, and dreamed of cleaning up politics. *Verguenza Contra*

Dinero—Honor before Money—had been the Orthodox slogan, and its logo a long-handled broom to sweep corrupt politicians out of office. When in 1949 a group of American sailors off a U.S. Navy ship docked at Havana, had climbed onto the beautiful statue of Martí in Parque Central expressly to urinate on Martí's figure, he'd called them "beasts, neither American, nor men."

But everything fell apart less than a year from elections, when they knew they'd surely win. In July 1951, Chibás accused Minister of Education Sánchez Arango of using school funds to invest in a Guatemalan real estate development. They agreed to debate on July 21 and some say he canceled at the last minute because he didn't like the conditions, but others say he showed up but was unable to enter the building while Sánchez Arango made a short, televised statement saying Chibás was a no-show. Next, Chibás promised proof of Sánchez Arango's guilt on his August 5 broadcast. Celia and her father had decided to drive to Havana for the event so they could celebrate with Chibás. At eight o'clock, the nation had gathered in front of radios, but Eddy kept bringing up other issues, and when the hour was over, he hadn't produced his proof. She felt sure that his colleagues, the congressmen who had the documents, the proof, refused to supply them and he'd been set up. Everyone listening had been bewildered, then found out that at the end of the show, Chibás had aimed a pistol at his abdomen and pulled the trigger. A sound engineer cut off the program because the show had run over its allotted time, and instead of hearing Chibás call out, "Forward! People of Cuba, goodbye! This is my last call! (*el ultimo aldabonazo*)," they heard instead: "Café Pilón, the coffee that is tasty to the last drop."

She stayed in Havana, couldn't leave Chibás as he held on, painfully, for ten more days, and did not let herself believe that he'd meant to kill himself. He died on the operating table at 1:57 a.m., August 16, 1951, and she went to the funeral parlor and stayed with his body until the lid of the coffin was closed and carried out on the afternoon of the 17th. Exhausted, she joined over 300,000 mourners behind the casket as it was carried to Colon Cemetery.

Even without Chibás, Celia did not drop her political activities. One of the founders of the Orthodox Party, Emilo, or "Millo," Ochoa, challenged Chibás's former running mate, Roberto Agramonte, for the party's presidential nomination, and so had a

This photograph was taken in Pilón in 1948, while Orthodox Party leader, Eduardo Chibás, was on the campaign trail for president. Celia and her father can be seen just behind the horse's head. *(Courtesy of Oficina de Asuntos Históricos)*

twenty-five-year-old lawyer named Fidel Castro, just then starting to attract attention.

She was shocked when Batista returned on Monday, March 10, 1952, to assume power by a military *coup d'état*. Ochoa, a senator, had called President Carlos Prio Soccaros and offered to send a plane to Havana to bring him to Santiago; he'd begged Prioto to stay in the country and make a stand against Batista, but both he and Prio ended up in exile. What Cuba was going to be like under a military regime hit home after Batista cancelled the June elections. There would be no legal means of reform through the ballot box for the people. She had felt depressed and powerless, but put out feelers, and started to find like-minded people who were against Batista and his military government. For the rest of 1952, from May to December, she'd driven all along the coast visiting Orthodox Party members to find out how they felt, to see if they viewed the present state of affairs as she did, and find out what they planned to do next. She discovered that among her former Orthodox Party friends everybody was willing to oppose the military dictator: there were those who were interested in joining a group against him (activists), those who wanted to focus on overthrowing him (militants), and then there were a few who had been willing to do whatever it took to end the military government (willing conspirators). She had conducted another one of her censuses.

During 1956, Celia would select militants from groups she'd worked with in the past. Attending an Orthodox Party meeting in Niquero, late 1948, she is seated in the center, with Israel Pela, Juan Sánchez Ramirez, Amparo de la Guardia, and others. *(Courtesy of Oficina de Asuntos Históricos)*

After Chibás, she'd believed in Ochoa, who wanted to return to Cuba from exile. She'd believed him capable of liberating the country from Batista, and she worked in the final months of 1953 and most of 1954 building a network to support him among all those activists and militants and potential conspirators she knew along the coast, persuading them to help "Millo" when he returned. For at least twelve months, she'd made contacts in Pilón, Niquero, Media Luna, Campechuela, and Manzanillo, going to Havana and Santiago to report on her progress and to receive instructions from various directors in Ochoa's camp. By the end of 1954, she had selected the people she needed and was ready for his arrival. Then, in the first days of November 1954, she learned that Ochoa had returned to Cuba by parachuting into Camaguey. No one in his organization even saw fit to inform her, so she'd gone to Camaguey to investigate for herself, taking a friend. They'd discovered that Ochoa had arrived by plane and gone straight to Havana. She realized that he had never meant to carry out an uprising, and at some point, without informing her, had given up his plan for using Pilón as his landing place. She was furious and humiliated. Changing plans is understandable, but not informing her showed complete lack of respect for the people taking risks for him, and questionable commitment on his part.

On November 11, 1954, Batista extended his presidency through fraudulent elections, and Ochoa, in Havana, was his vocal opponent, but she hadn't even considered forgetting about the months of work she'd put in, because, in her book, he was a traitor to her and everyone living around her. She contacted all the people on the coast, told them what had happened, and they began to regroup. She renewed old contacts with Orthodox Party members, and she founded her own secret movement, the Masó Revolutionary Movement, named after Manzanillo's own rebel, Bartolomé Masó Márquez. His message had been as simple and obvious as Chibás's broom: buy land, no matter how little, so the United States can't buy it, with whatever money you can scrape together; buy land as an act of patriotism, because the United States did not want a Cuban to own any more land than could be seen in "the shadow of the flag."

By January 1955, Ochoa had gone back into exile, in Mexico. He'd been living on a legacy of his younger days, and she'd fallen for it. In the end, he was unable to take risks, was too old, had a family, and didn't want to take chances.

As she waited for Fidel on the first day of December, 1956, Celia knew she wasn't the same woman who had volunteered so willingly to help Chibás in 1948 and Millo Ochoa in 1954. She hoped he was not the same kind of man either. Fidel seemed to be a different breed: he had been married and had a child, but he was a risk-taker, he thought like a young, single man and had proved it. He had risked his life at the Moncada.

When she had gone to see Frank in Santiago eleven months earlier, he knew all about her preparations for Ochoa and expressed admiration for her. He knew that her knowledge of people on the coast was extensive and her greatest point of expertise. He put her in charge of her own operations. He had assured her that he'd never leave her out in the cold—as Millo had done. She had demanded that. She understood that Frank would never fail her. But now, sitting at Crescencio's, could she say the same about Fidel?

7. DECEMBER 2, 1956

The Arrival of the *Granma*

THE *GRANMA* WAS APPROACHING, slowly. The boat had lost nearly a day plowing through rough seas off the Yucatán peninsula, and only passed the western tip of Cuba, at the remote end of Pinar del Rio Province, at 5:00 p.m. on Thursday, November 29. It then made even slower headway as it traveled east the length of Cuba, following a safe route, far to the south of the island and well out of view of the Coast Guard. Friday, while they were still on this route, their radio had picked up news of the Santiago uprising, but there was no way to increase speed and make up for lost time. Finally, they had seen their beacon, the light at Cabo Cruz, on the night of the 1st, and set course for it. As they approached their destination, at about three in the morning of Sunday, December 2, they hit rough seas and lost a man—a guerrilla named Roberto Roque fell overboard. The sky was dark, the water choppy, but with very little hope of finding Roque, Fidel decided they must try. Reversing then moving forward, and repeating this in a zigzag, they found Roque, but used up time and fuel and left their pilot, Onelio Pino, disoriented.

They approached Cabo Cruz with only enough fuel to last a few minutes, and as they started up the coast toward Las Coloradas, Pino told Fidel they would have to land. Fidel asked him: "Is this Cuba? Are you absolutely sure it isn't Jamaica or a key?" The pilot assured him that it was Cuba. They were very near their goal, having reached Los Cayuelos, less than three miles south of the port of Las Coloradas. This put them, as Celia would later dryly comment, at about the worst place imaginable on the entire Cuban coast.

It was around 5:00 a.m. when the *Granma* hit a sandbar and simply came to a stop.

THIS WAS PROBABLY THE SAME HOUR that Celia, Beto, and Cesar got into the jeep and drove away from Crescencio's house, heading for Manzanillo. She had stayed on at her Ojo de Agua headquarters knowing that Lalo would have called off the landing operation. She had still expected someone to show up on the doorstep Saturday with Fidel. It had been a long 24 hours: without a telephone or radio, no couriers, but knowing full well that Frank's uprising would have caused a wave of arrests in Santiago and across the nation. But she had risen on this morning resigned to the fact that she had closed down her end of the operation; now she was headed to Manzanillo to meet Lalo, learn the damage her clandestine operators—her militants—had suffered, and begin her next job of figuring out a way to protect them.

THE ORDER ISSUED TO BRING IN CELIA SÁNCHEZ dead or alive caused one officer (whose name I have never discovered) to feel such horror and conflict that, on receiving it, he tipped off the priest in Media Luna. The priest contacted Celia's brother, Manuel Enrique, who lived in Media Luna with his wife. Manuel Enrique had no idea what Celia was up to, but he got in his car and began driving from town to town, anxiously looking for her on this Sunday morning as she, Beto, and Cesar were retracing their route north.

When he arrived in Media Luna with Celia and Beto, Cesar Suarez left the jeep. Acting for Celia, he would make contact with the town's directors and get a report, find out what had happened and who was in danger. Beto and Celia continued on to Campechuela, where they were going to do the same thing: learn whether there had been arrests, ask what they'd heard about Frank's uprising, and whether they could shed any light on Fidel's landing.

Celia and Beto parted in Campechuela, but not before arranging to meet later that day. Neither realized they were walking into danger; both were sure they would be continuing on to Manzanillo in time for Celia to make her meeting with Lalo Vásquez. They agreed to meet up in the afternoon at a small bridge located on the highway leading out of town.

Campechuela is a classic Cuban mill town: one- and two-story buildings cram a couple of noisy commercial streets of ground-floor shops—a company store, bodegas, bars, cafes, one or two tailors, hardware and feed supplies. Campechuela's two main business streets (one of them the route of the highway) now, as it did then, straddle railroad tracks that run from the mill at the edge of town to the port, where boats load sugar. Celia stepped down from the jeep in front of a taxi stand on one of those main streets. She was wearing the chocolate brown skirt she'd put on five days earlier. She left the jeep at a crowded drop-off point, the one most people used when they arrived or departed from town. Sunday was market day, and the whole town was teeming with people, and, almost immediately, she noticed her brother, Manuel Enrique, as he drove by looking for her. She was completely surprised to see him, but relieved that he looked past and seemed not to see her. She headed for a nearby bar.

Celia walked slowly and naturally to La Rosa. The building is still there, now an urban planning office with a plaque on the wall to commemorate December 2, 1956, the day heroine Celia Sánchez stepped inside to talk with the bartender. La Rosa stood on a corner, and its customers could enter from either street. Both doors were double panels of solid wood, swinging open from ground to ceiling. The barroom was not large, with only a few tables. The bartender, Enrique de la Rosa, was one of Celia's hand-picked militants. Campechuela's city historian showed me a snapshot of Enrique taken on that day: twenty years old, he wore a white T-shirt, sleeves rolled up over his biceps to enfold a pack of cigarettes, and straight-legged Levis with six or eight inches of cuff. His blond hair was cut very short, except for a wave held in place with Brylcreem. In lieu of a bar proper, he did business behind a waist-high, glass-fronted display case (with open boxes of cigars on shelves below). Bottles of beer, rum, and a few canned goods lined a shelf on the wall behind him.

With all doors open, the bar was flooded with morning light. Celia had been inside only a short time when a jeep and two SIM (Military Intelligence Service) cars pulled up: officers jumped out, entered the bar, and arrested her while soldiers closed the doors, sinking the room into near darkness.

Celia recognized one of the men. He worked for army intelligence; his name was Hatuey, which he had in common with a Taino chief famous for his valor, but this Hatuey was noted more for his violence, especially with union strikers. His trademark, beating his victims with the flat side of a machete blade, had earned him the title "Machete King." Almost as quickly as they'd shut the place down, the soldiers reopened the doors, got back into their vehicles and drove off, leaving Hatuey and one other man behind to guard Celia. She knew him to be a member of Masferrer's paramilitary group, the *Tigres*, now doing much of the army's dirty work. Hatuey ordered her to sit down and not to move. He and the other man occupied an adjacent table.

She had come to the end of her life, she assumed, had been captured, defeated. She later recalled that her mind was frozen, dull, and her body felt leaden, although she claimed that fear wasn't the source of it. She knew she'd be tortured—all of the revolutionaries were aware of what would happen to them if caught—and that she had to do everything in her power to resist for 24 hours, the time her comrades would need to go underground. She would be taken away for interrogation. This was a given. She understood and accepted this, at least until a momentary glimmer of resistance swept through her. It proved just enough to clear her mind, to enable her to analyze her situation. It was odd, she thought, that Hatuey wouldn't look her in the eye; he didn't seem to recognize or even acknowledge her, although she knew him personally.

Celia had known Hatuey since she was a child. He was one of her father's patients. Why was he avoiding eye contact with her? He was the biggest braggart of them all, so why so quiet? And why were the three of them sitting in the open, on show, in complete view to people walking by on the street? Why were the doors open, and why had they reopened the bar after shutting it down? It hit her: she was being used as a decoy. The men were waiting to arrest anyone who might be coming to rendezvous with her. She willed her mind to function, to rise out of the stupor she felt in every inch of her body, and ordered herself to think of a plan. It took her only a few minutes to decide what she had to do.

AT 5:30 A.M., IT WAS STILL PRETTY DARK. Those on the *Granma* could make out a coast that appeared to be forested. As they looked east into the sun, soon rising, the trees along the shore were backlit. They had to cover the distance between where they'd run aground, on the sandbar, and the shore, and realized it would be impossible to carry all their equipment under the circumstances. In addition, some were too weak, debilitated from four days of seasickness. They all began to fight their way through what turned out to be fairly deep water, over the heads of some of the soldiers. Raúl Castro's rear guard platoon was the last to leave the boat.

They had started to disembark when it was still dark, and when they got ashore, about an hour later, what had looked at first light like a line of trees on dry land turned out to be a mangrove swamp. There was no actual firm ground to stand on. This alarmed them—they were, fundamentally, an urban bunch, and no one was from the area. One guerrilla, Rene Ramos Latour, had worked in the nickel mines in Niquero as an accountant, but he was from Santiago. Celia had been right to wonder how these men were going to get off a boat anywhere in Oriente and be able to find their way; she would have been an asset had she been permitted to travel with them.

Getting through the mangroves was not easy. They had to step on the roots rising out of the water. Each man needed both hands free to hold onto the trunks as he climbed over the network of slippery, tangled roots. Their uniforms got caught on the branches and were torn. Since the men had to maneuver through the grove singly, or at best in pairs, platoons could not go ashore in an orderly or organized manner. The guerrillas ended up scattered all along the shore, dispersed, having made their way through the trees as best they could. This cost them yet another hour.

At about 7:00 a.m., one of the men with Fidel, Luis Crespo, climbed a tree and saw a house beyond the line of trees. A group of eight got to the house an hour later (about the same time Celia was sitting in the bar in Campechuela) and Fidel greeted the man who met them, Angel Pérez Rosabal, with his famously grandiose "Hello, I'm Fidel Castro. We are here to liberate Cuba." This farmer was outside Celia's network and didn't recognize his name. On Miret's last trip to Mexico, Frank had sent word to Fidel to find Mongo Pérez in the lower reaches of the Sierra Maestra, but now Fidel needed to find the Sierra first.

AT THE TABLE IN THE BAR LA ROSA, Celia pulled a cigarette from her pocket. She asked her captors, in her soft voice, if they'd permit her to buy some matches. They agreed. She walked over to the bar—only a few paces—and got a box from Enrique. She returned to her chair, sat down, lit up, and smoked as naturally as she could. After putting out the cigarette, she said apologetically, possibly even smiling faintly, "Oh! I forgot. May I buy some Chiclets?" Again, they agreed.

The little boxes of gum were inside a small display case that stood on legs near one of the doors. She walked over to it, hesitated a moment in front of the case, then bolted outside. Both men came after her, firing their pistols.

The street was crowded, people shrieked, grabbed their children, shop owners rushed outside, saw the police, closed shutters, and some knowingly helped by dashing back and forth and causing confusion. She zigzagged through the streets, running from door to door, one street to another—"I ran like a rabbit"— until she recognized the sugar mill. In total dismay, because now she was on the edge of town and could go no farther, she dropped to the ground: "I came to an open lot, with sunlight, that was level and full of grass. I stayed right there and hid."

In Oriente Province people call such a place a *solar*, a piece of empty land that gets enough sunlight to produce ground cover. The grass was short, and the sugar mill, Dos Amigos, close enough that people were moving about in the area. She waited for the police to discover her, and when they didn't after an hour or so, she began to move just a few inches at a time, sliding, pressing flat against the ground, carefully, slowly, hoping that no one would see the grass move. It took hours. It was afternoon when she reached the edge of the lot, where she crawled into a spiny grove of trees—slightly akin to a cactus patch—and sought protection in a *marabu* grove.

Her hiding place at the base of this group of thorn trees was invisible only because the *marabu* is considered so detestable that everybody avoids its extremely hard, spiky thorns, which reach out threateningly from the trunk, the branches, and even shoot up from the tree's exposed roots. The species (*Dichrostachys cinera*) was imported from Africa in the nineteenth century as a cheap way to fence in roving cattle. Celia covered her face with her arms and crawled over the roots as thorns cut through her hair and dug into her scalp. *Marabu* isn't especially thick, and she wasn't completely out of sight, but she knew she was safe. Nobody ever looked at these sinister thickets, and Celia, with her shrewd country woman's instinct, expected the police would not bother to check there either.

FIDEL AND HIS GROUP OF EIGHT MEN spent the rest of the morning eating pork and fried bananas prepared by Angel Pérez Rosabal's wife. And then they rested. But as they rested, a Coast Guard plane flew in from the northeast and Fidel began to worry whether the army had already sent troops to the area. His guerrillas were so completely dispersed, broken up into such small units, defenseless, that he was afraid of being attacked by land troops. He decided to hide. He marched his group to a small hill and was surprised to find a few other guerrillas hiding there. At 11:00 a.m., Angel showed them a road to follow, and Fidel's group began their march east toward the Sierra Maestra, the heart of which lay 50 kilometers in the distance. At noon, they came to a small ranch and spoke with two farmers, Pedro Luis Sánchez and Juan Herrera. Sánchez offered them well water—repeating this offer throughout the day to all the guerrillas who came by—and showed them to the best road to follow.

BY THE AFTERNOON Celia had gotten her bearings and realized that her *marabu* thicket was not all that far from the highway, but on the other hand, it was dangerously close to the back of the police station. It would only be safe to move after dark, but soon fed up with that idea she took a chance and crawled out of the grove, this time backwards, reversing her painful route in. Once out of the *marabu* she scrambled, still on hands and knees, along a path to the highway, where she lay in a ditch. If she heard a car coming she would raise her head. She concluded that the military was traveling to the coast; she even saw planes overhead, and took this as clear indication that Fidel had arrived.

AT ABOUT 3:00 P.M.—around the time Celia would have been lying in the ditch—Fidel and his small group came to a clearing and rested. So far they had seen only one reconnaissance plane, in the morning. Now two Coast Guard Catalinas flew over. One machine-gunned a house, which they feared belonged to Angel Pérez Rosabal and his wife, who'd been so kind to them. As it turned out, the house attacked belonged to a farmer who knew nothing about the guerrillas and had no idea why his little coconut grove was coming under attack. The guerrillas had seen enough; they had to get into an area with better cover, but to do that they had to get across scrubland with low vegetation without being spied by any planes overhead. They decided to attempt this after dark.

HATUEY, THE ARMY OFFICER who had arrested Celia, drove down to Pilón that afternoon to speak with Dr. Sánchez in person. Hatuey informed him of her arrest and escape. "But I can assure you, the second time she won't escape," he told the doctor. He explained that she had been spotted very early that morning, and the call had come in while he was at the army post in Manzanillo. He'd gone to arrest her but, as he tried to make clear to Celia's father, he did not expect to find her so easily.

The hardened, brutal military policeman stood before the doctor, filled with remorse. His face was pockmarked, and one side was covered with a big scar; at times during his career he'd been evil incarnate, yet now he tried to apologize for what was happening. He claimed that he didn't want to have any part of what was going to take place if they found her. He told Dr. Sánchez his reason for coming: he was grateful to the Sánchez family, referring to a time when Dr. Sánchez had cured his father of typhus. Hatuey implored: "Try to get her out of here because they are going to get her, and torture her. They have to make her talk. She knows a lot. They are going to make her talk."

SOMETIME THAT AFTERNOON, General Pedro Rodríguez Avila, commander of army operations in Oriente Province, issued a statement: forty members of the 26th of July Movement had been annihilated, among them their chief, Fidel Castro. Their bodies had been collected, he said, but some of the bodies had been "literally pulverized" and were therefore unrecognizable. By this time the *Granma* had been confiscated by the government with the harbor maps that Celia had given to Fidel still on it.

IN THE LATE AFTERNOON Celia heard a car approaching; she lifted her head from the ditch and, recognizing the driver, an automobile upholsterer named Grana, leaped out onto the road to stop him. She asked for a lift to Manzanillo. He looked at the scratches on her face, her clothes covered in dirt and grass stains, and asked, "Celia, how did you get like this?" She supplied him with a scarcely plausible explanation—that her car had broken down "somewhere nearby"—and appealed to his compassion: "Look at me. It's been raining, look at the state I'm in. Just take me to Manzanillo."

Once they were on the road, she said she had a friend "who'd gone to buy a car part" waiting for her on a bridge ahead. And in fact, serendipitously, they came upon Beto Pesant. Grana stopped the car and he got in. As Grana drove on, Celia and Beto questioned him about the military activity, visible everywhere. He told them that the army had called that morning for a general mobilization and that the military had taken over the airport. He had seen many planes take off that day, and didn't know the reason because there hadn't been any news bulletins. He added that everyplace in Manzanillo was being systematically searched by the police. Hearing this, Celia knew they'd be caught if they stayed in his car; they'd eventually be pulled over or come to a checkpoint. She told Grana to stop the car. She quickly contrived a new reason—her family wasn't in Manzanillo, but waiting with a car at a farm nearby—and she and Beto got out. They hid in the underbrush at the side of the road until it was dark.

After nightfall, Beto took her to the house of a 26th of July Movement member who lived not too far from this stretch of the highway, where both husband and wife welcomed them. Celia was desperate for information, but the couple did not know much, although they knew through the grapevine that Frank's uprising had taken place. Around midnight (as December 2 turned to December 3), after they were sure that all traffic had ceased on the highway, Celia and Beto got back on the road and started walking toward Manzanillo under cover of darkness.

IN CAMPECHUELA, the police went to the house of the young bartender, Enrique de la Rosa, took him outside, and fired forty-two bullets into his body.

8. December 3, 1956

Felipe Guerra Matos

AT DAYLIGHT, on Monday, December 3, Celia and Beto Pesant reached the outskirts of Manzanillo. They hid in a cane field so that they could watch the airport, still under government control, and decided to stay out of sight for the rest of the day. Beto took her to the house of a sympathizer, on the edge of town. When they got there, they found the owner completely befuddled by grief. His father had died fifteen days earlier, and he'd barely eaten or gone out of his house since. They spent the rest of the day and night in this place.

The guerrillas—at least Fidel's group—awoke hungry on December 3, having eaten only cane juice and a little bit of food, including some corn, the night before. They took the road to El Mijial. By this time, they had reached an inland corridor off the southern coast of Cuba where the elevation rises in terraces and begins to form the mountains farther east. The terrain is covered with trees, which gave the men cover, but the ground was nearly impossible to walk on, covered in sharp rocks that cut through their boots. They had no water until they came to a house owned by Zoilo Pérez Vega, called Varón, who was not home, but his wife and children greeted them and gave them water. The guerrillas introduced themselves and one of Varón's sons, José Rafael Pérez, spoke up to tell them what his father had heard on a neighbor's radio. The Vega family killed some hens, made a nutritious soup with yucca, and offered them honey in the comb. The soldiers left with sweet potatoes and with Varón's brother, Tato Vega, and son, José Rafael, as their guides, who offered to show them a shortcut east to Beattie Sugar Company lands and a blazed trail, or *trocha*, that would get them to the mountains.

By now, they were marching in three platoons: the vanguard led by José Smith, followed by Fidel's platoon and Raúl's rear guard. On the road, they had met a *carbón* (charcoal) cutter (Fidencio Labrada), and considered him to be a good omen: if he met other guerrillas, he could tell them where to go. They came to a little village called Agua Fina, where three *carbón* cutters lived, and once again the guerrillas were fed; this time it was chicken with black beans and rice, for which the *carbón* cutters were handsomely paid $5. They spent a relatively calm night on December 3.

AS CELIA AND BETO PESANT were about to leave the next morning, Tuesday, December 4, they heard a milkman coming down the road and persuaded their host to go outside and buy a bottle of milk, which they shared. Then went on their way but right away ran into trouble. As they were going into town, a sentry recognized Pesant; they ran for cover and quickly separated so they'd have a better chance of getting away. Pesant told her how to find a dance hall in this part of town; he'd meet her there. They spent the rest of the day hiding out in the empty dance hall building, but when night came, the place filled up with prostitutes, and, at some point, they heard an argument followed by gunfire and were afraid the police would come and find them. They were desperate to leave because they were hiding in an office with only one way out, through a single door. Pesant thought the owner might have weapons hidden in the ceiling, so they spent the night searching frantically, and Celia would later describe the night, cryptically, as "very hectic."

BY THE 4TH, FARMERS WERE BEGINNING to hear stories: Batista's forces were in the area. The guerrillas still had not reached the *trocha*, and soon after 8:00 a.m. Fidel's group heard planes overhead, and their guide, José Rafael, had led them to terrain where the volcanic rocks were so cutting—Cubans call them *dientes de perro*, dog's teeth—that they made little headway. More *carbón* cutters came to their rescue (Jesus Luis Sánchez and his brother, Pedro Luis), providing food and water, and buying food for them in a bodega, as they kept marching eastward. The column spent the night of the 4th in a cane field, sucking on cane, which quenched their thirst and gave them a little energy. This was to be their undoing.

AROUND 5:00 A.M., on Wednesday, December 5, Celia and Beto left the dance hall. They had been in Barrio d'Oro, located on a bluff above the harbor, and now they carefully circled the hill moving toward the older part of the city. They separated, mindful that the sentry, who had seen them the day before, would have reported seeing them together. Completely out in the open and alone, Celia walked along the streets of Manzanillo and was greatly relieved to see one of the Larramendi brothers. He was stunned to see her, listened to her explanations (the same story: her car had broken down, she'd left it behind, could he take her home) and let her into his jeep, but started berating her for her political activities. "How can you do these things? You know what times are like. They are going to kill you." She ordered him to "let me off right here" and got out of the jeep.

She made it to Cira Escalona's house. Cira, one of her dearest friends, who had lived in Pilón but now lived in Manzanillo, called a young doctor, Lascos Vásquez, who gave Celia a tetanus shot as 26th of July Movement women arrived and began to remove *marabu* thorns with tweezers. She had a high fever and complained of severe headache, so her old friend, Dr. Rene Vallejo, came to Cira's and surgically removed thirteen thorns from Celia's skull. "Like Jesus Christ's crown of thorns," she'd say, later on.

WHEN CELIA'S FATHER HEARD that she was in Cira's house, he was overjoyed and wrote a long letter describing Hatuey's visit on the afternoon of her escape. In this letter, he told her that she shouldn't think of herself as different, or braver than anybody else, and he'd included his Colt 45. He advised her to use the pistol on herself rather than be tortured. This pistol (now housed in the Cuban Council of State's Office of Historic Affairs) is sheathed in silver and has the head of an Aztec warrior engraved on the stock. It fits into a holster made of thick, jet-black leather. A semi-automatic, the Colt was a very good gun and she was probably happy to have it, but closed her mind to her father's warning and ignored his pathos.

AT THIS POINT, THE WHOLE AREA SOUTH of Manzanillo— Campechuela, Media Luna, Niquero, and Pilón—was awash in speculation: was she dead or alive? Gossip flew from house to house, and town to town, linking the "doctor's daughter" to Fidel Castro, and the moment she arrived in Manzanillo she was the main subject of conversation, a hero. "When the landing happened, everyone started to talk about Celia and how she helped the guerrillas," explains Felipe Guerra Matos. He too had been inspired by the news of Fidel's open revolt against Batista and wanted to do his part, and like a lot of other people, he wanted to have the privilege of joining the 26th of July Movement. To do that, you had to talk to Celia. She became the person to see in that part of the country. So he put in a request to meet her. Guerra Matos says that people didn't use her name then, didn't call her Celia Sánchez: "We referred to her as the 'doctor's daughter' from Pilón. When we heard that she was in Manzanillo, everybody wanted to see her." When Elsa Castro heard that Celia was alive, she went to Cira Escalona's house to ask Celia to hand over the chocolate-brown skirt she'd been wearing. Celia was mystified, so Elsa explained: "This skirt is an important piece of Cuban history." It ought to be in a museum someday, "like Panchita's." Clothes worn by the wife of Bartolome Maso, a leader during the Second War of Independence, were kept on display in a local museum. "Burn it," Celia snapped. "You'll never see me in medals."

Elsa told me she still regretted not having ignored that injunction. She explained to me that Celia received many medals in her lifetime but never wore them. When she died, Fidel pinned these medals on a little cushion he placed by her coffin.

Even in the early days of the fight, Celia was suspicious of anything that smacked of a cult of personality.

ALTHOUGH SUFFERING SEVERE HEADACHES from the infection and toxicity of the thorns, Celia immediately began recruiting. Just days after her escape, she agreed to interview Felipe Guerra Matos. He introduced himself as the administrator of a rice mill, with many contacts among the rich farmers around Manzanillo, growers, mill owners, and rice producers. She responded by asking him to raise a thousand dollars. When Guerra mentioned the possibility that Fidel might have been killed, as the army reports were saying, he recalls, her voice dropped and she stated, quite coldly, that this was simply impossible. He watched the change come over her and thought he was going to be dismissed, until Celia explained why that information lacked validity. If they had killed Fidel, she reasoned, the army would have published a picture of his body in every paper, everywhere, "even pulverized." Guerra Matos was moved by her strength, her insistence, and says that her conviction carried the whole movement during those moments when people turned to her for strength.

Guerra was overwhelmed by her fragility. "I didn't have a proper description of Celia. I thought I would be meeting a big, strapping woman, but I met a thin, medium-tall woman instead, with a very refined manner. In bad shape. She had gone through a *marabuzal*. The first thing I said to her was, 'Have you been in a cat fight?'"

9. DECEMBER 5–16, 1956

The Farmers' Militia

THE GUERRILLAS WERE AMBUSHED on the afternoon of December 5. Chewed cane stalk marked their trail. A hundred Rural Guards armed with machine guns and rifles trapped them at a place called Alegria de Pio, in a field, then set fire to the field to flush them out.

In the battle that ensued, as Cuban historians explain it, two were killed in combat; nineteen were captured and immediately executed; and nineteen escaped one way or another, making it out of the mountains to safety as best they could, but did not return to the life of a guerrilla. Twenty-one were taken prisoner. Another twenty-one survived to form the rebel army.

Che Guevara wrote about his escape with four comrades: Juan Almeida, Ramiro Valdes, Reynaldo Benitez, and Rafael Chao. Three others, Camilo Cienfuegos, Francisco González, and Pablo Hurtado, joined them four days later. Fidel left Alegria de Pio with his second in command, Juan Manuel Marquez, a lawyer in his forties. They escaped into a cane field, but got separated. (Marquez wandered around, alone, for ten days, was captured and executed.) Later that night, Fidel caught a glimpse of Faustino Pérez and called out quietly: "Médico, médico." Now there were three: Fidel, Universo Sánchez, and the M.D., Faustino Pérez.

FROM DECEMBER 5 TO 16, Celia and everyone else in the 26th of July Movement had to live with heart-wrenching silence as to the whereabouts of the guerrillas. No one knew the fate of Fidel, or any of the survivors. It is estimated that over a ten-day period, until the 15th, Batista placed upward of 40,000 troops (counts vary) in the area. Platoons combed the open fields, set up roadblocks on all routes throughout the region. And in this atmosphere of stratospheric danger, when one would think that she would be frightened, careful, or at least circumspect about leaving Cira's house, Celia went to Santiago—within a week of her escape—to see Frank. Wearing a pair of harlequin sunglasses with white frames and black lenses, sporting a new short haircut with bangs, a maternity blouse to cover a chicken-wire stomach and a black skirt, she boarded a bus in Manzanillo. She later explained to documentary filmmaker Santiago Alvarez, "I had to go to Santiago to see Frank. . . . I had to see what he knew about the landing."

Several people had mentioned that she was at the top of the army's most-wanted list. This was confirmed by one of Batista's officers, who gave the reason: by mid-December, the army believed Fidel was isolated and harmless. Admittedly, he was still out there but, according to Retired General José Quevedo Pérez, the army thought snagging Celia would get them Fidel. Quevedo told me that Celia Sánchez was the number-one target on the army's radar, the first priority of the military intelligence unit, SIM, for that reason.

During the week she traveled, buses running between Manzanillo and Santiago were empty because nobody wanted to get involved with the national crisis under way. Most left empty and returned empty. When Celia caught the 6:00 a.m. bus from Manzanillo, accompanied by Eugenia (Gena) Verdecia of the 26th of July Movement, they were the only passengers. Every highway was blocked by military patrols, every car was subject to search, and the bus was halted at the checkpoints in every town along the route. When she chose her disguise, Celia had gambled that soldiers might respect a pregnant woman. When the bus got to the last stretch, near Santiago, it pulled into the military garrison at El Cobre. Soldiers invited the driver into the garrison for coffee. He turned around to tell his two passengers to wait in the bus.

Celia piped up, indignantly, "What about us?" and the driver asked the soldiers whether his passengers could have coffee, too. The soldiers agreed. When Celia climbed down from the bus, the soldiers saw that she was pregnant and expressed concern for her condition. They took hold of her elbows to help her over a barricade they'd constructed. She made it a jump. She later joked that when she made the leap, she had been afraid her wire belly would come loose.

Both women went to the garrison bathroom before entering the kitchen, where they were offered seats, in straight-back, cowhide-clad wooden chairs common in the Sierra Maestra. At some point Celia tipped hers back, balancing her chair on the two back legs, and one of the soldiers scolded her to take care, she might hurt herself or her baby.

She got a good look at the inside of the garrison and later was able to draw a floor plan that proved useful. She asked the soldiers where the troops were going. The coast, they answered, where the rebel landing had taken place. But the danger was over, they added. The rebel chief, Fidel Castro, was dead, and everything would be over soon. The others were dead or in prison.

She'd be sarcastic, later, in speaking of this incident, would say that it demonstrated how stupid the army could be. More to the point, she had been brazen, confident of their stupidity, sure they'd never recognize her. Maybe Celia put this spin on the story to avoid admitting that her trip may have been foolhardy, carrying unnecessary and excessive risk. Pedro Álvárez Tabío, director of the Office of Historical Affairs, a research archive devoted to tracking down this kind of information, is not sure which day she traveled to Santiago; he put it at sometime between the 7th and the 10th. The inconclusiveness leads one to infer that Celia wasn't all that forthcoming regarding this trip. Her sister, Flávia, says the scratches from the thorns had healed a little by the time of the trip, especially those on Celia's face (which she'd covered with her hands inside the *marabuzal*), but that her hands and arms— where the thorns had penetrated deepest—were still covered in angry, red scabs. The maternity blouse (housed in the archives) has short sleeves. It seems incredible that nobody considered this disfigurement odd in a pregnant woman, or thought it suspect. She certainly did not look normal.

MAKING IT TO SANTIAGO, Celia asked Frank what to do about her young militants who had been exposed waiting for Fidel, and now were in hiding. She explained that Cesar Suarez, on his stop in Media Luna, had found out that there were some whose families had denounced them when the police showed up, and she was determined to protect these people. Frank gave her his firsthand account of the Battle of Santiago, and told her to go home to Pilón and sit tight, to keep to the plan: wait for Mongo Pérez to contact her. No matter what developed, whenever Fidel surfaced, he would go to Pérez's farm, *Cinco Palmas*. Frank explained that he personally had asked Pedro Miret, on Miret's final trip to Mexico, to carry that precise message, in person, to Fidel: "Look for Ramon 'Mongo' Pérez as soon as you land." Celia was likely learning only now that this element of the plan had been put in place directly by Frank. That meant Fidel would go nowhere else.

In the end, Celia's carefully recruited network of farmers saved Fidel and his men. When Lalo Vásquez and Manuel Fajardo left the icehouse in Niquero on the morning of December 1, Fajardo, instead of returning to his normal life (Celia's orders), went instead to Guillermo García's house. He had no fear of being caught or pegged as a collaborator. In normal life he was a cattleman: "I'd be out of town fifteen or twenty days and nobody missed me. But I didn't go back." From the moment he heard about Alegria de Pio, he'd devoted himself to finding survivors of the battle. After the army moved in, when traveling about the region seemed impossible to others, Manuel Fajardo, Crescencio Pérez, and Guillermo García spent their days combing the countryside for dropped weapons or any sign of the surviving guerrillas. "We knew the area. We knew, by heart, how many trails there were, and that we could go anywhere. We rode on horseback and went on foot until it was impossible to continue farther."

ON DECEMBER 12, Fidel, Universo, and Faustino arrived on their own at Daniel Hidalgo's house. Hidalgo and his wife, Cota Coello, weren't members of the farmers' network, but they were sympathetic. They were aware that one of their neighbors, Ruben Tejeda, also a farmer, was involved in "something" with Guillermo García that was "anti-Batista" and gave Fidel directions to Tejeda's house, several miles away. The three guerrillas got there at dawn

In the end, Celia's carefully recruited network of farmers saved Fidel and his men. Guillermo García (photographed), Manuel Fajardo, and Crescencio Pérez spent their days combing the countryside for dropped weapons or any sign of the surviving guerrillas. Fajardo remembers: "We knew the area. We knew, by heart, how many trails there were, and that we could go anywhere. We rode on horseback and went on foot until it was impossible to continue farther." *(Courtesy of Oficina de Asuntos Históricos)*

on December 13 and Tejeda, following Guillermo's orders, took them to a farm that belonged to Marcial Areviches. From that moment, they were safely in the hands of Celia's official rescue network, as soon as Guillermo took over. A little after noon, his father, Adrian García, arrived with rice, turkey meat, bread, milk, and coffee in a bucket. Adrian García waited there with them for the rest of the day until the clock rolled over into a new day. At 1:00 a.m. exactly, on December 14, as Álvarez Tabío told me, Guillermo García greeted Fidel Castro, Universo Sánchez, and Faustino Pérez. Then he, along with the farmers Tejeda and Areviches, guided the three guerrillas from Areviches's farm to a place called La Manteca, where they hid in a cane field (on a farm that belonged to Pablo Pérez) for another twenty-four hours, or until the evening of the 15th.

In 2011, standing by the modest monument at La Manteca that honors this event, I marveled that Fidel and his companions had made it up and down this set of steep hills and valleys. To me, it seemed a nearly impossible route.

THE ARMY LIFTED ITS CORDON of the Niquero-Pilón road on December 15, and the three farmers led the guerrillas across it when Guillermo felt it was safe. He delivered Fidel into the hands of Ramon "Mongo" Pérez at dawn on the 16th, after having guided the group over twenty miles of very rough terrain and through the enemy lines. Mongo immediately set out for Manzanillo to tell Celia personally that Fidel was alive. Celia had moved from Cira Escalona's to Angela Llópiz's house. Ana Irma Escalona, who also lived there, says that Celia hugged Angela, and said "See, Angela, I told you so." With Fidel accounted for, Celia began running around town again. Ana Irma says that when Guillermo García arrived two days later with the news that Raúl and another group of guerrillas were okay, Celia was not there. She had slipped out of the house and nobody knew where she was, or what she was up to, and Guillermo had to wait until she returned. I asked Ana Irma whether Celia had presented them with an explanation or apology. Ana Irma's eyes rolled upward and the expression on her face told me: this was a futile question. Celia didn't offer explanations or apologies. Her kind of silence was simply one of the many ways she demonstrated her worth.

10. December 18, 1956

How Many Guns?

WHEN ACCOUNTS OF THE REVOLUTION were recorded, months and years later, Celia's network of farmers, fishermen, ranchers, and cattlemen was given a formal name: the Farmers' Militia. Nobody, least of all Raúl and Fidel, questions the fact that they saved the Revolution. Of the twenty-one survivors discovered by the farmers, sixteen made it to Mongo's place: three with Fidel on the 16th, five with Raúl on the 18th, another man on the 19th, and seven came with Almeida on the 21st. (Che has given a good account of the last group.) By December 21, the *Granma*'s scattered forces had reassembled.

THE MEN FIDEL HAD APPOINTED to command positions were dead or had been captured: Juan Manuel Marquez, José Smith, Candido González, and Jesus Montane were those he had relied on most in Mexico and during the crossing. The persons we think of today as leaders of the Cuban Revolution, Camilo Cienfuegos and Che, for example, were not so special then. Che was a member of Fidel's command platoon, but still only a rank-and-file soldier, though a doctor. Raúl Castro and Juan Almeida were platoon chiefs. Of the sixteen, Fidel sent Faustino Pérez to Manzanillo on December 23 to operate for him on the outside. In the end, fifteen remained in the mountains to stand beside Fidel and to form the core of what would become the Rebel army. Fifteen, sixteen, twenty-one—any one of those numbers is a fair interpretation, but there never were twelve, *doce*, expressly evoking the Apostles, as claimed by Carlos Franqui, veteran of the Revolution, and briefly editor of *Revolución*, a Havana daily.

IN CUBA, THERE IS THE STORY—a favorite story—of the conversation that took place between Fidel and his brother on the day they were reunited. Every Cuban can tell you, word by word, the story of Raúl's arrival. Fidel asked his brother how many guns he had. Raúl answered five. Fidel said that he had two, so that made seven. Fidel's summation, the punch line that everyone likes to deliver: "Now we've won the war." The story encapsulates unflagging optimism, complete conviction, the intimacy of brothers, relief, confidence—and the entire exchange consists of barely a dozen words.

On December 18, 2006, Cuba celebrated the fiftieth anniversary of that moment, televising the event to the nation. I was in a hotel room, watching. Fidel was in the hospital recovering from an abdominal operation, Raúl was running the country, and Guillermo García, Juan Almeida, and Ramiro Valdez were the guests of honor, standing on a wooden stage that had been constructed at the site of the real landmark, *Cinco Palmas*, Mongo's place, at the edge of the Sierra Maestra. You could see royal palm trees growing in one clump of three and another of two along the crest of the hill. Fifty years earlier those palms had marked the route, the final beacon. Students from the dance academy of Niquero, dressed as guerrillas, reenacted the terrible Battle of Alegria de Pio on the hillside above the temporary stage and below the palms. They wore green uniforms and carried wooden machine guns. I saw an incredulous look pass over Guillermo García's face as the young dancers pranced up and down the hillside, representing the survivors who had gotten separated and lost. Two dancers, as Fidel and Raúl, embraced as they delivered the famous "how many guns" exchange, marking the reenactment's finale. The camera returned to García, now looking delighted, finally on firm ground.

It had been the usual Cuban commemorative program: schoolchildren recited José Martí, party and union bosses were introduced from the podium, a choir sang, and the local head of the Communist Party closed the program, saying exactly what I wanted to hear: the real hero had been Celia Sánchez. And then Fidel's voice eerily came over loudspeakers and he explained in a high, raspy register, like a countertenor with laryngitis, what a difficult thing it is to make a revolution. He hadn't spoken to the public for months—it felt as if his ghost were attending the event. Guillermo García, along with all the people present—hundreds perhaps—raised little Cuban flags made of paper that rustled in the wind and had the overall effect of thousands of people, over a hill somewhere, clapping.

FIFTY YEARS EARLIER, in Manzanillo, Felipe Guerra Matos, good to his word, raised a thousand dollars among the rice growers. Celia, good to hers, had sent him to *Cinco Palmas* to hand the money personally to Fidel. This would have been a natural occasion for her to be present. Fidel was still the man she'd never met. But she sent, along with Guerra Matos, Rafael Sierra, and Enrique Escalona, the woman who had accompanied her on the daring bus ride to Santiago, Eugenia (Gena) Verdecia. Gena wore a big, circular cotton skirt that covered a petticoat stuffed with ammunition. (Fidel's biographer Tad Szulc writes that she carried three hundred submachine-gun bullets and nine dynamite cartridges.) This had recently become the 26th of July Movement's standard method for moving sensitive material: petticoats. Guerra Matos brought Faustino Pérez back to Manzanillo, so he could personally describe to Celia everything that had happened since the force had left Mexico. She and Faustino talked all through the night. The next day, December 24, Guerra drove Faustino to Santiago to see Frank. All this driving was conspicuous, but Guerra Matos explains how he got away with it: "I was a manager at a rice mill and I had a certain relationship with the police. There were some cops I liked to drink beer with."

THE GUERRILLAS LEFT MONGO'S FARM on the 25th rested, well fed, and aware that it had become dangerous to stay too long in one place. They began their final ascent in the Sierra Maestra with three newly inducted soldiers: the mountain patriarch, Crescencio Pérez, and the two young blades, Guillermo García and Manuel Fajardo. Crescencio and Guillermo were friends now, in the name of the Revolution. Faustino stayed on as Fidel's man in Havana, while on Christmas Day 1956, with an eighteen-man army, Fidel moved into the mountains.

11. January 1957
The Dove and the Zebra

AS A *CLANDESTINA*, CELIA BEGAN a new kind of life. Manzanillo's police force had a new captain, brought in from another part of Cuba specifically to capture her. She changed locations every few nights, and was managed by one person, a kind of keeper, a guardian angel. Guerra Matos ruminates on this. "She still had to keep in touch with the movement. But when you receive two or three persons in one place, there are security measures you have to use. Some of the people who visited could be arrested. And they could talk, because you never know. You cannot know how much [torture] a person can resist." Guerra concluded: "The life she led barred her from a lot of things."

WHEN SHE GOT BACK from seeing Frank, Hector Llópiz—shocked, perhaps, by Celia's having run the risk of a trip to Santiago—had taken her to stay with his sister, Angela. He simply assumed the role of her protector, not trusting the movement to do the job.

The arrangement had its genesis in the close friendship between the Sánchez and Llópiz families, dating back to 1914. That year, Manuel Sánchez had bought his first house from a member of the Llópiz family. The bond formed carried over to the next generation, and was consummated when Berta Llópiz made a trip to Pilón to visit Celia in the 1940s, fell in love with cousin Elbia's brother, married him, and stayed on.

So much of Celia's survival depended on family friends, and on Angela Llópiz and Cira Escalona in particular, who hid her from the military police. Photographed in 1928 are the older girls (back row, left to right): Silvia Sánchez, Angela Llópiz, Cira Escalona, and Chela (Graciela); front row: Griselda, Celia, in the middle, eight years old, and Flávia. *(Courtesy of Oficina de Asuntos Históricos)*

Hector could go unnoticed largely because he was quiet, middle-aged, short, thin, with hair beginning to gray. He was a family man with a wife and daughter. He'd been a teacher until a local businessman and dentist, Dr. Pepe Ramírez, began to admire his organizational skills and hired him to oversee his real estate investments. The job gave Hector a flexible work schedule and plenty of leeway to find hiding places for Celia. Surprisingly, finding hosts wasn't as hard as one might think. Felipe Guerra Matos claims that after the landing, when the government issued its statement that she had been arrested for assisting the guerrillas, this piece of news not only surprised everybody in Manzanillo, but inspired local social pages and gossip sheets to take up her story. It was such a sensational piece of information, according to Felipe, that a dozen or so people came forward, all from upper-crust families, offering to hide her. Still known as "the daughter of Dr. Manuel Sánchez," which helped, she was also the granddaughter of Juan Sánchez Barro, one of the richest turn-of-the-century Spanish merchants in Manzanillo; and it can't have hurt that she'd once been the town's beauty queen, sponsored by the leading social clubs. Those social steps had not been forgotten by the old families who were epitomized by Celia's aunts: three stately, unmarried sisters, icons of Spanish respectability. As Felipe said, it was hot news that one of the Sánchez daughters was up to something with the young guerrilla chieftain Fidel Castro. Women, rich and middle class, stepped forward offering—indeed vying—to protect her, obliging their Rotarian husbands go along. Had the press said nothing, Felipe assures me, it would have been difficult for Hector to find safe places for her. Elsa Castro makes a point of saying that things weren't physically tough for Celia during this clandestine period, since she stayed in the best houses all over town. The number of these houses varies, but the town's historian puts it at twenty-five. There are plaques on many. Schoolchildren take an inventory each year, inspect the signs, dust them off, and refresh the paint when necessary. If some houses she stayed in don't have plaques, it is, I suspect, because their owners have since decamped from Cuba—in the lexicon of the Revolution, have become traitors.

Clandestinos have their own idiom, too. Members of the underground often mention that he moved her "at the best time of day," which meant—it would take me some time to learn—when people were indoors having lunch, or when it was raining. Hector usually drove her himself, but sometimes his brother Angel, a schoolteacher, showed up in his jeep, entered the house where Celia was staying, changed into a different shirt, and the two walked out as a couple. Occasionally, Felipe Guerra Matos was allowed to perform this delicate task, but mostly Hector trusted only himself. Hector became the lion at the door, scheduling all Celia's interviews, making all arrangements, moving her daily. He used a code word for her, especially when it came time to relocate her, calling her "the Dove." I believe Hector kept her alive through this period.

DURING HER "CLANDESTINITY," Celia began to develop her own unique parallel network of helpers outside the movement. They worked for her as couriers, tailors, suppliers, shippers, party-givers, and letter writers (soldiers need mail). Drawn from among the women of Manzanillo, their work took convoluted and beguiling forms, like the wonderful courier system she orchestrated for carrying messages to Frank in Santiago. Since that route across the mountains was littered with checkpoints, Celia recruited especially pretty young girls to travel with Manzanillo businessmen. And, true to form, when a man was seen driving a big American car with a young woman, all dressed up, sitting in the passenger seat, Batista's soldiers checked the driver's papers but never requested the girl's, which would indicate a lack of respect for the man at the wheel. Celia had a foolproof system and knew it. Her bravery had clearly inspired admiration and a desire to emulate her. Celia reciprocated by putting so much confidence in these women, and, by the end of the war, no one had discovered her courier system. She was their hero.

While she ran her growing underground, Celia relied heavily on a telephone operator named Lilia Ramírez, whose second-floor window at the AT&T exchange directly overlooked police headquarters. Lilia monitored the cops' shifts, knew who was on duty, who went to lunch and when, and would phone Hector with the information so he was better able to plan Celia's move. More important, Lilia was the first person to take note of unusual, or stepped-up, police activity. If several cops left headquarters at once and piled into jeeps or squad cars, she'd alert Hector and often call Celia directly. Lilia usually knew *precisely* what was going on, since she—and other operators—listened to police and army telephone conversations. She, like Hector, was in the lifesaving business.

The new chief of police, Caridad Fernández, was unaware of Celia's new haircut (gotten for her trip to see Frank in Santiago), because for years she'd worn her long hair in a ponytail, and he began pledging, as he swaggered around Manzanillo, that he was "going to cut it off."

"If she—if any of us—caught sight of him, we'd call him Cachita, the nickname you'd give a woman named Caridad," Felipe says. Yet "Cachita" was no slouch. Probably on more than one occasion, but on one, which I was able to nail down, he nearly caught her. "Forty-seven guards came and jumped down from the roof," is Elsa Castro's version of this incident. "I was working a block away and saw the police go by with their legs hanging out of the jeep, their long rifles, and I thought, 'Oh my God, they've got her.' But she got away." Ana Irma Escalona once heard that Celia used a bed-sheet rope to slide from an upper-story window. But she didn't hear this from Celia, she says. It had been a close call, and typically, Celia refused to discuss it.

ANA IRMA, ALTHOUGH NOT A LLÓPIZ RELATIVE, had been raised in Angela's house, and when she was about seventeen, Celia began asking her to buy things like pencils and writing paper. "There would be a contact person in the shop. Celia would send me to that person, who knew I was going to buy specific things. Sometimes she gave me money, but other times these were people who helped the cause." Celia wrote on little pieces of pink paper, cut into 4-inch squares. (Elsa Castro supplied the paper, scratch pads her father sold to banks.) Eventually, Celia asked Ana Irma to carry messages. These, too, were written on the little squares, folded over several times. "You know what these times are like," Celia admonished, and ordered Ana Irma to swallow them if anybody stopped her. Celia, at the time, had been requesting donations; if people didn't pledge money, she would send Ana Irma back with another note to say that she'd be paying them a visit. Ana Irma says that people were frightened when they got a note like that, since Celia was the last person they wanted found in their houses. They usually sent money. They volunteered, but it wasn't voluntary.

Celia's great helper in Manzanillo was 21-year-old Elsa Castro who worked in her father's stationery store. "It was a beautiful war those women waged," one of Celia's friends, Berta Llópiz, told me. "If the police had figured it out, they would have killed all of them." *(Author's collection)*

Clandestinity hadn't dampened Celia's rebellious nature; in fact, it gave her more time to primp. She sometimes wore a dress that aggravated Hector: a pencil-skirted sheath made of wide black and white horizontal bands from bodice to hemline. It's a stunning dress (now in the archives). Hector implored her not to wear it since it was so conspicuous, and she ignored him. When she wore this dress, she was no longer his "Dove," and he'd grumble to her hosts, "Today I have the Zebra."

"IT WAS A BEAUTIFUL WAR THOSE WOMEN WAGED," Hector's sister, Berta, commented. "If the police had figured it out, they would have killed all of them." This was tough on women in the movement. Elsa Castro describes a night when she'd carried out an action. She'd come home wanting nothing more than to take a bath, go to bed, and put her head "under the covers," but the final step of her task required changing into a dress and high heels and sitting on a park bench in front of the cathedral—which is just across the park from the police station—in order to be seen by the authorities. She says she was sure that every person who glanced at her could tell what she'd been up to. The women's hearts were in their throats most of the time, she admits. Some of the women in the movement got so they couldn't control their bladders when they saw policemen. Elsa laughs softly recalling a time when she was carrying documents for Celia. She'd been sitting in a café and caught her reflection in a mirror. She could actually read the documents she was carrying through her new transparent nylon blouse. As they were so young, dressing well in the latest style was part of the thrill, and Celia's elegance part of their attraction to her. A realist, Elsa admits that "you lived with something very cold inside your stomach." She takes a deep breath, then tells me that her sister, also a *clandestina*, had not been able to stand the pressure and had committed suicide.

12. January 7–February 15, 1957

The Traitor

HAVING RESOLVED MANY OF THE ISSUES of the landing by getting Fidel into the mountains, Frank and Celia set about augmenting his depleted guerrilla forces. First they sent Beto Pesant, who led a small group of men from Manzanillo.

While awaiting Beto's arrival, Fidel's unit was finding sympathizers and becoming familiar with its new territory. Farmers and rancher known to Crescencio let them camp on their properties, got their wives to prepare food, and suggested where they might spend subsequent nights. In this setting, on the evening of January 7, the group arrived at the ranch of Eutimio Guerra, who invited them to warm up inside his house. Eutimio gave them hot coffee with cognac and honey, while his wife and a family friend cooked a pig. After dinner, Eutimio led them to a small outbuilding where they could shelter and sleep. Thus began, almost instantly, the love affair between Eutimio and the band of guerrillas—or between him and Fidel, anyway. Fidel's brother, Raúl, observed in his journal that Eutimio was between thirty-five and forty years old, and white. He also pegged the structure hidden in their host's pasture, where he'd taken them to hide, as a venue for cockfights. The popular blood sport was illegal.

Off and on, Eutimio Guerra began to help the guerrillas, becoming self-appointed facilitator.

Once Pesant and his ten new recruits met up with Fidel and his men, they headed toward the highest parts of the Sierra Maestra. It was from these far reaches that they swept down, January 17, on an isolated army garrison, located near the coast at La Plata. In their first high-profile victory, they killed five of Batista's soldiers and took two prisoners (whom they set free almost immediately); one of the garrison's defenders escaped. Following the engagement, the guerrillas evaporated into the vast Sierra Maestra forests.

This battle was a blow to Batista. But he stuck to his story that Fidel Castro was dead. So, showing the world that Fidel was alive became the 26th of July Movement's next goal, and soon an obsession. The M26 leadership seized on the idea that Fidel must become visible, alive and well, to the international press. Faustino Pérez had been sent to Havana to handle just this sort of thing. He sought contact with Ruby Hart Phillips, a stringer for the *New York Times*, offering an exclusive on Fidel's story. In the days following the landing, Phillips and her editor had fallen for the army's disinformation campaign, and the *Times* had printed Fidel's obituary on its front page. Fidel was alive, and the *Times* should acknowledge the fact.

MEANWHILE, EUTIMIO HAD STARTED to travel full-time with the guerrillas, as their mountain guide. But on January 28, he separated from them. He apologized to Fidel, leaving him and his fighters on their own only because his mother was ill, and pledging to return no later than the end of the week.

January 30 dawned cold—despite the latitude, temperatures drop surprisingly low in the upper elevations of the Sierra Maestra—so the guerrillas rose early and were already on the march at 7:00. A plane flew over; they recognized it as an army reconnaissance aircraft. Shortly after, more planes flew in, and they crouched in the foliage. The incoming squadron dropped bombs at precisely the spot where they'd been camped not an hour before. Shocked, they quickly made plans to reunite the following day, and scattered into the forest.

On February 1, Batista ordered three columns into the region: one to block off the western part of the mountain range, settling in near San Lorenzo; the second poured into El Mulato, the area where the guerrillas were hiding; the third landed on the coast at El Macho, to cover the south side of the mountain range. The guerrillas were unaware of any of this, possibly because they'd become so reliant on intelligence delivered by Eutimio.

Guillermo García soon knew about the army's presence. He informed the guerrillas, who then operated very cautiously. On the afternoon of the 4th, they were taken in by one of the more prosperous landowners, Florentino Enamorado, whose house at El Aji was large enough to bunk most of the guerrillas indoors. That evening, Enamorado's wife and daughters served up all the food the men could eat.

The next morning, the guerrillas split into two groups, for greater flexibility in the event they had to move rapidly. Crescencio took eight men, including his son Ignacio, and traveled away from the area, while twenty stayed with Fidel.

IN HAVANA, FAUSTINO'S PRESS EFFORT was moving forward. Joined by Rene Rodríguez, sent by Frank from Santiago, Faustino met with Ruby Hart Phillips on February 2. The location for their meeting was chosen to impress. Felipe Pazos was the country's leading economist and first president of the National Bank of Cuba, and a meeting in his office had been easy to arrange because his son, Javier, was a leader in Havana's 26th of July Movement. Following the conversation, Phillips cabled Emanuel R. Freedman, the *Times* international editor, who replied two days later that he would dispatch veteran reporter Herbert Matthews to Cuba. This was a coup, as Matthews had made his reputation covering the Spanish Civil War twenty years earlier, filing his reports from the guerrilla front as the Republicans fought Franco's Nationalist forces.

At the end of the week, on February 5, the guerrillas' best friend in the mountains, the ultra-sympathetic Eutimio Guerra, rejoined them, announcing he'd come straight back from seeing his mother. He was seemingly unaware of the army's presence, but his companions noticed that he was acting a little edgy, and carrying a pistol.

THAT SAME DAY, Celia met with a friend—a man who worked in Pilón and had driven all the way to Manzanillo to bring her information. The week before he was fairly certain he had seen

the man he'd been told served the guerrillas as a guide, Eutimio
Guerra, board an army plane in Pilón.

WEDNESDAY, THE 6TH, WAS PARTICULARLY COLD, especially
for the twenty men with Fidel, hiding out of doors not far from
Florentino's house, immobile and out of sight during the daylight
hours. At nightfall, Eutimio asked to sleep next to Fidel because
he was so chilled. Fidel agreed. The cold again drove them from
camp early the next morning. At 8:00, planes flew over and
bombed Florentino Enamorado's house, the residents presumably
inside. For 20 or 30 minutes, the guerrillas watched in horror.
Eutimio, apparently making a grim joke, said, "I didn't tell them
to attack here." Soon after the bombing ceased, he excused himself
and left the group again.

The previous week, when he'd allegedly visited his sick mother,
he'd gone straight to the army, been put in a jeep and driven to
Pilón (where Celia's friend saw him get into a small plane). From
the air, he had pointed out where the guerrillas were camped. Now
he headed for El Macho to give the army Fidel's new position.
The morning of February 8, the army column at El Macho moved
to less than 5 kilometers from the guerrilla camp. Che, writing
in his diary early that morning, notes that he's happy to see the
night patrol return carrying five chickens, so he must have been
unaware of the army's presence. He was still writing at 11:00
when planes flew in, surprisingly close, he notes. Little worth
recording in the diary seems to have happened for the rest of the
day. Che simply observes that it rained all afternoon (and so the
army postponed operations, pending better weather). Sometime
during the afternoon, Che records, Eutimio returned and spent
the night with the guerrillas.

CELIA, OPERATING FROM ONE of the houses Hector had moved
her into in Manzanillo, was extremely busy. Frank, following the
Times's confirmation (on February 4) that Matthews was coming,
had put her in charge of getting the journalist into the mountains
and out again. When Matthews and his wife, Nancie, arrived in
Havana on the 9th aboard a National Airlines flight, Faustino
Pérez immediately contacted Celia. She was in the middle of
preparing for the journalist's highly important visit when word

came that the guerrillas had been caught in an ambush. And not just any ambush: she was told that Fidel was dead. A 26th of July Movement ally inside the army, a lieutenant, was the source of her intelligence. She sent an inquiry to the informant and waited for his reply. By the end of the day, he confirmed that an ambush had taken place and all the guerrillas in the skirmish had been eliminated, including Fidel Castro. Celia's reaction was not hysteria or resignation, but skepticism. She initiated her own investigation, even though she found the lieutenant's report hard to contradict. Apparent facts went against her gut instinct. The army had released news of the ambush, but hadn't mentioned Fidel. She saw the twisted logic to this: since the government still officially maintained that he had died during the landing, two months earlier, they could hardly announce that they had killed him again. But she doubted both claims. Her thinking: if they'd killed or captured Fidel, such highly sensational news would find its way to light.

IN THE MOUNTAINS, on the morning of February 9, a farmer named Adrian Pérez Vargas was walking along the road near Fidel's camp, carrying two sacks of sweet potatoes. The guerrilla sentry, a new recruit, stopped him and—to be on the safe side—took him prisoner. He relieved Pérez of his machete and led him straight to Fidel. Fidel questioned the farmer, who insisted that a huge number of army troops were right down in the valley below, and had been there since the previous day. Fidel naturally wanted proof of this. "Can you take me to a place where I can see them?"

They set off, and in the course of their walk, the farmer mentioned having seen Eutimio Guerra that morning—down in the valley with the troops. Fidel and Pérez covered four or five kilometers to a point from which the rebel leader, astonished, observed the enemy through the scope of his rifle.

As he returned to camp, Fidel silently reviewed Eutimio's history: his trip to see his mother and other absences from camp; how easily he passed through enemy lines; how casually he'd been able to purchase things difficult to come by; the sick joke he'd made when Florentino's house went up in flames. As soon as he reached his men, Fidel ordered everyone who could leave to do so immediately. Only some six kilometers away he'd seen approximately 140 men camped around houses in the valley, supported by modern equipment, and armed with automatic and semi-automatic rifles. After issuing this order and giving the motivation for its urgency, he announced that Eutimio was a traitor. The guerrillas reacted with surprise and disbelief.

Fidel anxiously waited for two of his men out on reconnaissance to return. It was after 2:00 p.m. when they showed up, insisting while Fidel briefed them that they'd seen nothing out of the ordinary. During this exchange, the guerrilla on lookout, Ciro Redondo, called, "Quiet!" A moment later, Manuel Fajardo gasped, "It's Eutimio." A gun went off and a young farmer, a recent recruit standing just steps from Fidel, fell to the ground, a bullet in his head. Everybody ran.

Six men stuck with Fidel: Raúl, Fajardo, Redondo, Efigénio Amerijerias, Juan Francisco Echevarria, and José "Gallego" Moran. They followed a stream, hoping to get to the Macio River and cross it. The earlier group, Juan Almeida, Che, Camilo Cienfuegos, Guillermo García, Universo Sánchez, and Beto Pesant, had taken that route. They stayed on the run six days. On Sunday, February 10, Almeida's group crossed the Macio River and continued on through the night, finally stopping to hide at daylight. Che, in his diary, mentions that Fidel had ordered everyone to reunite in La Habanita (not far from Pico Turquino).

CELIA, MORE AND MORE convinced her gut feeling was right, telephoned Guerra Matos on the 11th. He still remembers feeling the force of her will as she told him, in a low voice (he says he had to concentrate to hear her), that it had been three days since the ambush and if the army really had Fidel, or his corpse, they wouldn't have been able to resist putting the picture on television. "Don't believe them. This is propaganda they are handing out," she said, ordering Felipe to drive to Mongo Pérez's farm, *Cinco Palmas*, to get firsthand information. Felipe told me he "absorbed her conviction," got into his car and drove to Mongo's prepared to wait until he had information to bring home to her.

FIDEL AND HIS GROUP got to the river on Monday, February 11, undetected. That night, Fidel knocked on the door of a house in a place called Tatequieto and the owner showed the rebels a good place to camp, hidden by trees, in a pasture on his land. The next day he suggested they stay on the property of some friends, offering to show them the way. There, his friends, two brothers, spent the day rustling up potatoes, beef, pork, and coffee to cook for the hungry men. The Almeida/Che/Pesant group got word that Fidel was nearby, and the Tatequieto farmer gave them directions. In less than an hour, the groups reunited. All these local farmers seemed to know about the guerrillas. They knew as well about Eutimio Guerra, and so the guerrillas learned— through this particular grapevine—that the stakes were high: in exchange for Fidel's life, the army had promised the traitor $10,000 and a farm.

ON WEDNESDAY THE 13TH, Fidel selected a soldier to carry a message to Celia in Manzanillo. He instructed the young man to tell her their present location, where they were going, and where he wanted her to bring Matthews; he had chosen a new location, a farm. Just as the young guerrilla, Juan Francisco Echevarria, left on his heady mission, another of Fidel's guerrillas, José Moran, simply walked off without authorization. This bit of outrageous behavior was noted by both Che and Raúl, who silently put their feelings down in their respective diaries. The independent entries come to the same conclusion: Moran was a deserter. On the 13th, young Echevarria showed up at *Cinco Palmas* and told Mongo about the ambush, mentioning that he had a message from Fidel for Celia Sánchez. Felipe Guerra Matos, who was present, relates how he grabbed the young man, put him in his car and took off for Manzanillo. In that letter, Fidel explained exactly where he wanted to rendezvous with Matthews and assured Celia he'd make it there on the 17th. Historians rarely mention that Fidel, in doing this, really upped the ante; he asked Celia to arrange for all the directors of the 26th of July Movement to be there, too. She must have been taken aback, as assembling the full leadership in one place ran enormous risk. Moving a famous journalist into the area suddenly became just another one of her worries. She whipped into action, asking Rafael Sierra, director of the Manzanillo branch since Beto Pesant's departure, to call a meeting for the next day. Frank sent Nicaragua (Carlos Iglesias, the young Santiago banker) to represent him. Celia, Enrique Escalona (the young Manzanillo banker), Nicaragua, and Sierra (who worked in his parents' dry goods store) decided that Matthews had been waiting in Havana long enough—since February 9—with no idea what was going on, so they'd get him to Fidel as soon as possible. D-Day was to be the 17th, the day Fidel promised to be at the new destination. Celia announced that Matthews should arrive just after midnight on the 16th, so he could interview Fidel as early as possible the following day. Nicaragua got on a plane for Havana (to help Faustino coordinate Matthew's movements), and Escalona drove to Santiago to fill Frank in on the details. After Frank heard the plans, he talked to Celia by phone (she was staying at the house of Dr. Rene Vallejo) and assured her that Rene Rodríguez was on his way to help her. Frank had sent Rene off so hurriedly that he didn't have film in his camera. Frank confirmed that he'd bring film himself (sending Arturo Duque de Estrada—probably as he spoke—to a camera store for several rolls).

IN HAVANA, AS SOON AS DIRECTORS Armando Hart and Haydée Santamaria found out that Fidel wanted all directors to assemble, they simply went to the airport and took the first plane to Santiago. On February 15, Vilma Espin drove the big three— Frank, Haydée, and Armando—over the mountain highway from Santiago to Manzanillo. Stopped at all checkpoints, they were completely conspicuous in the Red Threat, but to the soldiers they appeared to be two happy couples in a new red Dodge. The Red Threat rolled into Manzanillo in the afternoon, entering Celia's jurisdiction. Felipe was on the job, acting on her behalf, and when he learned of their arrival, he picked up Frank. Next he got Celia from her hiding place (she'd moved to another house, a Moorish-style palace a stone's throw from the police station) and transported them to Fidel's new location.

Los Chorros, the farm where the rendezvous was to take place, is located in the western foothills of the tallest mountains in the Sierra, and was owned by Epifánio Diaz. It turned out to be a very good place for rebel activities, and served the 26th of July Movement well for the rest of the war. The farmhouse had lots of windows, giving views in all directions; surrounding the house were coffee groves and pastures dotted with small stands of trees, good to camp in; best of all, Los Chorros was accessible by several roads, a main highway and back routes via farm roads coming from different directions.

Celia got into the car carrying packages that contained, among other things, slices of ham, cigars, candy, and as a present for Fidel, a Schaeffer pen Elsa Castro had probably swiped from her father's stationery store. Felipe had already loaded crates of bottled drinks into the trunk, along with a big box containing a wedding cake. This trip, carrying the bosses, Celia, and Frank, would be the first of many he'd have to make now that everyone was attending the interview. With the Rural Guard on the lookout, being stopped was inevitable, and his cover had to be credible. He and Celia had decided to say that one of Felipe's sisters was getting married on his father's farm (and point to the wedding cake as evidence). When Celia and Frank got out at *Los Chorros*, Felipe turned around immediately and headed back to Manzanillo.

ON THE SAME AFTERNOON, around 5:30, Javier Pazos telephoned the Sevilla Biltmore Hotel to tell Herbert Matthews to be ready to leave that night. Nancie Matthews, who has written an account of this trip, says she had just started to wash her hair when the call came, but stopped, opting to wear a hat, so they could go out to dinner immediately. The couple strolled up the Paseo del Prado, Havana's version of Barcelona's Las Ramblas, crossed Parque Central, and entered the restaurant El Floridita, where they ordered daiquiris and lobster. After dinner they returned to their hotel to wait for the call. At 10:00 Javier phoned from the lobby. Checking out immediately, Matthews informed the desk clerk that he was going on a fishing trip, calling attention to his rugged-looking clothes. He and Nancie got into a new Plymouth. Javier Pasos introduced Faustino and the car's driver and owner, Lilliam Mesa, as Luis and Marta. (Matthews wrote that he didn't know their full names and didn't want to.) The group took off into the night.

THAT NIGHT, FIDEL'S GUERRILLAS rested and ate well. They waited until it was dark enough to travel their last twenty kilometers safely, on foot. Meanwhile, the Plymouth en route from Havana skimmed the Central Highway, Lilliam and Faustino singing international songs to entertain Nancie and Herbert Matthews, stopping fairly often for "thimblefuls of Cuban coffee." About halfway, at around 4:00 a.m. on Saturday, February 16, Nancie felt cold enough to mention it to the others. Approaching the city of Camagüey, about an hour later, they stopped for breakfast. Lilliam had had trouble finding a place that was open, and had driven past the same policeman three times. Nancie Matthews recalled thinking, she's a charming girl, but a dangerous wife for a revolutionary. Finally Lilliam stopped and asked the policeman for directions to a good hotel. They ate fresh rolls, drank *café au lait*, warmed up a little, and were back on the road again by 6:00 a.m.

IN THE MOUNTAINS, just as it got light, Fidel ordered his men, sleeping in an open pasture on Epifánio's property, to get up and move out of sight. They pitched camp inside a stand of trees while Fidel, fully awake, and his bodyguard, Ciro Frias, headed downhill toward the house.

13. FEBRUARY 16 AND 17, 1956

The Meeting in the Mountains

CELIA AND FRANK SLEPT AT THE FARMHOUSE. Rising early and making their way up the mountain, guided by a couple of Epifanio's sons, they ran into Fidel and Ciro in an open field. It was still so early in the day that mists hung in places. There is no record of what happened next. Fidel had never met Celia, so Frank may have performed the introductions. He hadn't seen Fidel in four months, not since the previous October, in Mexico. Here, on this path, Fidel was finally face to face with Frank, his partner in revolution, and the lovely woman who had saved Fidel with her Farmers' Militia.

We can only fill in the blanks about what happened that day. We know that they walked as they carried on their conversation, and hesitated at one point to consider whether they should go down to the farmhouse or stay where they were. They decided it would be better to speak privately. We know as well that the conversation between Celia and Fidel continued all through this day and into the night. In a very real sense, it went on the rest of their lives.

EPIFANIO'S BOYS AND FIDEL'S BODYGUARD, Ciro, improvised a small campsite so that Celia, Frank, and Fidel could sit down. Celia probably assured Fidel that Matthews wouldn't show up until after midnight and he had the rest of the day to prepare. Later, when Celia and Frank were to go down to the farmhouse to wait for the directors, who would be arriving at various times, Fidel expressed his desire to take Celia up to the guerrilla camp, introduce her around. There she met Raúl, Almeida, Che, Camilo, and others. For Celia, it would be a reunion with Pesant, Fajardo, and Guillermo García, her old friend. After these introductions, the three went off on their own once again. This time they picnicked in a cane field. Celia must have sent one of Epifanio's boys down to the farmhouse to get food. Enshrouded by tall plants, they sat in their war room, speaking quietly, but letting the rustle from the slightest wind blanket their voices. After lunch, Frank left them. Stepping out of the role of chaperone, he went back to the guerrilla camp. He wanted to spend time with the troops: asking questions and inspecting their weapons.

CELIA AND FIDEL TOOK A LONG, meandering stroll. Now that they'd finally met, they had a lot to talk about, so many issues, some not so pleasant. She'd cut him loose, to fend for himself, when she called off the landing operation; besides reviewing events, situations, and decisions, they must have wanted to verify, clarify, re-trace, corroborate, compare, share, praise, or occasionally apologize. For years, they'd heard about each other. There were legends surrounding both. As they drifted through pastures, followed paths through woods, and walked along streams, they exchanged information. How long did it take to discover that they both liked to fish?

Celia was, for the first time, experiencing the full impact of Fidel's imposing physicality: a young giant, taller than most Cubans and with a heavy dose of high energy. He had all the classic features of a Spaniard: flawless white skin, symmetrical features, two dark eyes aligned evenly over a long, straight nose. His hair had a life of its own, dark and glossy, and he was just beginning to grow a beard, a scraggly version of a Fu Manchu. Photographs of Fidel from this period radiate warmth and good humor in a manner that is compelling. Look closely and you'll see a definite sweetness in his smile, a curiosity in his gaze. (Which is all to say, there was once a temperature in Fidel Castro that, over the last fifty years, has clearly plummeted.) And his immensely

This photograph was taken by Frank País on Epifánio Díaz's farm, February 17th or 18th, 1957. This is the first picture of Fidel and Celia together. *(Courtesy of Oficina de Asuntos Históricos)*

erect carriage is like that of a man wearing armor and carrying a sword: formal and somewhat elegant, Fidel is like a conquistador in work clothes.

Celia's features also reflected her Spanish heritage: intensely black hair, sparkling black eyes, and a finely chiseled nose. But she was his opposite. For one thing, her skin was darker; her body wiry and svelte by comparison; her personality quiet and secretive while his was expansive and open. Neither would classify as a particularly domesticated species. If he was a lion, she was a panther.

When they spoke, it was in whispers. If she told him a funny story, he couldn't have responded with a hearty laugh because they were in danger of being heard. Eutimio was lurking somewhere on the edge of their lives. Wherever he was, the army was assisting him, ready to pounce. This made the men watching over them, Epifanio's sons and Fidel's bodyguard, wary and on edge. The Eutimio problem has to have been high on Celia and Frank's agenda.

In Guerra's car, on the way to the farm, the two probably talked over the farmer-guide's betrayal, and the problem of Fidel's having trusted Eutimio so easily. I'm sure they concluded that they had to protect Fidel from himself. She would have provided the facts she'd learned from the young soldier Fidel had sent to her, Juan Francisco Echevarria, to help Frank in making his assessment. It's easy to forget that Frank, at the time, was the other director and could counter Fidel. But Frank was busy running the underground, the fight inside the cities. Had he told Celia, on their drive up, that she had to confront Fidel? She was the obvious candidate, and Frank's pupil; her credentials were pretty good in the department of managing men, or at least her father. She knew how to confront as well as coddle him, assist but also draw the line.

So it was likely Celia's first task to ask Fidel why he had picked Eutimio, and listen hard to his answer. As she walked at his side, did she think that she could be strong enough to talk Fidel out of things, particularly out of his flights of fancy?

Another issue at bay was her desire to join the guerrillas. She could be useful. Fidel was in her region, and she was the expert on this part of the Sierra, all completely new to him. In the mountains, moreover, she could demonstrate that she was up to living a soldier's life. If she was breaking this news to Fidel, that she planned to join him, it was with Frank's blessing. Her joining Fidel may have been Frank's solution to the problem of Celia's overexposure; in the Sierra, she'd be out of Manzanillo. More likely, she said nothing. If Fidel hadn't wanted a woman on the *Granma* to help him get safely into harbor, how likely would he have been to want one in his column of soldiers? In this first meeting, I surmise that she held off mentioning that she wanted to join his band of soldiers, or at least didn't express it straight out. She'd approach the subject, and make her case, by another means.

No doubt Celia arrived with questions and proposals to put to Fidel, not all of which would sit well. Surely, on some of these, they would not have agreed. Did they debate? I've had many opportunities to ask retired soldiers who served with both of them during the war. They always told me that Fidel and Celia conversed and argued. The old-timers assured me that Celia knew how to present her argument, make a case, and little by little bring him around. On this walk, they weren't alone but escorted by bodyguards, so it wasn't an occasion to question Fidel openly. They came upon an abandoned house and vowed to return to it later that night.

WHILE CELIA AND FIDEL WERE OFF in the woods, Liliam Mesa delivered Herbert and Nancie Matthews to a rice grower's house outside Manzanillo; Javier stayed with them, as interpreter. Guerra Matos was alerted to the arrival, went to pick up Faustino Pérez, and collected Vilma Espin, Armando Hart, and Haydée Santamaria to begin his second trip to *Los Chorros*. "It was a heavy load," he commented, referring to the political weight of his passengers, with a shake of his head. On his way back from dropping off Frank and Celia, he'd been recognized by a member of the Rural Guard—something he and Celia had anticipated—and he'd given the Guards his story. By all appearances, they believed a wedding was taking place on his father's farm. Now he had to maintain that fiction.

VILMA, HAYDÉE, AND ARMANDO RESTED in the farmhouse, making their way to the guerrillas' camp in the late afternoon. Celia and Fidel, when they returned to the guerrillas' bivouac, proposed camping that night in the abandoned house they'd seen earlier. They set off, retraced their steps, but couldn't locate the house again. As darkness approached, Fidel asked Ciro to construct a shelter made of branches, and, in the end, he and Celia camped out under the stars while some of the party drifted back down to the farmhouse. Enrique Escalona and Nicaragua arrived on their own, sometime in the evening. Frank spent the night at the guerrilla camp. Vilma, and possibly Haydée and Armando, camped with Celia and Fidel. One or two soldiers were there, too, to stand guard.

THE RURAL GUARDS pulled Guerra Matos over again, in Jibacoa, on his way after dropping off Vilma, Faustino, Haydée, and Armando. "Guerra, we've seen you make several trips." He explained that the wedding wasn't going to take place until Sunday (several days away) and assured them that he'd be making more trips still. He reminded them that his family knew a lot of people, all the rice growers (letting the implication of his family's wealth and position sink in), and invited the Guards to the wedding. "I told them I would pick them up, and we'd go get some beer . . . " At this, they waved him on.

AT MIDNIGHT, FELIPE WENT TO PICK UP Herbert Matthews; Nancie was staying behind. Felipe had promised to deliver the journalist to the *Los Chorros* farmhouse by 2:00 a.m., but now he was filled with apprehension. He told Javier Pazos that making this trip would be too dangerous. Horrified, Pazos claimed that Fidel would never forgive them if they didn't deliver the journalist, and Guerra reluctantly agreed. He couldn't take the same route via Jibacoa, so he chose a roundabout way through Yara, Estrada Palma, Caney, and Cayo Espino, turning onto one of the farm roads near Purial. All the same, they'd encountered plenty of checkpoints. Guerra would show his ID, explaining that he was the manager of a mill, and "the American" was going to Luis Gómez's farm to buy rice. Pazos was along as interpreter. (By some accounts, Rene Rodríguez, who worked for Frank, was also in the car, with his empty camera.) Matthews wrote that they drove across streams, went places only a jeep could go, and encountered swarms of mosquitoes. Guerra only recalls that the trip took too much time. He got to the farm after 5:00 a.m., instead of 2:00 as he'd promised Celia; no one was waiting for them at the house. Guerra says he nearly panicked until he could rouse one of Epifanio's sons (or cousins) who guided them, through the darkness, up the mountain. Matthews slipped while they were crossing a creek and fell. Guerra (then in his twenties) was sure the "old man" (Matthews was fifty-seven) had broken a leg. Matthews got up and gamely continued; they reached the guerrilla camp around 7:00. It was Sunday, February 17, an epochal date in Cuban history.

CELIA AND FIDEL HAD RISEN before dawn to prepare for Matthews. The young guerrilla chief put on gray work clothes provided by Celia; at the time, this was the 26th of July's uniform. He added a cap with a flat crown, more or less like General Charles de Gaulle's *kepi*, and was ready to meet the journalist. Matthews had on a black beret, evoking the spirit of Republican Spain's resistance to Franco. Fidel cracked open a box of export *habanos*. The two men lit up as Vilma Espin (who had studied at MIT) stepped forward to help Javier Pazos translate. The famous interview began with four people huddled together whispering, in two languages, wreathed in the smoke of good cigars.

Raúl managed the interview as if he were directing theater. Various platoons marched in, reported to Fidel as he talked to Matthews, then marched out of sight, changed their shirts, and returned from different directions. Matthews got the impression that Fidel had many more soldiers—a guerrilla army composed of several columns, he assumed—and jotted this down in a little black book. He talked to several soldiers (only Juan Almeida gave Matthews permission to refer to him by name) while Celia served ham-and-cracker sandwiches with tomato juice, followed by hot coffee in tin cups. After about three hours, the interview was completed. At Matthews's request, Fidel placed his signature and the date on one of the notebook pages.

Guerra, Javier Pazos, and one of Epifanio's boys led the journalist back down the mountain. Guerra drove them to Manzanillo, picked up Nancie, and took them all to the airport. Pazos joined the Matthewses aboard the plane for Santiago as "their son, Albert." From Santiago, the three flew to Havana.

AS SOON AS MATTHEWS LEFT, Fidel called together his directors and held a meeting that lasted some four hours. Armando Hart recalls that Fidel briefed him along with Raúl, Haydée, Vilma, and Faustino on issues he'd discussed the previous day with Frank and Celia. Mainly, Fidel was asking the movement for more men, enough to restore his guerrilla army to its former size of 82, the number with him in the landing. Frank placed another, entirely opposite, proposal on the table. He suggested that Fidel leave the country, arguing that he would be safer out of Cuba, and the movement could start all over again.

The mood, so ebullient among the directors after the interview and filled with the euphoria after having snagged the attention of one of the world's leading newspapers, now turned sober as Frank spoke. He faced the members of the group with a heartfelt and compassionate message: above all, we cannot lose Fidel. He, of all of us, must be safe. Now that the world knows he's alive, we've won a major battle and can take a step back. The time has come to move Fidel out of the line of fire, especially since Batista, faced with international pressure, will only step up the army's hunt now. Why take that chance?

Additionally, a reprieve would allow time for Frank to regroup, rebuild the movement in the cities. Frank, always so fearless, was advocating caution and responsibility: both to Fidel and to the cause. Frank, so selfless, was asking for time. How could they refuse?

More than sober, the mood would have taken on a sudden chill if Frank spoke openly about his visit the day before to the guerrilla camp. I've never seen this recorded, but several people have spoken to me of Frank's reaction to what he saw there. While Celia and Fidel had been out walking, he'd returned to the camp to inspect the men's rifles. He'd found them dirty and uncared for, so he had spent the afternoon cleaning the weapons. However coldly or silently he might have done this, there would have been no concealing his anger at this lack of discipline, so indicative of a fatal carelessness. Not simply on the part of the men, but of their commander. This was the same Frank who had insisted on uniforms at the Battle of Santiago, mindful of how his little army would be perceived, not just by the populace, but by themselves. How could he sanction such casual attention to details that meant life or death?

Tension mounted among the directors assembled in the guerrilla camp deep within Epifanio's farm.

Around 3:00 p.m., one of Epifanio's cousins rushed in to blurt out: "Eutimio's down at the farmhouse." Alone or with soldiers, Fidel wanted to know. But the young man wasn't sure. He hadn't waited long enough to look around; he'd rushed up to the camp as fast as he could, to warn them.

Fidel selected Mario Diaz, a guerrilla, to confront Eutimio and asked Epifanio's cousin to return with Diaz. The two set off for the farmhouse. In under a mile, they encountered Eutimio coming up the path. Diaz gave their old guide a big hug. "Where've you been? Fidel's been worried about you." To keep Eutimio away from the camp, Diaz suggested they go down to the farmhouse, where it was more comfortable. There, they'd be able to drink coffee, talk, catch up on news. Eutimio agreed. As they walked, the farmer-guide asked whether Fidel was around. Diaz assured him that Fidel was away, but he'd be back soon. "Tonight or tomorrow," he promised. Farther down the path, they ran into Ciro Frias, who appeared to be posted as a sentry. Ciro greeted Eutimio with a big hug—but didn't let go. Manuel Fajardo stepped from behind a tree, holding a Thompson machine gun, and frisked Eutimio. They found some papers in his breast pocket, and Eutimio said, "Don't read those. Shoot me first, but don't." The guerrillas bound his hands and took him up the hill to Fidel.

No words were needed after Fidel glanced at the document. It was a certificate of safe-conduct signed by Col. Alberto del Rio Casillas, commanding officer for the army's Sierra theater. Eutimio's actions had resulted in the death of one guerrilla and caused four days of running for their lives. Eutimio knew his fate. He asked Fidel to take care of his children.

Fidel had liked this man and enjoyed his conversation. "A simple man mentally unprepared to resist the promise of what seemed to be an unbelievable fortune: a farm and money." When Guerra Matos offered me this summary of Eutimio's story, I understood that he was giving me the present-day version, accommodating, yet leaving unsaid, the fact that Eutimio had also genuinely loved Fidel.

They executed Eutimio at the beginning of a torrential rainstorm, which continued well into the evening. Around 7:00 p.m., in the dark, Fidel and two unnamed guerrillas (we can assume that they were Universo Sánchez and Ciro Frías, then Fidel's bodyguards), Celia, Haydée, and Vilma left for the abandoned house, which they'd finally located.

The guerrillas had found a traitor among them, and they had shot him. They had been tough when they needed to be so, and only in the nick of time. Made vulnerable by the poor decision to let Eutimio be their contact, they'd paid a high price, but they had survived. In reality, what could their future hold without making some sort of drastic change?

The assembled directors met the following day. Frank argued his point further. He wanted to be sure Fidel wouldn't expose himself (and the others) to danger. It was an issue of security—and, of course, there was also the matter of the dirty weapons Frank had seen in camp. How can any soldier fight and protect himself if he doesn't love his rifle? This must have been an underlying refrain. What sort of commander sanctions carelessness when it comes to arms?

WHERE DID CELIA STAND? Surely her thoughts were similar to Frank's: that Fidel was in danger, and he posed a danger as well. Where did the others stand? Armando Hart and Haydée Santamaría, from Havana, were long associated with Fidel; Faustino was also in Fidel's camp. Then there was Vilma Espín and Rene Rodríguez from Santiago, longtime supporters of Frank, as was Carlos Iglesias, a.k.a. Nicaragua. Enrique Escalona, from Manzanillo, would have looked to Celia and Frank. (Guerra Matos was present as Celia's helper and would not have taken part in these discussions.) She was the tiebreaker, by my count. If she sided with Frank, then it's Frank's call. It was up to Fidel to convince Frank—all of them—otherwise. Fidel remained confident. He'd won the Battle of La Plata, and he'd learned when he'd swept down on the little garrison that he could make successful attacks and withdraw quickly. He knew he could win battles in the Sierra. If he could stick to the upper reaches of the mountains, he argued, Batista's army would always be vulnerable to his fire. We can assume he decorated his argument with flourishes of charm and gusts of boundless optimism.

In the end, the leaders came to terms: the movement would supply Fidel with an army, but its soldiers would be selected by Frank. Frank would send the recruits to Celia for initial training; he would provide arms and uniforms; she would do the rest and get them into the mountains. Fidel's job, for the time being, was to sit tight and wait for these new men to arrive. Once his army was restored, he could resume his hide-in-the-mountains, swoop-down-and-raid, lure-the-enemy style of warfare. Frank would continue to command the urban front.

Arriving at this deal had taken two days of debate. Celia was the oldest person present, three months shy of thirty-eight, fully mature; perhaps even an accomplished practitioner at deception to further the cause. Loyalty, diplomacy, these were her traits, and she knew how to keep her eyes on the prize. Everything I've learned about her indicates that Celia was unquestioningly loyal to Frank. Despite the strong pull of Fidel's personality, she was Frank's partner and I'm sure she felt as he did. Yet in this debate Celia must have been careful not to contradict Fidel, who came away convinced she was on his side.

The directors were still in the guerrilla camp on the 19th. A little after twelve noon, according to Hart, they heard a shot, from close by. Panic and fear struck. The army had found them

Frank País in his 26th of July uniform on Epifánio Díaz's farm, February 17th or 18th, 1957. The photograph may have been taken by Celia. *(Courtesy of Oficina de Asuntos Históricos)*

by following the steps of Eutimio. Faustino bundled together the papers he'd been holding, to destroy them. Fear subsided into confusion as the directors and guerrilla soldiers, as a group, quickly discovered something quite different. The shot had come from inside the guerrilla camp. José Moran had shot himself in the leg. Confusion was replaced by suspicion. Was this an accident? What were they to make of this situation? The same soldier had gone AWOL before their ambush ten days earlier. What were they to conclude? That Moran is a coward, that he had shot himself in order to desert and get out of the Sierra? Che, suspicious of Moran already, now stepped into his role as a doctor. He came forward to dress Moran's wound and observed that the bullet had passed through the muscle without touching the bone. He announced that Moran was in no real danger. Che could not say, for sure, based on the angle of the bullet, whether the shot had been an accident. Che, just days before, had stepped forward to shoot Eutimio when the others hesitated to do so, but he became circumspect here, less certain of what should come next. Traitors are shot. In war, that is the fate of deserters also. Were they to shoot everyone? Had this injury not been called into question, the course of action would have been automatic: a wounded man can't function as a guerrilla, always on the march, so Moran would have been billeted in some farmer's house to recuperate. Naturally, in light of the suspicion, they couldn't keep Moran in the mountains. Thanks to Che's tough mentality, we know they made another choice here: as guerrillas, justice may require that you shoot people, but there are situations with no perfect solution. Where was proof? Do we kill on assumption or suspicion? Are we that kind of people? Are we an army who blindly follows rules out of fear? Their actions came largely without discussion. Rather than become cold-blooded killers, they were willing to choose an uncertain fate.

This is where Celia stepped in. She offered a morally acceptable option. She told them that she'd arrange for Moran to be treated in Manzanillo by doctors running a clandestine 26th of July clinic. She'd be putting those doctors in jeopardy, but she offered Fidel and the movement a way out; and it would come back to haunt her in days to come. By doing so, she had taken on—for herself and for Rafael Sierra, Manzanillo's July 26th director—the obligation to absorb Moran into their organization. It was a huge risk, and caused problems later. But it was a defining moment in the Revolution. As a measure of how antagonistic the atmosphere in the camp was that day, Guerra Matos told me, he refused to transport Moran to Manzanillo. (Yet, as a member of the Manzanillo movement, he'd have to work with Moran there.) In the end, Nicaragua drove Moran to the underground clinic.

HERBERT MATTHEWS STAYED AN EXTRA DAY in Cuba to interview José Antonio Echevarria. That extension of his visit was somewhat in defiance of Matthews's editor, who'd urged him to get out of Cuba as quickly as possible. He and Nancie had gone to dinner at Mary and Ernest Hemingway's house outside the city on Monday night, near the village of San Francisco de Paula. The next morning, the 19th, as he got ready to leave for the airport, Matthews would note, he was filled with anxiety. He was afraid he'd be searched, that Batista's officials would take one look at his passport, which clearly stated he was a journalist, and go through his luggage. If this happened, they'd confiscate his notes. Hearing him express this concern, Nancie said, "Let me carry them." She slipped some pages of notes plus the little black book with Fidel's signature inside her girdle. When their plane was well outside Cuba's airspace, she went into the lavatory and took out the notebook. Matthews began working on his story while still on the plane.

IN THE MOUNTAINS, Celia spent the night in Epifánio's house. By then, the guerrillas had moved to a coffee grove, closer to the farmhouse. Guerra Matos showed up on the morning of the 20th to drive Celia back to Manzanillo. There, she set her sights on building the new army for Fidel. But, before leaving the mountains, she'd written a thank-you note to Ruby Hart Phillips, the *Times* stringer, and got Fidel to sign it. She sent it in a hand-woven basket lined with moss and filled with orchids.

14. February–March 1956

The *Marabuzal*

WHEN FRANK RETURNED TO SANTIAGO—after the Matthews interview and the meeting of the movement's directors—he informed his cells that he'd be selecting combatants to fight with Fidel in the mountains. Celia did the same, contacting operators in all the cities along the coast. Frank's guidelines were extremely clear: priority was going to members of the underground who had been detected, were in hiding, and no longer effective for clandestine work. Yet the recruits had to be capable soldiers, strong enough mentally and physically to withstand the rigors of guerrilla warfare. They had to have been "proven in action," to have a history of carrying out dangerous missions for the movement. And finally, Frank wanted only those men who were politically sophisticated.

Celia, in Manzanillo, expected the new men to arrive in twos and threes, and planned to hide them in private houses until she hit upon another solution. In the end, she devised a way to base her operation in a single location, with an imaginative approach much admired by the old revolutionaries. Celia's induction center operated throughout the war and was never discovered. Even after the Revolution, it remained something of a mystery.

Just days after her own return from the mountains, during the week of February 20, 1957, she was in the process of moving from one house to another, with help from her guardian angel, Hector

Llópiz. Hector decided to pay a quick visit, during the move, to his brother, Rene, who worked only a few kilometers outside Manzanillo. He took Celia along, perhaps to give her some time out of hiding, or maybe because the indirect route made moving her less suspicious.

They headed for *Finca Rosalia*, the rice plantation Rene served as manager. Hector and Celia drove out of town via the main highway, going east toward Bayamo. The land in the region is high and flat, with a view of the foothills and the distant mountains. They turned onto a county road, then into a private, perfectly straight driveway that led up to the farmhouse. The house was large and square, in full view of the highway.

Standing amid the vast openness of the rice fields, Celia took in her surroundings. Among the people of Manzanillo, the owners of these rice farms were well respected. For one thing, they were rich: these outbuildings sheltered expensive machinery, large U.S.-made tractors and other farm equipment. Celia was familiar with the properties in this area (often referred to as plantations), and the one she was visiting that day with Hector was similar to that owned by her brother-in-law, Pedro Alvarez. This farm's owner, like Pedro and his wife, Celia's older sister Chela, lived in town. The farmhouse at *Finca Rosalia* was not actually occupied as a dwelling by anyone. No one dropped by casually. Anyone arriving here came on business. Prosperous real estate encourages respect and remoteness.

Celia took stock of all this as she looked around her. The unoccupied house sat in full view of the highway, yet far enough off that no one driving by would see much of what went on there. There were no neighbors within sight. About a quarter-mile from the house, where the property was bordered by the highway they'd taken out of town, stood an imposing building she recognized as an army garrison. This facility was always active, as the army operated a prison there. *Finca Rosalia* felt safe, in part, and ironically, because the garrison stood so close.

The lone point on the property where anyone might lurk was a grove of trees behind the house. This grove held the one piece of the *finca*'s lands not under cultivation. Celia always viewed her surroundings through the eyes of a country woman, and she quickly grasped that this stand remained intact because it consisted of *marabu*, the same kind of thorn tree she'd hidden among after she escaped from the soldiers in Campechuela. But this was an unusual *marabuzal*. Its trees grew exceptionally tall and dense; she knew she was looking at a grove at least a century old. These old trees, covered in thorns, had been left alone because they were just too nasty to deal with, and would have presented a huge job to clear.

She'd found the right place to assemble, train, and house the new recruits. It was in plain sight of the army ("Let them protect us" was her way of thinking), an ideal distance from town, on a farm where trucks arrived and departed constantly, and conveniently located near the county road into the mountains.

She explained her plan to the Llópiz brothers. They agreed to her smart, albeit eccentric, proposal to house the soldiers inside the *marabuzal*. The trees rose over thirty feet and provided a thick canopy of leaves, guaranteeing that her soldiers would be hidden from small planes, no matter how close aircraft might fly overhead. The grove was extremely large; when Celia set forth her proposal, it covered an area about the size of a football field. And every branch and root was covered in thorns. Hector and Rene must have looked at her with consternation. She insisted that she could make the grove inhabitable. Right away, Rene sent his two sons into the grove with Celia, to help her carve out enough space for her soldiers' billets and their preliminary training.

She knew that wild animals moved within these groves, made paths over and under their spiky root systems, so there had to be a way in. She found a path, and Rene's boys, under her direction, widened it with their machetes, gaining access to the grove's interior. Inside, she found a spot that suited her, and had the boys clear underbrush and make space enough to string up hammocks. Because the grove was so dense, extensive clearing didn't change the way the grove looked from the outside. The boys cut out a series of open-air "rooms," and Celia rain-proofed them with large sheets of plastic suspended overhead.

Soon they had established four main trails: the first was the entrance; two more were for guard duty; and the fourth led to the "cafeteria." This was a clearing wide enough, just inside one edge of the grove, to let a horse pull in a cart loaded with food. When the time came to feed her troops, Celia did not prepare their

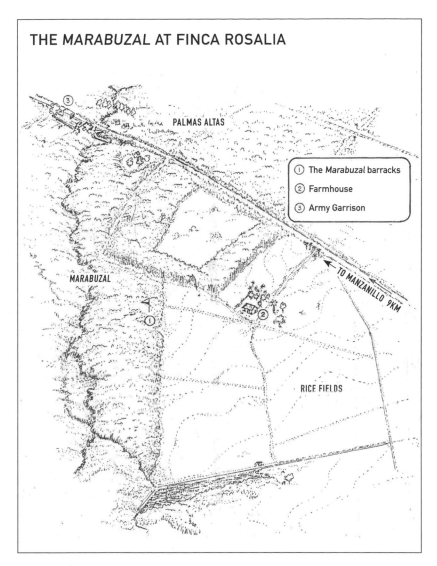

THE MARABUZAL AT FINCA ROSALIA

PALMAS ALTAS

① The Marabuzal barracks

② Farmhouse

③ Army Garrison

TO MANZANILLO 9KM

MARABUZAL

RICE FIELDS

(Map drawn by Otto Hernandez. Courtesy of Oficina de Asuntos Históricos.)

meals—not Celia, who had had a cook all her life—although I've often heard this story expressed. From Elsa Castro, I learned that Celia got Rene's wife, who dropped off a container of food for her husband's midday meal, to prepare the troops' food as well. Since Mrs. Llópiz left Rene's meal in a bucket by the mailbox at the foot of the long drive each day, she'd do the same when Celia's men arrived. She'd arrive at the usual hour, with her sons along to help her drop off a few large containers, and her husband would come down the drive with his horse and cart to pick up the containers. It would be unlikely that anyone passing on the highway would notice the difference.

JUST AS CELIA WAS PUTTING the finishing touches on her *marabuzal*, Matthews's article appeared on the front page of the February 24, 1957, edition of the *New York Times*. The movement had achieved a major goal: Fidel's photo and signature documented the presence of the guerrilla forces in the Sierra Maestra. Batista immediately denied that Fidel was alive, and pronounced the photograph a fake. The *Times* countered Batista's protest by publishing a second photograph of Fidel, sitting next to Matthews.

Two days following the article's appearance, the first group of soldiers arrived at Celia's *marabuzal*. They were guided by veterans Jorge Sotus and Alberto Vásquez, sent by Frank to train them. A miner named Eloy Rodríguez, who had been in hiding since participating in Frank's uprising, arrived a few days later. He and the soldier who came with him were driven to the rice farm by two young women, Vilma Espín and another one of Frank's female collaborators, Acela de los Angeles. "We reached Manzanillo—or the area near Manzanillo—and went to Guerra Matos's house," Eloy told me. "He had organized a party, or something similar, with cake and refreshments. We only stayed there about half an hour. Guerra took us in an open van along the highway, and then we took a detour and went to the *marabuzal*." Once inside the grove, Eloy spotted Sotus, who had led a successful offensive against the Customs House during the Battle of Santiago. He found the veteran's presence reassuring. "Sotus told me, 'Sleep here. Tomorrow I'll introduce you to your squadron.'"

Eloy says Celia, who was staying in the farmhouse, came to the *marabuzal* the following day and gave each man a tetanus vaccination. As she administered the injection, she talked quietly with each soldier. "She told us that in the Sierra, there was very little food and that the few men who were there were having a hard time of it. 'You are going to live the life of a nomad and I want you to be aware of the hardship.'" What she had to say shocked Eloy, already disconcerted by the *marabuzal*. "I was astounded by Celia's words because earlier, the American journalist Matthews had been up there, and he'd given the idea that there were lots of columns. No one knew there weren't."

Celia also explained that they would speak in whispers, in the mountains and especially here in the *marabuzal*. She emphasized that *sotto voce* would be the norm. Later, she'd brag that her men in the *marabuzal* were "quiet as mice."

Frank arrived in the first week of March, driving a truck and wearing a khaki uniform. Hidden under a cargo of oranges was a load of weapons, uniforms, and backpacks. Eloy was greatly heartened by Frank's appearance. "I had known Frank for a long time. I met him in 1953 or 1954. He used my group a lot. We were miners, and, as miners, we had access to dynamite, and we provisioned the 26th of July." Eloy explained that Frank was always concerned about his well-being, that Frank worried about all his men, and mentioned that he had started working with the movement at the age of fifteen. So at the time he came to the *marabuzal* he would still have been under twenty.

Frank stayed a few days, working with his recruits and making further plans. The time had come for Celia to leave the underground and go into the mountains, along with Frank's new recruits. Celia had always wanted to be a guerrilla and had been watching for an opportunity and this moment, when Frank was selecting recruits, presented itself as a natural, logical time for Frank to make the decision to send her. She and Frank were making good their commitment to replenish Fidel's army, and with this complement he'd have 82, the same number of men he'd had at the landing of the *Granma*. Celia was to be the 83rd. It was an important move within the 26th of July Movement since she would be swapping roles, from *clandestina* to *guerrillera*. But not unprecedented; women had served in the guerrilla camps in Cuba's wars of independence, about sixty years earlier. Aside from historic precedent, there were plenty of practical reasons Celia needed to get out of Manzanillo. She was in danger, more than ever since Matthews's articles had appeared and angered the military, and by leaving town she'd get away from Lieutenant Caridad Fernández, recently appointed Manzanillo's chief of police, specifically to capture her. Her prolonged presence in the underground was endangering others, most notably the entire Llópiz family, for Hector had enlisted his siblings Rene, Angel,

Angela, and Berta plus their spouses and children to protect Celia. As far as the Movement was concerned, this was a good time for closure: her job was completed, she'd brought Matthews up to the guerrilla camp, she'd set up her clandestine induction center and could leave it in someone's hands—Guerra Matos, perhaps— although I get the impression that the *marabuzal* at this point was conceived as a single-use facility, to be decommissioned after the group left. Her departure meant Hector no longer had to move her every day; all those households could breathe a sigh of relief. Getting Celia out of Manzanillo would quell all their fears that some unreliable person, or wrong move, would uncover her whereabouts or inspire a betrayal. Closing down the *marabuzal* operation would get Rene off the hook, too.

But I suspect there was something else at stake here, maybe even tacit, in Celia and Frank's thinking. Someone realized one of them would have to go into the mountains and sort those guys out. It was a long-term, highly specialized job, and couldn't be left to a proxy (Crescencio, for instance). Since Frank could not leave Santiago, where he needed to be in order to run the underground, Celia had to do it. Celia understood the gravity of the situation. She had to serve Fidel, but also to influence and protect him. Finally, having been one of them, she understood the psychology of the underground. Fidel's new army of guerrilla fighters was going to be made up of former members of the underground, who had been trained in covert operations but not in guerrilla warfare. Celia could shepherd these troops.

FRANK LEFT ON MARCH 9TH, driving the truck alone back to Santiago. Just outside the city, the Rural Guard pulled him over. He was carrying false identification, according to Nicaragua, and a gun. Nicaragua's account features the gun as a major character. It was an expensive little handgun, decorated in gold and silver, bearing the country's seal in enamel. It had been stolen, Nicaragua claims, from a high-ranking officer in Batista's army. Frank, found in possession of this distinctive weapon, was arrested and put in jail. Eloy's account is simpler: Frank had been arrested several times before, as a student organizer, and "they were looking for him."

Any hopes that Celia had of going into the mountains with the recruits were dashed when she learned of Frank's arrest. Shortly after a courier got the news to Fidel, she received new orders from the commander in chief: take over all of Frank's work and continue to supply him with an army. Celia would have to remain in Manzanillo, in the hazardous, frustrating role of the *clandestina*.

Part II

MANZANILLO

15. March, April, and May 1957

Clandestinos

DURING THE FOLLOWING MONTHS, the heat was centered on Celia. The new and embarrassing revelations by the foreign press only caused Caridad's police to step up their hunt for her in Manzanillo. One day, when Lilia Ramírez was looking out of the second-floor window at the telephone company, she saw a group of police leave headquarters. She quickly alerted Hector of a raid. Very likely, this was the day the police raided Angela Llópiz's house, only to find that Celia wasn't there. Ana Irma Escalona, who worked for and lived with Angela, describes the raid. 26th of July documents were hidden in the house, buried in the pockets of a couple of jackets hanging in a back-bedroom closet. Ana Irma was careful to say that Celia was never careless about leaving things around that might implicate the house owners, and that these particular documents were not important. Ana Irma had been ironing when the police arrived and left her ironing board momentarily to get the jackets. She placed them on a temporary clothesline she'd strung up, along with her freshly ironed clothes. The police searched everywhere, but didn't think to check her ironing, and when they found nothing, "made a fuss." They'd made a big show of finding a small statue (she thinks it was a bust of Mozart or Beethoven), but didn't take it with them, "just kicked over some small tables" and left.

Celia continued to stay in the farmhouse off and on. With Frank in custody, she had to pay house calls and lean on her network of friends to provide supplies he'd formerly given her, such as armbands. This meant that the Llópizes got further into trouble since the armbands were made at Angela's house for the new recruits. These armbands were carefully controlled items, being the guerrillas' means of official identification, and sewing them was akin to a covert activity. The task was relegated to the back of the house where the red and black material was kept well hidden, as was the sewing machine that was used to stitch M-26-7 in white thread. (In Santiago, there was a much-lauded sewing machine capable of producing circular stitches, and those armbands are today highly collectible items. That machine, during the Revolution, was guarded as if it were the Queen's diamonds.) Ana Irma casually mentioned that ammunition belts were also sewn at Angela's house, and transported to the farm "in the usual manner." When I asked what "usual" meant, she admitted that they were taken there "by a couple of young women," who turned out to be herself and "somebody else." Two slender young women had left Angela's house wearing twenty bandoliers wrapped around their hips under "our wide skirts," to step into Felipe Guerra Matos's station wagon. (When I asked Guerra for details, he denied it ever happened.)

Wringing information from these former *clandestinos* is like getting water from a stone. Until this interview, Ana Irma says she has never mentioned having participated in anything to do with the *marabuzal*, and only recently have people from the underground begun to talk to one another, and to tell their stories. From others, I'd learned their silence has something to do with the pride, or what boils down to *clandestino* etiquette, which goes something like this: everybody took chances; you were given a job to do, were highly trusted, therefore, it is out of place to brag or speak too much about what you did personally. I wonder why *clandestino* protocol is so markedly different from that which applies to the rest of the rebels, about whom a whole industry of lore and aggrandizement came into existence?

Elsa Castro is more forthcoming about her work with Celia. Even she didn't know about the *marabuzal*, although she knew, at the time, that Celia was outfitting a new group of soldiers selected from former *clandestinos*. Celia had enlisted her help, and Elsa started buying hammocks, toothbrushes, combs, and knives from a cousin who owned a small bodega and "didn't ask questions." Rafael Sierra (the director of Manzanillo's 26th of July) gave her shirts, blue jeans, and work pants from his family's store. Elsa got blankets from another source, and would put all these things into backpacks, never assembling more than two at one time. Someone would pick them up—sometimes this was Hector, other times Felipe Guerra Matos—everything wrapped like any other product going out of her father's stationery store. If anyone noticed, Elsa says she would have told them that she was making them up for the Boy Scouts.

CELIA HAD ACCOMPLISHED her obligation to Frank and Fidel. At *La Rosalia* farm, a.k.a. *El Marabuzal*, two trucks rolled up the driveway on March 15, 1957, and 53 *marabuzaleros* loaded into the back. The trucks lumbered onto the county road. Eloy Rodríguez described the specifics of this rarely described trip: "We went in a truck. We crossed rice fields, we took roads. We reached Cason, where we left the truck. We walked to Monte La O on foot. From Monte La O, we started up real mountains." They were headed for Epifanio Diaz's farm, *Los Chorros*, where Fidel had met Matthews. Che was waiting for them. He'd been instructed by Fidel to greet the new soldiers, bring them up the mountain slowly, while giving them some training en route. It took two weeks. At the end of the month, the new recruits met up with Fidel—or so goes the usual story. But it didn't happen as smoothly as that. When they got to Epifanio's farm, Che informed them that he was in charge, and Jorge Sotus had countered that "under Frank's orders" he was leader, therefore the only person responsible for turning these men over to Fidel.

Finally, the new men, and their feuding platoon leaders, got to a small hill named Dereche de la Caridad where, Eloy says, they waited for Fidel. As soon as he showed up, Che told him what had happened, stating that Sotus had been insubordinate. Fidel listened to Che and decided to hold a trial, did so, but took no action against Jorge Sotus. Instead, Fidel made Sotus a platoon leader, and for Eloy, and the others, this seemed to be a very fair resolution. "I personally think that Sotus was right," says Eloy, author of a book about this historic event. He has been reviewing his memories, talking to others, and shaping his thoughts on the issue. "Frank was head. Fidel had asked for these troops, but Frank had organized, selected, and sent them. With all the respect we gave Frank, I personally feel that Sotus was right, and Che accepted this."

While Fidel mulled over this conundrum, a state of shock, which Eloy openly describes, quickly set in among the new arrivals. Quite beyond the dispute, each of these men had been profoundly rattled by the situation they found themselves in. "Many of us," says Eloy, "thought that the war was going to last eight or ten months. A year, maybe. When we got up there, Fidel told us that this war is beginning now, with our arrival, and may last five, ten, fifteen, twenty years. 'The only thing I can guarantee, here, is that you aren't going to be run down by a bus,' is what Fidel told us. This was like a pail of ice water. It was so totally different from what we'd expected. We were shocked."

Their expectations, by and large, had been shaped by Matthews's *Times* article describing life for the guerrilla in the Sierra Maestra—that, and the sense of fulfillment at having been chosen by Frank. As Eloy explains it, being picked by Frank meant a very great deal. Each man was proud that he had met criteria Frank had set, had been selected because he could resist the hardships of the Sierra, and felt honored to be among the first *clandestinos* to join Fidel's army. Plus, it was a relief to leave the underground. "But we had to face a new life," Eloy sums up. Still, so much had depended on what Matthews had written, no one realizing that Raúl had organized the few men Fidel had into small platoons, marched them in to report to Fidel, then marched them out to march in from another direction. After Eloy read what Matthews had written, that there were several columns, he "thought there were going to be hundreds of soldiers there. We found only about 17, and these men had long hair, beards, ripped uniforms, a sack for a backpack. It was a deplorable situation. This made us sad. Then, what Fidel said [about the bus] killed us. But it was momentary. We got there with a uniform, an armband, a beret, a backpack. We looked like an organized army. We saw them, however, and our hearts sank to our feet."

CELIA, FILLED WITH PERSONAL ANGUISH over Frank's arrest, was unable to go to the mountains with the new recruits. With nowhere to go, she stayed on in Manzanillo, mostly at the farmhouse. There she received a second group of men Frank had picked before being arrested. She had to do everything alone, for now she was without his guidance, and probably felt like a boat that had lost its rudder. Just when she needed a partner, Felipe Guerra Matos was arrested one day, driving back from *Los Chorros*. Felipe's lawyers, who represented all members of the influential rice-growers association, immediately got him out of jail. But nothing remained the same after that arrest. He was being closely watched by the police, so driving to confer with Celia at the farm, for example, was out of the question.

IT WAS DURING THIS PERIOD, while Celia was at the farm, that the owner unexpectedly paid a visit to consult his manager, Rene Llópiz. The owner rarely came to the property. He knew nothing of the transformation of his *marabu* grove and unwittingly walked into the farmhouse to find Celia. He knew perfectly well, of course, that she was being hunted by the chief of police, and reacted as would any normal person: told her to leave his house because she was putting him in a lot of danger. Celia fired back that she had no intention of leaving. In fact, she said that he was the one who should go.

From his point of view, although he must have known that Celia was tough, being a guerrilla leader, she was still Dr. Sánchez's daughter. She was also the sister-in-law of a fellow rice grower, Pedro Álvarez. The owner was not going to turn Celia over to the police or military, but that didn't mean he wanted her to stay. From Celia's viewpoint, she had to throw him out of his own house. She had to get him out of there before he grasped what was going on. She was aware that he probably thought she was only hiding there, considered her to be a regrettable but temporary fugitive, an inconvenience. He could live with that, but if he stayed for any length of time, he'd figure out that she and Rene were involved in an organized operation. She must not allow him the opportunity of even sensing this. One of the upstairs bedrooms was what she called her "central warehouse" for storing uniforms and medicine. Of course, she also had a substantial number of men hiding in his formerly abandoned *marabu* grove, something he'd never figure out if she'd didn't let him. Therefore, he could not stay and she could not go. She threatened him. Historian Pedro Álvarez Tabío writes that "she insinuated fierce consequences that would supposedly come about if he used indiscretion or denounced them to the enemy." I never found out what those "fierce consequences" were.

WHEN THE FIRST GROUP OF SOLDIERS left the *marabuzal*, the nation had been focused on Havana because two days earlier, on March 13, José Antonio Echeverria's militant organization, the Revolutionary Directorate, had attempted to assassinate Batista. The attack was quite large in scope. It took place in two parts of the city. Echeverria and a small group of men stayed close to the university, which is located in the Vedado section of Havana. There they captured Radio Reloj (Clock Radio), which continuously broadcasts news bulletins every minute, punctuated by an announcement of the time of day, followed by the words: "Radio Reloj." Echeverria told the nation what was taking place, over the airwaves, as his soldiers machine-gunned their way into the Presidential Palace several miles away in Habana Vieja, the old part of the city. In order to defend two parts of the city, the army sent out over a thousand troops from Camp Columbia. By the time the army's soldiers and tanks got to the palace, the Directorate's men had gained access to the door leading directly to Batista's apartment (an elevator door, off the main courtyard). The Directorate's men were killed and the assassination attempt ended, but only because the elevator car happened to be at the top, according to historian Hugh Thomas, who tells us that had the elevator door opened immediately, Batista would have been killed. The attack at 3:30 p.m. was planned to coincide with Batista's lunch with his family. It lasted several hours, and various small battles took place in those two parts of town. The Directorate had snipers on the roofs of all the tall buildings near the palace, and these fired down on the army's troops. The same happened in Vedado, where small battles, generated from sniper fire, prolonged the conflict. Echeverria left Radio Reloj when he knew they'd failed at the palace, but he was gunned down on a street just outside the walls of the university. (A bronze plaque marks the spot on Jovellar, just off Calle L, and is covered in flowers every year on March 13.) A few of his men escaped and went into hiding.

AS CELIA WORKED TO ASSEMBLE a second group of soldiers, Fidel asked her to take on a new assignment. Robert Taber, a producer for CBS and a journalist, had sent word that he wanted to interview Fidel for television. This was a wonderful opportunity for the movement. Everyone with a television set would be able to see Fidel, in the flesh. Celia began making arrangements for Taber's trip, and elicited Felipe Guerra Matos's help. She devised a plan for Felipe to drive Taber and his cameraman, Wendell Hoffman, in and out of the mountains.

ON APRIL 15, Taber and Hoffman arrived in Havana. It was the beginning of Easter Week. They had to wait in a hotel until Maundy Thursday, when Haydée Santamaria arrived to pick them up. Armando Hart and Faustino Pérez were arrested as she watched through the windshield. Haydée acted as if nothing unusual had happened, even though she was married to Hart; she could do nothing but drive the journalists to Manzanillo.

CELIA WAS IN MANZANILLO WAITING for Haydée and the TV journalists. Pancho Saumell and his wife, owners of a rice plantation, had agreed to let her meet the journalists in their beautiful home, just off Manzanillo's Cespedes Park. She sat in the living room under Moorish arches, walls wainscoted with cobalt and bronze-luster tiles, with Nicaragua, who had been sent by Frank. (Frank, by April, was keeping up his general's role from jail.) Nicaragua would accompany the group, and when they reached Fidel inform him of a large shipment of arms that Frank had just purchased from the Revolutionary Directorate. Nicaragua's mission was to ask Fidel to name the best place for delivery of the weapons.

As Celia and Nicaragua sat there, expecting the journalists to arrive at any moment, there was a knock on the door. Enrique Escalona dashed in with the news that Armando had been arrested in Havana. The owners of the house, the Saumells, had been hovering and were having a change of heart. Perhaps their intention of doing something to help Celia had waned with

Nicaragua's arrival, especially if they overheard phrases like "extra guns" or "weapons left over from the assassination attempt" or "attack on the Presidential Palace." Expressing their reluctance, the Saumells, asked Celia and Nicaragua to leave before Escalona's arrival. What happened next must have confirmed all the worst flights of the Saumells' imagination. Just as Enrique was telling Celia and Nicaragua what he'd heard about Armando, a bomb exploded outside on the corner. Within minutes, the police poured out of headquarters, close by Cespedes Park, and began to enter all the houses in the vicinity. At first, Celia and Nicaragua tried to climb over a back wall, couldn't manage it, and came back inside. They left the house through a small side door that opened directly from the living room into the street, which was filled with policemen and patrol cars. They walked past all this activity very naturally, appearing to be curious but uninvolved onlookers.

Felipe Guerra Matos came out of a building nearby. He was unaware of what was going on. Later, the police found his car parked on the square with a pile of political pamphlets on the backseat. Escalona had borrowed Felipe's car earlier in the evening, had parked on the square "for a minute," thinking he'd just dash into the Saumell house with news for Celia about Armando's arrest. The police confiscated the pamphlets, and started hunting for Felipe Guerra Matos. (At this point in my interview with him, Guerra Matos, still angry about Escalona's carelessness forty-five years before, jumped to his feet. He had to walk around the room several times before he was calm enough to finish the story.)

Celia and Nicaragua returned to the Saumells' house when police activity died down, reasoning that it was the safest place to be since the police had already been there. By now the owners were adamant. Mrs. Saumell asked Celia to leave, and Celia, of course, objected. The two women were in the middle of their heated debate when another knock sounded at the front door; this time it wasn't the police, but a soldier. Celia and Nicaragua disappeared through the same side door. They returned at midnight. By this time, the owners were beside themselves and, according to Nicaragua, Pancho Saumell paced the floor, going around in circles and holding his head, but stopping fairly often to peek through the shutters to check the street, while his wife lurched back and forth in a rocking chair, sobbing and moaning that she was going to die. Celia took one look at the situation and announced that she was going to bed, leaving Nicaragua to deal with the distraught owners. When she got to her room she found the Saumells had dismantled the bed, so she simply went into the nursery and crawled into bed with their child.

The next morning, the Saumells woke Celia at 6:00 a.m. demanding she leave immediately, and she replied that she wasn't going anywhere without a cup of coffee. Celia had had a good night's sleep and was refreshed, whereas Nicaragua hadn't had a wink; he had spent the night sitting up with the owners, who were so unnerved he worried that they might call the police. Celia liked and respected the owners, but they were just a small detail in comparison with getting Fidel on American television. Downstairs, Mrs. Saumell refused to make Celia's coffee, on principle. Celia went to the kitchen and put water on the stove and was in the process of looking for the strainer when there was a knock at the door. Haydée Santamaria urged them to get into her car, but Celia refused, still insisting that she needed to drink some coffee first. She returned to the kitchen, compromised by sipping a bit of liquid through the grounds, and left, to everyone's relief. On the road, Haydée explained that she'd gotten away when Armando was arrested, had picked up Taber and his cameraman, and driven to Manzanillo. When she arrived, she'd looked for, but couldn't locate, Felipe Guerra Matos, then heard that he was in jail. Not knowing what else to do, she'd driven the Americans on to Bayamo, and left them at the home of a dentist she knew.

On the previous evening, when the police found Felipe, they jailed him for being in possession of political pamphlets. Someone notified Rafael Sierra of Guerra Matos's arrest, and Rafael quickly set out to find a replacement. He selected a 26th of July member from a landowning family like Guerra Matos's, who owned property in the mountains—in this case a coffee plantation— and had every reason to be driving around the countryside doing business with North Americans. Lalo Sardinas drove into Manzanillo as soon as he got Sierra's call. He saw all the police activity, had trouble locating Rafael, but eventually they got together and drove to Bayamo.

Now assembled in Bayamo, but without Felipe's roomy station wagon, they needed to take two cars to accommodate Celia,

Nicaragua, Haydée, Sierra, Lalo, Taber, and Hoffman, plus all the television equipment. They all had to reduce their luggage; even the journalists left pieces of equipment behind at the dentist's house. They got to the sugar mill in Estrada Palma that night. From there, they left on foot, walking along the only road from the mill toward Providencia, the next small town. They thought they'd be able to pass through the town unnoticed at night, but on the Saturday night before Easter, lots of people were out and about. By Celia's account, "People were dancing in all the houses, and each time a dog barked, Lalo worried we'd be discovered." Lalo had decided that six strangers (Sierra must have driven one car back) would be fatal and they'd have to change their route. Lalo had them walk in the fields to avoid passing through Dos Gruas and Naguas, although these towns contained very few houses. Walking in fields would have been hard going at any time, but it was especially grueling in springtime: the ground was soft and muddy, and they were carrying a weighty camera, a heavy tripod, large cans of film, luggage, and were traveling in the dead of night. The journalists and Haydée hadn't slept in 24 hours and were exhausted. Haydée was wearing a new pair of boots, and blisters soon formed on her heels. But Celia was fine. She had had a good night's sleep, liked being out at night, and was wearing a pair of flat-heeled cowboy boots embroidered with little stars (as documented by Taber and Hoffman, in a film now in the Museum of Radio and Television in New York City). In the morning, Lalo located a businessman (Chiche Lastre) he knew well enough to suggest he hide six people in his house.

IN HAVANA, ON THE SAME SATURDAY before Easter, the police stormed an apartment near the university where the few surviving leaders from Echeverria's failed assassination attempt were hiding. From this group, Frank (in jail) had arranged to purchase the Revolutionary Directorate's leftover arsenal. They'd been in the apartment at 7 Humboldt (now a museum) for over a month, since the Directorate's failed assassination attempt against Batista. The police killed all the people inside the apartment.

IN FIDEL'S CAMP UP IN THE MOUNTAINS, they heard that the army was searching for a group with two women, two gringos, and two others. Fidel was alarmed and ordered Camilo Cienfuegos, by then considered to be his most reliable platoon leader, to select "any man" (or so the story goes) but save the group, "no matter what." Later they heard, again through the grapevine, that the six had been discovered in a house near Santo Domingo, where they'd been hiding, and the house was under siege. Actually, Lalo's group slept all day and left Chiche Lastre's house after dark, following the Yara River, walking in the riverbed—a route that was both rocky and slippery, but much easier going then the night before, when each step they took had caused them to sink into the soft ground. They made good time, covering twenty miles on those two nights, and reached the property line of Lalo's farm early in the morning. Lalo hid Celia and Haydée in one of his coffee groves, warning them to stay out of sight because the Rural Guard patrolled nearby roads. Later, while Celia and Haydée were sitting under coffee trees, they thought they saw one of Batista's soldiers coming toward them. According to Haydée, Celia had been worrying about her father, wondering whether his instruments were being cleaned properly, as she watched the soldier approach. At first, only his helmet was visible, and they had to deal with their fear until they could see Camilo's big smile.

Interestingly, once Celia learned from Camilo that the guerrillas were broke, she sent money ahead to Fidel's camp, didn't even wait to carry it herself. She wrote to Arturo Duque de Estrada, covering for Frank in Santiago, before leaving Lalo's place: "These people need everything."

Tuesday, April 23, Camilo escorted them to the rebel camp. That day, Celia received her just reward: she was inducted into the rebel army.

I know nothing of this event, except that she was the first woman to be given that honor. It obviously was not freely or casually given, not a token gesture. It had nothing to do with impressing the journalists, otherwise Haydée, who had been with Fidel's original military group at Moncada, would have been inducted as well. The men had taken the serious step of including Celia as a member of their fighting force, and a month later she went into battle. Several members of the guerrilla force may have recommended her, but only one person could fully approve and carry out the commission. The celebration may have been quiet,

On April 23, 1957, Celia was inducted into the rebel army. Here she is in the Sierra Maestra, in early May 1957. Left to right: Abelardo Colomé Ibarra (from Santiago, he had just joined the rebels), Enrique Escalona (the young 26th of July Movement banker from Celia's organization in Manzanillo), Camilo Cienfuegos (who had come with Fidel on the *Granma* and became one of his most-valued commanders), Celia (planner of the landing, architect of the Farmers' Militia), Raúl Castro (Fidel's brother, then a platoon leader, later the commander of a column), Juan Almeida (with Fidel at the 1953 attack on the Moncada and on the *Granma*), Guillermo García (recruited by Celia to canvass the coast for farmers who would protect the landing guerrillas, who joined Fidel on December 25, 1956, and went into the Sierra Maestra), Jorge Sotus (a member of the Santiago underground, a veteran of the Battle of Santiago), Universo Sánchez (also on the *Granma*, a guerrilla who often acted as Fidel's bodyguard); crouched in the middle is Luis Crespo (who climbed a tree in the early morning hours of December 2nd, after the landing of the *Granma*, to lead Fidel safely to the house of a farmer). *(Courtesy of Oficina de Asuntos Históricos)*

or even unspoken, but Fidel tipped his hat to her by deciding to take the television newsmen to the top of Cuba's highest mountain, Pico Turquino. Fidel chose to be interviewed in front of the statue of Martí erected there by her father in 1953. It is the project she'd helped him realize. This gesture, on Fidel's part, was respectful, admiring, and generous.

They stayed in the upper reaches of the mountains for a week, all the time hosting the television newsmen. Celia never rested for a minute, writing to Arturo Duque de Estrada to order him to buy "two pairs of espadrilles, size 36, for Maria" (Haydée Santamaria);

"neo asthma pills" (sounds to me like medicine for Che); all the plastic tarp he can find since "it rains every day and there is nothing to cover with. . . . If it is 100 yards all the better"; three cartons of American cigarettes for the two journalists, "but not Camels"; a pair of glasses for Fidel "at the doctor's house where I left my suitcase" in Bayamo; a toothbrush "for yours truly"; and "A [Alejando/a.k.a. Fidel] says to send news."

Taber wanted her to retrieve his personal still camera for the trip down the mountain. Celia asks Duque to get the camera in Bayamo—but she also sends him to Hector Llópiz, in Manzanillo, to find out if Hector had received a large sum—"*la plata gorda*." If so, he was to get it to her, because "money is scarce." In her next letter couriered to Duque, she assures him that they are all having a good trip but wants to extract his promise to send everything she wants: "I want you to confirm, with this person who is taking this letter, that all the packages have been sent," ordering him around in a way she never would with Frank. She also asks him to send 1,000 cans of evaporated milk and tells him that, though she doesn't know when the journalists are going to leave the mountain, she wants him to have a car waiting for them with all their equipment (left in Bayamo) loaded in it when they do. She ends with: "Now look! Get together with this messenger and pick up all, all [repeated] packages," and sends everybody in Santiago "a hug." To use Felipe Guerra Matos's description of Celia: she was both imperious and impatient.

In her third letter to Duque, dated April 27, 1957, Celia complains that he's sent the wrong camera, a movie camera when "the one we asked for is for photographs." She then issues another set of instructions, and in the next sentence implies that if you can't do this, somebody else can. She encloses a message for Elsa Castro's brother (although the note is actually written to Elsa): "Have him [your brother] find a camera and film right away because Alejandro says that if they don't find it or screw up again, the work won't get done. This thing with the camera makes him feel embarrassed with the Americans. He's in some temper. We've sent the message with two different people so that the darn camera will get here, so, even if you find it, still go and pick up the one that Elsa is sending." (It's 1957. A lady does not swear outright, trusts her female friends, and has no problem giving orders.) "Elsa, I want you to lend me the best camera you have there. It's needed to make 'some perfect photographs.' Whatever you suggest will be paid, but it is very urgent," she wrote, expecting Elsa to take the camera from her father's store.

Last, but definitely not least, she remarks that Fidel's glasses had not yet arrived. This, too, is a threat, for Duque, as Frank's second in command, surely knows what this means, also. Although it must have come as a shock for Celia to discover that "Alejandro," when he was in a temper, would break his glasses. But she is going to deal with it, in her own way, of course. Since they can't win a war with a commander who can't see, Celia (probably at Frank's urging) has taken it upon herself to keep a constant supply of replacements on hand. She closes her letter to Duque with a list (in reality, a command): "Send now with Lalo: 1) The American's camera. 2) Elsa's camera. 3) Alejandro's glasses. 4) Cigarettes for the journalists. 5) Raúl's plastic [tarp] that I already sent for. 6) A toothbrush for yours truly. And nothing else."

In Taber's documentary film, the guerrillas present themselves well: a bunch of good-looking young men camped on a steep hillside, stylish in new uniforms—in other words, the opposite of what Eloy Rodríguez had encountered a month earlier. Taber interviewed three young Americans who wanted to join the guerrillas: Victor Buehlman, Chuck Ryan, and Michael Garvey. When Taber and Hoffman left Fidel's guerrillas, they took two of these boys to Santiago, leaving the oldest (Ryan) behind because Fidel thought they were too young and didn't want them to get killed. From Santiago, the two boys went home via the U.S. naval base at Guantánamo.

AFTER THE JOURNALISTS LEFT, the column marched eastward in the first week of May, getting in position to pick up the weapons. Frank had surmised there would be arms left over from the failed assault on the Presidential Palace, and that the Revolutionary Directorate would need to get those weapons out of Havana. He'd sent Nicaragua to inform "Fidel and make arrangements for the weapon delivery." Nicaragua had accomplished his mission soon after they reached Turquino and left them, going down the southern face of the mountain. From there, he took the coastal road to Santiago.

THE COLUMN, AT THIS STAGE in the Revolution, was divided into squadrons. The advance guard was led by Camilo Cienfuegos, and had a total of four men. Raúl's platoon came next. It was followed by Fidel's command squadron. In it were Manuel Fajardo, Luis Crespo, Ciro Redondo, Che Guevara, Universo Sánchez— Fidel's tall, handsome bodyguard—and Celia Sánchez. Behind them marched Juan Almeida's group, followed by a rear guard composed of four soldiers. Each group camped separately; each had a soldier who was designated as the cook. They descended the southern side of the mountain exchanging Sierra pines, palms, and hardwoods for feathery, subtropical vegetation that grows at the mountain's base. There they posted guards along white-sand beaches and camped under a clear blue sky with huge cumulus clouds overhead. This was documented by a Magnum photographer who joined the column. His photographs of Fidel and his men, armed and wearing uniforms, look like war played out in Paradise. On May 7, while camped on the beach, they got word that Nicaragua had been arrested shortly after he'd left them.

Much to their surprise, José "Gallego" Moran showed up, after leaving Turquino. He walked with a limp, although his wound had healed; his spirits were good; and he had a plan: Moran wanted to recruit men in Mexico and the United States. Fidel agreed, according to Che's original diary, closely analyzed by biographer Jon Lee Anderson. Perhaps Fidel actually thought sending him out of the country was a viable alternative. More likely, he was stalling. But Che was horrified by Fidel's decision; to Che, Moran was a deserter, but apparently he confined these thoughts to his diary.

In Santiago, on May 8, or the day before Frank was to go on trial, Taras Domitro implemented a plan to break him out of prison. At first, everything went according to plan: in the morning, Frank feigned illness and was taken in the jail's van to the hospital while his bodyguard, the big-boned Taras, waited on the street corner along with another July 26th activist. They would hijack the van and kidnap Frank en route to the hospital. As the van approached, something in the scene didn't look right to Taras. His instinct told him the situation wasn't safe, and he let the van pass by.

On the following day, Celia celebrated her thirty-seventh birthday camped at the edge of the Caribbean. It was May 9, and her gift was Frank's acquittal. This decision was something of a miracle, particularly if the authorities thought Frank had killed a policeman (although it was never proven). How could this have happened? Maria Antonia Figueroa explains that the police thought they'd caught just another student. "He'd been arrested because they were arresting anyone they thought might have taken part in the Battle of Santiago." The army's attention, several others claim, was elsewhere. It was focused on a small group of guerrillas who'd escaped from the *Granma* and been rounded up and were being held for trial. Since the trial focused on those guerrillas, as Figueroa points out, rather than students, Frank had been acquitted for lack of evidence of being a guerrilla.

Nicaragua has another version altogether. He explains that the two policemen who arrested Frank (as he drove from Celia's *marabu* barracks to Santiago) and confiscated the glamorous gold and silver pistol Frank was carrying, had kept the gun. They failed to turn it over. Without the gun, the prosecution couldn't produce evidence that Frank had been armed. But they knew that Frank was a student leader? Yes, Nicaragua nodded. They thought he'd probably killed the policeman in Caney, I asked, but Nicaragua didn't answer. He simply looked away. The police, he assures, were aware that Frank was a student leader, but they were unaware that Frank had been the architect of the Battle of Santiago. He had been charged with inciting the uprising, but there was no evidence to support the allegation. Frank had also been accused of carrying a weapon when he was arrested driving the truck, but was absolved because proof—the gun itself—"had evaporated." In short, Frank had been acquitted because the lawyers and the judge struck an agreement.

FOR CELIA, GUERRILLA LIFE meant camping on remote sandy beaches for a couple of weeks. I imagine she caught and ate fresh fish, while resting and toasting in the sun. The shipment of weapons arrived on May 18, and unloading the crate was a joyous affair. They had acquired three tripod machine guns, three Madzen automatic rifles, nine M-1 carbines, ten Johnson automatic rifles, and six thousand rounds of ammunition.

Also on May 18 Robert Taber's documentary aired. In it, other than Fidel, few individuals among the rebels were singled out, although Taber mentions an Argentinean among them. But he speaks of the two women with the guerrillas, "Celia Sánchez and Maria" (Haydée Santamaria), and of Celia, in particular, quite lyrically. He focuses on a bouquet of flowers pinned to her uniform. He calls it a corsage of woodland's flowers with the most beautiful odor, and gives them a name: "wild gardenias." At the time, all Cuban households with TV sets received the three American networks (ABC, CBS, NBC). Cuban viewers most certainly knew Taber was talking about mariposa, a wildflower that flourishes near water; Celia must have gathered near a mountain stream, or close to a waterfall, as they climbed Turquino. The blossoms grow on a stock and have a sweet, pungent smell, and look like small, white butterflies (mariposas) hovering upon a bright-green, hollow, slightly wooden stem. In the old days of the Mambisa army, Cuba's first guerrilla forces in their two Wars of Independence that started in the 1860s and ended in the 1890s, the Mambisa rebels hid tightly rolled messages inside these stems. Cuban botanist Alberto Areces explains that the flower is so famous, with such a historic reputation, that it was given the status of an "honorary combatant of the Independence Wars" for having played such an important part in the country's liberation. He says that women sympathizers, usually Afro-Cuban women, carried these surreptitious bouquets, filled with messages, behind enemy lines.

In New York, the three Girona cousins, Julio, Celia, and Inez, gathered in Celia Girona's living room that evening to watch the CBS documentary. Celia Girona worked in the Cuban Mission to the United Nations and eagerly looked forward to the CBS special program. Inez recalled that they had been stunned, but not surprised, when they saw Celia with the guerrillas. Both Girona sisters had visited Celia the previous summer (1956) in Pilón, just as Celia was knitting together her two clandestine networks, militants and farmers. They recalled that she'd spoken of her activities: the dinner parties, her committee activities to raise money for the toys, her great coup of getting the archbishop to visit Pilón during Easter Week, and of course her garden, as if these were the center of her attention. She'd built a rock pool and her sister Chela had sent her some large goldfish as a birthday present (not the kind of gift you'd associate with giving a revolutionary). The Gironas sat together long after the CBS program was over, taking in what they'd just witnessed; then Inez recalled Celia had bragged that she was so thin and fit she could run through a cane field and nobody would be able to see the stalks moving. They had discussed this little detail, while sitting together after the program, and concluded that she'd been "in training."

On May 18 no doubt most TV sets in Cuba (all major cities) were tuned to the special program about their country. When that program was over, the cat was out of the bag: Fidel had won another victory over Batista's censored media. That night, Celia finally graduated from being "the doctor's daughter" to Celia Sánchez, the woman who helps Fidel Castro.

16. MAY 28, 1957

The Battle of Uvero

WHEN CELIA HAD BEEN A MEMBER of the rebel army just over a month, she went into battle. On May 23, the rebel army was still camped near the beaches on the Caribbean when a boat loaded with men and arms, organized by the anti-Batista Authentic Party, tried to land. The *Corynthia* was quickly intercepted by the army, blown up as it landed, with only one survivor. Although the 26th of July Movement had had nothing to do with this landing, Fidel vowed he would strike back because the troops on board had been fighting against the same dictatorship, supporting the same cause. He vowed to let his presence be known and make the army pay for such easy annihilation. He would attack the army outpost at Uvero.

The garrison protected a small sugar refinery and a lumberyard located on the edge of the Caribbean; there was a small wharf for shipping. The garrison consisted of four guard posts and a barracks house. This clump of buildings lay in a cove, was backed by a high hill, and faced the water. It was isolated, served only by a single coastal road and a coastal ferry.

Fidel explained how they'd execute their attack. The trick would be to take the four guard houses by surprise; and this wouldn't be easy, since each one was manned by three or four well-equipped soldiers.

They got to Uvero on the night of May 27, Celia at Fidel's side. "She wore a uniform but nothing on her head," Eloy Rodríguez recalls, who traveled with Raúl's platoon. "Our groups reached the place at the same time. I saw her. She didn't look nervous. She looked very natural." She, with Fidel and the rest of his unit, set up command headquarters on the top of the hill. From there, Fidel could overlook the barracks below. Juan Almeida was to lead his soldiers in attack against the guard post at the bottom of the hill, directly below Fidel, and carry out the first strike. Raúl's and Camilo's platoons would move forward, take on the other guard posts, while Guillermo García and Jorge Sotus led their men against the barracks house. Crescencio Pérez and his platoon were posted on the coastal road, ready to hold off reinforcements the army would send in.

Among the rebel army's soldiers was tall young man recruited from one of the Sierra families, Pastor Palomares. Barely out of his teens, over six feet, he stood out among his comrades.

Celia carried an M-1. She had been allotted one of the most coveted guns, and Eloy Rodríguez remarked that some of the men were jealous. The M-1 semi-automatic carbine was a perfect gun for a small person like Celia: compact (35 inches), light (5 lbs. 6 ozs.), and accurate. The gun was manufactured by Colt at the end of the Second World War. The U.S. army moved on to a newer design in the Korean War, but the rebel army acquired M-1 "surplus" weapons whenever and wherever they could (Florida is often mentioned) preferring this gun above all others.

Fog filled the cove that night, and not all of the guerrillas moved into the correct places. It was still dark when the battle started. Fidel opened the battle thinking it was dawn. He located the barracks using the night-vision telescopic-sight on his rifle, and fired the first shot. The problem was, he could see the barracks before it was visible to the others. His first shot marked the location, but some of his shots landed near his platoons. "So we started the battle by shouting at Fidel, who was up on the hill, trying to tell him to stop shooting," Rodríguez recalls. "He was firing on his own troops." His shot also marked his position, and the barracks answered his fire. One of the army's first shots killed Julio Diaz, who (according to Eloy) stood next to Raúl.

Their battle was meant to be a classic guerrilla action: Fidel and his men would surprise the garrison, carry out a lightning attack, and duck out quickly. They'd leave Uvero before army

On May 28, 1957, Column 1 is leaving one of Batista's military posts after attacking it in the Battle of Uvero. This was Celia's first combat engagement. She stands with her back to the camera, facing Fidel, ready to make her way to Santiago where she'll explain to Frank all that has taken place. *(Courtesy of Oficina de Asuntos Históricos)*

reinforcements could arrive, simply melt back into the lower regions of the Sierra, and disappear. It was meant to be a short, sweet, bloodless battle, fought according to the basics of guerrilla warfare. Instead, the battle went on for almost three hours of constant engagement, and they lost several men. The longer the guerrillas fought, the more disconcerting their position became; they were aware that additional army troops were in the vicinity. When those reinforcements came, Fidel's command post would be the most vulnerable, isolated on the hill.

In the battle, Almeida attacked the most dangerous of the four guard posts, because it was closest to the barracks. He took out the post and positioned his men to cover Raúl and his men as they advanced. Almeida was wounded in several places early in the attack. When the soldiers in the barracks finally surrendered and the fighting had stopped, twenty men were dead (six guerrillas and fourteen from Batista's army); thirty-five were wounded (fifteen from the Rebel army and nineteen of Batista's men). The Battle of Uvero had lasted such a long time because army reinforcement never arrived. "The first shot did away with the enemy's transmission equipment," Eloy explains. The rebels only realized after the battle that they'd knocked out the transmitter; then army soldiers, after they'd surrendered, told them they hadn't been able to communicate out. "That enabled us to fight for the three hours," Eloy told me, "and gave us more time to leave the place. We used the lumber company's trucks and left after we buried the dead."

The guerrillas left with their wounded, except for two who were too injured to be moved, and drove to a place, not too far from there, where Che had established a medical camp. He stayed there all through June, bringing Almeida and the other wounded guerrillas back to health.

My sources tell me Celia fought well, but they provided no specific details. After the battle, she went to Santiago to brief Frank, disguised as a domestic going to the city to look for work. A few days later, Herbert Matthews flew in to hear their story; having read his article, I believe he was relying on her account.

She went to her sister Silvia's house. Pepín, Silvia's older son, then eleven, recalls seeing his Aunt Celia that day. After school, he'd gone to the Vista Alegre Tennis Club but found he needed something and had gone home to fetch it. He saw his mother standing in the doorway, and when she caught sight of him, she'd called out sharply, "Pepín, come here." This had surprised him; it was something Silvia never did. Then Celia opened the door of a car parked at the curb. He'd gone over to lean down and give his aunt a kiss. He claims he wasn't surprised to see Celia looking fully pregnant, but he had been disturbed by the woman in the driver's seat. When he went inside his mother immediately said, "Now, you can't say you've seen Celia," but he wanted to know why Celia was riding in a car with this woman, the wife of a famous medical officer in Batista's army. Silvia simply replied that Frank had sent the car. This left Pepín to conclude—later in life—that the officer's wife also worked for Frank.

ON JUNE 4, UNITED PRESS INTERNATIONAL reported that 800 U.S.-trained and -equipped Cuban troops were being sent to the Sierra Maestra. This caused some comment in the U.S. Congress, because it had approved weapons shipments for Cuba's national defense against an outside invader, not for Batista's use internally, against his own population.

IN JUNE, FRANK MADE PLANS to open a new front. He was on fire with new ideas a week after getting out of jail. He sent a memo, dated May 17, 1957, to all the directors: "I am going to create more fronts rapidly in order of effectiveness and importance; work with all the places in the provinces and cities in regions that could be used as future fronts, study them, make contacts."

He studied the geography of certain regions, considered locations for their access routes; he mapped all the possible ways of supplying a new group of guerrillas. Location wasn't the only consideration. He was looking for an individual who, like Celia, was familiar with his or her region. Soon he'd narrowed his list of locations down to Baracoa, Guantánamo, Mayari Ariba, and Miranda. Frank took care to reassure all the directors of the 26th of July Movement that he was creating the new front to distract the army and take the heat off Fidel, not to replace Fidel. On the other hand, he was making it known, candidly, that he was pretty fed up with all of them.

While in jail, Frank had had time to study the 26th of July Movement as an organization. He was critical of the way they had been using their money, and began to acerbically comment on their lack of discipline. In a conversation I had with her, historian Julia Sweig said, he spared no one, and let everyone know that he didn't like what he saw. He had already begun restructuring the organization on the national level while he was in jail. Now he worked around the clock to come up with a new national plan. This is why—or at least the reason given—Frank didn't leave Santiago for the relative protection of the Sierra Maestra. People feared for his life; they sensed that from the moment he left jail, he'd be hunted down by both police and military. Fidel wanted him to join him the mountains, where Frank could be protected. Everyone told him to get out of Santiago. To this, Frank clearly stated that he needed more time to get things right.

He called a meeting at the end of May to formally announce that he wanted to open his second front. He set a date: the middle of June. Present at the meeting were Lester Rodríguez (Fatty), Taras Domitro (Frank's bodyguard), and a young man named Oscar Lucero Moya. Frank thought Lucero could be turned into a version of Celia.

FIDEL URGED FRANK TO COME into the mountains. Now, whenever Frank went out, he was accompanied; often it was by an older woman, a member of the 26th of July Movement who posed as an *abuela*, a grandmother. She carried Frank's ID in a pocket sewn in her petticoat, and if they were stopped by police, she'd do the talking: "Officer, this is my grandson. He's taking me to the hospital. He didn't have time to get his wallet."

He moved frequently but to fewer and fewer safe houses. Yolanda Portunado recalls her family's anxiety when, out of the blue, their milkman observed that they'd been drinking a lot of milk. Frank had been staying with them, and Portunado's mother ordered more than usual. (Many years after this incident, Yolanda broached this subject with their former milkman, who couldn't recall the conversation and became very sad when he found out it had been Frank they were hiding.)

IN THE FIRST WEEK OF JUNE, Celia was back in Manzanillo—the place she didn't want to be. To soften the blow, she'd found a note from Fidel greeting her as *"Querida Novia"*—Dear Girlfriend. The short note was followed up by a long letter sent on June 15: "We have such pleasant memories of your presence here that your absence has left a real vacuum." Who doesn't want to be missed? The letter covers many issues, most of them about business, but Fidel expresses his professional gratitude to her and to Frank, and fears for their safety. "You and David [Frank] are our pillars. If you and he are well, then all goes well and our minds are easy." In three sentences he manages old-fashioned concern and last-ditch resistance: "Even when a woman goes around the mountains with a rifle in hand, she always makes our men tidier, more decent, gentlemanly—and even braver. And, after all, they really are decent and gentlemanly, all the time! But what would your poor father say?" And Fidel's brother, Raúl, began to write to her now; he addresses her in his letters as *Querida Madrinita,* which my translator swears is best construed, in this context, to mean Dear Little Patroness. Giving people what they need is something Celia had trained herself to do. Money is always good, but a pair of new boots can be even better, under certain circumstances. The same old revolutionaries who probably groused about her possession of an M-1 still shower her memory with praise for the little things she gave them: boots, a watch, a Catholic medal.

Back in Manzanillo, Celia had to confront two huge problems. One was José "Gallego" Moran. He had been around since the end of February, when she brought him down from the mountains to a Manzanillo clinic. Moran had not gone to Mexico and the United States, the assignment he'd sought from Fidel. He'd been working with the local 26th of July Movement in Manzanillo and moving about, whenever he felt like it, to the mountains and Santiago. They didn't know what he was up to, and he was someone they fundamentally distrusted. Frank had warned Rafael Sierra, who took over while Celia was with the rebel army, to keep Moran on a short leash. He did not: Moran had been popping up in various places since the rebels had left the CBS television journalist on Pico Turquino and come down to the coast. Moran was an ongoing problem. She had to solve it.

Upon her return, she encountered the second grave problem. Sierra had authorized some "boys" to join Fidel in the mountains. Only Frank and she had authority to do this. Although I don't have all the pieces of this story, I learned certain details: she didn't initiate this group, but she didn't stop them, either, and helped Sierra outfit them before they left Manzanillo. The outcome was disastrous. While Frank was voicing his disgust for the 26th's general ineptitude and lack of discipline, Celia, his star pupil, was providing him with a shining example. I gained a clear picture (if not a full understanding) of this situation from the letters Celia sent to Frank, asking him for help. The boys were unseasoned, she told him; they thought 40-pound backpacks were too heavy; they'd been barely trained; they lacked discipline, they ate up all their rations on the first days; and some "ran off" (she does not call it desertion) and threw their weapons and ammunition in the underbrush (which must have left Frank reeling). Celia, by now, had processed well over a hundred soldiers through her eccentric barracks, and had done so very professionally. Yet this one group of men jeopardized her *marabuzal* operation, which was becoming the lifeline of the rebel army, and she was faced with the responsibility of finding them, punishing them, and explaining why this group had become derailed.

IN SANTIAGO, FRANK SENT OSCAR LUCERO to the mountain zone of his birth. It was in a region northeast of Santiago, near the Miranda sugar mill, within the range called Sierra Cristal. Frank had already made a trip there, liked what he saw, and had informed Fidel. Fidel gave Frank his blessing in a letter written on June 4. In mid-June, a base camp was set up on a farm near the Miranda mill (today called Julio Antonio Mella) not far from the town of Palmarito de Cauto. In Frank's plans, the 26th of July Movement Second Front, or M-26 SF, would attack a small army garrison protecting the Miranda mill. After a lightning attack, his guerrillas would escape into the Sierra Cristal.

In Santiago, the movement's greatest threat came from the paramilitary force *Los Tigres*, led by Rolando Masferrer, who had issued a press release that infuriated Frank. Masferrer announced that he would be speaking at a recruiting rally in Santiago on June 30, and Frank decided that would be the date to launch the Second Front's inaugural attack at the Miranda mill. He also went to work on ways to disrupt Masferrer's speech during the rally.

On June 26, Frank's hand-picked forces began to leave Santiago; there were around forty men he'd assembled from clandestine groups all over the country, with Rene Ramos Latour (Daniel) as their leader. Daniel was the first to leave Santiago and head for a farm where weapons were stashed. He traveled with Oscar Lucero, familiar with the area, as his second in command. Taras Domitro was quartermaster; Raúl Perozo Fuentes, Miguel A. Manals, and Luis Clerge were platoon leaders; and José R. Balaguer (later to become architect of Cuba's famous health system) was their doctor. On June 28, the remaining M-26 SF soldiers left Santiago by train, and got off at two stations, Miranda and Bayate, a way station up the line. The group at Bayate waited, then left when no one showed to pick them up. They stopped a car going to Miranda and, anticipating who they might be, a clearly sympathetic driver said, "I'm sorry for you, but they saw you in the station. An army sergeant dressed in civilian clothes. He called the garrison near the Miranda mill to send a delegation to meet you." The army put troops in three stations in the region: Miranda, Bayate, and Palmarito de Cauto, and detained everybody who even went near them. The SF Bayate men broke up into two groups. One group hid near a cemetery, drew fire, and Rene Medina, one of Frank's soldiers, was shot and died shortly afterward. The rest made it into the mountains. Daniel, on the farm, ordered his men to remove all weapons they'd stored inside the farmhouse and bury them. Then they left, moving carefully through the countryside. That night, they were able to elude the army, and crossed the Rio Cauto by constructing a bamboo boat that carried two at a time, for seven crossings. Daniel was leading thirteen men; they made it out of the zone and sent a messenger to Santiago to get Frank's help.

In Santiago, *Los Tigres* got their rally rolling on Sunday, June 30, "in full battle gear ... with the backing of tanks, three thousand soldiers, and more than two hundred of Masferrer's thugs," as Frank described it. He'd devised a plan that called for his youngest brother, Josué, seventeen, to ride by in a car with two other boys, Floro Vistel and Salvador Pascual. The police recognized the three and sprayed the car with machine-gun fire.

The following day, unable to attend the funeral, Frank sat in a safe house composing a poem to his dead brother. "I feel my soul shattered," he wrote. "How much I always hoped to give you." Women of Santiago, in substantial numbers, went to the cemetery. It was too dangerous for young men to be seen there as they would be marked as supporters by the police. This became the pattern: women, and older people, would attend anti-police, anti-Batista events. On June 30, the day of the three burials, someone recognized an undercover agent for SIM. When the brother of one of the boys killed heard that an SIM agent was present, he assaulted the agent. Women—perhaps to protect him—joined in. Celia described what happened to Fidel: she said the women took off their shoes and hammered the man with their high heels.

CELIA WAS IN THE SAME DILEMMA as Frank after she returned to Manzanillo. She began living in another round of safe houses. Elsa Castro was ordered by the movement to take charge of feeding her in a couple of these houses because nothing, absolutely nothing, could call attention to where Celia might be hidden. Elsa explained that if a grocer noticed that an extra lamb chop had been purchased, he might say: "I see you have a guest," and speculate that the family was feeding an extra person, then mention this to the police. So Elsa would go on her lunch hour, when all shops were closed, to prepare something for Celia to eat. She'd carry a can of some imported Spanish gourmet product that her brother-in-law stored in his house, under a bed sheet, until he was ready to display these cans in his booth at trade fairs. She'd swipe a can, put it in her purse, maybe add an egg or two and make an omelet. She laughed recalling an omelet she filled with fruit cocktail: "Celia loved it." Like any pretty, well-dressed working girl of twenty-one, Elsa had appeared to be going to a friend's house during her lunch hour. She would ring the doorbell, be admitted at the door, and no one would have any idea what she was up to.

Hardship wasn't Celia's problem, Elsa says. "She didn't simply hide. Generally, she stayed in middle-class homes." Elsa wanted to clarify, as did others I interviewed, that Celia's real problems as a *clandestino* were insidious, and gave an example. "When she went to my cousin's house, there was a cleaning woman." Hector Llópiz had delivered Celia to Elsa's cousin's house, and the door was opened by a young girl who cleaned for the family, who exclaimed, "I know you! You're Celia." The girl became very excited at Celia's celebrity, claimed she'd seen Celia's picture in *Life* magazine. She bragged to Celia that her boyfriend was in the 26th of July Movement, and, in the manner of girlfriends, began to promote him. Now that Celia's cover was blown, and the girl knew who she was and where she was staying, Celia realized, to use Elsa's words, that "she'd have to lure her in, jeopardize the girl in order to keep her quiet." Celia apparently told the girl to bring her boyfriend by later that night. When the couple arrived, Elsa says, "She gave him an assignment. Told him—or maybe it was them—someplace to go and plant a bomb. They did. That way, she involved the girl and the boyfriend so they wouldn't talk. She compromised them and ensured their silence."

Situations like this are the stuff of urban guerrilla or clandestine warfare. I have taken Elsa's story at face value and see it as simply one more reason Celia was champing at the bit to get out of the underground, preferring battle as an alternative.

17. July 2, 1957

Thanks to Moran

ON TUESDAY, JULY 2, Felipe Guerra Matos was arrested for the third time as he drove into Manzanillo. He had just transported some men into the mountains, and his arrest was, he says, "Thanks to Moran."

During our interview, Felipe's voice dropped, markedly; his tone became soft, reflective. "It didn't happen overnight. A person doesn't come down from the Sierra one day and start working with the enemy the next. He worked for several months in Manzanillo. He worked with all of us." According to Felipe, Moran had been arrested by the police, let go, and after that "many of us were arrested and didn't know why." Mass arrests started on July 2 as members of the Manzanillo 26th of July Movement were taken to jail, one after another. Frank contacted Celia that he was sending someone to help her, along with "some packages." The next day Celia wrote a quick note to a woman she often worked with, asking her to take in packages. "We are in much danger with Moran. I have been in exile for three days. I'm counting on you to take care of my request." Frank's delegate got there, and the same woman contacted Celia. "Let him wait for a week," Celia wrote back, unsure when she'd be ready to meet with him.

On Friday, July 5, Frank wrote Fidel: "Things in Manzanillo aren't going very well. The Galician Moran stool-pigeoned on the whole movement. I warned Norma [Celia] and Sierra [Rafael] that the enemy was profiting by what Moran was regaling them with and that they had better execute him before he did more damage, but Sierra is irresolute by nature. Now the damage is done, and I think the least Sierra deserves is to be expelled from the movement for his constant negligence and incompetence." Frank had ruled out Sierra; that left Celia in charge. The delegate Frank had sent to Manzanillo would help her assassinate Moran.

Stalling perhaps, Celia turned to Elsa Castro for help. "Elsa, go to your friend Cabado and others who are always collecting blankets, sweatshirts—and flashlights, if possible, but not the small ones, normal size ones with replacement batteries. By tomorrow, I need four mountain knives with good handles because everything here has to be strong. The same goes for the blankets, the heaviest possible; the cold is so intense it will freeze your bones," which implies that she's either in the mountains, and needed these supplies, or was getting people out of Manzanillo.

In Frank's letter to Fidel, he confronted all the worst situations. When he sat down to write this letter, his hand shook as he picked up the pen, he told Fidel. When he was calm enough to write, he described what had happened to the Second Front, the failure at the rally, and his brother Josué's death. "Everything planned in such detail, everything so well distributed, and it all turned out badly, absolutely everything went awry, one thing after another. The time bomb, so meticulously prepared and placed, did not go off because it got wet a few hours before; the hand grenades did not work; the Second Front, organized with such secrecy, was aborted and we lost weapons and equipment worth more than US$20,000 [the peso and the dollar were equal at the time], as well as the life of a comrade. And we lost three more comrades here." Then Frank, in this letter, begins to describe what happened to the three boys, one of them his brother. "They were taken by surprise as they were carrying out a delicate operation. They preferred to die fighting rather than allow themselves to be arrested. The loss of the youngest among them has left me with emptiness in my heart and sorrow in my soul."

As more and more people were arrested in Manzanillo, and as Celia was trying to deal with Moran, Fidel sent her a message saying that some rolls of film would be arriving and he wanted her to get them developed and printed, and to be sure to put a package of prints on the first plane to Havana the next morning so they'd get in *Bohemia*'s weekend edition. She was furious but found a way to get it done. "Enough is enough: look, when the two rolls come, it's okay [this time]. . . . " she wrote Elsa. She asked her to tell Hector Llópiz the whole Fidel-*Bohemia* story when he came to pick up the prints, adding, "If Fidel wants his picture in *Bohemia*, next time he'll have to figure it out for himself."

ON SUNDAY, JULY 7, Celia warned Fidel that "a highly respected person" had come to tell her he had been approached by the government with a $50,000 offer to assassinate Fidel. But the man, after assuring the government's agent he didn't know how to find Castro (let alone assassinate him), contacted Crescencio Pérez to warn them of the government's offer. Crescencio sent him to Celia. She thanked him after listening to his story. Before leaving, the man had warned her to be careful, because "that kind of money is tempting."

In four letters, written between July 7 and 16, Cella pours out her problems to Fidel. She analyzes why that one group from Manzanillo had been such a failure; mentions that $10,000 is missing, a matter that she and Frank are investigating; and moans that Rolando Masferrer planted a company of his paramilitaries in the Sierra disguised as 26th of July soldiers wearing false armbands. She is extremely upset about this, since mountain people—farmers, ranchers, and small business owners—assist the 26th of July Movement. They are the ones who are going to get caught in Masferrer's trap. But Celia had good news to offer as well: she let Fidel know that she was sending guns and ammunition (the contents of the packages from Frank) and adds: "I want to continue preparing and organizing well in case I am not around." (Does this mean she's vulnerable, as in death, or is she reminding him that it is high time she moved out of there and into the protective geography of the Sierra?) She closes her letter with, "I love you and remember you," but the "you" is plural and she means "all of you."

On July 11, she writes: "I think I told you before about this. . . . Luis Sardina here in Manzanillo, his real name is Rafael, [is] a gangster; at present he is talking to Moran and organizing a group. . . . We have to fear all these people because they are capable of anything."

Two weeks had passed, and what had she done about Moran? "You can't imagine the problems that come up daily," she writes Fidel. "Moran is exhausting! He lives at the Moncada garrison, is always with the head of the SIM in Santiago; when he came here it was with someone else. He owns a jeep, two pistols and two machine guns, and it hasn't been possible to eliminate him." This letter to Fidel was written on the 16th. She treats Moran as a predicament, that is, a problem that comes up daily, but is defensive in case Fidel has forgotten that everybody in Manzanillo has been getting arrested (while he was interested in getting his rolls of film developed). She adds, with a certain amount of drama: "He left us here with 49 arrested and others in hiding. . . . He left me alone and out in the street."

As to the assassination, the person Frank sent stayed two days. "The delegate came to exterminate 'Gallego' [Moran] and, I repeat, it was not possible." I'm sure Fidel got this the first time. Then, in a separate paragraph, positioned on the page in a way that the words stand out clearly, she assures Fidel that "it is impossible for him to get the papers I have." She briefed Frank, in a separate letter: "He [Moran] says he has nothing against the movement, only against me for not giving him his passport and address book," meaning Moran spoke to her or passed messages to her. "In it, he has all the addresses of people in charge in the U.S. He says that he is getting a new passport and will be transferred to New York and before that is going to Mexico. He's already left here for Santiago."

I CAN ASSURE YOU THAT most of the old revolutionaries I interviewed did not want to remember Moran, let alone talk about him. It took a long time to collect all the pieces to this story; I wanted to discover if the movement—to me this means "the men"—permitted women to carry out assassinations. I admit that I was wary of talking about assassination, but the veterans of the early movement were not. Still, when talking to the never particularly forthcoming members of the underground, I'd always ask about Moran; it was just one of the questions I asked. One day I hit the jackpot, and found out why Moran's passport and address book were "impossible for him to find." Elsa Castro had them. In January 1959, she handed an envelope over to Celia. Only then did Elsa discover what she'd been safeguarding.

In guerrilla warfare, assassination is one of the duties attached to leadership, under certain circumstances. When Nicaragua took on the job of describing for me the steel-tempered aspects of Frank's character, he started with, "I want to tell you a story." He selected a situation in which he, Nicaragua, had been in charge of storing arms "in one of our cells," meaning within the group he was responsible for, and two of its members sold some of the weapons. "Some young men in the cell, who were poor, were brought over by [another group that included] people with money." Frank had just assumed a leadership role with the movement when this happened (on June 22, 1955). He went to see Nicaragua at the bank where he worked as a teller and stood in line at his window. When he got to the head of the line, he passed a deposit slip to Nicaragua with this written on it: "They stole your weapons and the measures we take have to be exemplary."

After work that day, the leaders—"We didn't leave this to other people"—traveling in several cars, had gone to the houses of the boys, searched, found the boys and "arrested them and set them free." After a pause, Nicaragua continued, "It hurt us to do what we did," and he skipped the details. I realized that he expected me to fill in what must have happened, so I said: "They were shot, right?" "It was a painful thing to do, but it had to be done," he answered. It is basic, in a clandestine military movement, that members cannot sell weapons. That I understood. He waited as my mind edged forward to fill the gaps. I sought clarification: "Setting them free" meant letting them go, but only so they could get away from home, out of sight of their families, when they were assassinated? Nicaragua nodded. He explained that "the leaders" had left the bodies on a hill in the Loma Colorada section of Santiago (near the Hotel Versailles) as an example, so that other cell members and everybody in Santiago knew that the 26th Movement was tough and couldn't be messed around with.

Celia was supposed to assassinate Moran. She didn't, says she couldn't—not even with the help of Frank's "delegate"—because it was too dangerous. Instinct tells me that she would not do it, and didn't have to. She knew full well that being Celia Sánchez didn't require bravado since she'd already played an important role in this revolution, and she didn't have to assassinate someone just to please Frank and Fidel. They were all equals. She also knew that they had to accept it. She'd been through this before, when she rescued Moran and brought him to the underground clinic in Manzanillo. "It's not about Moran," she seems to be saying. The important thing is this: we, the 26th of July Movement, are not killers.

It is interesting to take note that, after telling Fidel that she could not eliminate Moran, she immediately changed the subject. In the next line she informs Fidel that Errol Flynn is premiering his movie in the Sierra Maestra town of Estrada Palma and Flynn sent someone to Manzanillo to make sure they were all invited. End of story—let's not talk of assassinations.

It took me a long time to find out whether Frank had killed the policeman at Caney. Frank is so beloved, I realized, that this wasn't a question for everybody. Finally, I slipped it in when interviewing Eloy Rodríguez. He paused, looked me in the eye, and nodded.

JUST HOW FRANK HAD BEEN ABLE to assemble US$20,000 worth of weapons for his Second Front is a mystery, but a fairly strong clue lies in his letter to Fidel dated July 7, 1957. Discussing Lester Rodríguez, who has been trying to get out of Cuba, Frank writes: "You probably know that, at long last, after so much work, El Gordito [Fatso] Rodríguez left today for the United States. The very meritorious and valuable American embassy came to us and offered any kind of help in exchange for our ceasing to loot arms from their base [at Guantánamo]. We promised this in exchange for a two-year visa for El Gordito and for them to get him out of the country. Today they fulfilled their promise: the consul took him out personally, and the papers, letters, and maps he needed were taken out in the diplomatic pouch. Good service. In exchange, we won't take any more weapons from the base (anyway, security there is now so tough, we couldn't possibly get away with it), so we will only take ammunition (they didn't mention that). The weapons, if all goes well for us, will be brought directly from the United States."

18. JULY 12, 1957

The Manifesto

FRANK HAD BEEN REALIZING one of his greatest political
achievements during the two weeks he helped Celia with her
problems in Manzanillo. He had charmed a couple of high-profile
Cubans into going up to the Sierra to talk with Fidel: Raúl Chibás,
Eduardo's brother, and Felipe Pazos, former head of the National
Bank of Cuba. Frank initiated this project after his brother's death,
and carried it to completion in less than two weeks.

"The idea you proposed is a good one," he compliments Fidel,
"precisely because the 26th of July Movement lacks respectability
among the general populace." People of Cuba might hate Batista,
but were hesitant to endorse the 26th because it was too militant.
Frank continued: "I think it necessary for you to have a General
Staff with certain outstanding personalities to give it prestige and
an even greater aura of danger for all the sectors of the nation
who look upon you—romantically, perhaps?—with certain
reservations." Having talks with opposition leaders, Frank points
out, would cause the general population to reconsider the rough-
and-ready guerrilla leader in a new light, "when they see you
surrounded by people of this kind." Frank wanted a broader
political base, uniting the two major parties, Authentic and
Orthodox, behind the 26th of July Movement. "No one doubts
that the regime will fall," Frank states assuredly, but "what

concerns them is the quality of the engineers that the 26th can mobilize to construct the new edifice."

Chibás and Pazos readily agreed to meet Fidel in the mountains; and Fidel asked Celia to take care of the logistics. As usual, she got these distinguished gentlemen visitors in and out of the mountains but with a distinctly feminine touch. She sent handwritten notes to their wives, once the men were in the Sierras, telling them not to worry.

Frank, by this time, had already established a wide social network in Santiago to support his M-26 underground. This, too, had been created during another precarious moment of his life (while lying low after the Battle of Santiago, waiting for the *Granma* to arrive). The Civic Resistance Movement was composed of Santiago professional business owners and their wives who'd been talked into raising money and giving shelter to his militant movement. Frank, this twenty-three-year-old schoolteacher, made them feel that they were supporting their country and being patriotic. Civic Resistance Movement had grown nationally, and now, as Frank threw himself into his new alliance-with-politicians project—almost as an antidote to his brother's death—these politicians, within a week, had hammered out a public declaration, in which Fidel promises to hold elections and choose a nonpartisan provisional president within one year after defeating Batista. They signed the Manifesto of the Sierra Maestra on July 12, 1957.

JULY 12 MARKED THE BEGINNING of a personal upheaval between Fidel and Celia. As soon as the Manifesto was signed, Fidel sent word to her that a messenger, carrying the Manifesto to Havana, would be coming by to say hello; on the following day, he added, another messenger would be coming through Manzanillo with another copy—in case the first one got lost. Celia was outraged. Fidel had so little confidence in his messenger that he was sending a backup? It wasn't his job to make these arrangements. She and Frank selected everyone, including messengers, not Fidel.

Hidden away, in a cocoon of pine trees on his mountaintop, Fidel kept making capricious demands and ill-advised choices—or so it seemed. Every move he made could easily end up costing lives. All those people out there, operating in cities, were staying in houses located just minutes away from police stations, as was Celia herself.

Fidel might be a giant among men, a genius, a charmer, but he was proving to be less than a great judge of character. He seemed to have a penchant instead for colorful personalities. Proof: the first messenger left Fidel's camp and headed straight for Santiago, having taken it upon himself to deliver a letter for another soldier, to the man's girlfriend. In Santiago, he let it be known that he was carrying a manifesto to Havana. "Everybody asked questions, he talked . . . !" Celia later wrote to Haydée. "Santiago found out about the manifesto before it got to Havana." She complained to Frank that the whole messenger thing was insufferable, including the second messenger Fidel sent, even worse than the first.

She composed a letter to Fidel. "Dear Alejandro: This messenger arrived and continued on to Havana. I thought his mission so cute that I wrote David [Frank]. Later, M [second messenger] arrived. I was glad to see him. With him I am like one of those women in love with men who abuse them. They become indignant and afterward . . . they love the men more. He is such a liar and has such a loose tongue! But he is so useful!" She's chagrined, choosing her line of attack. But what is she saying? I suspect that Frank cautioned her against confronting Fidel too directly, speaking too harshly, being overly critical. In any case, she ended up writing a coy letter—but her tone leaves clear her frustration. The second messenger, she complained, chatted to anyone who would listen to him in Havana, and turned up in Manzanillo again, on his return trip, informing Celia that lots of people would be coming to join the war because he'd told them who to contact when they got to Manzanillo. In fact, she told Fidel that one of his so-called recruits had already arrived there. Clearly, things were getting dangerously out of hand. She describes that messenger to Fidel: "He came on the boat with his boots on, telling all the passengers that he was sure he'd be taken prisoner on arrival because of what he was wearing. He stopped at the doctor's house, then walked freely all over Manzanillo, endangering that family that is so useful to us." (She may be referring to Dr. Rene Vallejo, Dr. Manuel "Pitti" Fajardo, or to Fajado's mother, also an M.D. and active supporter of the 26th of July Movement.) "The doctor sent me a message to take this person out of the house at night, and we had to really search, since finding houses [to hide in] is critical here. We couldn't even find one for me," she adds accusingly.

She might as well have added: "Don't you get it, Fidel? Don't you have any idea what it's like to be here, always in plain view? *Clandestinos* are always taking chances in order to support you and your men. We are living our lives a step away from arrest, always near the military garrisons. How can you pick such people as messengers and send them to us?" But she didn't write this. Celia knew that unless she could educate Fidel, and do it quickly, they'd all sink into even deeper danger, if that were possible. She was confronting the fact that the movement had now increased in scope to the degree that such episodes were somewhat inevitable— and she and Frank would not have time to micromanage.

IN MID-JULY, CELIA CHANGED HER NAME, adopting a new *nom de guerre*. It was a smart thing to do after all the arrests, since too many people knew her old appellation, Norma. Frank changed his *nom de guerre* around this time as well. "Even the dogs know me as Norma," she complained, in a letter to Haydée Santamaria. Frank chose Cristían (as in Christian soldier, or Christian martyr), and Celia changed hers to Aly. She gave no explanation then, or after the Revolution, for its origin or meaning, and no one I've spoken to could say, for sure, including the historian Pedro Álvarez Tabio, why she chose this name. Álvarez Tabio commented that Aly— spelled that way—isn't a Cuban or Spanish name. Yet, it's hard not to notice the obvious: Aly is a little piece of Alejandro.

WHEN JULY 26 ROLLED AROUND, Elsa Castro says that she and Celia needed to let off steam. They went onto the roof of the house where Celia was hiding and released a bunch of balloons they'd gleefully marked up with "M-26-7" in black ink, to commemorate the date of Fidel's attack on the Moncada. They were near Cespedes Park and wanted the balloons to float down in front of police headquarters.

To commemorate the 26th of July, Frank wrote to Fidel on that day, "Give my thanks to all the officers and comrades for their sincere and brave note; it was especially meaningful to me." All the men in Fidel's column had signed a letter of condolence over Josué's death. This would have been a very revealing document had the army gotten hold of it. It was a brave document, indeed.

CELIA FINALLY SENT FRANK a long report on her own investigation of why the one group of *marabuzaleros* had gone haywire. She laid out what had taken place, factually and psychologically, explaining bad choices and how she'd resolved the solution. She takes the blame, but points out how vulnerable those new men had been. "They saw themselves under siege, mortar fire, airplanes overhead, etc. . . . Of the 88 or 89 men, only 20 were armed. Ten of the rifles weren't working," and assures him that "we've sent them to be repaired." We are the guilty ones, she argued. "They found themselves in a terrible situation, under the influence of the surrounding environment. Weight is heavy when one is not accustomed to walking a lot, 40 pounds feels like 80 [up] hills and [carrying] weight. . . . What I cannot forgive is that they threw away bullets. Why didn't they throw away the food, the blankets, etc.? For that, I find them all guilty." They hadn't had enough food, had eaten their rations too quickly, got lost; fifteen days passed and they were starving. "As far as one meal [a day], I find this natural," she continued, "nothing was lacking; later, yes, they had to start thinking about becoming accustomed to discipline." Frank must have seen through Celia's observations about food—she herself seemed to eat almost nothing. After reading her report, Frank, her boss, explained the situation to Fidel, without being critical of Celia. She solved her problems characteristically; she'd stuck with the people she trusted. She'd sent Felipe Guerra Matos into the wilds to take charge of the men. She asked him to wait with them until a new guide arrived. Then she had the guide escort them to the old patriarch himself, Crescencio Pérez.

For all their pitfalls, Fidel and Company appeared to be on a road to success when the new issue of *Bohemia* came out on Sunday, July 28, with the Manifesto story. It appealed to all manner of people throughout Cuba, asking them to back the new front, the Civic Revolutionary Front. The response to this appeal was immediate. Suddenly, even very bourgeois institutions, such as garden clubs, began to support the 26th of July Movement.

19. JULY 31, 1957

The End of an Era

IN SANTIAGO, DURING THE FIRST TWO WEEKS OF JULY, the police started daily searches, apparently looking for Frank, as if intending to cover the whole city, neighborhood by neighborhood, house by house. Fidel, listening to the radio, wrote Frank: "I am overcome by a feeling of suspense every time I listen to the radio and hear that some young man was found murdered in the streets of Santiago. Just today they announced they had found the unidentified body of a young man, about 24 years old, with a mustache, etc., etc. This will worry me for hours until I know the identity of the man." Frank had been switching from one house to another, always protected by young men and women from lookouts posted throughout the city, who would let him know the exact location of the police at any given moment and based on this, would make a decision where he had to move.

Then, mysteriously, the hunts stopped. In the last days of the month, Frank had been staying with a couple and the wife was pregnant, according to an account given by Vilma Espin. When Colonel Salas Canizares suddenly resumed neighborhood raids again, during the final week of July, the woman became overly anxious, tormented that Frank was going to be caught. He worried about her condition and made the decision to leave there and go to the home of a member of the Civic Resistance, businessman Raúl

Pujol. Pujol, with his wife and child, lived in a quiet neighborhood only a few blocks away from Maria Antonia Figueroa's. Pujol's house was off limits to everybody in the Santiago 26th of July Movement as too dangerous—there was only one way out, through the front door, to the street. The proscription had been issued by Frank himself. As word spread that he'd gone there, members of M-26 became confused and disturbed: why was Frank staying in this house he'd expressly forbidden everyone from using.

Maria Antonia Figueroa told me Frank sent her a note on July 30, instructing her to send money to Pedro Miret. Miret had been living in Mexico for some time, and Figueroa, the treasurer, always sent him money via a movement member (Rodríguez Font), who flew via Caracas. At the bottom of this note, Frank added, "Stay by the phone, I want to speak to you."

Rene Ramos Latour, a.k.a Daniel, went to see Frank that morning. Daniel's mission was to get him out of Pujol's house. It was a month to the day since Josué's murder. Frank was lonely, homesick, and acutely aware of being separated from his mother, Rosario, and his girlfriend, America. In the last house where he'd stayed, he'd been able to see them, although from a distance. He'd ask his mother and girlfriend to stand on a particular street corner, where he could see them through an antique spyglass.

A photograph shows Josué's body covered in blood, lying on the ground by an automobile, with a few members of the police (or paramilitaries) standing nearby. Maria Antonia told me that Josué didn't die right away; and when the police discovered this, they dragged him behind a car.

Daniel left, and another July 26th member, Demetrio Montseny (now a general in the Cuban Revolutionary Armed Forces), arrived almost immediately in a pickup truck. He told Frank to get in, that the neighborhood was being surrounded, but Frank refused, calmly explaining that he'd already heard about this from Pujol, who was coming in a taxi. "I'd better go with Pujol," Montseny recalls him saying, "you go first." When Pujol arrived, Frank remained inside. Pujol had to go into the house to look for Frank and precious minutes were lost. Maria Antonio, at home awaiting Frank's call, heard the shots as they echoed through her neighborhood.

Frank's death, to Cubans of a particular generation, is similar to that of John F. Kennedy: they can tell you exactly where they were and what they were doing when they learned that Frank País had been assassinated. At the scene, there were several people present (Pujol's wife and thirteen-year-old son walked right behind the two men), yet details are mixed up, and there's no clear consensus of what exactly happened. Emotions are still just as ragged today. It seems that Frank and Pujol were struck by rifle butts, pushed into an unmarked car and driven two and a half blocks. Nena Pujol ran after the car, screaming, and people came out of their houses. Reaching an alley, the police took the two men out of the car and killed them. Witnesses say that Rene Pujol tried to cover Frank's body with his own.

People began to gather, seemingly coming from every direction, before Colonel Salas Canizares arrived. The army brought in someone to identify Frank's body (incredibly, they still weren't sure). An old classmate named Randich (whom the 26th of July would later assassinate), confirmed it was Frank País. The police cordoned off the area and ordered everyone to leave.

Maria Antonia says she went out on her porch thinking that the shots came from the next block, and that her messenger (on his way to contact Font) had been shot. "When I heard no more, I went back inside my house. Someone came and said, 'Frank País has just been killed.' I picked up the phone and called a man who was close to Frank. I said, 'Has anything happened to Frank?' But, of course, I used another name, I used Cristian. He answered, 'No,' and to this day, I cannot forgive that person. If he didn't know for sure, why would he say that?" Her final comment—expressing a grudge she has carried for fifty years—sums up the pain, guilt, and remorse people still feel when they speak of Frank's death.

Daniel sent Celia a written report within hours, stressing that Frank was fully aware that Pujol's block was being searched and since two police cars were parked in front of the house, had decided to leave on foot. Daniel was under the impression that Frank would have passed unnoticed, had it not been for one critical element of bad luck: the ex-classmate who worked for the dictatorship and recognized him. "This is the version we believe and it is backed by Mrs. Pujol's statement," Daniel informed Celia. Over the years, various pieces of information have surfaced. Armando Hart recently reconstructed Frank's death as it likely took place, including additional information supplied by Vilma Espin. When

Frank moved into Pujol's house, a woman on the block—described as the mistress of well-known *batistiano* Laureano Ibarra—saw him enter and called the police. They took time to protect their informer (therefore the lull in the searches), transferred the mistress to another house, and waited until they could find a ship about to depart. When they found one bound for Santo Domingo, they put Ibarra's mistress aboard and then went after Frank.

"If I'd been there, I wouldn't have let Frank stay in the apartment," Nicaragua claims. "I was in a high-security prison in solitary confinement on the Isle of Pines when he died. I was next to a hospital ward. A male nurse told me that a 'colonel of the revolution' had been killed, and that the population had filled the street. I knew then that it was Frank." Nicaragua spent several hours on this interview with me, but couldn't hold back his tears when we got to this part, and was mortified. Apologizing, he began once again to explain what had happened. "He was in a house that I had forbidden him to use. When they killed his brother, he felt isolated. That was a contributing element. He was still grieving. This didn't contribute to his safety. It is my personal opinion that the people around him should have known his manner and ways [seen his depression] and said no." If he'd left in the pickup truck, he might have outfoxed them.

July 30, 1957, was extremely hot. The midday sky had bleached to white, as word spread through the town. Civic Resistance— "bosses and workers, everybody"—was the first to suggest that businesses shut down, says Vilma Espin. Owners began to lock up. "At last I got Rosario on the phone. I told her: 'You have to go down and fight any way you can, with your teeth—anyway you can—so that they hand over Frank's body to you.'" So Frank's mother, "a woman of great courage, went down there with enormous forcefulness."

Acute anxiety about recovery of the body had to do with the death of William Soler, still on everyone's mind. In January of that year, the fourteen-year-old, acting alone after school, put a firecracker in a milk bottle and placed it in the gutter on a street corner, a few yards from his house. He and his mother lived in the same neighborhood as Figueroa and Pujol. When the firecracker didn't go off, William went to inspect it. The police picked him up. They took him to headquarters and he never returned home.

For the record, William Soler was a white, middle-class schoolboy, the child of a single parent—his mother, Maria Louisa Ledea, was divorced. Did the police really think this juvenile had been making a Molotov cocktail? They never gave an explanation. William Soler was tortured to death. In police custody, he suffered the pressing of hundreds of tacks into his body. His young mother demanded an open coffin, making all of Santiago witness to what had happened to her son. Now, only six months later, people felt sure the same police would mutilate Frank. The sanctity of his body always figures in accounts of his murder.

Rosario García went to the coroner's office, accompanied by one or two of her friends. She found a small crowd gathered outside, and the coroner released Frank's body to her. She took it home. Maria Antonia Figueroa insists that when Frank's mother saw the bullet holes in her son's body, she cried out, "My son was a teacher, not a gangster!"

BY DUSK ON JULY 30 Santiago had turned into a ghost town. After 10:00 p.m., the streets were so free of police that Frank's girlfriend America and her brother Taras moved his body to their house. The police had withdrawn from the streets, confined to their barracks, which Vilma Espin calls "the one sensible thing they ever did." People are still stunned by this. "Just imagine," Maria Antonia remarks, "the police were afraid," although considering what they'd done and the feelings of the populace at the time, it seems almost like common sense. She added, "They fled. They hid."

At the Domitro house, America and Rosario dressed Frank's body in his white linen jacket, a white shirt, and a maroon tie. Then Vilma arrived and insisted on his 26th of July Movement uniform, the same green-gabardine uniform he'd worn on the 30th of November, when he commanded the Battle of Santiago. They did, and laid a beret on his chest, adding a white rose.

A death mask—plaster cast—was made. Photographs of this mask are in the archives. They reveal that his face was almost a perfect oval, with the widest part at the cheeks. Heavy eyebrows arched over eyes that were wide apart, and he had a normal nose, straight but not too long. His disguise, the tiny mustache that grew over his wide and beautifully shaped mouth, was left unshaved. His hair was cut short, except for a small wave just above the forehead.

That morning, friends, members of the press and of the movement began to fill the street outside; they all wanted to see Frank's body. One writer noticed a slight smile that had appeared on Frank's face (which the writer attributed to rigor mortis), and mentioned this in an obituary, published the morning of the 31st, titled "*El Universo no es Ajeno*"—"The Universe Belongs to Everyone." This clipping, without a byline and surely from an underground publication, is archived at the Council of State's Office of Historic Affairs, with "by Miguel Angel Sague?" penciled in the margin. The author establishes that Frank wrote poems and composed songs based on Galician folktales and music that his mother taught him. He mentions Pablo Neruda's poems, the love songs Frank had asked the author to read while Frank played the organ and they both sat in the empty Baptist church. "So there he was in his olive-green uniform and his black tie. The sign on his chest was red and black, 26th of July in white letters. The three stars [his rank equaled that of Fidel] were shining. Later, they replaced this with his beret. Then his lips formed a slight smile. Death dressed him in greatness."

The obituary's continuation speaks to me in the collective voice of the movement: "His vision and comprehension of the revolution was not mediocre. For him, the end or the final goal was not the overthrow of Batista. This was, in reality, only a transition. His vision went much further. As a lover of Martí's work, he saw Cuba in its broader sense, welfare for all Cubans. Our generation's revolution is a compulsion: its mission is to carry out the work of the *Independistas* [referring to Cuban, mostly guerrilla, soldiers who fought in the Wars of Independence] of the past century. Cuba today, long freed from Spain, has to get to know herself, and has to use her natural assets. She has to be Cuba, definitely Cuba. Cuba needs to retake her historical evolution: the need for militarism and despotism has to disappear. . . . The mission of the present generation's revolution is getting Cuba out of this chaotic phase of the West in which we are immersed. It should reduce the influence of the problems of Europe and Asia. . . . The revolution has a national objective, without hostility to any other nation, and an international position to maintain. Cuba has to convert its smallness into a continent."

This statement ends: "Frank knew, with the delicacy of his soul, the seriousness of these problems. He knew that our Cuba needs integral reform; that she should acquire full autonomy. The fall of Batista (with all the evil that was brought on by his coup d'état and those that followed) is the definite step that has to be taken. After this, the road will be clearer. The vanguard will start an incessant forward motion. The past will dissolve into oblivion. . . . Cuba's liberty will exist. Even beyond the international idea of home[land], it will be a fact." And the final thought is this: "The universe is not somebody else's, it belongs to everyone. It is still his. . . . Democracy is far from a police state under which the universe is only one small part. Where heroes fall, the universe is also ours."

MANY OF SANTIAGO'S BANK TELLERS, on the morning of July 31, announced they'd be leaving early to attend Frank's funeral: without tellers, bank managers were forced to close their doors. Since nearly all banks in Cuba were foreign, mostly U.S.-owned, their locking up before the standard 3:00 p.m. closing time, people often told me, made quite an impression.

At midmorning,the crowd outside America and Taras Domitro's house had changed, no longer limited to members of 26th of July or the press. This was the first indication of just how large Frank's funeral might be. All through town, members of all the Masonic lodges and civic institutions let it be known that they were going to take part in Rene Pujol's funeral and pay proper homage to this well-respected businessman. By midday, the two groups had decided to join their two processions: Pujol's coffin and mourners would follow Frank's on the route to the cemetery.

QUITE INDEPENDENTLY, a protest was to take place in Santiago that morning, having been planned before the assassination. The demonstrators planned to confront the newly appointed U.S. ambassador to Cuba, Earl Smith, who was making his first appearance in the city that day, at a reception held in Government House, on Cespedes Park. Various women's groups, working in secret, were going to greet Smith with placards demanding an end to violence, and a stop to U. S. support of Batista. All morning women arrived downtown, ostensibly to go shopping, but dressed in black. In photographs, they appear to be wearing high heels, carrying purses, in dark glasses against the glare of the sun, and clearly come from Santiago's upper classes. When Smith and his wife came onto the balcony, only then did the women materialize and raise their placards. One photograph shows firemen on the balcony with the ambassador, not in the street, as one would expect, turning hoses directly on the women demonstrators from above. As soon as the first dozen protesters were arrested and led off to jail, another group, who'd been quietly waiting in another part of the park, walked over and took their place. Around two hundred women joined the protest that morning, and by noon fifty were in jail with more still arriving. For his part, Smith was astounded at what he saw and his wife was horrified. He protested to his hosts, arguing that such force was hardly necessary—and was told to mind his own business; it was an internal matter.

"The only thing that worried the arrested women," Vilma Espin reflected many years later to Armando Hart, "who were soaking wet and bruised, was that they would not be set free in time to attend the funeral." Espin had pronounced Frank's funeral—in her 26th of July internal report the most important and colossal demonstration of mourning ever seen in Cuba. Not exactly, since 300,000 had reportedly marched behind Chibás's casket in Havana in 1951, but it was not hyperbole; even by the most conservative estimate 60,000 marched behind Frank País's and Rene Pujol's caskets. While Havana's population was 1.5 million, per the 1953 census, Santiago's was only 163,000. Such a turnout was colossal, with one of every twenty citizens taking part, walking or riding behind the cortege that day.

Six young women led the procession, schoolteachers who had studied with Frank. They carried garlands of flowers linked by a band of wide silk ribbon. The procession wound through the oldest part of the city, entering Heredia, an ancient and narrow street. Here, people began to throw flowers from the balconies onto the procession below. In photographs, the crowd seems endless. Civic groups, made up of members of various lodges and business organizations, filed behind Pujol's coffin. Many were on foot, but hundreds of cars eventually joined the cortege.

"For hours during the route, people sang the Cuban national anthem, thus breaking the absolute silence that had filled Santiago de Cuba for months," Francisco Vallhonrat wrote. Mostly, he was surprised at the range of people he saw there: "boys, adolescents, young people"—the very groups usually not seen at public demonstrations for fear of reprisal—"middle-age and old people of both sexes, white, Negroes, yellow, mestizos, tall, short, all marched together as if a violent decision was pushing them."

Many people sympathized with Frank's mother whether they agreed with the movement or not. Here was a woman who had lost two sons in the course of one month. Rosario García walked at the end of Frank's cortege; behind her, a group of Catholic women, dressed in mourning, said the rosary for the entire route. Inevitably, as the marchers increased in numbers, political sentiment escalated. "People kept calling out 'Death to Batista and His Regime,' slogans against the army, alternating this with 'Long Live (Viva) Fidel Castro and the 26th of July Movement,'" wrote Vallhonrat. When they reached the cemetery, even before entering, people could see the outlawed 26th of July flag (half black, half red) flying from the tallest monument. The procession brought all traffic on Central Highway, the east-west road that runs the length of Cuba, to a standstill, outside the gates of the cemetery. Furthermore, at the end of the day, the city did not go back to work. "Movie houses were shut, store windows dark, cafes were closed, even kiosks. Even the shoe shiners' chairs were empty," Vallhonrat observed. This response—the equivalent of a general strike—had been Frank's dream and his invention as much as the Civic Resistance had been. Frank had always advocated general strikes and armed warfare as necessary urban guerrilla strategies. On this, he had been very clear, feeling that one couldn't exist without the other. He'd never managed to pull it off in his lifetime, but his death became the catalyst, and the city, without him, seemed to declare a strike on its own.

Unions stepped in where business owners and members of Civic Resistance ended: transportation halted, buses pulled over and simply stopped. By evening, city after city had joined Santiago; the next day, there were strikes in Holguín, Camagüey, Santa Clara, and Matanzas. Only Havana failed to respond as members of Havana's Civic Resistance ignored what was happening across the rest of the nation. According to Enrique Oltuski, a member of the 26th of July who tried to raise interest in a strike there, businessmen left town, to spend the weekend at their beach houses or on the golf course at the country club. They alone seemed indifferent to Frank's death.

Most demonstrations were repressed. On July 31, the first day of the strike in Holguin, the notoriously cruel local army chief, Col. Fermin Cowley, responded by shooting nine people he had accused of causing a power cut. In Santiago, the police eventually emerged, laying low, but killing a few people when they got the chance. ("Took some as they could," as one of the old residents described the situation deftly, "knowing they could not shoot everybody.") The strike lasted five days in Santiago, during which time, generally speaking, the police were subdued. The real test came on Monday, August 5, when people had to return to work. Only then did the western end of the island—Havana and Pinar del Rio—join the strike, and only, according to Oltuski, because television and radio stations had been discussing what happened throughout the weekend. Havana, Oltusky says, wanted to catch up. In Santiago, Vilma Espin claims, the 26th of July Movement's directors came to the conclusion that a prolonged strike would only reap repression. They ordered all members to return to their jobs on Tuesday. Some went back in tears, Vilma recalled.

In Cardenas, the strike crippled the sisal industry; in Matanzas, students led the strikers, stores closed, followed by spontaneous acts of sabotage, such as burning tires, setting cars on fire, even buses; in Manzanillo there were similar acts of resistance. People often call this general strike "Frank's last battle," and remark that it had been won because Cuba's general population realized it had the power to topple the regime. After experiencing the general strike, they learned—or perhaps you could say, felt within their hearts—that it was possible to get rid of their government. They just had to do it.

20. August 1957

After Frank

WRITING FROM THE MOUNTAINS, Fidel instructed Celia to take over. "For the moment you'll have to undertake, in regard to us, the better part of Frank's work," and carry on with "all the things that you know more about than the others"—this until the 26th of July Movement could designate a replacement. She—numb with grief, and on the very day of Frank's funeral—duly began to compose a report for the movement's national office. Over three days, she added to her draft, finally completing the letter on the 2nd of August. She addressed her thoughts to Haydée Santamaria. At first, she apologized for not communicating earlier, then tried to clarify certain things that had gone awry—such as the chaos caused by the messenger Fidel had entrusted with the Manifesto. That covered, Celia touched on national affairs. The tone of her letter is warm but businesslike, without the newsy tales of threats and treason or the gossipy style she had used in correspondence with Frank. She acknowledges her pain over Frank's death, but adds almost dismissively, "Why talk about it if I know that we are all in pain?"

Celia had, since her childhood, consistently dealt with the death of people she deeply loved by stiff-arming grief. She experienced her first trauma of separation at age six, with the loss of her mother. Her near-refusal of death can be traced from then on, chiefly through her letters. Family members say that when the Sánchez Manduley children's mother died, their father carefully explained what had happened. While Celia verbally acknowledged the fact, the older children discovered her frantically searching all the rooms in the house to find their mother. While this reaction is far from unusual in such young children, Celia became ill, developing a temperature and symptoms of anxiety. When, at seventeen, she had watched through a hospital window as her boyfriend, Salvador Sadurni, die on the operating table, she denied her grief the opportunity to surface. Confusion over this reaction had caused relatives to debate her love for Sadurni. When her favorite uncle Miguel (Sánchez) died in 1950, she informed her brother, Orlando, then living in New York, that she didn't want to talk about it; a year later, when Eddy Chibás shot himself, she wrote to Orlando, that she could not accept the suicide and "I don't want to remember."

Fidel, not yet well enough acquainted with Celia to understand this dynamic, wrote a letter in which he poured out all his grief and compassion. "It's hard to believe the news. I can't even begin to express my bitterness, my indignation, the endless sorrow that overwhelms us. What barbarians! They have no idea of the intelligence, the character, the integrity of the person they've murdered. Not even the people of Cuba are aware of who Frank País was, what greatness and promise there was in him. It's painful to see it happen like that, finished off in full flower."

His vehement emotion only angered her. And she was no doubt hurt, when, on the following day, edited a bit, the text of this ostensibly personal letter formed part of Fidel's radio broadcast. He changed the ending, closing with an appeal to all Cubans to unite against the dictator. It would be many months before she could acknowledge Fidel's private communication to her about Frank's death—and when she did, it was to berate Fidel for thinking he could approach the subject.

In early August, while she remained trapped in Manzanillo in what she describes as "deep hiding," her colleagues one after another getting locked up, Fidel was out in the forest, living in relative insulation, surrounded by armed men. While he, too, faced danger, his life bore no comparison to those of the militants outside the Sierra, nor to the dangerous life Frank had led. Yet Celia, intelligent and (usually) rational, knew that in guerrilla warfare, the underground fighters in the plains were the dedicated support system to the guerrillas in the hills. Both elements of the movement knew this. A great many members of the July 26th movement felt this inner conflict. Historians speak of it as the battle between the mountains and the plains (*sierra y llano*), but I am willing to venture that Celia and Fidel were playing this battle out personally.

Among colleagues, and in all her actions, she nonetheless focused on the war's eventual outcome and the necessity of Fidel's leadership.

Current historians suggest that during the week or so following Frank's death the movement's balance of power shifted. Fidel favored Faustino Pérez to step into Frank's role, but the national directorate put forward Rene Ramos Latour (Daniel). In this extended moment of crisis, Celia mediated for both sides. While she might have been grief-stricken to the extent that her emotions were a bit crazed, her loyalty to Frank made support for Fidel as fundamental and unlimited as it would have been for Frank. Frank had been Fidel's confidant and military partner; now, whether she wanted it or not, the role of Fidel's confessor became hers. While she would discharge this role strictly in a secular sense, her letters written over the rest of that summer spell out the conflicts she faced, and it is from them that I get my sense she had landed a role she hated. It was a bequest she'd inherited, and an obligation no one else could fulfill. Among the leadership she alone was up to the job. Mentored by Frank, she was one of Fidel's few intellectual equals (in the old guard, Che and Camilo belong on that list, but their close relationships with Fidel were to evolve later). Celia, as well as a skilled communicator, was a natural diplomat.

Her qualifications for this reluctantly accepted new role included Fidel's admiration for her, and the respect the underground had for that admiration. It is clear that, even before Frank's death, following Celia's adoption of the name Aly, members of the 26th began to defer to her as their best conduit to Fidel.

On August 11, Fidel wrote to her again: "Today I put on the new uniform you sent me, in which I will begin the fourth campaign." His letter declares public reaction to the recent assassination "a rehearsal, unmistakable proof, a beautiful explosion of Cuban dignity, a well-deserved homage to our Frank." He also tells Celia that he accepts the national directorate's choice of Rene Ramos Latour, referring to him as "Daniel." "I believe our comrades in Santiago can continue Frank's work. They are inspired, and I'm certain they will do it well. I myself am going to work harder and help in any way possible. I urgently need to get news of the doctor"—Faustino Pérez, his candidate as Frank's successor—"and Jacinto [Amando Hart]: their plans, ideas, immediate projects. I have great confidence in what they can do." He wanted Celia with him, in the mountains, when he talked to Daniel: "And you, why don't you make a brief trip here? Consider the possibility of coming as soon as the upcoming days, days of observation and expectation. A big hug, Alex."

As mediator, she conveyed Fidel's sentiments to Daniel, in Santiago, waiting it seems for approval direct from the mouth of Mars. Within a couple of days, Daniel composed a letter to Fidel (dated August 14) clearly relieved at his acceptance: "I've waited until today for news from you. Your silence had us worried. We're trying to keep you informed through Aly. We received your warm, inspiring message and have spread it throughout the Movement."

Underneath those sentiments, recall that just before Frank's death, Daniel had given Fidel the exact breakdown of the guns they'd rescued from the Second Front disaster. This cache of weapons more than anything else held Fidel's interest. He wanted Celia to be the go-between, and wrote Celia the same day he heard from Daniel—the 14th—about getting down to business: "I insist, as I did in my previous letter, that a directive must be given to the movement right now concerning the war: 'All weapons, all bullets, and all resources are for the Sierra.' Weapons must be sought everywhere. . . . Tell me to whom I should write to and what I should do. . . . You know that with Frank gone, we'll have to be more directly involved in the work that he carried out so brilliantly. There is no shortage of courageous comrades, but one doesn't acquire that authority, that initiative, and that experience in a couple of days. For that reason, I'm ready to write whatever letters, papers, or recommendations are needed from here. . . . Now I realize that I should help you where and when you need me in order to facilitate your work. P.S.: Take great care! I don't know why, but I feel sure that nothing can happen to you. Our misfortune with Frank was too great for it to happen again."

Two days later, he asked her once again to come to his camp in the Sierra. But she remained in Manzanillo. The army had stepped up the heat on the underground, and she was, in her own words, "out in the street," under greater threat than ever and literally on the run.

21. SEPTEMBER 5, 1957

The Maps

IN THE MIDDLE OF AUGUST, SIM launched a widespread investigation in Pilón. When they got to the offices of the sugar mill and began to examine files, they came upon the empty folder with maps signed out by Celia Sánchez. The government's agents quickly confirmed that these missing charts were those discovered on the *Granma*. Although the army had for some time accused her of supporting Fidel Castro, here in hand was concrete evidence. An order was issued to search Manuel Sánchez's house. Soldiers arrived in jeeps and trucks; they confronted the doctor by holding up the empty map folder and—in a strange tactic of psychological intimidation—a girdle. The prop aimed at making Celia's father think they had captured and raped her. Her father stood by as they searched his house, upending furniture, breaking things, and going through his medical files. Taking some papers, they departed. Dr. Sánchez stayed at the house just long enough to determine that the documents they'd taken were of no significance, and that taking them had been mere bravado. He got into his car and drove to Manzanillo.

For the Sánchez family, the SIM's discovery of the source of the *Granma*'s maps marked the end of an age-old way of life. Celia had been submerged some time in clandestine activities, but members of her family had not fully realized it, nor grasped just why she had sent her father out of the country. Nothing normal, or benign, would figure in the existence of this family for a long time to come.

IN THE MIDDLE OF AUGUST, a farmer made his way to Fidel's camp to report that forty to sixty soldiers from the Cuban army had pitched camp near his house on the Palma Mocha River. Fidel chose Crescencio's son, Ignacio, to lead a small vanguard squadron and go with the farmer to the site. They were to make contact with the enemy, but Fidel sent them primarily to determine the location of the camp the farmer had reported. They left around 10:30 p.m. on August 18, 1957, taking with them the promising young fighter Pastor Palomares, who had been with Fidel and Celia in the Battle of Uvero in late May. Still just twenty, he'd served also in the Battle of Estrada Palma, under Guillermo García's command. The guerrillas reached the mouth of the river at 2:00 a.m. on the 19th, but found no army troops camped there. The squadron advanced along the river until they saw army guards posted on the shore.

Ignacio's squadron launched a commando attack, and the army's guards quickly abandoned the area. Following their surprise assault, the guerrillas moved farther along the river, to the house of another farmer. Finding abandoned weapons (including a bazooka) in the house, they were now well armed, equipped to overtake the enemy camp and force a surrender. They had to accomplish this before daylight, so as to get out of the area before the army's planes could spot them.

At first things went smoothly. Before sunrise, not having succeeded, they prepared to retreat. An order come from Fidel: hold their position as he was sending in another platoon. Although they had lost a man during the night's battle, the squadron was strong; no one had injuries, and Batista's soldiers seemed disorganized. When dawn came, however, the tables were turned: the enemy's troops established order and the rebels saw they were facing far more enemy troops than expected. Around 250 army soldiers had been in the hills long enough to dig trenches. With light enough to see, those troops opened fire on the rebels from well-protected positions. In addition to such a disadvantage in numbers, the rebels faced a new weapon, a rifle grenade. Fidel's troops took further losses: Juventino Alarcon, Yayo Castillo, and Pastor Palomares. Palomares was moving between several of

Fidel's squadrons, carrying their single and highly prized 50mm machine gun, when a grenade hit him directly in the legs and lower abdomen. His comrades carried him out of the battle, laying him by the river, and Fidel ordered a forced retreat. Efigenia Amerijerias, the rear guard platoon leader, knelt by the dying soldier as Fidel covered the retreat. Pastor whispered that his wife was pregnant and, with Amerijerias as his witness, asked that Fidel raise his child.

Local farmers buried Pastor's body several days later, after the army left. In doing so, they discovered that a hand was missing. The army had seen this tall, sturdily-built young man, moving among squadrons, and had been confident they'd killed Fidel Castro.

BACK IN MANZANILLO, the Sánchezes convened a family council and drew up a plan of action. Manuel should behave normally. He should go about his business, taking his vacation in September, in Havana. Flávia, in Manzanillo with her family on holiday, volunteered to stay a few additional days and accompany him. She, her husband, and their daughters usually left before the end of August, so there was time to get the two girls ready for school. Flávia offered to stay until the 1st of September, when they could all take the Havana-bound train. Midway along the island she and her family would transfer to a branch line south to Cienfuegos, and Dr. Sánchez would continue on to the capital.

On the appointed morning, Dr. Sánchez, Flávia, her husband, Rene Otazo, and their two daughters, Elena and Alicia, went to the railroad station, where military police arrested Dr. Sánchez. They took him to the army garrison within sight of Celia's *marabuzal*, where they locked him in a cell. Flávia and her family were ordered to remain in Manzanillo. The union of physicians, alerted to the arrest, soon appealed for Dr. Sánchez's release. Their respected colleague had, since 1925, been a delegate to the National Medical Assembly, representing Oriente Province's entire southwestern coastal region. The city's mayor arranged the release and, based on Dr. Sánchez's age, the union negotiated a two-day house arrest, contingent on his departure thereafter from Manzanillo.

The morning of September 5, 1957, the Sánchezes went again to the station. This time they boarded the early-morning train for Havana. Acacia had joined the party, to accompany her father all the way to Havana, once Flávia and her family changed trains for Cienfuegos. The Sánchezes were unaware that on this same day, a group of Batista's naval officers in that city were initiating a mutiny.

Frank had known about the planned uprising. Daniel mentions it to Fidel in a letter written on August 17; thus Celia must have known as well. Though she was in hiding, she had, according to Flávia's daughters, been in contact with the family during the days after her father's arrest. Yet she didn't warn them of the impending mutiny. She must have known that Flávia and Rene were to return home, and find themselves in the army's sights.

Certain navy officers had joined with a few members of the army, plus other anti-Batista forces including members of the 26th of July Movement. For a few hours, the mutinying forces held the oldest part of Cienfuegos, the port area, but their plans had been discovered and their rebellion was cut short, crushed. History records that following the revolt the army brought in bulldozers and hundreds of unidentified bodies were buried in ditches.

Word of the suppressed revolt reached the train by radio and the engineer conveyed the news to the passengers. "Right away, we knew the police would be after us if we went back to Cienfuegos," Flávia explains. They had little doubt that the army would take revenge on them, linked as they were to Celia. Flávia recalls that after the announcement, she and Rene looked at each other, knew they'd have to go into hiding, and got off the train in Santa Clara. Through the railcar's windows they could see soldiers on the highway en route to Cienfuegos, their home city.

Flávia says they went to a friend's house, to take cover until they could figure out what to do. She told me, as we sat sitting in her large, well-furnished penthouse apartment overlooking the sea, near the Hotel Riviera, that she could still not accept those losses, and had tried over the fifty years that had passed not to think about their house in Cienfuegos. In our conversation, she made a brief inventory of what "home" had meant, filled as it was with antique furniture inherited from both families, wedding gifts, important family papers like their wedding certificate and daughters' birth certificates, mementoes such as baby pictures, furniture she and Rene had acquired carefully, cautiously. The last thing she spoke of was all the expensive, not-yet-paid-for, state-of-the-art equipment that had filled their dental clinic. They had in one morning lost their home and their livelihood, and had very little in savings. On September 8, they left Santa Clara, heading for the northern coast, to a spot near Havana where Rene's brother owned a vacation house. They would live in "the green bungalow," careful to give out no further details.

22. September 1957

Chaos

THE BATTLE OF PALMA MOCHA was one of the worst battles of the Revolution—and, from Fidel's letters, it is clear that after he returned from this battle he'd anticipated getting a reply from Celia. He heard and received nothing and stopped writing for the ten days remaining in the month. But, on the 1st of September, when he heard that her father had been arrested, Fidel sent a man to Manzanillo to pick up Celia and bring her back to his camp. After this concerned gesture things started to fall apart. She left Manzanillo with Fidel's man, confident that she was going to join Fidel, but because of the army's crackdown following the mutiny traveling got tough. The army threw a cordon around the area and used aircraft. She couldn't get to Fidel's camp, and waited at a place he often went, expecting Fidel to come for her. But he didn't show up. It is painful to read their letters, written in October, after it was all over, and when they were trying to sort things out.

CELIA'S FATHER HAD BEEN ARRESTED on September 1 and on the next day she left Manzanillo with Rafael Castro (no relation to Raul or Fidel), sent by Fidel to guide her to a place she thought they'd meet. Because of the army's reaction to the attempted mutiny on the 5th, they got caught in a place called La Maestra. Batista's forces quickly retaliated by sending troops to "lay a dragnet"—block the highways. Planes began to drop bombs in various parts of the Sierra Maestra, as she explained to Fidel (in October): "On the 5th and 6th [starting] at 6:15 a.m., five planes bombed the area, and on the 7th and the 8th they continued to do so. By then I had no place to hide. On the 8th troops came up, according to the news [she probably means rumor] to make a siege. They shot mortars and machine guns all they wanted to."

She waited in La Maestra—which was a code name for the place in "The Sierra" and a general geographical location, not the name of an actual village, where Fidel often camped—and because, as she put it, "I didn't want to leave, waiting to hear from you," she stayed on after Rafael Castro left. Celia joined up with other fugitives who, like herself, were on the run. She was trapped there until the 17th of September. She and the fugitives lived in caves, and couldn't leave the area because it would have required getting through the cordon of army troops set up to block all the roads. At one point, eighteen people made up what she called their "caravan," barely armed, or if armed, without bullets. For nine days, between the 8th and the 17th of September she existed like that, and with little or no information. "We were not sure whether there would be troops on the road," she would later explain to Fidel, "we heard that there were," and thought about leaving, but one of the members of the caravan "deserted" and "we heard five shots and then I really resisted exploring the road."

So where was Fidel? On September 10, he and Che took their columns to a place called Pino del Agua, after receiving intelligence that the army was about to move into this place. Fidel and Che decided to set up an ambush, with Fidel marching his column into the area first, making sure everybody knew about it, then moving them out again. Fidel would create a lure while Che and his men quietly set up an actual ambush. They waited for the army to appear, which it did on the 17th; Che and his men captured a few trucks, which they burned, and some weapons.

Going strictly by the documents, it appears that Fidel panicked when he discovered that Rafael Castro wasn't with Celia, because he ordered Daniel and the Santiago Movement to find her. Daniel and his men did everything they could think of, couldn't locate her, and were in despair. On September 15, Daniel reported to Fidel that they had failed. "With Aly missing and . . . the five army companies blocking the way to the area that we had been using for our communication route, we tried to make contact with Guevara," thinking she might be with him. Then they exhausted other possibilities: "We tried to locate a girl here in Santiago who, according to what was reported to us, was the person who had delivered the letters. We couldn't find her anywhere. Then we hunted for the person who had replaced Aly in Manzanillo." The Santiago 26th men finally made contact with Celia on September 17, and, still expecting to be rescued by Fidel, she became rattled. Why was Santiago trying to find her? As she explained to Fidel weeks later, "When I received a note saying that Jorge [Sotus] urgently wanted to talk to me . . . I was filled with confusion." But Sotus did not find her. She left the caves and made it to Santiago, apparently guided by her famous survival instinct. Celia got there on September 19, seeking out Frank's old comrades. She learned that Jorge Sotus had tried to find her in Manzanillo. Sotus had been the one commander who'd been successful at the Battle of Santiago. He was a loner, from a bourgeois background— his father was a merchant—but he was a scrappy character, exceedingly tough, and a very good fighter. It is to Sotus that she turned when she got to Santiago, and to Daniel. They filled her in. "After talking to Ulises [Jorge Sotus] I was even more confused," she wrote Fidel, which prompted this query: "How come, if you had sent for me and paved the way for me to the Sierra, how could it be that it was Ulises who came looking for me in Manzanillo? I don't understand these things." She either didn't understand or wasn't going to let him off the hook.

The Sierra Maestra, that September, was close to anarchy, with roving bandits; in short, it was a very dangerous place for Celia to be. If not caught by Batista's army, she was "a temptation" to bandits, a wanted person attached to a nice reward for anyone who could capture her. I don't know the amount, but the government had just placed a $100,000 reward on Fidel's head. The reward on hers was less, but the army always thought that she was key to finding him.

ONCE AGAIN, FIDEL SENT RAFAEL CASTRO to pick her up in Santiago and bring her to him in the mountains: "At 9:00 p.m. on September 19, he showed up saying that you had sent for me. . . . [I did not go because] for the first and only time someone had come to pick me up." This was her way of saying, "He didn't lead me to you the first time, why trust him now?" She didn't go because, on the 20th, having sent Rafael Castro packing, she, Daniel, and Jorge Sotus sat down to compose a memo to Fidel.

The preamble read: "In what follows, we are going to set forth a series of requests that we hope will be given special attention in view of the serious upheavals and troubles we have experienced in our work because of not having anticipated these small details that, at first sight, seemed insignificant but nevertheless, in practice, have caused very serious problems." Six points followed. They addressed the poor quality of Fidel's soldiers and their lack of discipline, and the fact that there were sixty men waiting in Santiago "from all over the island" (left over from Frank's Second Front, needing to get out of Santiago and into the protection of the mountains) who wanted to join the guerrillas and could not because "[you] confer overriding powers on many people who have gotten to you by disregarding discipline and acting irresponsibly." Celia, Daniel (Rene Ramos Latour), Sotus Frank's disciples— had decided that the time had come to be like Frank and to bring their (surviving) commander into line. "And so we ask that all individuals who are sent out on negotiations or special missions be sent to the Directorate, where we would gladly offer them our cooperation through our existing organization."

Next, the three of them laid down the law on Fidel's ad hoc messages as well, announcing that from then on, all his letters had to go through their hands to avoid spreading false or improper news. If the "General Staff" dismisses a soldier, the Directorate must be notified "in order that these people not be considered deserters." Names of deserters, they said, must be reported immediately so this information could be circulated. Now, referring to him in the third person, they observed that "there are many cases of individuals who have taken advantage of Fidel Castro's signature on papers of no importance, which, however, have been used by irresponsible parties to pass themselves off as direct representatives of our leader, simply by flashing his signature." They concluded their memo with "For the triumph of the Revolution."

Celia left Santiago. You can almost hear her saying, "Forget him, I'm going home." When she got around to explaining how she felt, she told Fidel: "On the 22nd of September, I reached Manzanillo," but that was when they were on writing terms again. Once again dipping into her women's network, she summoned Elsa Castro to come for her in Santiago (or at least Elsa describes a situation that seems to fit this date). After Celia telephoned, Elsa filled her car with young women and drove to Santiago, returning very late on Saturday night (which would have been the 21st); they were stopped at every checkpoint, and pretended to have been at a party. Elsa says they giggled a lot, asked one soldier if he'd like a piece of cake, and only once did a pair of soldiers actually shine flashlights directly on their faces. But the soldiers didn't get a good look at Celia, who was crowded in the backseat, and the group got to Manzanillo before dawn Sunday morning, the 22nd.

In Manzanillo, she faced an interesting problem. From Havana, her father wrote that he'd made friends with Lina Ruz, Fidel's mother. Both parents wanted to come home, and Manuel Sánchez had written to Celia that he and Lina Ruz were going to travel back together and would like to visit their children in the Sierra Maestra. From Celia's point of view, this was an awful idea. She asked him to stay in Havana because the army would arrest him again if he came back. She suggested, very gently, that he be patient.

She was aware that such a message called for a carefully considered response, and she wrote to her father as if she were filing a report to her commanding officer. She describes life in the rebel army, reassures him that they are as secure and well organized as General Antonio Maceo (in the nineteenth century) had been, and includes detailed information. She writes as if she were an officer in the field, in a remote country, addressing headquarters, and thus better equipped to evaluate the situation and disabuse the recipient of any desire to journey to the front. Part general, part daughter, she claims she is safer than he is: "Today you are in much more danger than myself; no one can find me, whereas your situation is dangerous." Flattering and to an extent true, since it is now thought that the army had wanted to use Manuel Sánchez, capture him, in order to extract a promise, in an exchange for his release, from Fidel Castro that the rebel army would not attack Pilón.

Her father had enclosed a snapshot of himself and Fidel's mother. Celia makes no comment about this memento, nor does she even touch upon their desire to visit the guerrilla army in the mountains. She had to deal with her father's longings, and Fidel's mother only complicated matters. Both these old parents were homesick for Oriente Province, plus they wanted to see a bit of action and hang out with their famous children. But she knew the desperation of such a trip and suppresses real news—and does not mention having been trapped by the army, hiding in caves, getting caught in places where planes were dropping bombs overhead, having no place to go, living hand-to-mouth, feeling a heart-sinking possibility that someone might betray her—and, having lied to her father about how nice and safe she was, stresses how well organized members of the rebel army all are.

She waited a week in Manzanillo, until the 29th, before beginning to compose her messages to Fidel—the better to summon her ire and lambast him. The opening lines are completely professional, as if she were complying with rules of communication laid down by Alberto Bayo (the Spanish war veteran who'd trained Fidel's guerrillas in Mexico), which required that the first section of reports contain weapons statistics. "You'll receive 5,500 five thousand five hundred—M-1 rounds that came last night from Santiago in *presillas* [clips] of 10 bullets each," she begins. But soon enough her thoughts are personal; she promises to enclose newspaper clippings from a Miami paper, send him a leather jacket ("I ordered one made in olive green, very light and warm"), canisters of calcium tablets ("Take them, they will be good for your cavities") but isn't above observing that he isn't the only person with a toothache: "With the persecution that I'm under with these bandits I am forced to continue with this pain in my molar," implying he might do the same. She tells him she's well hidden ("More than hidden . . . I'm buried alive") and gives him news of a shootout—two members of the Santiago 26th of July Movement have been assassinated. She mentions a bill she's found in the mail for his eyeglasses (a reminder of his bad habit of breaking his glasses when he's angry), the availability of a journalist, and what's this about your having no money? He's asked her for money. She reminds him that she has been sending him money all along. She signs off with "a hug" (*abrazo*) a typical way to close a letter among Spanish speakers, just as common as "Yours truly" in English, and not to be confused with a warm embrace.

The next day, September 30, she wrote to Daniel: "My trip was very good, but upon my setting foot in Manzanillo, somebody informed [the police] of my arrival and they searched for me day and night." Not finding her, the army went after her sister Griselda, surrounding her house and forcing her to leave Manzanillo. "Two trucks and two jeeps of soldiers went to my sister's house. What a fuss!" In Celia's "I'm so safe" letter written to her father, she doesn't mention that his other daughter is being harassed by the police, was then run out of town, when in fact they had been searching for Celia herself. She employed the same type of thinking (or is it deception?) when she didn't warn Flávia of the upcoming mutiny that Celia surely knew would be taking place in Cienfuegos. In other words, she's safe. The Dove had returned to the Ark. The Dove's keeper, Hector Llópiz, was finding safe places to hide her. With the paradoxical logic of a guerrilla, her attitude was, I'm okay, let them figure it out.

Two days later, she started another note to Fidel, beginning with a few paragraphs about 26th of July business, then asking him to apologize to Raúl, his brother, for not sending film, and ending, ironically, with "Please write!" These two relatively short letters were a mere warm-up for a long letter she was composing simultaneously—a complicated, private manifesto that she'd been working on since she got back. It is dated on its first page October 1, but midway through, she asks: "Have you noticed that we are almost at the end of September?" Here, she allows herself to describe being alone and on the run, to tell him what it's been like, for her, between late July and the first days of October, including the arrest of her father. It's clear that she is angry with Fidel, but she pours it all out. These two letters—one to her father, the other to Fidel—confirm how tough but diplomatic she could be, how good she was at masking her own vulnerabilities, standing up for herself, giving orders, and meting out criticism. It's a pity Celia never had a turn at being president. She was educated for the job, particularly as relates to her knowledge of Cuban history, of medicine, her unwavering commitment to social justice, and her popularity. Combine these with her war experience, both in the underground and as a soldier, and you have a powerful package. She could talk like a politician: The Revolution is in motion but nothing can stop it now, is the central theme of the letter to her father. But her future role as presidential advisor emerges as she writes to Fidel.

"HOW WE NEEDED A REVOLUTION," she tells her father. "How we've struggled for recognition! But that's history now," because the people know what they think, are aware of their feelings, and have given the Revolution priority. "Cuba always follows a leader. It is a fact of life," she muses, and pragmatically observes that they've needed Fidel. "I was always afraid he'd be killed, and people would abandon us," but claims this is old news "now that the people back the revolution." As for coming home, "you know how to wait." She asks him to have patience, be serene in his suffering, and promises that the day when he can return isn't far away. Celia is too adroit to use such a contentious word as *no*.

She doesn't mention that the 26th of July had been having trouble exerting control over volunteers flocking to the Sierra in hope of joining the rebels, nor the problems they faced with the influx of paramilitary forces, under Rolando Masferrer, who were posing as 26th of July soldiers. Instead, she reassures her father that farmers had organized the territory into zones to protect the rebel army and were supporting the movement by stopping infiltrators, interrogating suspicious characters, taking them prisoner, and condemning them. Continuing in this "we are in complete control" vein, she writes that these same farmers have closed the zone to outsiders and nothing can be sent up to them, "not even a bottle of medicine."

Then she tells him a story about two of "our men" who with pistols—not rifles—shot at 150 armed men and slipped away before the army, confused, had time to take up position to return fire. "Fidel always used to dream about this sort of thing and I'd always argue with him, never thinking that incidents like that could take place." For the rest of the letter she sticks to the joys of guerrilla warfare. There is some truth in what she says—rebel army commanders Escalona and Ochoa emphasized the huge advantage they had had operating alone or in pairs, always striking from higher ground—but she masks the fact that, at this stage in the war, they were completely trapped.

As a way of further reassuring her father that they are okay, she claims, "We'll never die of hunger because the ranches have pigs, fowl, and we have warehouses with food, but money is scarce," and she admits that they have to figure out a way to solve this problem, the crux of the matter.

Money to meet their needs had become a huge issue for Celia, who essentially was the supply officer of the rebel army. In the following paragraphs of the letter, she documents her plans for securing money. She suggests "threats," that is, terrorism, which in my opinion gives her great credibility as a guerrilla leader. Cubans from the current generation remark that she wasn't very political, just a good organizer, and cite Fidel as the catalyst of all radical ideas. But this letter refutes that. She tells her father that she can't stand the idea that Cubans with money are unwilling to hand it over to the 26th of July Movement. How could they not? "I can't forgive big capital," she writes, because they won't sacrifice for the country or for a just cause; on the contrary, they always take, and only give us what we ask for "through terrorism." They'll give to a colonel (referring to an officer in Batista's army), they'll pay for a political campaign "for any shameless individual," she complains, but they won't pay "to save the country." Borrowing a theme from Fidel, she claims that "we" never wanted to make our revolution with dirty money, but don't have enough weapons and that's why this fight is costing so many lives. We don't want to obtain money by force, she continues, because "it sets a bad example, especially to young people," and we can't get caught doing something we're fighting against. But big capital doesn't understand, so "I am encouraging us to begin to apply terrorism. It is what they are accustomed to." All of this is an admission on her part that she has decided to threaten local big business—rice growers and ranchers as well as merchants, owners of sugar mills—in other words, some of the wealthiest men in the nation. As a coordinator of the 26th of July Movement for the Manzanillo region, Celia was in the position to make that call.

Their victory, discussed so matter-of-factly here in 1957, is more than a year off. Yet to read this letter you'd think it had already happened. This attitude was verified in several interviews I made over ten years with soldiers who spoke of her prescience, marveled at her conviction they'd win even before they'd begun to fight. Start with Guerra Matos's recollection of the days following the landing; everything indicated that Fidel might easily be dead, but she'd heaped scorn on Guerra Matos for his lack of faith. Yet her evidence was mostly instinctual. She describes their upcoming victory with confidence. What concerns us, she tells her father, is how to control "sentiment" (which really meant bloodbath and retaliation) after victory. Fidel has his platoon captains read Curzio Malaparte's *The Skin* to prepare for the first moments after their triumph, and she assures her father that the rebel army must—at any price—avoid letting people lose their common sense. We want to control their passions; we do not want to create chaos, she writes. There will be no need for vengeance, since we are the ones who have suffered most of the cruelties, and we will set the example; there will be no "tomorrow's heroes" (to use Malaparte's phrase) on our side handing out vigilante justice.

Returning to the present, as if it were a newsy aside, she asks her father what his views had been on the mutiny in Cienfuegos, but she does not mention Flávia, or Flávia's family who lived there. Celia simply does not allow other members of her family to enter her war. She says she's heard people expressing their shock that the army would bomb one of Cuba's own cities, but what about the Sierra? Aren't we people too? We've been bombed daily for ten months—forest, family homes. She tells her father that people had been collecting empty shells to show her. They were stacking them in their backyards, like trophies. Then Celia, like any good politician, closes by expressing pity for her opponent: "So many arms, so many troops, yet they are nothing compared to us." She had come to this conclusion because the army had resorted to dropping flyers, offering reward money that she calls pitiful and "indecent" and predicts they'll have no takers.

Again, she addresses the impossibility of her father's return, echoing his words, written after she escaped in Campechuela, when he advised her (along with a gift of his Colt 45 pistol): Don't think you are the only one; don't think for a minute that the way the army acts won't be applied to you. "Stay on a little longer," she urges, "you've done it before"—previously he'd extended his Havana vacation because he had been having a good time. Circumstance, she says, evoking a word used by Martíto to explain nearly everything, requires the high road. "Love and kisses, Aly," her *nom de guerre.*

After she'd finished this masterpiece to her father, she polished her letter to Fidel, a letter that is well over 4,000 words. She explains what happened in September, beginning with her father's arrest, her leaving Manzanillo to find Fidel, and ending up being confined to the forest. In his August 16 letter, he'd sarcastically asked her: "When are you going to send me the dentist? If I don't receive weapons from Santiago nor Havana, nor from Miami or Mexico, at least send me a dentist so my molars will let me think in peace," and when she read this, after what she'd been through, hiding in caves, and so on, it clearly got on her nerves. He'd tried to be funny, too, but she failed to notice or acknowledge it: "Now that we have food, I can't eat. Afterward, my molars will be okay and then there won't be any food." And he'd been sweet: "I don't blame you. You do more than you can handle." She was having none of it. She tells him she found a dentist who'd agreed to go into the Sierra but changed his mind (*pero el se arrepinteo*; the verb she used is "repented") at the last minute, but promises she won't go again without bringing along a dentist. And again she sourly reminds him that he is not the only person in the world with a toothache . . . but she is sending "calcium tablets, take them, they will be good for your cavities, I have a hundred of those cans."

The real trouble between them was money. While Celia was in the mountains and on the run, she'd come across undelivered letters containing money she'd sent Fidel at three houses located in the Sierra. From her viewpoint he had needed money and she had sent it. But the person Fidel sent to pick up the money (which didn't arrive), was the same person Fidel had sent to rescue her in Manzanillo (and didn't arrive). She takes this opportunity to say that the arms she'd taken into the mountains, when she went with Rafael Castro, had been distributed with the understanding that "when we got to you, we'd turn them over, and you'd hand them out as you saw fit." But Rafael had selected a coveted M-1 for himself. And still has it, she says. "He and the rifle are still strolling the Sierra in search of you."

She was winding up this letter on the night of October 1 when Felipe Guerra Matos showed up in Manzanillo, sent by Fidel, to find her. So she pens, adding on the front pages: "What a surprise to see Guerrita, and even more to know why—because you hadn't gotten any money for two months." She explains that in the beginning of August, when he first asked for money, the banks were closed and she could only send $500 on the 7th. (The reason, of course, was the general strike following Frank's assassination, when the banks were closed.) In Manzanillo, the banks reopened on Saturday, August 10, and she took out $1,000 that she sent him on August 11 via Rafael Castro. Then she edges into her main, or most obvious, reproach, the reason she, Daniel, and Sotus had composed and sent their memo. She tells Fidel that they've heard about the "famous group" that went into the Sierra on its own, and that he'd incorporated into "our rebel army," and reminds him that it isn't "his rebel army," implying he can't just make monarchical decisions. It was bad for me and bad for you, she points out: "You already know the consequences this had for me and they were bad for you"—using *ustedes*, meaning "all of you."

She softens her tone after that, and tells him that it had been a "balm" to read his letter inviting her to the Sierra. But soon she returns to the money theme, and describes how she got hold of another $1,000 and sent it August 24. She assures him that she did write back, she wrote as soon as she got his last, August 17 letter, and that it had arrived on the 26th. She even reminds him what he asked her to do: find information for him about property titles, which she'd done. She'd even sent an example of one, she says, and other things he wanted. She has enough to do running her own life: "This is the way I ended August, so busy, despite the intense heat, that I didn't even have enough time to fan myself."

After this comes the painful part. She tells Fidel that these have been bad times for her, the arrest of her father, what happened after his arrest, and she states that rather than stay in Manzanillo she had gone with this questionable character she's been ranting about, Rafael Castro, because it was "more important to be with you than stay and defend his [my father's] life." (What could be more flattering or manipulative than this?)

After that preamble, she describes the terrible trip she made through the mountains trying to reach him, planes dropping bombs overhead, the caravan of eighteen people she'd lived with while waiting for him to show up in La Maestra, hiding out where she could,. But she tells him: "On the road I kept finding letters of mine that had not reached you, [there were] up to three." She had found $1,000 in one letter lying in someone's house, claims that she wrote from La Maestra saying that she'd go back home, but only if she had to. "I wrote you that I would turn around, but regretfully, and if you saw no problem with it, I'd continue."

She was, she told him, really confused, especially since she kept finding her letters along the road, also a letter from Daniel, propaganda from Marcelo Fernández (one of the leaders of the Manzanillo movement), a report about the mutiny in Cienfuegos, and "eyeglasses for you." But money is the issue here. Although I have not read the message Fidel sent her via Felipe Guerra Matos, it is fairly easy to imagine its content. He must have accused her of not writing, not sending money in two months, and (I deduce, from the way she answered, that after he'd been kicked verbally by the memo she, Daniel, and Jorge Sotus sent) implied that she was not doing her job responsibly, neither for him nor for the national organization in Havana.

Shortly before his death, Frank had complained in a letter to Fidel: "Funds are down a bit (it would have to happen right at this moment!), so we'll have to find a way of getting more. Havana spends too much: 4,000 pesos a month, sometimes more." Fidel's inquiry may have been reasonable, but she responded defensively: "Through my many letters which are on the way and which probably haven't been lost—you'll receive confirmation that at no time have I abandoned anything having to do with you (all). Since David has been missing"—notice she cannot bring herself to say dead—"I have intensified my work." For two months, she tells Fidel, she has dedicated herself to his cause. But, at this point, she stops short of defending herself and simply tells him to figure out what she'd been doing when he gets the letters she sends, and "let the others account for what they are doing."

Then she goes in for the kill. Appearing a lot like an illustration of a thundercloud, set apart from every other sentence, she underlines the word *treasury*. You can actually see the force of her pen pressing into the paper. Then she proceeds to set down a history of their finances together, starting on the day they first met face to face, waiting for Herbert Matthews and the *New York Times* interview. "The money raised has never been fantastic," she writes. "The first time Santiago donated something for the Sierra was on the 16th of February, when Frank and I went up [to meet with you in the mountains] and we argued over one thousand dollars; he, because he owed them, and I because I wanted him to leave them in the treasury. We finally gave the money back to Vilma [Espín]." Celia goes on to explain how the two organizations, Manzanillo and Santiago, raised money, and how she and Frank had handled their accounts. She points out, with a pat on the back, that Manzanillo had supported his revolution with far more money than Santiago ever had.

Then, and it is hard to imagine that she wasn't hurt by the implication this refutes: "In reference to my personal expenses, I want it to be quite clear to you that I've never caused any expenditures to the movement. My expenses have always been paid for by Papa and my brothers; they all help the treasury of the movement corresponding to where they live, and the money they send me is for my personal expenses. I don't use it because my expenses are minimal. They have always been spent on extras that I send to the Sierra." (And here, one has to stop and consider what those extras might have been. The first thing that comes to mind is the olive-green leather jacket she had ordered, and mentioned in her last letter to him.) And there you have, in one fell swoop, the paradox of your basic, successful nearly always middle-class revolutionary: ready to slash and burn and terrorize, but supported by Daddy, and who never forgets to buy and send expensive presents.

With her family in hiding, she reminds Fidel, she's had her own financial problems, since her relatives are scattered, "but in spite of this I have not made use of anything from the movement. I know how to do without." This is followed by two sentences with lots of space around them, so that they stand out on the page: "I would have preferred not to reveal all this but you've forced me to account for everything. This time, Fidel, you really have judged me unfairly." He had gone too far. No use of his protective alias is deserved here. No need. There is no way that Guerra Matos would have been able to swallow this stack of pages, had he been caught on the highway driving back to the Sierra Maestra.

Finally, before she ends this letter, she brings up Frank: "We've all reacted differently to Frank's loss—you, myself, all of us have been deeply affected by it. You've been trying to prove what it meant for you while I've been doing my best so that you wouldn't feel the impact of it; you were acting above the movement and very differently from how things are done. You are the ones that were affected. You cut all communication after August 17. You started to act unwisely and you are all suffering for it." But Fidel hadn't cut communication—he'd been defeated in the Battle of Palma Mocha. But what she said is true: he'd let people into his army and didn't have the authority to do so: they were admitted by Frank. Now this would be handled by Frank's surrogates.

She ruefully admits to being a gofer with nothing to show for it. "The Sierra is a large place and you've made me work in a crazy manner sending letters and an endless number of things all over the place; there are $6,000 in different places. This is the insanity you've caused. I continue sending the weekly magazines and some article or other that might be of interest to you. And when I analyze all this, I see the effort I've made over the past two months has been of no use, since it's only created this state of chaos."

Completely spelled out, Celia has told Fidel that he is unwise and unjust, full of himself and out of order, and, deep down, she is probably thinking that he is definitely not Frank. Besides those scathing observations, she implies that he is a bad judge of character and can't even pick a guide to carry letters, deliver money, or rescue her. She claims that she's sent money she doesn't have, meaning it was hard to get hold of, therefore can't afford to have it lie around somewhere. (She had a point: chances are Crescencio or Guillermo could have suggested better delegates.) She slips in several little barbs, a reminder that she always has to replace his glasses (because he is such a brat and breaks them), and because I did not ask the curator of Fidel's papers at the archives for his response do not know what nasty and mean things he wrote back to her. One thing is clear: there was now so little objectivity, so many freely flung accusations stirred up between them, and delivered with so little humor, as if they were falling in love.

As if the thunderclouds had lifted and the grand finale is about to begin, she ends with these lines: "I hope you really can understand what happened during the last two months, and that everything will be forgotten. Let's reach an agreement for your well-being and my peace of mind." And that is what they did.

There are a few more sentences, mostly end-of-letter add-ons. Lightheartedly, she suggests that he not agitate Agitado (her nickname for Guerra Matos) too much (whom she'd sent to

Santiago to pick up money to send Fidel), and "he'll show you a little map." That map marked the location of where she'll be sending his next group of soldiers.

Sixty or seventy men would be going into the mountains led by Jorge Sotus (who had raced off to Havana to raise money for these troops). They would be veterans of Frank's Second Front—and she assures Fidel that she'll outfit them as well as she possibly can. And, "without your even asking, seven days ago I ordered two pairs of glasses. I called Havana and they are being sent by plane, should have arrived today but didn't, and we called again. Tomorrow they'll be here for sure." (Stamp on your glasses, Fidel, but get used to it: Frank's men and I are back in the business of choosing your soldiers. End of story.) Then she tucks the picture of his mother and her father into the letter, and hands it over to Guerra Matos. It was their last letter—this truce, this personal report—because less than two weeks later she went to live in the Sierra Maestra with Fidel and the rebel army. She remained with him for the rest of the war. They do correspond again, but it would be several months later, while preparing for the summer offensive. They begin again to write to each other daily because he is on one mountain and she is on another.

Part III

SIERRA
MAESTRA

23. OCTOBER 17, 1957

Celia Leaves the Underground

CELIA LEFT MANZANILLO for good on October 17, 1957, accompanied by Hector Llópiz, who flew into exile to Costa Rica, where he lived until the end of the war. Both took an escape route via a particularly pretty country house owned by local Coca-Cola executive Rene Suarez. Their host was arrested almost immediately; he quickly left for the United States, along with his wife, Teresa Marinol, and teenage daughter.

Celia would always recall this period in the Sierra Maestra as the best time of her life, something wonderful, as if she had entered Paradise instead of a war zone. After reaching Fidel's camp, she left immediately with a guerrilla who guided her to another part of the mountains where she visited a newborn baby—the daughter of Pastor Palomares, who as he lay dying on a riverbank, following the battle at Palma Mochain August, had asked Fidel to raise his child. The baby had been delivered by the child's grandfather, Angel Palomares, in La Jutia cave, since the whole area was under constant aerial attack. Angel Palomares was a famous herbalist in the region, who treated members of the rebel army (even Che was one of his patients). He explained that he'd stuffed the baby's mouth with coffee leaves to muffle her cries because the Rural Guards patrolled a path on the hillside above the cave. The child's mother, also there, had remarried and planned to leave the baby with the grandparents. The old herbalist informed Celia that the baby couldn't breast-feed and had rejected cow's milk; Celia sent the rebel soldier who'd brought her there back to Fidel's camp for canned milk, assuring the old man that she'd supply the baby's food from then on.

The baby's birth seems to be the reason she finally took leave of Manzanillo—the place she'd been trying to abandon since December 1956—and it seems likely that Fidel asked her to get there in a hurry, on learning that Pastor's baby had been born, because she left Manzanillo carrying baby clothes.

As soon as she got back to Fidel's camp, the entire Command Column 1 "José Martí" traveled to El Coco, a village on Pico Caracas, where they held military trials. These trials were being held so a soldier known as "The Teacher" could defend himself (for impersonating Che, calling himself doctor, and raping a young woman), and a gang in the business of theft and extortion (who'd been wearing fake M-26 armbands) could have their say.

Hungarian photographer Andrew St. George, then associated with the Magnum photo agency, documented the trials (negatives and contact sheets are now in Yale University's Sterling Library). Celia, a member of the jury, appears to be hanging on every word, and looks as if wheels were spinning in her head; her expression incredulous and skeptical. In one picture, her mouth is open, presumably offering her opinion or making an observation. The jury sits on the ground. Fidel is in the middle: his back is erect, his legs are folded in a kind of semi-lotus position under him, and his jaw is drawn down as he keeps his eyes straight ahead. His expression is perceptively indignant; one finger is raised as if making a point. Raúl Castro balances on a tree limb, his legs are stretched out, while he writes in his diary. They all focus on the prisoners, who appear to be a sad bunch of rascals. Some were executed that day, while others were merely frightened (in a mock execution). A couple were set free to be drafted (or incorporated), right then and there, into the rebel army.

When the trials concluded, the rebel army traveled back to their favored part of the mountains. Celia and Fidel, along with a priest, Father Guillermo Sardiñas, took another route. They hiked to La Jutia cave, where they baptized Pastor's baby. They named her Eugenia—as the story goes, not for the child's mother.

Celia washing clothes in the river at Las Vegas, 1957. *(Courtesy of Oficina de Asuntos Históricos)*

There, Fidel assured Angel Palomares that he and Celia would raise the child in compliance with his son's wishes. They made it clear they'd do this after the war was over. The child's biological parent, the mother, left after the ceremony with her new husband to live in another province.

CELIA BEGAN HER NEW LIFE as a nomad. Comandante Dermidio Escalona, then a newly enlisted soldier in Fidel's command column, describes it: "We would walk for ten or twelve hours every day in the rain, going up and down mountains," dawn until dusk, changing locations constantly; they'd camp somewhere at night, eat, sleep, and move the next day. The men were shocked to find out she was going to join them. To the soldiers, her extreme thinness had been disconcerting, and Escalona ruminates that "Celia seemed so fragile. . . . We assumed she'd stay in a village and live in a house with a mountain family." Instead, she marched beside Fidel. "We couldn't conceive of someone as fragile as she being able to stand such a hard life."

Escalona also says that Celia immediately began to take care of Fidel, would prepare his coffee before he got up in the morning, made sure his uniform was clean, the buttons sewn on, rips and tears mended, and boots cleaned and repaired; and, she always had an extra pair of glasses on order. For her, these tasks were effortless, second nature, after all those years of looking after her father. Hers was a traditional Latin role: she'd drawn her father's bath, brought him a cup of morning coffee, organized his medical office, carefully scheduled patients according to his or her special needs—and it wasn't hard for her to transfer this routine to Fidel. "She wouldn't go to bed until after he did," Escalona told me. Once the soldiers in the column had seen how gracefully she managed to blend in, perform many and varied tasks, and live among them with such simplicity, they were happy, particularly since Fidel was so pleased to be the object of her attention. He was easier to live with, thanks to her presence; it made life easier for everyone. Although Haydée Santamaria, a national director of the movement, occasionally spent time in the mountains, generally speaking, Celia was the only woman in Fidel's camp.

IN THE EARLY DAYS OF THE REVOLUTION, Fidel's column must have been something of a road show. They traveled with several medical doctors. Some were hiding, but doctors were living with the guerrillas for a number of reasons: they had been caught providing treatment to guerrillas or collaborating with the rebels in some manner, such as donating medicine; or they might have had to go underground for giving testimony of police brutality. And some, of course, chose to be there. Doctors were a rarity in the mountains. When Fidel's column reached a town, the *medicos* would receive patients no matter what time of arrival, day or night, according to Ricardo Martínez, a radio announcer in the Havana underground who'd been transferred to the safety of the Sierra. He told me that Celia was the key to this community outreach: "We would reach a small valley where maybe there were five to ten houses. The women and children would come to wherever the rebels were camped. Celia would see a child who might be sick, and she would ask the child to bring its father, or maybe the grandmother." When the guardians arrived, she'd ask permission to let the rebel army examine and treat the child and summon one of the doctors. It was 26th of July policy to leave medicine for further treatment, and Celia was the source of much of this medicine.

She was modifying a role she'd played most of her life, because from an early age she'd brought children—poor children—home with her. According to her sister Flávia, Celia nursed children

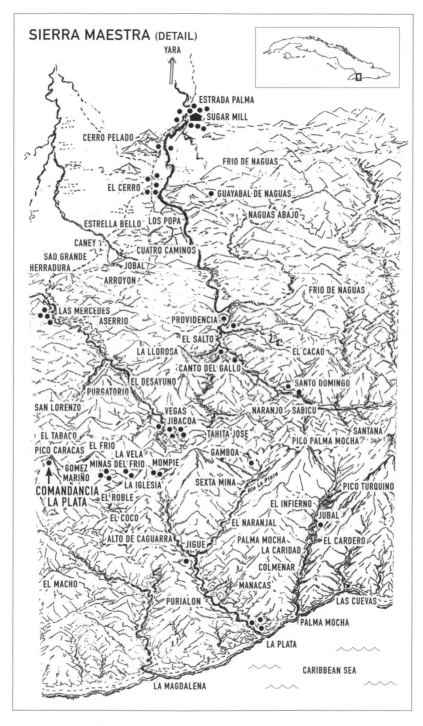

(Map drawn by Otto Hernandez. Courtesy of Oficina de Asuntos Históricos.)

Father Guillermo Sardiñas joined the guerrillas in late 1957 or early 1958. "Because people knew we had a priest among us, they would ask to be married, or to have their children baptized. And because Celia was present, they'd ask her to be the godmother, and she'd accept," Rebel Radio's Ricardo Martínez related, in describing his travels in the mountains with Column 1. *(Courtesy of Oficina de Asuntos Históricos)*

barely younger than herself, and would give them baths, delouse their hair, dress them in her own clothes, emulating her father. Now, in the Sierra, she was aware of the psychological benefits this outreach would have for the rebel army. Celia had a shrewd diagnostic eye, and what she observed she passed on to those accompanying doctors. All this contributed to the rebel army's reputation, and soon, when guerrillas showed up, mountain people flocked to their camp because they thought the rebel army could work miracles. It didn't hurt that priests were there also, the second ingredient in this successful social recipe.

Three priests, in particular, took turns going into the mountains to be with Fidel's column: Fathers Chelala and Rivas from Santiago, and Guillermo Sardiñas from the Isle of Pines. Other priests did stints with the guerrillas, encouraged by their parishioners, laypersons active in the 26th of July Movement; but of the three, Father Sardiñas is the most famous. He is described as *celestial* (meaning absent-minded), and sufficiently so to be a handicap because Raúl Castro usually appointed a soldier to keep an eye on this priest. He might just start smelling the flowers—

Lydia Doce, four years older than Celia, managed Che's camp, El Hombrito, near San Pablo de Yao. In September 1957, Che asked her to be his courier. *(Courtesy of Oficina de Asuntos Históricos)*

to quote Ricardo Martínez—wander off, get lost, and fall into a ravine. Sardiñas dressed as a guerrilla priest: his soutane was olive green, embroidered with a red star, and had been designed by Camilo Cienfuegos (who had worked in El Arte, a stylish men's clothing shop located in Havana behind the Capitol, before becoming a guerrilla). Martínez told me: "Because people knew we had a priest among us, they would ask to be married, or to have their children baptized. And because Celia was present, they'd ask her to be the godmother, and she'd accept." He says that Fidel would step in to take his place as the godfather (and here Martínez sighed, as he related this), causing a certain amount of fanfare every time they camped. Don't forget, they all looked rather biblical, with their long hair and beards. Plus it didn't hurt their glory that the "doctor's daughter" was with them wearing mariposa blossoms, the old Mambisi army symbol of resistance and liberation pinned to her uniform. Nor did it hurt that the rebel army paid for everything in cash.

Martínez described how each day ended: they were exhausted and footsore, having been on their feet for nine or ten hours, and wanted only to undress, bathe, and find a place to string up a hammock before dark. Most of all, he says, they were always desperate to know whether the cooks had started a fire, wanted to be reassured of having something to eat before going to sleep. Martínez returned to his theme: they'd be trying to make camp and people from the area would drift in. "They would ask Fidel if he would be godfather, and he would be godfather," he recalled grouchily, but with fondness. "Other people would need a doctor," and they could get no rest.

Father Sardiñas officiated at weddings and baptisms and masses all over those hills while he traveled with the rebel army, even though there were no Catholics in the Sierra. The people who came to the rebel camp were spiritualists, primarily, and Seventh-Day Adventists with the occasional channeler. Spanish priests who were sent to Cuba had never bothered to go into these out-of-the-way villages, so there were no Catholics per se. But that didn't matter, because as soon as someone spotted the guerrillas making camp, word went out, and country people would start to arrive from the surrounding area. Martínez pointed out, "You have to keep in mind that most of us were not communists then. I am confident in saying that we have all become communists along the way. All of us, with the exception of those who were Marxists, had chains with medals of the Virgin Mary. I still have the rosary that Father Sardiñas gave me that I used to wear on my uniform. Fidel had chains with medals. We weren't the only ones." Then, he added, after a long moment of silence, as if rousing from a somewhat bizarre memory, "This is a true story."

WHEN CELIA BEGAN LIVING with the rebel army in mid-October 1957 she was, in fact, following closely in the footsteps of another woman, Lydia Doce, four years older, who worked for Che. Lydia managed Che's encampment at El Hombrito after he'd been appointed commander at the end of July, when he'd set off on his own, leaving Fidel's column to make a permanent camp in another part of the mountain range. It was north of the areas Fidel usually frequented, on the other side of Bayamo. One day, Che went to the small town of San Pablo de Yao to find food, and later wrote: "One of the first houses we saw belonged to a baker's family." A month or two later, he asked the baker—Lydia Doce—to organize his second camp, where he'd hidden his men inside a coffee plantation.

In late September, Che sent her to Santiago on her first mission. Che was unacquainted with Frank's replacement and asked Lydia to make diplomatic contact with the new chief, Daniel (Rene Ramos Latour). Like a pro, she went to a friend's house first for a complete makeover, changed the color of her hair, and put on a dress. She was plump but had a pretty face; and some photographs of her suggest seductiveness. Getting to Santiago meant navigating roads controlled by the army. And these she had maneuvered with ease, only running into problems in Santiago. There, the 26th of July rejected her because they couldn't identify Che's signature. But Lydia was resourceful; she found an outsider to introduce her to Daniel, and after this episode, Che decided that he wanted her to carry all his messages. She became an executive courier, and within the rebel army this was a high-status position.

She became "radicalized by the experience," as Cubans frequently comment when speaking of Batista's coup d' état. She had been living in Havana but left the capital when Batista took over in 1952. She moved back to Oriente Province in 1955, opened a bakery in San Pablo de Yao, where she encountered Che in 1957. She'd married at sixteen (in 1932) and had three children with her first husband, Orestes Parra (two daughters and a son named Efrain, who joined Che's column). She divorced her second husband, Sebastian García, after fourteen years of marriage, before moving to Havana in 1952, and had been managing on her own for five years before working for Che.

Che's camp was stationary (unlike Fidel's, which was always on the road), and Lydia took care of it. She secured food, medicine, and uniforms for Che's men—much as Celia had been doing for her outdoor barracks in Manzanillo—was known in the community, and could do this underground logistical work discreetly. She oversaw about forty soldiers in Che's Column 4 (named Column 4 because Fidel wanted to suggest there were more columns by skipping a few numbers). As Che put it, Lydia "could be tyrannical" and Cuban men found her hard to handle. One of his soldiers complained that she had "more balls than Maceo" because she was excessively reckless, and advised Che to watch out, she'd bring them all down. Che admitted that her audacity had no limitation.

ANOTHER AUDACIOUS FEMALE was Celia's oldest sister, Silvia (often spelled Sylvia in the archives). She had been living quietly in Santiago, in spite of Celia's ever increasing notoriety, with her husband, Pepin Sánchez del Campo, a pharmaceutical salesman, and their two sons. Silvia taught at the Santiago Teachers College. It was a private school, and Frank País had been an intern in her classroom, and he had recruited her. Today, both of Silvia's sons remember Frank, his sweet face and his charm, and chortle as they describe the first time they saw him. Silvia had organized a meeting in her house to introduce Frank to a prominent member of the Santiago community, so Frank could ask him to buy weapons, and they were there. Their father, Pepin, came home after work, and Silvia introduced him to Frank. As soon as Pepin got a chance, he pulled his wife into the kitchen to ask her, incredulously, "Are you planning to carry out a revolution with children?" Young Pepin and Sergio then started to discover things around the house: they found armbands in a drawer and surmised that one of the outlawed M-26 sewing circles must be meeting there, too, and decided not to confront their parents— better to keep their eyes open and discover more about what was going on. One day, Sergio, the youngest, came home from school just as Frank's bodyguard drove up outside their house, got out, and removed a spare tire from the trunk of his car. He knocked on their door and handed Silvia the tire (filled with pistols and ammunition) and told her to get rid of it. Without any pretense, she'd asked her eldest son, Pepin, then eleven years old, to help. She handed him the box of ammunition and told him he'd have to take care of this. She explained the route he'd take, which went right past a policeman, but said: "Don't let him see it." The box hadn't been small; it had been about the size of a large cigar box, or a collegiate dictionary, but he managed.

Soon after Celia went into the mountains, Silvia's quiet life began to explode. "My father was arrested twice," and Sergio began to describe his family's odyssey. Through the spring and summer of 1957, Silvia was pregnant. In November, "my mother was in Santiago's Los Angeles Clinic and gave birth to a daughter who died at birth." (Silvia had been RH-negative and the baby was RH-positive, creating antibodies at birth; this was the second child she'd lost at delivery.) The day after she left the hospital, her husband was arrested. "We arrived home from school, my father wasn't there, and a lot of neighbors were going in and out of the house. We asked our mother what was happening. She answered that our father was in Guantánamo, and that was all she said. Going to Guantánamo was normal, since he was a pharmaceutical salesman," but when the neighbors left, she explained what had happened.

That morning, the head of the army in Santiago, Col. José Salas Canizares, the man who officially killed Frank País, arrived at their house accompanied by soldiers. They searched all the rooms and found medical samples—no more than normal for a pharmaceutical salesman—and then arrested Pepin and took him to the Moncada. She'd telephoned the mayor, a friend of hers, who was high up in the pro-Batista government. The mayor, Maximilian Torres, and Silvia had been in school together and often chatted at social events. Torres drove to the Moncada and got Pepin released, but Canizares had been tough (according to Sánchez lore) and asked the mayor sarcastically, "What do you think you are doing at Moncada making inquiries about an arrest that is an army affair?" In other words, you might be the mayor of Santiago, but I am head of the entire eastern division of the country. Wasting no time, Canizares informed Mayor Torres that the army had finished their interrogation and were aware that Celia Sánchez had stayed in Pepin's house at Alta Vista. Furthermore, they knew that Pepin was sending medical supplies to the Sierra Maestra, even though Pepin had denied everything. Still, Canizares said, he would release him. Torres, confused by the about-face, related all this to Silvia, who rejoiced that her husband was free.

Three days later, soldiers arrived again. During this search, Silvia got a call from a doctor saying her husband had just been arrested while making a sales call. Silvia again telephoned Maximilian Torres, who went to the Moncada for a second time, where Canizares greeted him coldly, saying that "Pepin is alive only because there are no battles in the Sierra Maestra at the moment." Again, the army released Pepin to the mayor's custody, but Canizares warned, as Sergio Sánchez told me: "The next time you get here, you are going to find Pepin with ants in his mouth."

Nobody in Santiago at that time would have doubted the threat behind this kind of statement. Torres hurried to Silvia, related what had happened, and implored her to leave town immediately. It isn't a threat, or even a warning, he said, "It's a prophecy," and urged them to leave Santiago that night, at the very latest.

They didn't actually get away until around five the following morning, and were accompanied by their next-door neighbor, Pepe Boix, because Boix actually had Pepin's medical supplies, which he had been shipping to the Sierra Maestra. Boix, who owned a hardware store in downtown Santiago, also shipped all Celia's supplies to the rebel army directly from his warehouse. For years, he had shipped Celia's King's Day toys, which she bought in bulk in Santiago, putting the packages on the coastal boat to Pilón. Nothing had really changed: Celia recruited him the way she recruited everybody. It was easy, and he was glad to help. This is a good illustration of how she developed her own personal network, through expediency mostly, often bypassing the 26th of July Movement. She would get her family and friends to buy oil, lamps, blankets, boots, plastic, and ammunition—all the things the rebel army needed—and let Pepe Boix do the shipping.

On the night of Pepin's second arrest, neither Rene nor Pepe knew if the army had discovered Boix's involvement. They felt the army might know, but were turning a blind eye, temporarily, since Boix's brother was a colonel in the army. Boix's brother was the army's public relations officer for the eastern region, a well-known officer in those parts, so Boix proposed they both get out of Santiago while he could still talk his way through Central Highway checkpoints by merely mentioning his brother's name. Both families fled: four adults and four children, with luggage, crammed into Pepin's car. Both families locked the doors of their fine Vista Alegre houses, hoping for the best, and when they reached the first checkpoint, Pepe did the talking. They passed through easily, as he'd predicted.

Silvia was weak from childbirth, still bleeding, feeling sharp abdominal pains, and she was physically exhausted after having spent the night packing, getting her family ready to leave. Mollified from their checkpoint experience, they decided it was safe to stop at a roadside café outside the first major city they came to, Holguín. They settled down in a booth, when, through the windows of the restaurant, they saw armed jeeps and patrol cars racing down the highway. Obviously something extraordinary had happened. Holguín was famous for its violence, and reprisals were par for the course. They reckoned that this was something big, and they'd better get out of town, so they left the café immediately.

On the far side of Holguín, all cars were being waved into the army's garrison. Seeing this, Silvia took command and told her husband, who was driving, to stop the car so she could speak to the soldier directing traffic. "Don't drive into the garrison, no matter what they tell us," she ordered Pepin as they pulled abreast. She leaned forward, looking past the driver's seat to sweetly inform the soldier that her children were about to have their tonsils removed and she was taking them to Havana. They had a long trip ahead, she reminded him "with a mother's urgency," Pepin remembers. Silvia started to describe the appointment schedule for the tonsil operations, quoting the hours, etc., and explain why they needed to get to Havana as soon as possible. Convinced, the soldier waved them on. "Our mother had lost her baby, and her house, but she was not going to lose her husband," Sergio concluded, also saying that their mother "looked soft, but could be just as strong as Celia." Later that day, tuning the car radio to Radio Reloj, the 24-hour news station, on the car radio, they learned that Holguín's notorious army chief, Colonel Fermin Cowley, had been assassinated that morning, and had they pulled into the garrison, neither Pepin nor Pepe Boix would have come out again. I asked if that meant they would have been put in jail. "No," Sergio and Pepin answered, incredulous at such a tepid suggestion. "They would have been killed, because the army didn't ask questions."

Pepin burned up the highway, and 970 kilometers later, he dropped the Boix family at the Hotel Lincoln in Central Havana. Then he'd turned east, and drove another hour to Flávia's hideout, "the green bungalow," arriving on the night of November 22. Silvia's family moved in with Flávia, Rene, their two daughters, the youngest sister Acacia, who'd arrived in late September, and Griselda with her small son, Julio César, who showed up in early October after the police ran them out of Manzanillo. Pepin drove into Havana the next day to meet the director of the Analec Pharmaceutical Laboratory, and told him their story. The director found an office for Pepin and put him to work immediately as a Havana salesman. Of the eleven people now living in the beach house, only Pepin was bringing in a salary.

IN NOVEMBER, SOME "ACTION" MEMBERS from Guantánamo's M-26 finally ran José "Gallego" Moran to ground; they assassinated him, carrying out the order Celia had assiduously avoided.

By early December, the 26th of July Movement national director, Armando Hart, officially and pointedly asked Celia when she was going to return to Manzanillo: "I am tasting the bitterness of incomprehension. . . . Aly, we thought you were going to keep your promise to return. . . . Without your very able collaboration, they have had to make superhuman efforts to keep the supplies going to the Sierra." He reminded her that Daniel was overworked while she was away (thus Hart did not know that staying there had been her plan). By December, the situation in the cities was quite dangerous. When the seemingly untouchable Colonel Cowley had been assassinated, the people of Holguín had rejoiced, and their reaction caused increased repression in all cities. In Santiago, when Salas Canizares heard that his Holguín counterpart had been murdered, he sent tanks into the streets. Celia's *clandestino* colleagues were encouraged to keep up the pressure. The underground started a new campaign: to burn the sugar crops around the nation and heighten subversive activities. Around November 28 it began, and the movement operating within cities began suffering losses as many clandestine fighters were killed. Celia did not return to the underground and take part in this particular stage of the Revolution. She stayed in the mountains with Fidel, keeping his buttons from falling off, his mind engaged, his coffee brewed, and a box of cigars ever ready to keep his mind stimulated and his behavior mellow. Women's work? Not if you speak to the retired comandantes and other alumni of Colunm 1. Everyone that I spoke to concedes that this work badly needed doing, to keep Fidel on an even keel, and is one of the crucial ways she helped win the war.

24. JANUARY–JUNE 1958

Planning War

DURING THE FIRST MONTHS OF 1958, Celia and Fidel planned a defense strategy. The 26th of July had an informer within the Cuban army and knew it would be staging an all-out offensive in the upcoming summer months. This piece of intelligence gave Fidel time to make preparations.

By January 1958, the rebels held most of the mountains of southeastern Oriente. After a year of rebel army harassment, the Rural Guard had pulled out of nearly all the smaller garrisons in the Sierra Maestra. Now, with this geographical zone in their possession, it was up to the rebel army to look after all the people who resided in it. Fidel put Celia in charge of some managerial duties in the *zona libre,* or free zone. Her main responsibility was to figure out how they would acquire enough food to feed everyone in the zone should Batista's army wage a long and effective blockade against them—a blockade lasting months, maybe even years. She already provided for about one hundred people, Comandante Delio Ochoa told me, rebel army soldiers and specific Sierra families who were working for the guerrillas. In January, with an eye to the future, when they would be under siege and she would be supplying everyone, she set about obtaining cattle from ranches outside the mountains. She began by canvassing ranchers south and east of Manzanillo, where she knew many of the ranch owners.

She sequestered the herd on her family's farm first—the Sánchez Silveira 40,000-acre ranch at San Miguel del Chino—but tapped all owners, demanded or bargained for cattle, which were paid for with a graciously written I.O.U. penned by Fidel promising payment after victory.

Fidel suggested setting up warehouses along the western slopes to store food and other supplies. In 1956, when Celia had been planning the landing, she'd urged farmers to buy extra kerosene and bury it. Now she began to visit mountain farmers in various places, asking them to grow food, encouraging fields of malanga— big plants with exotic leaves and edible roots—on mountain slopes. It was a plant that blended in well with the scenery. She ordered some families to raise livestock. "I started out with a small farm with pigs, hens, turkeys and pigeons," she wrote her father a few months later. "They are now giving us such good results that we are going to develop them in each zone. We've got pens, chicken coops, grain tanks for corn. I found an empty house and a rebel couple to take care of it and do all the work. Each farm is going to have a corn field." After gathering stats, taking one of her censuses, she drew up a plan for distributing the confiscated cattle by placing them in convenient places within the free zone. She tried to spread them equally among families.

None of this was easy; Celia had a lot of trouble getting those cattle from the ranches into the mountains. Soldiers from the rebel army borrowed horses to drive the cattle and didn't return them to the owners. Her letters to Fidel provide a glimpse of what was going on. She complained that the guerrillas were getting to be as bad as Batista's guards, taking whatever they wanted, and he shot back: "It is almost as though it is my fault that the people who borrowed the horses didn't return them." Humberto Sori Martín, the rebel army lawyer, was in charge of the civil government of the free zone. "Sori came to me with this problem," she wrote Fidel, and "I thought it best that civilians [local people] under the order of Sori's representatives [rebel soldiers, platoon captains] should be in charge of moving and looking after the cattle, protected by our troops, but [I told him] not to determine anything until Che arrives." Fidel definitely did not like the idea of the locals being in charge, but went along with it. He let Celia and Che work it out.

Fidel decided that he, like Che, wanted an executive courier. He chose a farm girl, Clodomira Acosta, who, as a messenger for the rebels, had been caught and arrested, and famously escaped from the Cuban army. Celia, thinking Clodo was sixteen, was ambivalent about Fidel's using someone so young (Clodo was actually 21), but still did everything she could to help her. In this picture, taken in Guayabol de Nagua in early 1958, Clodo, on the left, avoids looking at the camera; Pilar Fernandez is in the middle, and Celia, in doorway, listens to Luis Crespo. *(Courtesy of Oficina de Asuntos Históricos)*

She and Fidel developed a work pattern: she ventured out to take care of projects while he stayed in one spot, concentrated on planning the defense of the rebel army. Her presence, as members of the rebel army repeatedly told me, "freed him up to win the war."

FIDEL SOON DECIDED HE, like Che, wanted a courier. He found the right person when a farm girl showed up at his camp in late January. Clodomira Acosta Ferrales was born on February 1, 1936, but looked much younger than twenty-two. (Celia thought Clodo, as she was called, was sixteen or seventeen and was ambivalent about Fidel's using someone so young.) Her parents, Estaban Acosta and Rosa Ferrales, had an orchard farm on the Yara River.

She was the third of eight children, and had briefly worked as a maid in Manzanillo, but hated it and returned home to help cultivate fruit trees. The nearest town didn't have a school, so she was uneducated. She lived with Sergio Pena briefly, when she was about seventeen, in a common law marriage that lasted a few months before she left him. One day she saw a couple of Rural Guards arrest a boy and knew he helped the rebel army, so she had gone up to the Guards and shouted: "Let him go. Don't you see that he's nobody?" Like everybody else in the Sierra, she'd experienced Rural Guard brutality, saw how they treated farmers: stealing animals, raping women, burning houses, and probably experienced or heard about unreported incidents that had ended in murder. In the heat of the moment, this impetuous young woman had sealed her destiny, and become political. She joined one of the rebel army platoons, where they found a job for her as a messenger. Clodo was caught and arrested, interrogated, and locked in a cell. Her head was shaved, but Clodo managed to escape right under their noses after setting a couple of backpacks on fire with some matches she'd hidden on her person. In the smoke and confusion, she jumped out of a high window, but she landed safely, and traveled on foot through several towns, with a shaved head, until she could join another rebel army platoon at La Vega de la Yua. Once again, she worked as a messenger.

Clodo was arrested again, escaped once more, but this time—in January 1958—she'd headed straight for the commander in chief. Fidel and Celia had heard of Clodo, since her ability to escape had become legend. Story has it that she'd been caught carrying a wounded rebel army soldier, screaming dramatically, "Hang me! He can't walk," until one of Batista's soldiers had threatened to hang him if she didn't shut up.

In February, Fidel asked Clodo to scout the Sierra del Escambray, which is in the middle of Cuba, and make contact with the Revolutionary Directorate (*Directorio Revolucionario*, or DR) Echeverria's group, which had barely survived after their attack on the Presidential Palace. Fidel was acting on information that its new director, Faure Chamon, had arrived in the Escambray on or around February 8, and gave Clodo a letter of introduction. It said,according to Faure Chamon in a document in the Council of State's Office of Historical Affairs Archives: "To the Rebels in Las

February 1958: European journalist Enrique Meneses takes this picture of Celia riding into camp, behind Juan Almeida, burlap sacks stuffed with food fastened to her saddle. *(Courtesy of Oficina de Asuntos Históricos)*

Villas in Escambray, the person carrying this message can fill you in on details and events of interest." Fidel asked Clodo to find out what sort of people were fighting with the DR, and to try to get some idea of what they were doing there.

MEANWHILE, CELIA HAD BEEN TRAVELING around the mountains asking people to establish new vegetable gardens and build pens to raise chickens and pigs, and trying to explain, all the while, that the fruits of these labors wouldn't be for them, personally, but for everybody. She tried to convince these farmers that should they all become isolated and cut off from the rest of the country, they'd be able to survive a siege if they had these surplus products. Although logical, it was not an easy argument. Later on, educating the Sierra farmers in the fine art of animal husbandry became the real test. When she tried to tell some of the host farmers that the cows she was giving them represented future food, and furthermore they could expand their herds by producing calves, some slaughtered their animals, giving the excuse that the cows had broken their legs. But she confiscated the meat, set up a curing house in a place called Jimenez, and took over two industrial-sized refrigerators (from a businessman who had decided it was best to leave the area). These were subsistence farmers, not used to being engaged in agricultural production, and always having trouble feeding their own. Many had been run off their property by the army or Rural Guard and taken refuge in the Sierra.

BY THE END OF FEBRUARY, nearly all of Celia's sisters had moved out of the green bungalow. For six months, the four families had been trying to look normal living in the same house. Silvia's husband had been their only envoy to the outside world. Plainclothes police watched the house from the beginning, according to Flávia, but the neighbors had always helped out by giving hand signals to indicate who the police were, and where they were stationed. There had been several house searches (after someone had thoughtlessly made a phone call to Santiago), which indicated that the phone was tapped, but nothing much happened. Yet, Flávia says, they were aware that the police wouldn't be putting in all those hours without coming up with something to show for it, so they decided to go their separate ways. Flávia's family left first; then Griselda and her small son, Julio César, slipped away. Acacia moved in with the Gironas in Havana. Silvia and Pepin waited, with suitcases packed, until the neighbors signaled one morning that the coast was clear: no police were on duty. Then Pepin quickly put his wife, boys, and their suitcases in the car and drove away. Flávia told me that she and Rene had reached the point that they needed to find an income, so they opened a dental clinic in Havana. They bought a house on a major artery road, Santa Catalina. It was on a corner, next to a fire station, across the street from a bar, and in such a completely busy neighborhood that no one had time to notice their two names hanging on the shingle and connect them with Celia. Like Frank's red car, their house went unnoticed because it was so obvious.

CELIA WAS BACK IN FIDEL'S CAMP in February for the arrival of a European journalist they'd permitted to visit the column, but only because they wanted him to document the arrival of Dr. Leon

Ramírez, senator from Manzanillo. Ramírez was making the journey to Fidel's camp to propose a peace plan. "I noticed that something odd was going on," the journalist, Enrique Meneses, later wrote. "The cooking smelled better, the rebels were polishing their boots and cleaning their arms with more care than usual. . . . Sentries were posted along the length of the road which Leon Ramírez had to take, and every so often the Senator and his guides were stopped and asked for their papers in order to give the impression of a territory under the control of a perfectly correct and well-organized rebel army. Leon Ramírez arrived. After greeting those present, he gave a pistol to Celia Sánchez. 'I have met and have the greatest respect for your father, Dr. Sánchez. I had thought of bringing you a more feminine gift, but under the circumstances, I feel that this will be more useful.'"

MEANWHILE, HIDDEN IN THE ESCAMBRAY, Faure Chamon heard that a girl from Fidel's Sierra was looking for him. He decided to make contact with her and suggested she come along with his group as they moved farther into the mountains, since they were constantly on the move. With Clodo, they headed into an area where numerous groups of anti-Batista guerrillas were hiding, and Chamon recalled that Clodo had asked him: "Who are you? What are you like? What do you call yourselves? Are you students? Who are the others? Where do they come from?" (These must have been, quite literally, Fidel's questions.) Chamon recognized that she was bright—his description was "quick"—decided to take a chance, and explained his situation with transparency. Two or three days later, they were ambushed by Batista's forces (at Cacahual), and Clodo became separated from his group. But she knew the geography of the Escambray well enough to make it on her own, ended up joining another section of the DR, led by Ramon Pando Ferrer, and questioned him for a few days. When she'd learned enough, she bade farewell and headed back to the Sierra Maestra. Fidel was delighted with the intelligence she'd gathered, and after this, began giving her assignments.

AT THE BEGINNING OF FEBRUARY, Fidel gave Celia jobs that were distinctly military. First, he decided to put in some fortifications in the spot he considered a possible "point of entry" for the enemy.

This most vulnerable spot was near the village of Las Vegas de Jibacoa, farther down Pico Caracas. There she moved into a house with a family, oversaw trench digging, and then got to work establishing an armory. She found a building in El Naranjo that suited her needs, and began doing what Fidel asked of her: she procured land mines, detonators, cables, and bombs, and stored them there.

IN MARCH, COLUMN 1 "JOSÉ MARTÍ" broke up into separate columns, although Che had left earlier due to his frequent attacks of asthma and inability to be constantly out marching; but now, with several new columns, Fidel could expand their sphere of influence. All this was in keeping with Frank País's goal when he established the second front: grow the rebel forces, confuse the army by occupying new locations, and, simultaneously, take the heat off Fidel's column. Finally, the rebel army was ready to carry this out, and Raúl Castro left with his own column by March 16. He began networking with freelance guerrilla groups in the Sierra Cristal near Guantánamo, the same groups Frank had scouted earlier (in June 1957), reorganizing them to fit in with the rebel army. He noticed that—unlike his brother's always-on-the-move column—these groups had never marched, always lived comfortably in houses, and he adopted their style. "I still miss him so much," Celia wrote her father. "Raúl is the best and most affectionate person that anyone can imagine. . . . For me, for all of us, Raúl's departure was sad." In my favorite photograph (shot, it is thought, by Frank), Celia stands beside Fidel, but Raúl's hand is on her shoulder. "Good officers stayed behind," she writes, but "he departed with the best captains and the best men, chosen by him, as well as the best weapons." She tells her father: "Their standard of living is higher than here, in the Sierra. They don't use plastic, always [sleep in] houses and beds . . . they have telephones, cars," she observes longingly, and, I suspect, is resolving to make a change to her own quality of life.

The authority of the 26th of July Movement guerrillas had expanded from the highlands, on the western flank of the Sierra Maestra, where Fidel was generally located, to the territories near Guantánamo, to where Raúl had established his second front "Frank País," into the southern section of Oriente Province, where

Juan Almeida's new column held the mountain range outside Santiago. Eventually, the rebel army would grow to eight separate commands. Also in March, Che moved his camp to be closer to Fidel. This also meant that Che's courier, the forty-two-year-old Lydia Doce, was nearby, and could take Clodomira under her wing.

Celia worried about Clodo, and thought the young woman was sixteen (when, in fact, she was 22); when she learned that Fidel was sending this young farm girl to Havana to liaise with Faustino Perez before he and Fidel began to plan a general strike scheduled for April 1958, she intervened. Celia declared Clodo too vulnerable, too young, and would stick out in Havana as a tomboy. She sent Clodo to Santiago to one of her friends (Maria Lara) with a note: "Take Clodo to a dentist and have her teeth fixed; then take her to a beauty salon." Clodo returned to the camp to show Celia her new look before leaving for the capital. She had to cross through heavily enforced enemy lines to get to Manzanillo, but went with confidence: she walked into an army garrison and informed the chief officer that her mother was gravely ill in Manzanillo. He ordered a soldier to drive her there, and when she left the jeep, sang out, "See you later." She took a plane for the first time in her life; found Agustín Guerra, the poet who was Celia's father's friend, who helped Clodo contact Faustino Perez; then went to see Flávia. Flávia told me that she had made a "general offer" to supply the rebel army with "some things" and had been a bit taken aback when Clodo appeared carrying a long wish list from Celia but resigned herself to filling Celia's requests. Soon after this someone in the movement found a sympathizer who drove one of the Havana-Santiago long-distance buses. He'd agreed to haul materials, but not weapons, and constructed a false ceiling in his coach to transport Flávia's items. She says she sent books for everyone; asthma medicine and inhalers for Che; plastic dishes, cups and saucers for Celia; yards of plastic for everyone—much loved as it kept their sleeping hammocks dry; and—not to be forgotten or left unmentioned—cans of peaches for Che, because Celia knew he loved them. Flávia thinks the bus driver left his cargo at a drop-off place somewhere along the Bayamo highway, and is under the impression that Camilo Cienfuegos would come down with a few of his men to pick it up all the parcels she sent.

IN EARLY APRIL, CELIA DEVELOPED her famous inter-mountain delivery network of mule teams. These teams, whose owners pledged absolute loyalty to her, played a big part in the Revolution's success. With them, the rebel army could get all the essential materials up the steep mountains: guns, ammunition, gasoline, kerosene, oil, boots, uniforms, and medicine. The teams became the lifeline of the guerrilla army, and some were made up of as many as twelve mules. They transported freight as far as 100 kilometers (still within rebel army–held territory) allowing Celia, in certain instances, to provision the outer columns. Of course, now that the owners of these teams were working for her exclusively, this meant that the mules, owners, and their families had to be fed, paid, and kept happy. Along with being the guardian of all the precious items the teams hauled, she was in charge of goods in the warehouses she set up in private houses to be distributed later on, when the war heated up. Celia also used the teams to haul up furnishings she used to decorate command headquarters.

IT WAS IN EARLY APRIL 1958, while Celia was away, that Fidel decided to set up a permanent headquarters. He quit moving his column through the countryside in order to fully concentrate on planning a defense strategy against the army. A summer offensive—the Cuban army's strike against them—was fast approaching when Fidel broke ground on his new command post. He got a few soldiers to build a rough wood cabin: a place in which he could sleep and work. Ricardo Martínez, the former radio announcer, was on the construction team, although he knew nothing about building or carpentry. He followed the orders of a couple of local farmers who were helping them. Martínez says that the farmers cleverly picked trees in various parts of the mountains so no discernible clearing could be seen by army planes, and harvested enough boards to create a cabin. When Celia came back, she took one look at the building and declared herself architect. Thereafter, she exerted design control over all future structures (of which there were several), and although the men weren't aware of it immediately, began to landscape the place as well. Martínez says she noticed that the hillside had become slippery, and that it was hard to get anywhere without falling down, so she ordered some of the guerrillas to construct handrails. She demonstrated how to do this, showed them where to make paths; then she suggested covering the paths with small, leafy branches. They were amazed that getting around could be so easy and then she proposed stairs. Doing this design work was a pleasure for Celia—for all of them, as they recall it now. She continued landscaping the new headquarters and never stopped: the final *Commandancia*, as the result, is a masterpiece. Even though fifty years, and many hurricanes, have whittled away at it, Fidel's command headquarters at La Plata is a place of beauty.

While Fidel worked on war strategies, Celia had quietly created a surprisingly large military complex, covering a square mile. First she concentrated on a field hospital, the largest building in the unit, and practically invisible as it subtly hugged the contours of a hillside, roofed in palm branches. It is camouflaged even today to those walking nearby, and completely blends into the landscape. She had proposed to the men that they construct an entrance that was a separate building—a kitchen set apart from the other structures, sort of a decoy. It links via a walkway to a dining pavilion and leads to the hospital. The objects in the foreground distract the eye from the large infirmary, surgery, and pharmacy that is pinned against the side of the mountain and nearly hidden under a thatched roof. The hospital was large by necessity: it had to accommodate rebel army wounded, plus soldiers from Batista's army that they'd captured wounded, and function as a clinic for the local population as well. The hospital was rough but not primitive, because, thanks to the mule teams, there were standard metal hospital beds, assembled on-site, covered in white linen bedding. They named the facility *Mario Munoz,* for a doctor who was killed at Moncada. This hospital would be duplicated west of the La Plata River, at Habanita, and was called *Pozo Azul,* Blue Well.

The next set of buildings to be constructed was quite a distance from the hospital: a civil administration building (the equivalent of a small courthouse) to deal with collecting taxes (a form of income) and judicial issues, plus a few small facilities, located farther up the mountain, under civil administrator Humberto Sori Martín. At about the same time, Radio Rebelde put up in the mountains an antenna that could be raised and lowered. The engineers often slept in Mountain House, where, starting in April 1958, the rebels transmitted radio programs.

Celia was now architect plus supply chief, mule team *jefe*, and communications director. She had put herself in charge of taking care of all the messengers who were now threading their way throughout these precarious mountains to rebel headquarters, and her special couriers, a group of people she picked (mostly women, I think), began to supply intelligence reports. She'd leave the Sierra occasionally, to interview people, if she thought they had something to tell her, but mostly she communicated through little handwritten messages, carefully folded several times. "I asked her one day," reminisces Comandante Delio Escalona (a veteran of Column 1, who would later be in charge of his own column in Pinar del Rio Province), "why do you write on these little pieces of paper instead of sending messages by word?" He thought her female messengers would be detained, her notes confiscated, and the rebel army endangered. "Escalona," she replied, "they carry the message in a place where nobody can find it," thereby ending the conversation. He chuckled and commented that Celia could be very mischievous.

Celia had arrived in the mountains in mid-October 1957. By the following April, she'd become the voice of Fidel, confirms Escalona: "For us, she was like the boss." He instantly modified this to: "For us, she was the boss; very sweet, but with a very strong temper." A second commander, Delio Ochoa, said, "Most of us considered her to be second in command in the Sierra Maestra," and supplied the reason: "Because Fidel never revoked her orders." Ochoa explained that men had confidence in what she told them, because she was so in tune with Fidel's way of thinking they couldn't go wrong following her orders. Whereas "with Che, there was—sometimes—certain points where he and Fidel differed, and which Che would discuss even though Fidel had stated them, because Che was very analytical. But not with her." His point: she knew what Fidel had in mind, and when she spoke, it was with understanding and authority, and he did not have to deal with what might be Che's interpretation.

Ochoa—Comandante Delio Gómez Ochoa is always referred to by his mother's surname—said, "Let me give you an example." He explained that in April 1958 Fidel had gone to Che's camp. Celia stayed at the *Comandancia* and from there she ordered Ochoa to travel to the coast to meet an airplane that was going to land near

May 1958: Celia is in the window of Bismark Reyna's house in Las Vegas de Jibacoa, where she has moved in order to assist Fidel in preparations for the upcoming summer offensive. Here, she is midway between Fidel's command headquarters and Che's. In Las Vegas, she oversaw the digging of trenches and installed a telephone system to link Che and Fidel. *(Courtesy of Oficina de Asuntos Históricos)*

Las Coloradas Beach. She handed him a written order, which she'd written on one of her small pieces of pink paper, to take all measures to ensure the plane had a safe landing and that, in his absence, Fidel's headquarters was fully protected. "So I left some squadrons there, and put the rest of column 1 in trucks. We had to travel all day and into the night so that we could be there, waiting near the place where they expected the plane to land. We waited for about a week, then I got a note [from Celia] that the plane wasn't coming. But I want to prove with this example, that I, myself, was second in command of the Column then, but I followed her orders, even though I knew that Fidel didn't know about any of this." Ochoa added that her name recognition, by that time, was national. "In Havana, people knew of Celia Sánchez, and Che. Not just Fidel."

By May 1958, Celia was in Las Vegas de Jibacoa—the locale thought to be the most vulnerable place in their territory—where she was midway between Fidel's command headquarters and Che's, overseeing trench construction. "What arrived here, for me, were picks, shovels, iron bars, a sledgehammer, files, machetes, pipes, 24 rolls of wire, and school supplies of all types in large amounts," she wrote Fidel. She was setting up seven schools to instruct children, parents, and soldiers in and around the Las Vegas area. She tells Fidel that she is expecting there to be forty students in the morning, forty in the afternoon, and however many grown-ups show up for night classes.

Celia celebrated her thirty-ninth birthday on May 9, away from the *Comandancia*, and received sad news from Fidel, written in a state of agony. The store, house, and coffee warehouse of one of his friends, Nassim Hadad, a Lebanese who immigrated to Cuba from the Dominican Republic, had been burned down by Batista's soldiers. Nassim supported the rebel army but maintained a civil relationship with members of the Rural Guard, until they discovered that Nassim had been buying supplies for Fidel, and destroyed his property. Celia traveled, probably on horseback, to Nassim's charred house at Guayabal de Naguas. Delio Ochoa arrived ahead of her, also sent by Fidel because Ochoa was nearby. He found the bodies of Nassim's two boys in the ashes: a white boy, who was Nassim's adopted son, and a black Jamaican boy Nassim had been raising. The black boy's body had been tied to a post. She didn't have to tell Fidel what had happened because Ochoa filed the report. She purchased Nassim's herd of animals consisting of many species, and gently wrote Fidel that she'd acquired "a Noah's Ark."

Either there, near the ruins, or somewhere en route back to Las Vegas, she wrote to her father. He had been moved to a special wing of Calixto García Hospital, reserved for members of the medical profession, which alerted her to the fact that he was entering the final stages of lung cancer. She gives him an honest appraisal of the war. "The reprisals are tremendous . . . we are living Malaparte's *La Piel*, only our war is not on the road toward denigration." She refers to the Italian Curzio Malaparte's book *The Skin,* which describes Naples in all its deprivation at the end of the Second World War. The rebel army was using the book to anticipate the very worst that could happen. Ochoa told me they were developing their own set of rules based on ethics, a set of rules for that time when they'd be victors. *La Piel* was a kind of primer for how all their soldiers should not behave after victory. She writes: "Cayo Espino was bombed from two to six thirty in the afternoon." And continues,

"When the bombing was over we went [there], spent the night, took out the dead and wounded. . . . We did not find a house that had not been hit by bullets, some were like colanders . . . The small town of El Cerro was completely burned, some 32 houses. Another small neighborhood, San Juan, was burned, two kilometers from Estrada Palma. There, it was 36 houses. All of these families are coming toward the Sierra with nothing but themselves, grateful for having saved their own lives." A young woman had come looking for a doctor: "A 17-year-old girl came to our camp in search of a doctor because she was injured. I asked her [what happened] and she told me that while she was breast-feeding, soldiers came looking for her husband, and because he is with the rebels, they shot her baby girl and the same bullet went through her breast."

When her father was first admitted to the hospital, Celia had sent Clodomira to see him. "What do you think of Clodo?" she asks. "You can believe the things she tells you." Celia had discovered that Clodomira was illiterate. Clodo always kept a notebook in her breast pocket, which Celia had assumed contained their wish lists from Havana. But then she picked up Clodo's shirt, which she saw lying somewhere, thinking she'd go over the list. Squiggles filled the pages, and Celia recalled that Clodo usually climbed a tree and sat on a limb when she wrote in her notebook. Celia talked to her, offered to send her to school, but Clodo declined. Celia promised to be silent, though Clodo continued to climb a tree whenever she made her notations. Celia wrote to her father: "She told me that if she knew how to read, she wouldn't be so shrewd."

I think it very likely that Celia wrote this letter alone, perhaps accompanied by a bodyguard, while still in the vicinity of Nassim's burned-out house. It is a letter of death and destruction. She, who avoided speaking of death, was looking it in the face. She made her way back, probably stopping in Che's camp. Lydia Doce carried the letter to Havana and personally handed it to Celia's father.

THE NEXT PROJECT CELIA CARRIED OUT—miraculously— was the installation of a telephone system so Fidel could get in touch with the front from his headquarters. She began collecting equipment and managed to get cables, battery telephones, and other components needed. Ricardo Martínez, who was there, has no idea how she accomplished this. Probably, we decided, the same

The directors of the 26th of July Movement convened for a meeting in early May 1958 at El Naranjo farm in Santo Domingo. Among them is Nassim Hadad, Fidel's friend. Seated, from the left, is Haydee Santamaria and behind her, Celia and Vilma Espín. In the center is Nassim Hadad, Fidel, and Faustino Perez. At the back, standing, are René Ramos Latour (aka Daniel, who succeeded Frank), Marcelo Fernandez, and David Salvador. *(Courtesy of Oficina de Asuntos Históricos)*

way she did most other projects: through her personal friends and contacts. She always had her own network of followers outside the 26th of July Movement, composed of people who wanted to help her personally. We deduced that in Las Vegas, she wasn't too far away from the plains and her old subversive Bartolomeo Masó colleagues from her early 1950s action team and from the *clandestinos* who worked with her on the landing of the *Granma*. No sources are able to tell me. But I think I know how she did it. It seems very likely that the telephones were stolen from local sugar mills. The road that ran north of Pilón was so narrow that drivers had to stop and call ahead from one sugar mill to the next, and it's not hard to imagine some of her friends sneaking out to "collect" a battery telephone or two, and any other "necessary" equipment she wanted. Martínez told me that she personally supervised the installation of the phone lines using 26th of July soldiers.

Fidel wanted the telephone system to extend from La Plata to "key points" on the front lines, meaning wherever he thought Batista's troops might be able to penetrate. At the time, the "key point" was Las Vegas, directly down the mountain from his headquarters. Although the telephone system was makeshift and the reception poor, it would prove to be immensely effective. During the offensive, these telephones connected Fidel to his spread-out forces and allowed him to reinforce his units at a moment's notice by sending additional men into critical areas. By using the guerrilla army telephone he could effectively move equipment from one site to another. Martínez said that the rebels had only one 50-caliber machine gun. "That machine gun fought in all the different fronts. We would have it one place today, transport it to a different place tomorrow, and bring it back. Then we'd take it another place so that the enemy thought we had several."

In April, Fidel moved Radio Rebelde from Che's camp to the *Comandancia*. Its purpose: to get coded messages to Fidel's outlying columns. The radio's weak signal traveled to Venezuela, then was beamed back to Cuba, much stronger. Ricardo Martínez says they never anticipated any other use, but before the offensive, on Mother's Day (which was May 11), the engineers asked the Medina family of musicians (who lived—and still live within the *Comandancia* La Plata complex) to perform, and Radio Rebelde soon had a popular following. Their style of music is known as *punto cubano*; singers make up their lyrics to suit the occasion. After that initial program, on Sundays Fidel would give the Medinas the war news, and the quintet did the rest, setting Rebel army news to popular music. The station was picked up and rebroadcast by Cuban stations around the region. Half the island was listening to Radio Rebelde, Martínez claims, by the end of May, when Batista's summer offensive was supposed to start. Using their radio, the rebels, openly acknowledging that a bloody fight lay ahead, started asking for volunteer doctors and donations of medicine.

Old soldiers and current-day historians are in agreement: the telephone was strategically important to the war's outcome. The new, stationary command headquarters at La Plata with its communications system marked a qualitative change in the rebel army's ability to carry out guerrilla warfare. Cuban historians go a step further: they say that Celia's importance lies in the fact that Fidel by this point trusted her implicitly and could ask her to do things, and he would no longer worry about them. They feel confident that Fidel knew that whatever he asked her to do, she'd complete the task.

She'd been instrumental in acquiring a permanent, strategically located headquarters (the location of which is attributed to Celia); an interlocking and complementary communications system of couriers (Celia); a telephone system (largely provided by her); warehouses of food and ammunition (ditto Celia); mule teams to supply the *Comandancia* (Celia); victory gardens around the mountains to sustain the rebel army and their followers (Celia).

25. June–July 1958

The War

CELIA WAS STILL IN LAS VEGAS when the enemy began to advance toward fragile, rebel-held territory. After a few days, in early June, the army had moved so close that she traveled back up the mountain to the command post for safety. There she helped Fidel contact his commanders as he sent orders to the various columns engaged in battle. Seeing how important it was to have someone at the front—Las Vegas, their most vulnerable location—he and she came to the conclusion that she'd go back. She went to Mompié, where she installed a battery telephone, and there, in Mompié, she became the person in the middle, the contact between Fidel and his captains who were fighting in the northwestern sector. Crescencio Perez and his company are one example; the old patriarch was operating close to the Las Vegas front, but mainly she went there to be closer to Che, so she could link him to Fidel.

She was in Mompié on June 5, 1958, when Cuban air force planes, loaded with napalm-headed rockets supplied by the United States, destroyed the house of a farmer named Mario Sariol, Fidel's friend. When this happened, Fidel wrote his most-quoted resolution: "Dear Celia, When I saw rockets firing at Mario's house, I swore to myself that the North Americans were going to pay dearly for what they are doing. When this war is over, a much wider and bigger war will commence for me: the war that

I am going to wage against them. I am aware that this is my true destiny. Fidel."

Aware of her own destiny, Celia seemed to harden her resolve to create an archive of their war documents. Subconsciously, perhaps, she is paying tribute to her dying father who taught her how to study history, the joys of discovering and collecting primary sources, and she'd learned from him how to manage records. In short, he'd taught her all the techniques as well as the pleasures of being a good historian. She'd been making copies of Fidel's messages for quite some time, and now began to ask the other commanders to do the same, and give copies to her. This project was by no means rubber-stamped by Fidel. Nor did it go by without discussion by the others. If anyone were to capture these documents—an altogether reasonable argument against her project—it could be disastrous; it increased the vulnerability of the rebel army, therefore it was too dangerous. Maybe it was Fidel's letter, declaring his destiny, and she reflected to herself that she knew her own contribution. Some commanders were already sending her material. Camilo Cienfuegos asked her to send him an accordion file so he could start collecting documents from his column, and she seems to have decided that the time had come to confront Fidel. "Tell me if you've taken care of this," she wrote, and handed her letter to a messenger at 2:00 p.m. Fidel answered her letter at 5:00 p.m., probably as soon as he got her message, demanding: "What is all this sermon about papers, the archive?" But he didn't say no, and she never let Fidel's grumbling stop her.

DURING THE EARLY BATTLES—throughout June and July 1958—Celia's strategic importance was getting messages from Che that provided Fidel with accurate information of the Cuban army's advance. Che would send her letters by courier, and she conveyed Che's messages to Fidel via telephone. Likewise, Fidel would call Celia with orders for Che, she'd write them out, and have a courier take them to Che, who'd moved his column closer to the Las Vegas front. There were days in June that were the most precarious of the war: Fidel held onto a few square miles of northwestern slope of Pico Caracas because Che, closer to the mountain's base, held off the advance of Batista's troops. Las

Vegas fell to the Cuban army on June 10, but Che continued to move back and forth, striking wherever he could. Batista's forces poured into the area in huge numbers, but partly because of the effectiveness of the telephone, the Cuban army could not gain a foothold. We can see a piece of that story unfold, moment to moment, because of Celia's archives.

Che moved around from skirmish to skirmish; on June 8 an American showed up in his camp in Las Vegas and Che quickly sent a note to Celia, asking Fidel what to do. She replied the same day: "Fidel says to leave the gringo there. According to our intelligence he's from the FBI and has come to eliminate Fidel." According to Cuban historian Pedro Álvarez Tabío, it was Frank Fiorini, who became famous during the Watergate break-in when he worked for the CIA under the name of Frank Sturgis. "Since you are coming in the morning, I'm not writing [at any length]," Celia added, as a postscript, and "Today I've heard a new word." The rebel leaders could be completely flummoxed by the sometimes apocryphal language of the mountains, and amused, as was probably the case in this instance. "Until tomorrow, Celia Sánchez 6/8/58."

Cuban army troops were advancing on all fronts: from the east, they were pouring into Estrada Palma, which was too close to the rebels' training school at Minas del Frio. "I've just talked to Fidel," Celia writes him from Mompié, at 3:30 p.m. on June 10. "He says he hasn't had time to write you . . . he only said to tell you to choose someone responsible there [the officers' training school]" to lead a defense.

Two rebel soldiers told Celia they'd seen an army tank going up the mountain toward Las Vegas, and had counted, along with the tank, twenty-five foot soldiers. She quickly fires off a note to Che; "They say that the tank stopped when some soldier yelled out to be careful, that in those branches there was a mine. The tank stopped in front of the mine and the mine exploded, the explosion was not great . . . but something happened. . . . According to what we've heard, after the mine exploded the soldiers continued to the peak and later retreated. If this is so, they were coming as an advance."

Rebel platoons scattered around the base of the mountains held onto the area. On the 15th, she wrote Che that she'd got his message "in code, half is missing; Fidel says for you to come here, and if that's not possible to quickly send a copy of your code and an explanation of it." Then the Cuban army made another drive.

On the 17th, planes hit a rebel hospital. Fidel called at 11:15 a.m., and she took down this message: "Che: Fidel sends this message over the telephone for you: The soldiers are going down toward Lucas's house, send the seven men with automatic weapons. . . . We've been fighting since 7:00 a.m., Fidel." She adds her own intelligence: "You also must hear the plane flying over the place where Horacio is. We hear mortars and sometimes we hear machine guns. It seems that the soldiers are advancing through there." She notes the time as 12:10 p.m., and hands it to a courier. Che answered her at 2:10: "Celia: Tell Fidel I'm carrying out his orders . . . We have to remember that there is a hospital with wounded. For now, I am going to take them outside. I also have given orders to Raúl [Castro Mercador, no relation to Fidel or his brother] to extend his lines and to Fonso [Alfonso Zayas Ochoa] to make a gradual retreat. I'll let Crescencio [Perez Montero] know what's happening. If you think some weapons can be left here, let me know. I'm sending you the ones you asked for, and I'm reminding you that we have a tripod here with 500 bullets." Then writes: "Commander in Chief: Tell me what my job is."

About seven hours later, she got this: "Celia: I'm sending you the book [for the code]; try to send me the first volume. Pass this message to Fidel: Commander in Chief: I am ordering the immediate transfer that you ordered but I'm letting you know that because it appears that resistance in the area of Las Vegas has been set up, our advance troops are at Loma de Desayuno. I gave orders to take the summits around Las Vegas. . . . If you have a detonator I need it here. I have three personal bombs and five grenades. Che June 19, 9:25."

The next morning she wrote: "Che: I received your message and I sent it over the phone to Fidel. He says that all the changes are very good. Tell Crescencio's group to retreat toward La Maestra... and to move the hospital back, he thinks the best place is El Roble, he doesn't think La Plata is safe... Last night Fidel told me that he could not send you a detonator [but] that he'll send you a car battery; it was low on charge and recharged this morning. . . . Another thing that Fidel keeps asking for is the reinforcement he requested yesterday. Celia Sánchez 6/20/58 11:25 a.m."

Meanwhile, Fidel had received a report of the Cuban army's advances from the sea. They were unloading troops to advance on the *Comandancia* from the southern side of Caracas Mountain. He must have been out in the field because he wrote her a note. "Celia: Send Che the entire message from Pedrito so that he can understand the situation here."

The following day Fidel wrote, "Send the two large bombs to the little store [Tiendacita de La Maestra] and send for the large square bomb that was left behind in Las Vegas."

She composed a note, fixed the time at 11:58 a.m., and sent it to "Che: . . . soldiers are fixing the road with tractors, Fidel says to make trenches for the tanks and put the mine near a ditch." In the afternoon, she sent another. "Che: Gello brought news that Las Vegas was taken; that from Minas del Infierno, with binoculars, you can see soldiers. I paid no attention to this. We haven't heard one shot. Now we can hear some sort of celebration. Fidel says to select the ten best men from the school; he is going to arm them and give them Beretta practice. He wants you to start moving Raúl and Anelito's group to the road toward Las Minas del Infierno and Mompié. Cover those positions with Crescencio's men; Horacio and Lara's people should reinforce Raúl and Angelito; he, Fidel, will come [down] to give the weapons of those who were in Las Vegas, Horacio and the Laras, to the ten boys he asked you for, and the five from Las Vegas that he's bringing and who are already trained in shooting. This will be when we learn the motive of or how the entry to Las Vegas occurred. . . . The reinforcement of the seven boys arrived here 15 minutes ago. I told Fidel that they are going to eat now, sleep, and leave at 5:00 a.m. They are tired." And she added a postscript: "I received the [code] book. Celia Sánchez 6/20/58 5:45 p.m." She adds: "Tomorrow two men are going to install a telephone there to connect only us. This is going to resolve [the problem of having so] many messengers, even though we are the only ones communicating."

On June 23 and 24, another battalion (the Cuban army's eighteenth) started moving up toward Fidel's command headquarters. They'd landed on the beach and were making their way up the La Plata River toward the *Comandancia*. From higher ground, the rebel army's Captain Ramon Paz attacked and drove off the battalion, although he was fighting with a single platoon of men.

ON JUNE 24, CELIA'S FATHER DIED in Havana. A news bulletin was read hourly over Radio Reloj, the powerful 24-hour news station broadcast from Havana: "The longtime representative from Niquero to the National Medical College has passed away." The announcer was Mas Martín, a 26th of July member (who would later marry Inez Girona). Che heard the broadcast and wrote: "Celia: I suppose you've learned of your father's death. I wouldn't like to be the bearer of this news. Between us there is no space for formal condolences; I only remind you that you can always count on me. A brotherly hug from, Che."

THEY WERE IN SUCH DANGER that Fidel called in Camilo Cienfuegos and Juan Almeida to help him resist the army's advance. On Wednesday, June 26, he came down the mountain to get Celia in Mompié. They waited as Che made his way from Las Vegas. The rebel army was conceding territory. Fidel ordered Che to stay with them in Mompié, because it was too dangerous for him to go back to Las Vegas. By the next day, Thursday, June 27, Las Vegas had been overtaken. Defeat and her father's death had arrived at the same time for Celia.

IN HAVANA, BEFORE HER FATHER'S DEATH, a last-ditch attempt to capture Celia Sánchez was mounted by the army. They were so convinced that she would appear at her father's bedside, that during the last weeks of his illness they put plainclothes detectives inside the hospital (from both police and military forces). Clodo and Lydia had been posing as friends from Media Luna and switched their guise to family from Santiago. Visiting the hospital was a menacing prospect for Celia's sisters, so the Girona cousins went to see Dr. Sánchez, and many people traveled from Oriente Province for that purpose, such as Elsa Castro and Maria Antonia Figueroa. They went for Celia. Figueroa says she made friends with an Oriente family who often visited another ward, so the guards thought she was one of their family. Then she'd slip into Manuel Sánchez's ward at night, where the nurses were 26th of July supporters.

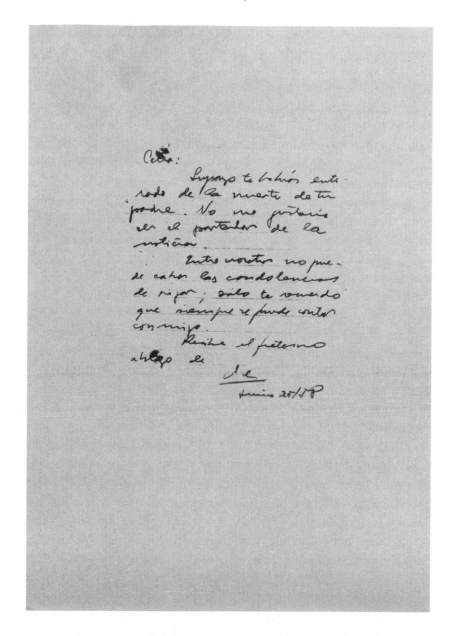

On June 24, Celia's father died in Havana. A news bulletin was read hourly over Radio Reloj. Che heard the braodcast and wrote: "Celia: I suppose you've learned of your father's death. I wouldn't like to be the bearer of this news. Between us there is no space for formal condolences; I only remind you that you can always count on me. A brotherly hug from, Che."

Gossip played heavily in the army's attempt to catch Celia, and they bought the news on the street that Celia Sánchez was going to make an appearance in Havana. Unable to capture her at the hospital, the army thought their final chance lay in her appearance at her father's funeral. They cordoned off the street around the funeral parlor. In Cuba, funerals take place within a short period following death—usually no more than a single, day-long viewing period, since bodies are buried without the usual elaborate embalming process. Mourners' identities were checked at the door of the funeral parlor, which offended many of the distinguished poets, politicians, artists, and physicians who numbered among Manuel's friends and consequently resulted in complaints to the army. A Manzanillo senator telephoned Batista, and the identity checks were lifted, but the army posted men holding rifles around the parapet of the building, which was located right in the heart of Vedado.

The funeral parlor was on La Rampa, at the time a stylish street with airline offices, which runs like a ramp from the sea up to M and Calle 23. The funeral parlor was next to the entrance to the Polynesian Room on the Rampa side of the Havana Hilton. When the service was about to begin, every seat was taken. Since the 26th of July Movement had sent a huge wreath, with its name prominently displayed on the ribbon, people assumed that all these unrecognizable guests were members of the underground. Flávia told me that she and Acacia, both blondes, had dyed their hair black and dressed "uncharacteristically" in blouses with big flowers to look like country women from Oriente Province; and that she and her husband, Rene, sat apart. Silvia and Pepin came (neither family allowed their children to attend). No one in the family could identify most of the people in the room. Mariano Bofill arrived. Bofill was the owner of the largest foundry in Manzanillo, which manufactured parts for sugar mills. Griselda was briefly married to his son, and they had a child, Julio César; Bofill still kept ties with the Sánchez family and his grandson. He came in minutes before the service began, looked around for acquaintances from Manzanillo to sit with, and saw no one until his eye fell on Silvia and Pepin. He whispered in Pepin's ear: "It's too crowded." Then, suddenly able to recognize the crowd, he'd growled in a low voice, "This is disrespectful. Come with me." In the hall, Pepin confirmed that none of the guests were from Santiago, and Bofill, who was close to Batista, dialed the president's number. Bofill's early fortune, from the 1920s, was based on scrap metal, and one of his suppliers had been the young Fulgencio Batista. According to Silvia's son, Sergio, when Batista wanted to enter the army, Bofill had furnished a recommendation. The two men had close social ties and most people assumed that Bofill was a *batistiano*, but both he and his sons made substantial contributions to the guerrillas in the Sierra as well.

Bofill stood at the bank of telephones in the lobby of the funeral parlor, with Pepin next to him, and his conversation has been passed down to the next generation, as if scripted: "I'd like to speak with Fulgencia, this is Bofill calling," It was not lost on Pepin that Bofill had Batista's personal telephone number. "Fulgencio, I'm at the service for Celia Sánchez's father. You know I have ties with this family. This place is full of people from the SIM, and I feel that it is disrespectful to the family. I'd be very grateful if you'd take care of it." And, according to the story, Bofill put down the phone without waiting for Batista's comment. Minutes later Tabernilla, the obese, much-hated and greatly feared officer who ruled over Havana, waddled in, clapped his hands twice, and the unknown guests left. Soon only a few people were left in the room to attend Manuel's funeral.

Flávia gave me a general outline of what happened. I'd known about the police on the parapet, confirmed Flávia's description with that of the Gironas, and tried to find someone who could recall being at the service on the day of the funeral. Sergio was under the impression that Delio Gómez Ochoa had been there. He was Fidel's man in Havana, and married Acacia after victory. When I asked him, Ochoa looked at me in astonishment. He answered that of course he wasn't there; it would have been "suicidal" to have put in an appearance.

This part of Celia's life story, so far removed from where she actually was at that moment — in Mompié — unfolded with textbook precision. Here was the nation's army throwing its resources into capturing a woman who was unlikely to make an appearance — an army caught in a trap, trying to keep up its reputation. Having let Celia slip through their hands once, at Campechuela, the army was plagued by its mistake and was always trying to make sure it wouldn't happen again. The generals, it seems, couldn't take a chance that she wouldn't come to Havana, so they ended up doing what traditional armies often do: spend a huge amount of time, energy, and money on something that is unlikely to happen. Guerrilla armies are effective if only because they allow the establishment to overextend itself, in just this kind of effort. Here was proof of it.

Just as the Cuban military was caught up in an age-old Bismarckian set of behaviors, futile and predictable, so, too, in its own way, was the Sánchez family. After the secret police left, there were very few people in attendance, and one of the unrecognized guests introduced herself to Manuel's children. She had, for a decade or so, been Manuel's lover. One of the grandchildren thinks the affair began in Pilón in the 1940s, and that the woman moved to Havana, where Manuel spent most annual vacations. Manuel's other children had no idea of her existence, and were shocked when she approached them. But the Gironas say that Celia always knew about the affair. For all her apparent closeness to her siblings, she chose not to inform them.

None of the members of the family who attended the funeral are alive today. I cannot ask Flávia for details, because she died (of cancer) in 2004. Griselda's son, Julio César, who was the first person to tell me about his grandfather's lover, is also dead. Sadly, so are the Gironas, who were a worldly lot, and of the opinion that Manuel, widowed at the age of forty, would have been happier had he married. Instead, Dr. Sánchez had a long affair with a woman he couldn't marry, because he never ceased touting his wife as "the love of my life." Where these fabrications left off, the Manduley women took over. The Gironas told me that no extra women were allowed in that family after Manuel's mother-in-law and sister-in-law moved into his household. I would discover that anger erupted that day along with anguish over Manuel's death, and not just over the SIM and the girlfriend.

Chela, Manuel's second daughter, wasn't at the funeral because her husband, Pedro Álvarez, had taken his family to Spain, allegedly on vacation, but in truth he'd gone away to avoid the funeral. Pedro himself told me that his wife had been too nervous to attend. He'd been worried about her to the extent that he'd taken her away from Havana, for her health. Pedro cited the genesis of Chela's fears: she was arrested on Galiano while shopping for jewelry because the police thought she was Celia. The police had released her almost immediately. Yet Pedro—forty-two years later—was still wrapped up in concern for his wife's anxiety symptoms, describing her occasional blackouts after she was arrested and said he'd taken her out of Havana on doctor's orders. Pedro still didn't understand, when we spoke in Miami in 2000, how much this had annoyed the others. In his mind, he'd solved any further confrontation between his wife and the police by taking her away. To me, it makes some sense, since the police had been anticipating Celia's appearance in Havana all through April, May, and June following her father's diagnosis.

Retired comandante Delio Gómez Ochoa, who became Pedro's brother-in-law after he married Acacia, considers the decision Pedro made to have been cowardly—although he didn't use that word. He said that Pedro's behavior was "not good enough"—even in this unusual situation.

Ochoa himself is something of a hero. In the first year, after victory, he led an expeditionary force against the Dominican Republic's dictator, Trujillo. The first time I interviewed him, it was on the wide verandah of the Writers Union on 17th in the Vedado section of Havana. Filmmaker Lisette Vila, the union's director, arranged for us to be at the front table, nearest the elaborate iron gate that marks the entrance. People appeared out of nowhere wanting to shake his hand: union members and people even came in from the street; they thought nothing of interrupting my questions to say hello to this old warrior. For the second interview, we sat in his sunny dining room in Playa, and were interrupted only once, by a messenger from Juan Almeida bearing a Christmas card.

Ochoa reminded me that Manuel Sánchez Silveira had been an exceptional man, and an outstanding father. Speaking of history first, Ochoa pointed out that Manuel had had every chance to leave Manzanillo when he graduated from university: he could have spent his life in Havana. And, because he was so charming, Manuel would have become a rich, successful, urban physician. But Manuel had chosen instead to be a public health doctor. Dr. Sánchez had worked among Cuba's most impoverished people, in one of the country's most out-of-the-way places, and had spent a lifetime battling conditions that were the result of bad governments: malnutrition, addiction, and complete absence of social justice. He'd confronted these evils bravely, and had taught his children to face these circumstances head on. Since those elements are the mother of all revolutionaries (paraphrasing José Martí), Ochoa continued, winding up his explanation, by saying that he couldn't understand how one of Manuel's children could not choose to be near him at his death. No one who understood or admired Dr. Sánchez would have taken a vacation when they knew Manuel's death was imminent—or that is how Ochoa felt about it.

From Pedro's point of view, it hadn't been quite that easy. He had worked out a kind of compromise: he'd made an agreement with his wife before leaving Cuba that they'd fly home for the funeral if her father died. Various grandchildren filled in the rest. When the telegram arrived, Pedro didn't give it to Chela, and she did not find out that her father was dead until they returned to Havana. Angry, she threatened to divorce Pedro. Sergio Sánchez says, "She became so intent upon divorcing him that the family intervened." Pedro must have reasoned that if the police are so sure Celia will come to Havana, who am I to say otherwise? He probably envisioned her popping up in his apartment in the Focsa building, then the flashiest building in town. Chela, for her part, must have buried her head in the sand because she could have made telephone calls, if not to her sisters in hiding, then to the Girona family, or she could have phoned Calixto García Hospital from wherever she was vacationing in Spain. Chela simply did not, because her husband was in charge of everything. When I interviewed them in Miami in 2000, I would turn my head directly to face Chela and explicitly ask her questions, but Pedro would answer them.

FROM JUNE 27 TO JULY 10, the rebel army held their ground against the Cuban army—but barely. Gradually, things began to change for the guerrillas; they were getting better, although they seemed to be worse. Attacks now came from two directions. Under the command of Major José Quevedo, the Cuban army now had a company of men directly below La Plata, and were going up the mountain toward Fidel's headquarters. Numerous companies were closing in on the rebels on Che's side of the mountain, coming from the north and east. As Quevedo and his men ascended the mountain, Fidel realized that here, at last, was a chance to pick them off, one by one. He sent for Celia on July 8 and they rendezvoused at the rebel army's military academy in Minas del Frio. She stayed with him during the following month as he directed battles, she in a role akin to that of handmaiden to Mars. On July 10, they had reached the slopes above Quevedo's soldiers, who'd established an enemy position at El Jigue; here, Fidel decided to establish a command post to battle Quevedo. Celia set up his headquarters on the 11th: she found the site, made sure Fidel had a table and chair, a lamp, a first-aid station, food, a safe water supply, cigars, extra pairs of glasses, etc., and was around to greet soldiers when they arrived, give them Fidel's orders, and field their questions. That way, Fidel was free to think, to make plans for the hours ahead. It worked well, mostly because she was so adept at keeping people out of his hair. Commanders have told me that they got into the habit of speaking to her first.

Two days later, on the 13th, she sent a message to Che: "I only had some change . . . and a one-thousand-peso note that someone took to change, and it won't arrive [back] until Tuesday. Everything is quiet here." The tables have turned: it is Celia who sends notes by messenger to Che, and he is the one with the telephone. "Tell Camilo to send us 20 pairs of shoes from the ones Medina purchased. He is the only one there who can give them out and do so exclusively to the troops and the messenger." Che will call the *Comandancia* La Plata, which is being defended, in Fidel's absence, by Camilo Cienfuegos, and discuss the shoes they'll need for the upcoming battle.

By the middle of July, the guerrillas had begun to operate from the advantage of a superior location. "One guerrilla soldier in the mountains is equivalent to ten regular soldiers," Comandante Delio Gómez Ochoa said, trying to teach me guerrilla warfare conceptually. "Why? Because in the mountains, soldiers can't disperse, they have to go in a single line, one after the other. One bullet that hits its target is more dangerous and can cause more disadvantage there." In the heights above El Jigue, the guerrillas knew every inch of the mountain landscape. There, a handful of rebels began to pick off Quevedo's men, one by one, until Fidel and his column were able to cut the company off, isolate them, and keep them from either retreating or being rescued. As the Cuban army moved other companies in—landed them on the beach and sent them up the mountain to rescue Quevedo—it, too, suffered the same fate. They were cut off. The paths up the mountain were narrow and the rebels were so well hidden that they could shoot at Batista's soldiers from above and below the paths. On July 18, the army tried to come to Quevedo's aid approaching from the opposite side of the mountain. A battalion composed of veteran troops made a forced drive from Estrada Palma. But this battalion was stopped by Che, who defended the Las Vegas side with several rebel army platoons that he would move very rapidly from one place to another. He'd have them strike in one spot, then another, back and forth through the valley. Che held the rebel army's line. On the 19th, with change for the 1,000-peso note, Celia wrote: "Che: I am sending you $500 [pesos]. Last night we received the *malanga* [root vegetable] and it suited us perfectly. Irene is going to Manzanillo tomorrow in case you want to send something. I'm ordering cigars, pipe tobacco and other stuff for you and Fidel." And though Che is commanding several platoons, and Batista's soldiers are breathing down his neck, she tells him: "Olga Mompié's husband wants to go to town for his wife's operation. I'm sending him to consult with you first." In the end, Che halted the Cuban army's attempt to ascend the northwestern face of the mountain, saved the *Comandancia* La Plata, and presumably gave his best medical advice to Mr. Mompié.

"FIDEL TOLD US, WE DON'T HAVE TO KILL any soldiers." Ochoa emphasized this point as he lectured. "What we have to do is injure enemy soldiers. An enemy soldier who is injured has to be taken out of battle. They have to carry him in retreat. They have to use four men for each injured soldier, so you should ambush them from behind. They start screaming and this demoralizes the rest of their troops." Then he asked if I knew why it is better to have five prisoners than one enemy dead. "Why? Because it generates more weapons," he answered himself. And how? "You shoot for the legs." They had done this as Quevedo's soldiers climbed up the steep paths. "Of course, an injured soldier is out of combat, and the first thing he does is leave his weapon behind. He starts screaming, 'Don't leave me behind!' The others go to him, and it is then that the guerrillas come out of the trees and capture all of them."

Quevedo's troops waited, trapped and isolated, for help to arrive. Planes dropped food, water, and medical supplies, but as soon as a helicopter dropped the packages, the guerrillas—hiding among trees—stole them. The army landed more replacement companies, but their fate was no better. The rebels just took more prisoners. In the end, they had hundreds.

Quevedo explained his side of the story as we sipped tall glasses of cold water and drank tiny cups of black coffee one afternoon in 2000, in his house in the Nuevo Vedado section of Havana. Batista's former officer wanted to make it clear that he came from a military family, that his father had been in the army, but mostly wanted to point out that when he knew he'd been defeated, his military heritage had made him reluctant to surrender. Surrender was too contrary to his upbringing. In addition, he felt he had "owed the rescue unit the right to do their part." Therefore, he waited, cut off, without food or water. "But so did Fidel," he softly pointed out.

"Fidel's strategy," Ochoa explained, "was to wait and collect prisoners." In the course of picking off Quevedo's men, the rebels took over two hundred prisoners within a week. They had no place for them, so they created a holding area, called it a jail, and gave it the name Porta Malanga.

"Fidel waited until he knew that we could hold out no longer," Quevedo stated, and began giving statistics for how long a man can survive without food, without water. Both he and Fidel knew when the time had come for surrender. Using one of Quevedo's captured soldiers as a messenger, Fidel had sent a letter asking for surrender. He'd also sent along some food (or maybe Celia did this) and a pair of horses. Quevedo said he ate the food "for strength to travel," but, because he had not eaten in such a long time, had vomited. Feeling "very weak," he had to rest "until I could get up enough strength to mount the horse and travel to make the surrender."

He and his aide set off. When they reached the rebel army, a battle was in progress: "Aircraft were bombing overhead," and he had been surprised to see a woman standing beside Fidel— not because he hadn't heard about Celia Sánchez, he assured me, because "every army officer knew about Celia Sánchez." Rather, it had been her ease in those surroundings, and the calm she showed that dumbfounded him. He claims that a bomb fell nearby and she took no notice. He and his aide-de-camp accompanied Celia and Fidel to a cave, where they discussed the surrender. As they walked, he was struck again by how utterly unfazed she was by the noise and danger.

Quevedo admittedly was rattled: not so much by the surrender (he says that he had resigned himself), but by the way Fidel was handling it. Fidel acted as if they were friends. This made Quevedo ashamed. He had taken law classes at the University of Havana in a special program for army officers (they worked from a reading list, with no lectures) on Saturday mornings. Each officer/student met with a teaching assistant to discuss the articles they'd read during the week. Quevedo's teaching assistant had been Fidel Castro. Just as he was trying desperately to come to grips with surrender, Fidel was now asking him if he remembered their classes together. This is what flustered Quevedo most: "No one asks a question like that," he snapped. He told me that his first reaction had been that Fidel was crazy. This chattiness had come at "the worst moment in my life," when he was weak, sick, dehydrated, and emotionally devastated. But it had only been an opening, he admits, so that Fidel could take the opportunity to turn on his full personality. Quevedo had been defeated first; then humiliated by charm. But his story wasn't over.

After the official surrender, on the morning of July 21, 1958, the four of them, Celia, Fidel, Quevedo, and his aide, walked toward the *Comandancia* La Plata. Quevedo would be held prisoner there. They were taking the same path that Fidel had described to Pedro Miret, and they soon came to a place where the path forked. When Quevedo came to this part of the story, he sat back in his chair and stroked his chin, and his whole face relaxed into a wide, contented smile. Retired now, Quevedo has served Fidel's government since the rebels came into power, primarily as military attaché for the Soviet Union. Every reason for his faithful service seemed—at least metaphorically—to spring from this moment that he was about to describe. When they came to a fork in the path, Fidel asked Quevedo if he wanted to visit his men—the soldiers the rebels had captured that were being held at

Porta Malanga. And Quevedo had answered yes, he would like to do that. Fidel had sent him unguarded, accompanied only by his own aide, along one of those paths, while he and Celia took the other. Fidel let him keep his pistol, which simply follows military etiquette, but Quevedo thinks that, in this situation, it had been "a great kindness," for it had allowed him to arrive at Porta Malanga with dignity, a commanding officer, unguarded and still armed. He had been able to stand before his men with self-respect, "like a gentleman."

Celia and Fidel took the path that led them home, to the *Comandancia*, triumphant. What they'd feared might be lost was now safe: Radio Rebelde, the hospital, their house, the various administrative buildings, and their land-mine and grenade factory had all survived intact. They didn't stay at the *Comandancia* for long; Celia accompanied Fidel during negotiations that took place between Batista's army, the rebel army, and the Red Cross on July 23 and 24, when she, Fidel, and Che went up in one of the army's helicopters to verify the large number of prisoners they'd captured (which had grown to over 400) at Porta Malanga. The three rebel commanders witnessed the Red Cross making the exchange of prisoners in return for medicine. The Battle of El Jigue, and this exchange, is considered to be a turning point in the Revolution. They moved on. Celia soon set up another command post for Fidel, this time at González's sawmill.

From the sawmill command post, she describes to Che what is going on: "Fidel says that there have been some things that have been like scenes from a movie; for example, Duque [de Estrada] got lost last night with five men and ended up at one of the patrols thinking they were rebels, and the [army] soldiers thought they were soldiers. They even talked to each other; when Duque realized this, he was about to cock his machine gun when the guards jumped on him. He was in body-to-body combat downhill for more than ten minutes. He had been given up for dead [by us], but last night he appeared with a blow to the head and all mangled." She wrote this on Monday night, July 28, at 10:30 p.m. In a few days she would take part in the Battle of Las Mercedes in the first week of August.

The tide had turned. She continues to explain this to Che: "Fidel says that it has been a titanic effort to destroy Mosquera's full battalion, which struggled desperately to save itself, leaving dead along the way. Today they got support from a reinforcement battalion on the outside, and cut through our siege at Providencia, fleeing in all directions. Mosquera had been evacuated by helicopter a little while before; the fighting has continued during the day."

She probably wrote this letter while waiting for Fidel to finish his plans. Most likely, he sat at a table with an oil lamp, smoking a cigar, while she wrote her letter to Che, a cigarette and a tiny glass or gourd of coffee at hand, holding a pen and describing their news. Then, when Fidel had decided what Che's orders will be, she begins another paragraph. "[Fidel says:] Tell Che that we are going to surround, from the lower side, the troops that will advance from Arroyones and Las Mercedes toward Las Vegas, and, if possible, cut them from exiting in San Lorenzo. I cannot give you a full report of our losses because I am waiting [for] news from [Ramon] Paz who was located beyond Providencia, and who might have had a fierce struggle with the reinforcement. We've only had one dead and several wounded. We've taken weapons, bullets, mortars, etc.; [Batista's commanding officer] Mosquera's men burned many of their dead's rifles."

The "one dead" was still too painful to mention by name. It had been Daniel, Rene Ramos Latour, Frank's apostle.

After the Battle of Las Mercedes, which took place during the first week of August, Celia and Fidel returned to the *Comandancia* La Plata. Their prisoner, Quevedo, lived there for the next four months, and he told me that Fidel never spoke directly to him again, for the rest of the war. He'd send messages through Celia once or twice about military matters. She visited Quevado occasionally, and always made sure he had a box of *habanos*, fine export cigars, befitting an officer and a gentleman.

26.

The House that Celia Built

EXCEPT FOR A FEW BREAKS to go into battle, Fidel and Celia stayed at the *Comandancia* from late July to November 1958. They lived in the third and final house, the only one that Celia completely designed and furnished. It is simple, quite beautiful, and you can see her hand in every detail.

The military complex, which covered a square kilometer, was always being changed. They constructed new buildings and moved the old ones to more secure locations. The Cuban army still didn't know the exact location of the *Comandancia*, yet knew, generally, where it was, and every day around 10:00 a.m., B-26s flew in from Guantánamo and dropped bombs. They'd start with a meadow that lay above the Medina family's house, then they'd fly eastward toward Pico Turquino. The bombs never actually touched the *Comandancia* because planes could not fly that close to the side of the mountain, but constant air activity meant that the rebels couldn't cook—and there were a lot of people to feed—without making sure that smoke would not escape above the trees. Ochoa says Celia counteracted this by giving out big protein pills she'd purchased from U.S. army surplus. After a while, they figured out the Cuban army's bombing pattern and learned to live with it.

Since the Cuban army's best bet for finding Fidel's headquarters was to get someone into it, there were always spies. Some visitors just showed up; others had proper clearance but weren't who they claimed to be. Once, a so-called journalist arrived (described as a Cuban who was a U.S. air force veteran), and Fidel spotted him right away, knew he was there to spy. As soon as this person left, Fidel ordered the *Comandancia* "transformed." Several people recall this incident because they actually moved a couple of buildings. But what sticks in everybody's memory is a stand of trees they dug up and replanted on another part of the mountain. This clump of trees had always functioned as a guiding landmark, and they moved every one of those trees to another spot. The rebels were rewarded for their effort, because the next time bombers came in, they blasted the trees out of existence.

I WAS GIVEN PERMISSION TO VISIT the *Comandancia* in 2003, after three years' repeated requests to the Council of State. In the interim, I kept trying to persuade prominent Cubans to speak on my behalf and did not give up, since every soldier I had interviewed from Column 1 spoke about the place in the most nostalgic manner. Architects Dolly Gómez and Mario Girona explained that it wasn't necessarily the buildings the soldiers had been praising, it was the site, particularly the landscaping. Gómez said, "Celia was a great fan of the land. It was how she planted flowers at La Plata that you must see. That is how you will get to understand her." When permission came, a letter arrived stating that I'd be escorted by the curator of the property, who would meet me in Manzanillo. Pedro Álvarez Tabío, director at the Council of State's Office of Historical Affairs, inquired if I would need a mule to travel up the mountain. He explained that he'd need to book the mule in advance, as mules were not always available. I thought, if those *clandestinos* from Havana could walk up the side of that mountain, so could I, a New Yorker.

I had invited a friend along, and we met at the airport in Havana. By the time we left the city, the sun was setting, and it took us some time to find the right exit. We got lost on the belt road; there were absolutely no signs other than the ones that proclaimed "*Victoria o Muerte*"—Victory or Death. We could tell which were major roads by the intersections: people were standing by these, waiting for a lift on a bus, a truck, or a car. Eventually we found our way to Santa Clara, but it was pitch dark and raining heavily by the time we arrived, too late to get food at the hotel, El Caney, which replicates an Indian village and was one of Celia's projects. The next day, we drove on a Soviet-era highway, with two lanes in each direction until it came to an abrupt halt: the end of the Soviet Union had materialized before us in a single lane. They came, they built, and when there was no more Soviet Union, there was no more road—an amazing image. A makeshift detour led to the old, American-built, east-west, two-lane Central Highway. By midafternoon, we were in Manzanillo.

Felix Zamora is responsible for the maintenance and well-being of the landmark. He met us in Cespedes Park that June afternoon and we made plans to meet the following day. He arrived in a jeep around 5:30 a.m. The hotel, built by the Revolution in the 1960s, is located on a steep hillside in the old Barrio d'Oro section of town and has a variety of Cuba's native snakes—made of painted cement—artfully placed under the hotel's raised foundation. We were soon into rice growers' country, drove past La Rosalia, the farm that hid the *marabuzaleros*, and continued toward the mountains. Zamora, in his forties, is a member of the new generation that works for the Revolution (that is, the government). We picked up Erasmo Olivera, who took part in the Revolutionary War and has been designated as the *Comandancia*'s official guide. Soon, we were on the lower slope of Pico Caracas traveling on a road constructed by the rebel army after the 1959 victory. As we climbed upward the roadbed became deeply grooved; an ordinary car could not navigate this part of the route. At one point, the corkscrew curves became so vertical that all the passengers had to get out and walk. And then, out of the mist, from around a tight curve, a mule train appeared. Big reddish animals, whose bloodlines traced back to Celia's mule teams. The road ran out, and the old Russian jeep (a Volga, I think, with two shift levers, one restrained by a leather belt) could go no farther; Zamora parked. We followed a rocky road for a bit then started up a so-called path. Erasmo apologized for being able to see the path and commented that it hadn't been like this—meaning so visible—during the war. He grumbled that the path had grown too wide, was too obvious. But it seemed invisible to me, partly because I had to concentrate on each step I was taking, in places gingerly placing my weight on one wobbly rock, then another.

Starting in April 1958, Celia built a house for herself and Fidel. It was Fidel's command headquarters and the heart and soul of the *Comandancia La Plata* military complex. During the war, the ledge, where they stand, was something akin to a miniature public square where Fidel issued orders to his soldiers and met visitors. In this photograph, Fidel works at a small table while Juan Almeida, standing, awaits orders. Another guerrilla, Manuel Fajardo perhaps, sits in Fidel's willow chair and reads a newspaper. Quietly standing guard is Universo Sánchez, at the corner near Celia's balcony, which begins beyond the open window in the side wall. Photograph by Andrew St. George. *(Courtesy of Oficina de Asuntos Históricos)*

Eventually, we arrived at the Medina house and sat on a porch while two members of the new generation (also musicians) sat with us as their mother made coffee. She began by grinding the roasted beans with a wooden pestle, pointing out the tree that produced the beans. At the time, I didn't know that we'd reached the official entrance to the *Comandancia*. Zamora stayed there, handing my friend and myself over to Erasmo Olivera, who led us the rest of the way. It was at least another hour's climb before we came to the open field that marks the entrance.

In 1958, by November, there were sixteen buildings. The rebels kept constructing as the war progressed. We visited the hospital first, since it was the nearest, almost invisible as it wraps around the mountainside, in various states of decay. Since my visit, several hurricanes have struck this part of Cuba. That day, the beams were strong enough that we could walk through the hospital's rooms; marvel at the size; gaze at a few medicine bottles on cobwebby shelves. From the hospital, we began another steep climb, but suddenly I recognized stairs with banisters, saw hibiscus plants, grown leggy over all these years. The house where Celia and Fidel lived comes into view unexpectedly, and lies below the path. It is wedged against the side of the mountain. The site alone is wonderful: perched on a precipitous ledge, a simple house with a roof made of palm branches, near a gentle waterfall, like a poet's house in an ancient Chinese painting.

During the war, the ledge was something akin to a miniature public square. It is just large enough to hold a couple of benches and a small group of people. Here Fidel would meet his visitors. He would take a table and chair out to the rock slab. Only one room is completely visible from the ledge, and only when both doors are open. After opening these, Erasmo got busy propping open windows up with sticks. That main room, which you see from the ledge, is furnished with the same furniture it had then: a table with two benches, a tall cupboard that served as a bookshelf and writing desk. There is a photograph of Fidel seated in front of this cupboard, its shelves decorated along the edges with gingham-checked paper and holding snapshots of his son. Everything about it shows a woman's touch. The room also holds a big gasoline-fueled refrigerator with bullet holes in its door. Zamora said that the refrigerator was strafed by an airplane as mules hauled it up the mountain. Walk through this room, and you'll come to Celia's private room, or enclosed balcony, which is completely out of view from the ledge. The outer walls are covered by latticework—each strip of cedar sanded smooth and carefully joined together by a boat builder Celia brought from Pilón. A ladder drops to the ground and the path that leads to the waterfall. Erasmo showed me a trapdoor in the floor and lifted the lid so that we looked down into a vault where she stored the documents, the letters she collected to make a future archive. Then he pointed to a rack on the wall that still held a set of glasses, each one thick and small, and told me that Celia used these glasses for coffee. He said that this is where she brought guests; and I noticed several nicely curved corner shelves. The view from Celia's balcony looks directly onto the tops of palm trees growing far below on the steep side of the mountain. She could descend the ladder, step onto the path, and walk to the waterfall. Or she could climb down to enter a room directly below that is a bath house: spacious, cedar-paneled, with a tall ceiling. It felt fresh and light and clean, the wooden bucket sat on a shelf, ready to be filled or refilled. It felt as if the house's old inhabitants had been there recently.

Fidel's room is completely out of view. It is located in the part of the building that hugs the mountain; where windows, along one side, open into the tops of trees and sun bounces off shiny, bright-green palm fronds. Two chairs, crafted from willow branches—a big one for Fidel, a small one for Ceila—are stored here. They'd traveled wherever their masters went: on the balcony, out on the ledge, down to the waterfall. The rest of the space in this room is taken up by a big double bed.

This was the first presidential palace of a government that had not yet established itself. In the spring of 1958, when the house was built, the rebels had no way of knowing that the war would be over within a year. They thought it possible that the Sierra Maestra Free Zone would become a separate government, a virtual island cut off from the mainland, and that it might be in existence for several years, with the *Comandancia* La Plata as its capital and this tiny building its presidential palace. Erasmo asked if I wanted to go up to the mountain house used by Radio Rebelde, but I chose to sit by the waterfall instead. It had been their safe water supply, guarded day and night, beautiful and a lifeline.

Later in the day we returned to the Medina house and were reunited with Felix Zamora. We'd made a rapid descent, but we'd stopped at a place in the woods with a few stumps to sit on, their ritual resting place, where the two men responsible for the landmark, that is so close to the heart of Fidel, began to reminisce. Zamora commented that Fidel hadn't been there in some time. Ten years, he calculated, looking at Erasmo, who didn't contradict him. I saw them smile. Memories were washing up, as the two men recalled Fidel's last visit. Finally Zamora broke the silence and declared, "Good. It's a good thing. Whenever he comes, he gets far too emotional." They both laughed, and with that, we got up and continued our way down the mountain.

But I knew I was missing something. "Look at the plantings," Dolly Gómez had told me. It was the landscaping that had made the place sensational. I'd spoken with Otto Hernández, a former combatant and the official geographer at the Office of Historical Affairs, who pointed out: "During the war, while planes were bombing, you could walk into this place and be served coffee . . . Celia had her own special storage box with tobacco, cognac, wine, special food for visitors, only for visitors. But all the same, they were shocked by all these things. Planes overhead, and they were being offered a glass of wine. Celia knew it was politically important that those visitors feel the power of the installation. To see a refrigerator. To know that Fidel slept on a good bed. She was thinking about comfort all the time. She would write to Havana and ask them to send her this, and this, and this, anything to make the *Comandancia* comfortable; and to display that comfort." When I spoke of orchids she'd cultivated there, Otto simply said: "It's easy to have orchids in the mountains. But Celia had the feminine touch."

"The whole idea of La Plata was Celia's," Hernández continued. "She knew the area, she knew the region . . . Celia's father was interested in geographical issues: the land, the Indian settlers, the last Mambisas. Manuel had taught her how to love that type of life, living among trees, camping out. Manuel had loved nature. And she was very cultured. Many women become guerrillas, but only Celia knew how to make life better there. She knew the pleasure of living well, in camp, in war. Only Celia could create something like this."

A film was shot at the *Comandancia* about a decade after Celia's death. Hernández let me discover the final piece of the puzzle in this video. She had planted coleus along the long walkways. Each leaf shouted out for attention, from pink to deep purple to fire-engine red, and each plant glowed in that hot tropical light. I knew that coleus thrives well in shade, grows easily under trees, and grows quickly from cuttings. Like her soldiers in the *marabu* grove, planes couldn't see these plants. They were blocked by the tree canopy. Celia had sent out a message that she planted cuttings, Hernández says, and women from all over Cuba sent them to her. There were hundreds, planted in straight rows. "It was all very military," Hernández added, and he reminded me that she was

Ricardo Martínez, right, often confided in Celia. Before arriving in the mountains, he'd been a radio announcer in Havana, but was almost caught working for the 26th of July Movement underground. At the *Comandancia La Plata*, he was a member of small but highly successful guerrilla broadcasting team, Radio Rebelde. On the left is Luis Orlando Rodríguez, director of Radio Rebelde, and in the center, Orestes Valera, also an announcer. *(Courtesy of Oficina de Asuntos Históricos)*

appealing to people who knew military history, and that long lines of red flowers are in keeping with a proper military installation.

THE FIRST HOUSE FIDEL BUILT, in early April, stood near that original clump of trees. Celia had instantly seen that it lacked even basic security and took matters into her own hands, organized the construction of house number 2, and moved Fidel's bodyguards into the first house while the new one was being constructed. (Later, she would put members of the press in that vulnerable building.) The third house is the gem. It was constructed with the help of the boat builder from Pilón. She'd brought him in to do the job in May, and he helped her design the small building. He built it while she was overseeing the digging of trenches in Las Vegas and setting up warehouses around Mompié.

Nighttime was best for a really determined person to slip into their military area, so at night no lights were used, and no one spoke. Delio Ochoa says they got through the night "by not saying a word," and listening to the forest around them. He and Ricardo Martínez both explained that, from the beginning, members of

Column 1 spoke in very low tones even in the daytime, and only called out when there was a real calamity.

The army's offensive finished on August 6, when Lt. Col. Fernando Neugart formally made the army's concession: "You may have the mountains, but we are waiting for you in the valleys," records historian Paul J. Dosal, who gives a vivid account of the meeting between Neugart and Fidel Castro. What I can add is information on the location: the two days of negotiations Dosal said took place "at Fidel's headquarters" was not at his and Celia's headquarters (the third house). They rarely allowed outsiders near the headquarters or needed to, because the guerrillas had the use of two farmers' houses. Both were on the edge of the *Comandancia* complex, yet both were called Fidel's headquarters. The Medina house is referred to as the first point of entrance, but there was a large house, farther west on the mountain's slope, belonging to a rancher, known as the second point of entrance, or the Santa Claritan's house. Most important meetings with outsiders took place at this large bungalow; the cease-fire negotiations with Neugart and the land reform laws were signed here after the war. Even after the war, Fidel protected details concerning the *Comandancia* La Plata from common knowledge, and only very special visitors or members of Column 1 would go there.

BETO PESANT WAS KILLED IN ACTION on August 8. He'd been at Celia's side during the nerve-racking days as they waited for the *Granma* to arrive; he'd steered her home, to Manzanillo, after she escaped from La Rosa, the bar in Campechuela. Celia's only consolation must have been that he had lived long enough to see the Cuban army retreat from the mountains.

On August 13, Fidel celebrated his thirty-second birthday, and Celia threw an elaborate surprise party for him in the intense heat and humidity of a Cuban tropical summer. On a mountain in the middle of nowhere, she served him pieces of ice-cream cake delivered by one of the members of the 26th of July members from Manzanillo, packed in dry ice. This cake symbolizes Celia's way of bringing spirit to a military life. Like Mariana Grajales, the mother of Antonio Maceo, who managed the field camps during Cuba's guerrilla War of Independence, Celia was carrying on a Cuban tradition of women who went to war, and was adding her own footnotes to that history. She enjoyed doing things in style, but more than this she was making a point: the head of state, in the newly formed Capital of the Insurrection, was celebrating an official birthday, and she thought it imperative to mark the occasion suitably. It isn't too hard to imagine the pleasure this brought Fidel.

RICARDO MARTÍNEZ PROVIDED a personal story about Celia at the *Comandancia*. He had been grateful to be alive and out of Havana, but nonetheless was terribly homesick for his wife and daughter. He often spoke to Celia of his longing, and had specifically lamented at not being able to see his daughter grow. One day a courier arrived on horseback with an amazing message: his child was going to be on a television program that night, Faustino Perez's child as well. The woman messenger told him that the program started at 7:00 p.m. "I was excited and went to find Celia. She smiled, but in a way that makes me think she was behind all this. I asked her, but she wouldn't say." She and Fidel had a little television set in their house. "Tell Fidel that I need it," and she told him he wouldn't be able to get the channel featuring his daughter and he should take the TV set up to the mountain house: "Don't worry. Take it. Go now. Get it set up there and I'm sure you'll be able to see the show." At seven everybody was there, and Celia was in the front row. "We all ended up crying. Even Celia. The host knew what was going on. He was from the 26th. He told my daughter and Faustino's: 'Give your Daddy a kiss. He's in Miami.' "

Mariana Grajales

CAMILO CIENFUEGOS LEFT THE MOUNTAINS and headed west with his "Antonio Maceo" Column on August 21, and ten days later Che Guevara followed. Che's column was fighting in the name of Ciro Redondo, one of the *Granma* veterans who had died in battle at Mar Verde on November 29, 1957. It was up to Camilo and Che to take the war outside the Sierra, to the plains, to meet Batista's forces head on, and to cut the island in two—as Antonio Maceo had done in 1896—ensuring that the 26th of July would control the entire eastern side of the country. Fidel, Camilo, and Che would take on the western side. The old guard will tell you that Fidel let Raúl and Almeida (commanders of his second and third fronts in the Sierra) do whatever they liked, gave them his full trust, accepted (agreed to admire) whatever they did. During the preparations for the offensive, Camilo was at headquarters where he and Fidel talked all the time, every day; Fidel, at the same time, wrote to Che every day, because they—Che and Camilo—were his eyes and ears and anticipated everything. Now they were leaving him behind.

Celia sent a letter to her youngest sisters, Acacia and Griselda, on August 17, carried by Lydia Doce: "I began this letter one day during the combat at Arroyones, when the troops at Las Vegas surrendered." That would have been on June 20, four days before their father died. "I started it in a bomb shelter, things got complicated, and I couldn't continue because there were endless things that had to be done." It had taken Celia nearly two months to write because this meant coming to grips with her father's death. "I haven't written to you since April, Acacia. Only to Papa. During that time I got your letter about Papa's illness, which paralyzed me completely." She is forthright: "I was very cowardly and didn't have the courage to write to you." Then she repeats her old mantra that she used for the deaths of her Uncle Miguel, for Chibas, and for Frank: "What could I have said, what could I have done, and what consolation could I have given you if it was such a great pain for all of us?" She admits that she'd wanted him to die quickly when she thought about the pain, "even if I never saw him again, that wasn't important anymore," and is full of denial: "I was confused when I was told that he was better, that he was in the clinic," then vents her anger: "You didn't write, no one from there wrote me a line" she continues imperiously, "I still doubt all of you, although it absolutely doesn't really matter to me what anybody thinks." She doesn't understand how confusing and overwhelming she can be for her younger sisters, who only wanted to emulate their superhero sister. They, too, worked for the movement. Celia barely manages to soften her tone, but finally assures them that she knew they would "behave well and do the right thing," that her father wouldn't have lacked anything, and mentions, "I received a very long letter from Silvia, and I was grateful for all the details. It allowed me to live through those moments that I wanted so much to know about."

Luis Mas Martín, editor of the Communist newspaper *HOY* visited the *Comandancia* in the middle of August (almost family, he was about to marry Inez Girona). He reported that so many people were traveling up there that the foot traffic impeded the mule trains bringing up supplies. The *Comandancia* was crowded with outsiders. Everybody wanted to see Fidel. Some wanted to join the war; others—farmers, Fidel's commanders—went to La Plata to ask for things they needed; politicians came to plan the future; journalists wanted a good story. Celia channeled these emissaries much the same way she had scheduled her father's patients. She decided who had precedence and set the parameters so they wouldn't overwhelm Fidel. As more and more people arrived, she became alarmed at the situation, at Fidel's vulnerability with Che, Camilo, and their well-seasoned soldiers gone. The command headquarters really wasn't protected, and she pressed the issue. Instead of being disconcerted by the problem, Fidel became energized solving it. His commanders always like to say he leaned on history—and, evoking the memory of Mariana Grajales, he formed an all-women's combat unit. Ricardo Martínez bluntly observes, "I, for one, didn't like it. In those times, there was a lot of machismo, and it was not understood that women could do those things." On the 3rd or 4th of September 1958, if Martínez recalls rightly, Fidel said: "I know what I'm about to suggest the majority of you are not going to like or agree with," and told them to assemble the next night. Everyone gathered at the hospital. Fidel, inspired by adversity, became even more enthusiastic as some of the men argued against the unit. "There were still a few men without weapons," Martínez explained, who "argued that they had priority." The women spoke for themselves; most had carried out extremely dangerous actions, more so than most of the men present, so the debate came down to the weapons. Fidel ignored the men's arguments, and a women's unit was established.

28. September 1958

Lydia and Clodomira

BEFORE CHE LEFT, he told Lydia to get in touch with him as soon as he reached Las Villas. As he explained, she was going to be his primary means of communicating with Fidel at the *Comandancia*. He wanted her to go ahead of him to Havana, to set things up before he got there. The Office of Historical Affairs collected information about Lydia Doce and Clodomira Acosta well into the 1970s, and I have taken most of this account from OHA compiled reports.

Soon after speaking with Che (who left the mountains on August 21), Lydia made her way to Havana. She went to the house of her brother-in-law, Carlos Parra, and was there on September 5, when 26th of July Movement action groups staged a protest against the government by stealing the Virgin of Regla statue. The black-skinned Madonna, with a white baby Jesus in her arms, is housed in one of Havana's oldest churches. The protest was meant to humiliate the much-loathed chief of police, Estéban Ventura, who accompanied the statue in the annual festival-day parade and liked to think of himself as the Virgin's protector. After stealing the statue, the action group hid it in a bodega located across the street from where Lydia was staying, at 3 Villalobos. That is how she heard about it. The festival took place on September 8 with a substitute statue Ventura purchased from La Nueva Venecia (a store on Neptune between Gervasio and Escobar, which is still there), although he had widely announced that the old statue had been found. But the people of Regla, who regularly prayed before the Virgin and left her offerings, knew he was lying. They, too, asked far and wide what good are police if they can't protect our beloved Virgin of Regla?

Lydia thought it important to find a better place to hide the statue than the bodega, although she was supposed to stay out of this sort of thing. Her position as an executive courier precluded her engaging in street activities of any kind, and much less with the Havana underground. But she helped Celia's younger sister, Griselda, organize the removal to the statue from the bodega in broad daylight to the small, ancient church in central Havana known as the Caridad. Lydia Doce, Amado del Valle, Victor Tejedor, and Sergeant Blanco—who was actually in Batista's army—were in the first car, with the statue; Griselda drove the second car with Ismael Suarez beside her in the passenger seat. On Pepe Antonio, the two-car caravan caught the eye of a policeman standing on a corner, so Lydia yelled: "*Que paso mulatto, buena gente?*" (What's up, mulatto, you sweet guy?*)* to distract him. When they got to the church, a patrol car came alongside Griselda and Ismael's car. Father Boza Masvidal (who later left Cuba) realized they were being followed and signaled them to go inside the church. Griselda posed as a Catholic whose Protestant husband wouldn't let her wear a Caridad medal, but who nevertheless wanted to give thanks, having survived an operation. The police listened to some of this and left. Griselda was quite frightened because the lead car, carrying Lydia and the statue, was nowhere in sight. But Lydia had noticed two people doing an elaborate pantomime of taking down their license plate number and knew she was being warned that informers were around. They'd taken the statue to the Marinao section of town (to the house of Victor Tejedor, one of the people in the car), a densely inhabited pro-Batista neighborhood. At midnight, they moved the statue into the house where it remained until Tejedor's family refused to keep it any longer. Then a mechanic took it to Rancho Boyeros, where it stayed until the 26th of July Movement arranged a return.

On Lydia's last day in Havana, September 11, she followed departure protocol. She went to Delio Gómez Ochoa, Fidel's representative in the capital, to report what she'd accomplished.

She told him how she planned to return to the Sierra Maestra and he had her picked up and taken her to the movement's treasurer,who gave her $50 for the trip back. At noon, she met several women (Ernestina Otero, Eneida Diaz, and Griselda Sánchez) at the 5 & 10 cent store at 23rd and 12th, where Humberto Sori Martín's wife waited for them (probably with a letter for Sori). Ernestina Otero and Lydia went shopping; they went to El Encanto, the famous department store in central Havana, then decided to have lunch at a 5 & 10 across the street. Lydia told Ernestina that she was famished, and proceeded to order soup, an entrée, and dessert. The waitress brought everything to the table at once, including a Lolita cup made with two little custard flans side by side, topped with small scoops of ice cream—Havana's reference to Nabokov.

As soon as Lydia started the meal, she began to sob. Nudging her, Ernestina said, "Didn't you say you were dying of hunger?" and she replied that "my people" in the Sierra have hardly anything to eat, "how selfish of me," as tears ran down her cheeks. Finally, they left with Lydia's food largely untouched, as the waitress commented, "That woman is crazy." Ernestina took her to get her hair color changed on Concordia, then to an apartment at 27th and O, in Vedado, where Griselda and a 26th member, Reinaldo Cruz, kept her company until seven that evening. They drove her back to Carlos Parra's house, and to Lydia's delight, she found Clodomira Acosta sitting in the living room when she arrived. They hugged each other, caught up on news for the next couple of hours while Griselda and Reinaldo listened. Griselda left, reminding Lydia they'd meet the next morning at nine.

At eleven, Lydia had an anxiety attack and said she couldn't spend the night in her brother-in-law's house. She was too afraid. She wanted to go to 451 Rita, the address of a 26th of July safe house in a nearby Juanello neighborhood. Reinaldo Cruz (who had stayed to guard her) called Gustavo Mas, who informed him that the house on Rita was off-limits. It wasn't safe, and no one could use it, on movement orders. Finally, they settled on going to a bar called the Catacombs, on Virgen del Camino, where they could hang out for the rest of the night.

El Joyero (The Jeweler), a well-known police informer, was assassinated that night and police started arresting anyone they could. Soon Lydia, Clodomira, Reinaldo Cruz, and Alberto Álvarez left the bar, frightened by the police activity. They went to 451 Rita just before dawn. Two boys (Onelio Dampier and Leonardo Valdes), on the run, showed up there and Lydia and the others let them in. It was a bad move; in the next hours—it was now September 12—Ventura's men arrested José Antonio Pinon, called "Popeye," who, under torture, gave them information including the address of this house. The police took him back to Rita, where Reinaldo Cruz recognized Popeye's voice, opened the door, and was killed immediately by rounds from a machine gun. Everybody in the apartment was armed. They killed four policemen. Lydia got hit with a bullet in one buttock, and Clodomira alone came out unharmed. Reinaldo, Alberto, and the two boys were killed. The two women were taken to the 14th Precinct police station in Juanelo and kept there for the rest of the day.

Lydia could barely stand, and one of the police gave her a shove where she'd received the bullet but she didn't cry out. Infuriated, he picked up his club and hit her in the back of the neck, knocking her unconscious. Clodomira turned on the police, biting, punching, and scratching the policeman who'd hit Lydia. Both women were taken to the La Chorrera 9th Precinct, located near a fifteenth-century tower and the sea wall.

The rest of this account was given by one of Ventura's policemen, called Carratala, who was interviewed in his cell in La Cabaña Fortress after the January 1959 victory. Carratala stated that Ventura, chief of police, admitted that his "boys had gone a little too far" and recalled that Clodo had bitten him on the shoulder (the report states that he showed his scar to the interviewer). "She was a real beast, that one." He then described how Lydia and Clodomira were placed in bags by 9th Precinct policemen who then filled these bags with sand, lowered them into the sea near La Chorrera and would then pull them out again. The third time Lydia was submerged she died; they gave Clodomira a *coup de grâce*. Then their bodies were thrown into the sea.

This account was verified later, with only slightly different details, by one of the prisoners captured at the Bay of Pigs. A former member of the police (Calvino) said that Laurent, in charge of the precinct, had tried to get information from the women that "the others had not" by taking them in a boat offshore, where they were put in sacks into which sand was poured; and that Laurent had them dunked in the water and brought up again. Lydia, "whose eyes were almost out of their sockets," had died right away but the "younger and tougher" one had resisted.

When Lydia didn't show up the next morning at the meeting spot, Griselda immediately got in touch with Monsignor Raúl del Valle, secretary to the Cardinal of Havana. He made arrangements for Griselda's M-26 partner, Ismael Suarez, to go to the morgue, where he found Reinaldo Cruz's body. He counted the number of bullet holes in his body—52 from the waist up—saw the bodies of the other three men, noticed that their hair was standing straight up since the bodies had been pulled by the feet down the stairs of the apartment building and the hair, already stiff with blood, dried upright. Suarez didn't find Lydia or Clodo, so Monsignor de Valle made arrangements for Suarez to go to the cemetery. So many bodies had arrived that morning that some had already been covered, but the grave diggers were able to confirm that no one fit Lydia's or Clodo's description. Other reports say they had been sighted in a police car—which is possible—being given "a macabre tour of the streets," as Che described it, to force them to give up information. Their deaths are usually dated September 17, but if you believe the prisoners, they died as early as September 13, 1958. Over the years, Celia's staff at the Office of Historical Affairs collected evidence. A short biography of Lydia was published in 1974 as a pamphlet, which states that there are many versions of how she and Clodo were murdered and none is certain. The writers of this pamphlet were reluctant to quote—as I have done— anything from the mouths of *batistianos*, particularly policemen, or from a prisoner.

The Triumph

CELIA LEFT THE *COMANDANCIA* with Fidel and did not return there for the rest of the war. Neither seems to have regretted trading paradise for the battlefield. Fidel was about to command his final battle against Batista's forces.

They traveled slowly, stopping at the rebel army's training school in Minas de Bucycito first, and on the 17th were approaching Guisa (inland and to the northeast of Pico Turquino). In that town the army maintained a significant garrison, which the rebels were ready to engage. On the 20th, Celia left Fidel to start receiving and assigning recruits, at a place called Mon Corona Farm. She had gone ahead to set up his field headquarters and chose the hamlet of Santa Barbara, just west of Guisa.

The rebel army had grown enormously in the final months of 1958, and, at Guisa, Fidel deployed two of his all-women squadrons from the Mariana Grajales unit trained at the *Comandancia*. He'd be using five hundred troops, a major force for the rebel army, but they were outnumbered ten to one, and most of them were new to combat. But they had spirit. "The Battle of Guisa was one of those events that proved nothing was impossible for that small army," Fidel said in 2000, when he commemorated the battle's 42nd anniversary. The army's 5,000 well-trained, well-armed soldiers were supported by air power and tanks. But Batista's troops were low on morale.

The Battle of Guisa, a bloody engagement and not easily won, was waged from November 20 to 30.

THE ARMY GARRISON WAS LOCATED right on the main east-west highway. By taking the Guisa garrison, Fidel wanted to demonstrate the vulnerability of the army's headquarters, which was just down that highway, in Bayamo. Fidel's troops didn't attack the garrison directly; they ambushed the army's reinforcements trying to reach it, and did so with small contingents posted along the route. Their most useful point of defense was a hill—not a large nor a high one— with just enough elevation to see Batista's convoys as they came up the road. The rebel army lost and recaptured this hill many times during ten days of battle, but used it to strategic advantage; at one point, so the story goes, every fighter in one of the little rebel bands managed to fire his or her rifle in unison, and they brought down a plane. At the peak of combat, the rebels surrounded an entire enemy battalion loaded into fourteen trucks and protected by two light tanks, simply by attacking from every direction.

"We have a strong line of defense between Bayamo and Guisa," Fidel wrote to Ricardo Martínez (a letter he treasures) who had stayed at the *Comandancia*. "It's like Jiguani, but at the doors of Bayamo. Here, our fight is against tanks; one has been overturned. The veterans aren't with me," he added, referring to former battles when Che, Guillermo García, and Crescencio Perez had been at his flank or elsewhere nearby. Now his most seasoned comrades were leading their own troops, in other parts of the country. "But the troops are behaving well. Cordolun has turned into a lion. He has opened more than 200 trenches. We have picks and shovels all over the place. The people are good. Everybody is anticipating being able to buy something, [because] in Guisa there are many goodies. An embrace for all of you, Fidel Castro." He apparently handed the letter to Celia who closes with "A hug, Celia Sánchez."

At Guisa, Captain Baulio Coroneaux, called "Cordolun," operated the rebels' one and only .50-caliber machine gun, apparently with great effect, until he was killed by a precision shot from a tank. The troops, Fidel noted in 2000, were "children of workers and farmers; most of them could not even read or write. And in their training, they had hardly made any real shots. They

The evening of December 31, 1958, Fidel, Celia, and Pedro Miret sit at a bar in the city of Palma Soriano, waiting to negotiate with the Cuban army and end the war. Celia's stalwart assistant, Felipe Guerra Matos, stands behind her. They watch an admirer who has come to speak to Fidel. *(Courtesy of Oficina de Asuntos Históricos)*

had learned and practiced shooting theoretically." His reminiscence recalls the early 26th of July actions, when Frank País drilled his men for the Battle of Santiago with "no bullets" exercises.

The heaviest fighting came in the last three days, when the army sent in B-26s and F-47s, from bases in Havana and Camaguey, to bomb the area and rescue their battalion. To create a "zone" for the government forces' escape route, the army unleashed thirty hours' air support, showering the rebels with bombs. But the rebel army, in Cordolun's trenches, held out.

To rescue the besieged battalion, in the end, the army was forced to abandon the garrison. The rebels had their victory, and Bayamo lay within their sights.

Celia's two younger sisters, Acacia and Griselda, had traveled to the locale to experience a battle firsthand. Shortly before the intensive bombing started, Griselda, who hated noise, took refuge in a cave outside the city. Celia, even as the battle raged, sent a note to them, remarking that the army was shooting as if it were the end of the world. The Gironas, in Havana, received a postcard from Griselda. She wrote that she was vacationing in lovely Guisa, and: "Wish you were here."

CELIA AND FIDEL THEN TRAVELED EAST. On December 2, 1958, they stopped in Charco Redondo, where Celia set up another field headquarters. The date would have been significant for her: the second anniversary of her escape from the SIM in Campechuela and the bar La Rosa. Now, with several victories behind them, she and Fidel waited for Camilo and Che to conclude their long march across the island, heading for Havana. By December 20, Fidel and Celia had moved onto a sugar estate called "America." They left to spend Christmas with Fidel's oldest brother, Ramon, a farmer who sat out the war, returning to the America sugar mill on the 28th. There they rendezvoused with one of Batista's generals, Eulogio Cantillo, to discuss ways to bring the war to an end. While Fidel and Cantillo talked, Ricardo Martínez says that he and Celia waited in a room filled with sugar-processing machinery. Fidel emerged confident that he and the general had come to an agreement, assured that Batista would remain in Cuba.

On the final day of the year, they drove to Palma Soriano, up in the mountains, and the last town of any size on the way to Santiago. There they learned of Batista's escape. Fidel was furious. They went to the local station (an affiliate of Radio Progresso), from which Fidel broadcast an appeal to all citizens of Cuba, imploring people not to take the law into their own hands. Following the broadcast, he ordered an advance on Santiago. Simultaneously, across the nation, members of the 26th of July Movement, the Revolutionary Directorate, and other anti-Batista groups occupied police stations. At the news that Batista had fled, cheering crowds came out into the streets. Unpopular members of the police and military were assassinated; some were jailed to await trial; others quickly got out of Cuba. Historians consistently remark on the fact that there was little violence.

When Fidel met in a final parley with the army's commanders, Celia took part. On January 1, 1959, at El Escandel, an outpost northeast of Santiago (now within the National Park Gran Piedra), Colonel José Rego Rubido, regimental chief, surrendered Santiago de Cuba and its forces to the rebel army.

On the morning of January 1, 1959, Celia is joined by her sisters, Griselda and Acacia, in Palma Soriano. *(Courtesy of Oficina de Asuntos Históricos)*

No more fighting would be necessary. Fidel and Celia prepared to enter Santiago.

FROM THE FEW PHOTOGRAPHS I've seen, it looks as if there were few in the party that drove down from Palma Soriano to Santiago: the two comandantes, Fidel and Celia, a few bodyguards, Celia's stalwart helper, Felipe Guerra Matos, her sisters Acacia and Griselda, and two radio engineers, packed into a two American cars. Celia donned her 26th of July uniform, rather than the olive green tunic and trousers she usually wore, and a cloth cap, perched on the back of her head so the bill stood up. (The detail makes her easy to find on contact sheets.) She is talking to soldiers in jeeps, most likely telling everybody what they're to do next (and which they receive as orders). In frame after frame, she's surrounded by hundreds of soldiers, all in rebel army uniforms. By nightfall, columns from the entire eastern end of the country came pouring into Santiago. By midnight, most had arrived.

The victorious 26th of July leaders made their way to the balcony of the town hall, on the edge of the old Plaza Cespedes. People crammed the verandah and balconies of the old Hotel Casa

Grande; they filled rooftops, side streets, the steps of the cathedral. Strings of bare bulbs hung around the square, and a pair of klieg lights illuminated Fidel as he prepared to speak—accepting the surrender of Santiago's garrison.

"What greater glory than the love of the people?" he began. "What greater reward than these thousands of waving arms, so full of hope, faith, and affection toward us? . . . No satisfaction and no prize is greater than that of fulfilling our duty, as we have been doing up to now, and as we shall always do. In this I don't speak in my name. . . . Physically, Frank País is not here, nor many others, but they are here spiritually—and only the satisfaction that their death was not in vain can compensate for the immense emptiness they left behind them."

BEFORE DAWN, Celia and Fidel left Santiago. They traveled in a motorcade of just a few cars that seem in photos to be emerging from a fog, at the front of the caravan composed of the command staff, followed by guerrilla soldiers loaded into trucks and jeeps confiscated from the Moncada (driven by ex-*batistiano* soldiers). Slowly, the victory march rolled along, stopping in each city to accept the surrender of former government forces. At each stop, Fidel would explain everything, the future and the past. The caravan grew as it continued westward, army regulars, in numbers, joining the rebels—Cuba's new army.

The slow pace was strategic, writes historian Hugh Thomas, to allow Camilo Cienfuegos and Che Guevara to get settled in Havana. Camilo had seized the Cuban army's military stronghold in Havana, Camp Columbia, at approximately the same time Fidel led his victorious troops out of Santiago; Che arrived in the capital on January 2, and took command of the ancient La Cabaña fortress. The 26th of July was, by design, occupying seats of military power closely associated with Batista's ascent.

Nothing happened fast. At each stop, local boys who'd taken part in the war as members of the 26th of July Movement, soldiers and *clandestinos*, slipped back to their neighborhoods, welcomed as heroes. Photographs provide a sense of these small celebrations: a house filled with candles and flowers, on the table a cake covered in icing; young girls dressed up in their prettiest clothes; and neighbors crowded in along with mothers, aunts, sisters, fathers,

Celia in Santiago, on January 1, 1958, dining in the home of Arsenio Cervea. The fighting is over, Santiago has surrendered, and she is about to take her place in the victory cavalcade, west to Havana. *(Courtesy of Oficina de Asuntos Históricos)*

brothers, uncles—all with radiant faces. The local hero, wearing a 26th of July armband, stands before them, savoring this unrepeatable moment. Those young heroes would leave again at dawn, to rejoin their squadrons and continue west with Fidel, to the next towns and provinces, and eventually Havana.

Manzanillo's women quickly raised $5,000 (a staggering sum) and presented Celia with a gold Rolex wristwatch, in remembrance of her years among them—planning the war, hiding in their homes, asking for support. They wanted her to have something elegant, and useful in her new life in Havana. They no doubt anticipated she'd become Cuba's new first lady. The richest of them kicked in the most but, as I understand, everyone gave. They were proud of Celia, and proud of themselves. She'd asked them to risk their lives to make this revolution. As young wives and daughters, they'd donned high heels and their nicest skirts to smuggle, in their petticoats, everything from film to explosives. Older women had carried passports and documents; farm girls had served as the backbone of the rebel army's communications system; young women had served as telephone operators; others had done whatever they could as saleswomen, housewives, and maids to flummox Manzanillo's police force and the local garrison. They'd often defied their families. Fidel clearly cast a larger-than-life presence in these stops, but in some cities along the route it was Celia the people most wanted to see.

The victory cavalcade moved so slowly that it only got to Camaguey on January 4, having covered less than fifty miles a day. Photographs show people waiting by the highway for a long string of vehicles to appear, for their chance to throw flowers, while others wait in their newly washed automobiles, eager to join the caravan. The foreign press poured into Cuba to cover the story, traveling east from Havana to meet Fidel's triumphal march. They encountered the 26th of July's ad hoc protocol: journalists who wanted to see Fidel needed to speak first to Celia Sánchez. They met a woman in uniform, notebook in hand, cigarette between well-manicured fingers, and the story goes that when they heard she was Fidel's command partner, at least some of them thought of "Maid" Marion, Robin Hood's soul mate, the woman of the forest who helped him rob the rich to help the poor.

FROM MY PERSPECTIVE, this marks a watershed in Celia's life story—not that she was aware of it or would have cared. Having finally reached the point that she was known by those around her as Celia Sánchez—a figure in her own right, though to an extent still "the doctor's daughter"—in foreign eyes she was becoming identified as "Fidel Castro's . . . something." No one could pin down that "something." For various reasons, the questioners found it vexing, and a mystery emerged: "Who is this unusual figure, relative to Fidel?" For Cubans, it's not irrelevant, but hangs somewhere in the background. She was Celia, their heroine. All, or so many of them still feel, knew her personally. Celia Sánchez Manduley is too formal, almost an insult. When I started this project, people would correct me: Celia is Celia just as Che is simply Che, and Fidel only Fidel, etc. But the mystery persists. It played a part in my attraction to her life story, and though I don't imagine I've solved it definitively, I believe I've been able to shed some light. The greatest illumination reached me, to my surprise, not in retracing Celia's life in the mountains, during the war, but in

Early in January 1959, somewhere on the victory cavalcade route, Felipe
Guerra Matos stands by Celia as she speaks with Dr. Bernabé Ordaz. Ordaz
was a physician who, as a clandestino, was imprisoned on 13 different
occasions before coming to the Sierra Maestra, where he was in charge of
the hospital Celia designed at the *Comandancia* La Plata. Ordaz also took
part, with Fidel's Column 1, in battles, and shortly before this picture was
taken, had received the rank of comandante. Perhaps they are discussing
Havana, where Ordaz would become director of the psychiatric hospital.
(Courtesy of Oficina de Asuntos Históricos)

following her through victory when she lived in Havana, a leader
in post-Batista Cuba. It was to prove radically different from her
rugged existence in the mountains, and, in my estimation, far from
the life in the capital she had probably anticipated.

WHILE EN ROUTE TO HAVANA, and the next chapter of her
life, Celia kept a part of her heart in the Sierra Maestra. She
arranged for the purchase of toys in late December, as she had
for years, and made calls to her old vendors in Santiago even as
she waited in Palma Soriano between Christmas and New Year's
Day. She intended to pull together her King's Day festivities for
less privileged children, just she had in Pilón. On January 6, at
her behest, a Cuban air force plane flew over the war-torn parts
of the Sierra, targeting the houses of families who'd supported
the rebels, and dropped toys. Buying toys, locating a plane and
pilot—charming a former *batistiano*—and advising him where

to drop his payload was among the things with which Celia was occupied, notebook always in hand, in Santiago and on the march west. Her friends from Pilón don't know who helped her that year, and suspect she made all the arrangements on her own. Celia was sending her comrades in the mountains a message: I will not forget you or your children. Thank you for your help. Together, we have won the war.

Celia's decision and effort to sustain the tradition she'd established for King's Day exemplifies her role after victory. She interprets victory in her own manner and decides how best to serve the Revolution. She chooses her own projects, and quietly goes about achieving them, for the rest of her life. It is safe to say, thanks in some measure to the power she held as a member of the revolutionary government and her close association with Fidel, that most of Celia's projects got accomplished. She always seemed to remember what winning the war meant, that the 26th of July had obligations after victory. In this way she remained loyal to Frank, to the people who helped her, to the combatants and *clandestinos* and friends who had been with her in Manzanillo and Pilón.

Part IV

HAVANA

30. January 1959

Arrival in Havana

THE HUGE CAVALCADE ARRIVED in Havana on January 8 via the old industrial city of Guanabacoa, wending its way on the old harbor road past freight yards, factories, and refineries along the port, to the Presidential Palace. The country's new leadership was to give a press conference there, in the Hall of Mirrors. The newly appointed president, former judge Manuel Urrutia, was waiting with his wife. Celia and Fidel joined them on the stage. I'm not sure when—maybe it was before Camilo Cienfuegos arrived from Camp Columbia—Fidel looked around at the mirrors and rococo moldings, and at the gaudily painted ceiling, and told those assembled that he didn't like the idea of having a palace, but since they couldn't afford to build another seat of government, "We are going to try to figure out a way for the people to have affection for this building." Between his fingers he held a long, slender cigar.

After the press conference, Celia, Fidel, and Urrutia left for Camp Columbia. They got into the head car, one of Batista's, driven by Batista's driver, and rode through old Havana. When they reached La Rampa, the street that ascends from the sea to the heart of Vedado, the first street to be lined with tall buildings housing airline offices on the ground floor and underground nightclubs, Fidel spontaneously declared that he didn't want to ride in Batista's car any longer. The vehicle was closed in by tinted windows and had been bullet-proofed. He leapt out, got into Juan Almeida's open jeep, directly behind—also driven by one of Batista's soldiers—where he could see and be seen; from there, he could drink in the pleasure of the crowds.

Celia rode in the front car, and when it reached Camp Columbia, the driver took the wrong entrance (by the San Alejandro Art School) but immediately realized his mistake. Before he could turn around, Celia got out and went into a house just inside this gate. Almeida's jeep pulled in behind, and he and Fidel also went inside the house, as did the next group of commanders coming off the parade route. They'd been traveling since dawn and were exhausted. Some chatted, some took quick naps, until they all agreed that they'd better get on with the official ceremonies. In the distance, they could see the stage that had been constructed for the event inside Camp Columbia, and decided that the least complicated way to get there was over the fence, then walk to the podium and get the ceremony—their official acceptance of control of the camp and of the Cuban military—under way.

All the men went over the fence: Fidel, Raul, Almeida, Dermidio Escalona, Felipe Guerra Matos, and many others. But Celia noticed a tree farther up the fence. She climbed the tree and got onto a limb. Her safe transit of the fence required all the men to pull on the limb to move it to their side, so she could hop down. The story offers a metaphor: in the years to come, the men would often come up with a plan and rush forward while she chose another, possibly less immediate but more practical route. In power as in opposition, they pursued different ways of arriving at their destinies.

IT WAS WIDELY ASSUMED that the new government would establish its headquarters at the historic residence of Cuban presidents, the wedding-cake-shaped Presidential Palace. When Fidel commented that they'd have to find some way to get people to love the Presidential Palace, no one expected that he would abandon it. In the weeks to come, people began snapping up apartments on Calle Zulueta and the Avenida de las Misiones, to be nearby.

The situation, however, was complicated. The 26th of July Movement couldn't move in because the Revolutionary Directorate held it. But Fidel had no intention of moving into the place where Batista had nearly been assassinated, and turned to the newly built Havana Hilton. It became a military zone for the rebel army territory, renamed Hotel Habana Libre, and the top floors became his command headquarters.

The determining fact, though, was simpler: Celia and Fidel had no place to go. They both hailed from the far end of the island. Fidel had spent his high school years in Havana, at the Jesuits' Colegio de Belén (Bethlehem). While still at university, he'd married and lived with Mirta Diaz-Belart. But the marriage and apartment were long gone, and he had no place to call home.

In the beginning, Celia's idea was to establish an official residence for all five members of the rebel junta. Living along with her in this place would have been Fidel, Che, Camilo, and Raúl. After arriving in Havana, she started to look for a large house to rent, one that was modern and elegant, for just this purpose. Two pieces of furniture are surviving mementos that she bought for this project: a huge black marble-topped dining table and a 1950s modern sideboard with Chinese detailing and black Bakelite trim. She'd been working out this idea, where and how to live, for some time. Once she'd felt confident victory would come in the near term—basically, this seems to have been at the end of July, after the spectacular success of the rebel army at the Battle of El Jigue—she asked her sister Silvia to find an apartment "with at least two bedrooms, someplace central, for herself, for Fidel, also, and maybe for the others." It had to be expandable, and Celia instructed Silvia to furnish it with their father's furniture, which friends had rescued and sent to a Havana warehouse, where it had been stored since September 1957.

Not long after this, police had surrounded Silvia's building (the Aparthotel on the corner of 8th and 19th, in Vedado); Silvia's husband thought they'd come for his family but they arrested another resident. The SIM took the hotel register, and she and her husband were frightened enough to leave that same night. They went to the home of a politically sympathetic doctor, who welcomed them and their two sons, Sergio and Pepin. But the doctor's house already had too many people crowded into it. So Silvia began to look in earnest for an apartment she could live in and turn over to Celia following victory. With help from the

26th of July, she found a vacancy on Once (11th Street). The lease restricted children, pets, and Afro-Cubans (at the time, a fairly standard Vedado lease), but the owner saw fit to make an exception, given his revolutionary sympathies. Silvia and her husband and boys moved into Calle Once, No. 1007, at the end of August 1958, along with Ernestina González, Celia's Afro-Cuban cook from Pilón. Expediency, not design or style or glamour, had been the criterion for Silvia's selection.

Celia would move there in February 1959.

IN THE WEEKS AND MONTHS that followed the dramatic arrival of the rebel army in Havana on January 8, 1959, the 26th of July Movement was contested by other groups. The Revolutionary Directorate, the university-based clandestine organization originally directed by José Antonio Echeverria, occupied both the university and the Presidential Palace and had done so since Batista fled, and continued to hold these two strategic locales after Fidel entered the city. Its leader, Faure Chamon, complained that Fidel hadn't consulted them when he set up a provisional government during his victory speech in Santiago. Meanwhile, another group, the *Directorio Estudiantil*, collected arms and prepared to challenge the 26th of July supremacy. Both opposing groups claimed that unity belonged to everyone, not just to Castro's group, and that left the third group, and possibly the strongest organization to be won over, the People's Socialist Party, second in size to the 26th of July Movement, the most prestigious party among the trade workers. Even though Fidel had no intention (because of security) of moving into the Presidential Palace, he didn't have the consolidated power at the time to do so (a fact that is rarely mentioned). In the end, no one could match Fidel Castro's charisma, or his magnetism.

IN JANUARY, CELIA WAS OFFICIALLY appointed Secretary to the Commander in Chief and this meant, in practical terms, that the new ministers, formerly members of the revolutionary army, could still rely on her to interpret what Fidel wanted. This may not have been apparent, initially, to *habaneros* and even to those new rebel army soldiers who, although they might be winners of battles and heroic commanders, hadn't been there since the beginning; that is, they had recently joined up and were not the elder statesmen

In early January, 1959, days after victory, Fidel, Camilo, and Celia listen to Randol Cossío, who, as a member of Batista's army, had provided statistics to Celia and Frank as they prepared for the landing of the *Granma*. Cossío was recruited by Celia in 1956. In this picture, he appears to be advising the three leaders of the 26th of July Movement. *(Courtesy of Oficina de Asuntos Históricos)*

of the founding 26th of July, *Granma, Comandancia* La Plata club. This new group apparently didn't know how Celia and Fidel had operated in the Sierra Maestra, but original members of Column 1 "José Martí" realized how much Fidel trusted her, and were greatly relieved to see Celia at his side in the capital. They had witnessed Fidel and Celia's ability to communicate as a team, recalled what it had been like in early days, when he gave her military orders, asked her to do things like build trenches and install a telephone—military duties. Those same rebel soldiers were now somewhat scattered, were taking up completely new and overwhelming duties around Havana, a city they didn't know, and were reassured to be able to go to Celia to get orders or permission or approvals from Fidel. She could always give them an answer. As in the mountains, they could count on her to explain just what it was that they were supposed to do. It is usually said that Che is the one who initiated this practice in Havana. If he wanted to speak to Fidel, he talked to Celia first, or sent his message via Celia as he'd done in the Sierra. It could have been a courtesy, or a way

In early 1959, Celia converses with Commanders Calixto García Martínez and Che Guevara. Following the custom established in the Sierra Maestra, commanders who wanted to speak with Fidel contacted Celia, or sent their messages via her. It is usually said that Che is the one who initiated this practice in Havana by speaking to Celia first, as he'd done in the Sierra. *(Courtesy of Oficina de Asuntos Históricos)*

for the two of them to keep intact their friendship. Anyway, it was a procedure that stuck.

Yet, after arriving in the capital, by necessity the small group of commanders went separate ways. Raúl Castro and Juan Almeida left Havana and returned to the eastern end of the island to take up posts with their columns in the regions of Santiago and Guantánamo (to protect the Revolution against invaders). Celia and Fidel became a unit as the others paired off. Raúl got married first (in Santiago); Che married next, but continued to live in the Cabaña fortress. Camilo lived at Camp Columbia. That left Celia and Fidel, of the original five commanders, so Celia gave up on the plan of the house for all of them, which would have been fun, something on the order of a radical clubhouse. It definitely would have been interesting in the evolution of state residences. Biographically, it's a milestone: she gave up on what she had wanted.

AT HOTEL HABANA LIBRE, members of the rebel army patrolled the lobby. Journalists wanting to see Fidel killed time in Las Canas, the big second-floor bar that faces the swimming pool, although Fidel did not use this bar. He favored the deeply shaded, grass-ceiling-and-walled Polynesian Room, oddly reminiscent of the interior of the *Comandancia* La Plata in its materials and dark protectiveness. After all the lean years (in prison and as a guerrilla) he liked the luxury of pork loin slowly cooking in barrels. Fidel was the conquering hero, glorious, not about to resist pleasure. He started an affair with a young woman, Marita Lorenz, the daughter of the captain of a German cruise ship, who moved into an adjoining room on the top floor of the Habana Libre.

AT THE END OF THE FIRST MONTH of 1959, the 26th of July government had secured its place as victors; and Celia felt she'd made her mark, done her duty, and declared that she was happy with their victory and was going to get on with her life. From the 23rd to the 26th, she visited Venezuela as part of a large delegation invited by President Larrazabal, to commemorate Venezuela's first anniversary (after having overthrown Marcos Perez Jimenez). In photographs documenting this trip she's the elegant face of the Revolution, dressed beautifully, with the look of refined elegance. She's attending receptions, or speaking to the Venezuelan president, or riding on a tank. She created a stir, and the men in the rebel army were proud of her.

Flávia says that when Celia got to Havana, she had very little to wear except her uniform. She hadn't worn a dress since October 1957, and wouldn't have wanted to go back to her zebra dress or any of her *clandestino* clothes, even if they had been shipped from Manzanillo. She went to El Encanto, the best department store in Havana, where some of her friends—members of the 26th of July underground—were saleswomen. There she bought four dresses, one in navy blue silk chiffon with white polka dots, and purchased several pairs of high-heel shoes with pointed toes. Havana had expected a woman who was tough and heroic, but Celia turned up looking delicate, lovely, and expensive. Many people remarked on this, impressed. Writer Miguel Barnet saw Celia Sánchez for the first time at a cocktail party. He says that he had been unprepared for her elegance; although everybody talked about her, nothing had given him the idea that she would be so refined, how softly she spoke. He explained that drinking martínis was in style then, and that people in Havana felt the very act of drinking this cocktail signaled modernity and sophistication. He'd been stunned that she drank nothing, remembered how thrilled he'd been to discover she'd be representing his country, and soon after this composed a poem about her—inspired when he saw her driving down Linea in a jeep, completely alone. In Havana, Celia made sure to appear as the woman the world wanted to see. Or, as Maria Antonia Figueroa described it: "The people knew only that she could withstand the life in the Sierra, which is hard, isn't the same for a woman. And then they found out that she was a sophisticated, educated woman, who had traveled abroad. There is a big difference there."

CELIA LEFT THE HABANA LIBRE when the Revolutionary Government got back from Venezuela. She wanted a place of her own and moved into the Calle Once apartment in the first days of February. Not missing a beat, or unable to function without her, depending on how you want to look at it, Fidel started showing up there, daily.

RIGHT AWAY, WITH A PLACE to spread things out, Celia hauled out her collection of documents collected in the Sierra. There were battle plans, pieces of correspondence, tapes from her adding machine, notations for her expenses dating back to the landing of the *Granma*, messages from her Manzanillo helper Elsa Castro, Fidel's and Frank's letters. She'd kept this collection close at hand for such a long time. It is a collection of materials that Pedro Álvarez Tabío describes as "born in Celia's knapsack and the most precious treasure of the Revolution." This collection, from its inception, is something she had gone about making with the steadfastness of a woman on a personal mission. She'd argued her way around any and all opposition, including Fidel's, and less than a year before, on May 3, 1958, as they began the offensive, she'd written a letter from Las Vegas de Jibacoa describing exactly why she wanted this collection: "There are many papers without importance today but in the future and for history, they [will] have great value. I am interested in this; when history is

The members of the new government went to New York City in April 1959. Fidel accepted an invitation to address the American Society of Newspaper Editors in Washington and a large delegation accompanied him to the United States. Here, Celia was photographed by Raúl Corrales as she made notes and took phone calls in a room in the New York Hilton on 54th Street and Sixth Avenue. *(Courtesy of Oficina de Asuntos Históricos)*

written it is real and there is no more proof than documents, for all are important later." From the storage vault constructed under a trapdoor in the floor in her section of the house at the *Comandancia*, to the battlefield she'd carried her documents from one place to the next inside a nylon bag during the last stages of the war. That bag came with her to Havana, stuffed into a canvas postman's bag she kept under her bed until she was able to begin to organize its contents at her new Once apartment, in the early days of February 1959.

About a month after this, writing from her new abode, she told Camilo Cienfuegos, "I am making an archive of the war with the original documents. Afterward, the archive will be filmed to be used and for our museum, it will be complete, from before Moncada. I also want to be sure that Fidel, all his speeches, all his writings, his letters, to the last paper [is included]. You could help me. Agreed? I'm interested in all your writings, your letters which are interesting because you write well and interestingly. A hug, Celia Sánchez M. [P.S.] Don't put anything in order."

She was finding a suitable role for herself and writing her own job description, as she began her new life as a member of the Revolutionary Government.

A COUPLE OF MONTHS LATER, from April 15 through May 8, Celia was in the United States, a member of a large Cuban delegation. Fidel had accepted an invitation to address the American Society of Newspaper Editors, and traveled at the behest of the American media, not the U.S. government. Still, he wanted to shake hands with the president. Eisenhower did not meet with him, and left that up to his vice president, Richard Nixon. Castro's biographers and historians have dreamed about what would have happened if the young warrior had met the old general. The new 26th of July government, a.k.a. the Revolution, was reaching out to the United States. Two months earlier, Camilo Cienfuegos and eight members of the new Cuban government had visited New York City on a goodwill tour scheduled to coincide with George Washington's birthday. Camilo's trip was unnoticed but important: it prepared the way for Fidel's grand tour and sent a message to the United States that Cuba would like to be friends. In photographs, Camilo and his group look more like members of the Parks Department than representatives of a country; in contrast, Fidel and his entourage are somewhat stately.

They visited Mount Vernon, George Washington's home, where Fidel talked to women volunteers and visiting schoolchildren, and they went to the Lincoln Memorial. Celia stood alone, contemplating Lincoln's statue, and was photographed by Alberto Korda (although this photograph is rarely shown). They traveled to New York and were met at Penn Station by a crowd of 20,000 people, there to catch a glimpse of revolutionaries. They attended an event in Central Park and Fidel received the ceremonial keys to the city; they went to City Hall, the United Nations, the Empire State Building, Columbia University, and the Bronx Zoo. They took a train to Princeton and Fidel spoke before a group of students. Celia was given a wrist corsage, which she wore on the upper sleeve of her uniform, converting it into a floral armband. They headed to Boston. In Bridgeport, New Haven, and Providence, Fidel got out of the train to shake hands. In Boston, he spoke before 8,700 students at Soldiers Field, while Celia went to see a Girona cousin who worked as a librarian at Harvard.

Celia was the caretaker of Fidel's cigars, and had brought along a few extra boxes of Havanas. In Boston, they had enough to give a few to railroad porters and policemen as an expression of gratitude. These were not normal cigars. Fidel had found a shape he liked that was not too thick (that is, it wasn't a fat businessman's cigar, like the Churchill), long, and a bit like a knife and slender, a shape he called *lancero*. For security, it was rolled by one man. This cigar was made differently, too, rolled from a leaf that was blond as opposed to dark brown, and tasted smooth but was strong from extra fermentation. Fidel's cigar had a new look: it was slim and new and powerful, like the Revolution. It was a young man's cigar.

In one of these cities, Fidel met an Argentinean psychologist named Dr. Lidia Vexel-Robertson and started an affair with her of sufficient heat that, according to biographer Leycester Coltman, Dr. Vexel-Robertson made plans to move to Havana immediately.

31

See the Revolution

WHEREVER THEY WENT, Fidel urged his audience to visit Cuba and promised they'd find a low-cost, see-the-Revolution-at-firsthand vacation in the sun. If speaking to college students, he'd invite them to come to Havana on July 26th. Celia and he hatched this plan for a new kind of tourism, then went back to Havana and worked out the details. Here, for the first time after victory, she seems to have found a modus operandi. It became a pattern for how she worked with Fidel: he'd express an idea, and she'd put it into action. In the decades to come, she would play out the role of facilitator, the person he could count on to get his projects off the ground—and she threw some of her own into the mix.

"She was the engine," Raúl Corrales, who worked many years for her, explained. On a practical level, this meant that Fidel would articulate a dream, a proposal, an idea, then he'd go on to the next meeting to address other issues, and Celia would pick up the phone. In this instance, directly following the trip, she started to work in INIT, the national tourist institute. There, she began spearheading their new kind of tourism for Cuba. (First, however, she and the rest of the delegation flew from Boston to Canada on a friendship tour, then on to Brazil, Argentina, Uruguay, and Trinidad and Tobago.)

The first tourist project under her authority was the installation of 8,000 lockers at Varadero Beach. It was a supremely practical and political gesture, and neither her idea nor Fidel's, but one that had been proposed by the Orthodox Party leader, Eduardo Chibás, a decade earlier. The lockers were quickly installed and quite soon those fabulous beaches—with sand literally the color and consistency of refined sugar at the edge of miles of shallow, aqua-tinted water—were, for the first time ever, available to every Cuban. The beach front had previously been privately owned by U.S. or European citizens, and, as strange as it sounds, most Cubans had never seen it. Nor had the beaches been developed. Soon the new government decreed that workers had the right to have a vacation at the beach, and instituted buses that went there daily. "Elegant, affordable buses that served coffee and sandwiches on the trip," my translator, Argelia Fernández, told me, with a tone of longing in her voice. Not long after installing the lockers, Celia had tree houses, or more precisely a series of sleeping platforms, built into some of the palm trees along the beach, so people had a place to sleep high above the sand. At the beginning of the Revolution people camped in tents on the beach for long periods, several weeks or a month, whatever vacation time was allowed them.

Celia promoted *Cubanismo*, pro-Cuban sentiment, emphasizing Fidel's promise of a low-cost, see-the-Revolution type of vacation. At the same time she was pointing to a new kind of vacation, which wasn't just for foreigners, since Cubans needed to get to know their country, too. Seeing Cuba became a goal that was promoted by her design teams, who quickly set about making other, previously off-limits venues available to the general population. "Celia worked in the INIT, the national tourist institute, while I was the accountant for that group," Roberto Fernández explained. "She worked on a project called *La Vuelta a Cuba*, which translates best, although not literally, as Get to Know Cuba First, because people didn't know the country. Many people had been to Paris, Miami, New York, but hadn't traveled in Cuba."

32

The Urban *Comandancia* and the Zapata Swamp Resort

STEADILY, THROUGH THE EARLY MONTHS following victory, Celia was building a home for herself and Fidel. By mid-1959, most of the other tenants in Celia's apartment house had moved out as she took over the building. Her own apartment grew into an urban command post, with security guards stationed on the ground floor (and both ends of the street). Her first apartment, vacated by Silvia, was on the ground floor, but she soon got an apartment on the first (above ground) floor, and there installed a kitchen and a dining room with a big, easy-to-clean countertop, plus a few banquettes for seating, and filled planters with Sierra Maestra flora. Then she took the apartment across the hall—a two-bedroom apartment—for herself and furnished one of those rooms with a small library of books and a few pieces of her father's furniture, his carved-walnut bed, and gave this room to Fidel. The turn-of-the-century carved furniture that her father had purchased in the early decades of the century was mostly too large for any of the rooms in this 1950s apartment building. Most of it was sent back to storage.

"When we were young, we spent our weekends at Once," Flávia's daughter, Alicia, told me. I was to hear this from several of the nieces and nephews, from Chela's son, Jorge, and Silvia's sons, too. Everyone congregated in the kitchen and dining room apartment. "Fidel used to be more spontaneous. He would sleep in the next room, on my grandfather's beautiful antique bed brought from Pilón. When he woke up, he'd go to the kitchen like any normal person, in his pajama pants. He'd get coffee. He was very natural. That life changed. It didn't last long. He was still an idealist," Alicia added.

The apartment building on Once was a far cry from the victors' clubhouse of Celia's imagination. At Once, she kept the lifestyle simple and didn't bother to disguise the mundane architecture. "I went to her apartment weekly in the 1960s," recalls her accountant, Roberto Fernández. "It was austere. Two chairs hung on the wall like in the country." Time-saving efficiency became her new style.

Fidel was particularly interested in making public a legendary fish-and-game preserve in the Zapata Swamp (Ciénaga de Zapata), thought to have the best hunting and fishing in all of Cuba. Here again, Cubans had never actually experienced its bounty since this property had been privately owned since the sixteenth century by either Spaniards or North Americans. One of the first *La Vuelta a Cuba* projects became the Guamá tourist center in the Zapata Swamp. Celia took over this project that Fidel initiated, which was meant to be a theme resort that resembled an Indian village. It can be seen in the opening scene of the film *I Am Cuba,* directed by Mikhail Kalatozov in 1964, a Soviet-Cuban production, as the camera zooms over thirty-eight palm-thatched cabins that stand on stilts above a lake, joined by a network of bridges.

Construction began in 1959; then everything came to a standstill when the project architect suddenly left the country. Since Guamá was Fidel's special project, Celia didn't want a similar embarrassment to happen again. She needed an architect she could trust, and brought in Mario Girona—brother of Julio, Inez, Celia, and Isis—who was a society architect in Havana. Only a couple of years prior to this he'd designed the Hotel Capri for Meyer Lanksy. Girona explained his new role in the Revolution: "Professionally, as an architect, I worked with Celia, but first I want to make something clear: my grandfather and Celia's father were cousins. Both were from Manzanillo. I am from Media Luna. My sister, Celia Girona, and Celia were children together in Media Luna."

Fidel was particularly interested in making public a legendary fish-and-game preserve in the Zapata Swamp and began promoting this project almost immediately. Here, in a boat on Tesoro Lagoon, he and Celia display their day's catch. *(Courtesy of Oficina de Asuntos Históricos)*

The Girona and Sánchez parents and children had been the closest of friends, and Mario Girona was not going to leave Cuba.

Celia had telephoned Mario to ask if he would come to the Once apartment and told him they'd be meeting about a project. Both Fidel and Celia were there, and each explained the need to finish the Guama tourist center, which was far from finished. Girona said that "there was really nothing there. They had a house for the workers, the beginnings of a cafeteria. They had done some cabins. It was all being constructed in wood. I never worked with wood." Fidel explained that the idea was that Guama would be constructed from wood, and that all the wood would come from the Sierra Maestra. Groups of trucks were hauling it in, and the wood for the foundations was so hard and dense it could withstand years in the water. Mario agreed, and before he left this meeting Celia gave him the project of installing lockers at Varadero (8,000 were still there in 2000). "People need to change their clothes," she told him, but cautioned not to disturb "the beach flora." Girona took care of this job immediately so he could get to Guama as soon as possible.

Celia hired Havana society architect Mario Girona to complete the Guama Tourist Center, Fidel's project to open up the Zapata Swamp to the public. Girona was Celia's cousin and someone she trusted. Celia put all her power and energy into realizing this project. In the photograph, he is on the left. Emilio Aragones stands behind him while Celia speaks to her longtime friend from Manzanillo, who had become Fidel's personal physician, Dr. René Vallejo. *(Courtesy of Oficina de Asuntos Históricos)*

"I worked there for three years. You have no idea what it was like," Mario Girona continued, explaining the difficulties of getting the project off the ground. "We communicated by radio to Havana. Archaeologists found *pilotes* and pottery. The *pilotes* were the foundations placed there by Cuban Indians. The archaeologists found an Indian town." An Indian theme had been given to the project before it was discovered that it was an archaeological site, and Girona had to make changes so as not to disturb the historic areas.

"I needed a boat—a rapid boat for the lagoon, and a car to get to and from Guama. I called Celia and explained that I couldn't oversee the project without a car to get there, and a boat to get around in. She told me to see a particular person and pick up a boat [from the marina] on the Almendares River. The car I selected was a Plymouth, and I picked out a fast boat that had belonged to the Tropical Brewery owner. With a call from Celia, I could pick out anything."

TO THE MEMBERS OF OLD VEDADO SOCIETY, Celia and Fidel looked like a couple. Members of Column 1 knew the relationship was a bit more complicated than that, but citizens of the capital saw them standing side by side in parades, boarding planes together to travel abroad, and eventually found out that they were living together but were not husband and wife. Good at being revolutionaries, this important couple was breaking the rules of the town. Many conservative people (although radical enough to stay in Cuba and support the Revolution) were not amused by the Bohemian lifestyle displayed by the couple at the helm. They did not approve of Fidel's staying in "his secretary's apartment," which was, according to interior designer Maria Victoria Caignet, the most common sentiment at the time. They weren't entirely critical of Celia, however. *El Diario de la Marina*, the most Catholic and conservative of newspapers, put a flattering picture of her on the front page, and Mas Martín, the editor of the Communist newspaper *Hoy*, declared that it was the only time *El Diario* got it right. The apartment house was part of the problem; it was not on one of the lovely lettered avenues, like F or G; it was made of poured concrete and hadn't been designed by an architect of note. A nicer house at a better address would have been a more acceptable approach to their new lifestyle: a grand house, preferably with columns (of which there are plenty in Havana), with a wing or two. Tactically, Celia should have created that clubhouse she wanted for herself and "the boys," as Flávia always described it. Celia could have furnished it fabulously, and this might have created a smoke screen. But Celia knew her man, and had the right instincts as to how to set about creating an in-town field office reminiscent of the Sierra Maestra. Besides, she was a hero, and a victor and in charge now; and that held some sway. The trouble with Celia and Fidel was that neither of them had the mind of a common or ordinary person. They were hopeless when it came to doing what was expected. Their behavior got on the nerves of the old bourgeoisie more than the communism that was to follow.

"SO I GOT THE BOAT, but I had to get it to Guama," Girona said. "I told the person at the marina that I needed to take it to the Zapata Swamp, and he gave me a trailer. I had a suitcase of clothes, and my drawings for the week ahead. When I got to Matanzas, two policemen stopped me and told me to return to the marine military post in Havana. [They] accused me of wanting to leave the country." Girona had considered the long drive back to Havana with the trailer and boat, the bureaucratic haggling that would ensue, and the time lost while he could be working on the project. "I told them to please call the comandante who gave me the boat and they'd find that it had been confirmed by Celia Sánchez. When they heard that, there was no problem." Girona continued: "Everything was wood. I had never worked with wood. Wood construction was used by farmers. But Celia wanted to use wood because she wanted to employ people from the Sierra Maestra, and because she liked wood and wanted to recreate the Sierra Maestra."

THE NEXT GENERATION, who grew up with the Revolution and were teenagers in 1959, think of Celia and Fidel as a pair, not a couple—a pair of heroes. And heroes are not ordinary. To that first revolutionary generation, Celia is a mystery, mysterious and powerful, the closest thing to him. When I asked the current generation about the living arrangements in the apartment house in Once, they couldn't imagine why I asked. "It is the one place he could find shelter," was one reply. "Neither Fidel nor Celia cared for material things," said another. Underlying their answers was a simple reminder: ordinary politicians need presidential or stately residences, but heroes don't. Offended at my question, especially coming from an American, one person snapped, "We were learning to defend ourselves. Modesty was appreciated in 1959."

Gone were the beautiful dresses; Celia wore her uniform. She didn't move out of the poured-concrete apartment house, and the public took notice of the fact that she'd chosen an ultra-simple house. By the end of 1959, it was clear that a certain kind of revolutionary etiquette had been established: Celia and Che refused to live the life of privilege. "They were normal and humble when," as one person put it, "all these people, and everyone around them, lived with privileges. The ministers were an elite corps with no housing problems, they had access to cars. [With these things] you feel superior." But that was not true of the country's larger-than-life heroes, Celia, Fidel, and Che. They lived in their own glory.

By the end of 1959, it was clear that a certain kind of revolutionary etiquette had been established. Celia and Che refused to live the life of privilege. Her old Martíano upbringing, the philosophy and ethics derived from Jose Martí ingrained by her father, was kicking in. Gone were the beautiful dresses: Celia wore her uniform. *(Courtesy of Oficina de Asuntos Históricos)*

She'd changed. Her old Martíano upbringing, the philosophy and ethics derived from Jose Marti ingrained by her father, was kicking in. She could see the fallout from the Revolution everywhere, especially in Havana, where the professional classes were leaving daily: medical offices closed, nurses and secretaries were looking for other work; by the 1960s, the bourgeoisie were leaving daily. Their servants—mostly women—were left with no employment. If lucky, they'd be given a couple weeks' salary but were unable to find other rich families to work for; most did not know where to turn. Celia had power, and was in the position to help. She threw her heart and soul into setting up large and small businesses to hire women, and she also reached out to all professionals, grateful that they wanted to stay in Cuba.

"SHE WAS VERY FINE AS A CLIENT. She convinced you it was the best thing to do. When you finished talking with her, you were one hundred percent in agreement." Architect Girona was speaking about Celia's persuasive qualities, the same qualities that had served her so well when she was setting up the Farmers' Militia. "But, when you think about it, she was also respectful of what you did."

SHE DROVE TO WORK EVERY DAY in an Oldsmobile painted "*blanco con crema*" (now aged to faint lavender and preserved in a car museum). Her office was on Revolution Square in one of the large governmental buildings. She had both desk and air conditioning removed, preferring a couch as a less intimidating place to discuss problems people brought to her. She sat with her staff as well, knew the names of all their children, along with the state of everyone's heath. And later, perhaps a decade later, she had the desk reinstated—but not an air conditioner, preferring a ceiling fan instead, and added plants to increase the humidity.

She wasn't a minister like her colleagues, the men who had fought in the war. It is often said that Fidel wanted her to be the minister of education, but she declined. As far as I can determine, she was Celia Sánchez, a member of the government who took care of what she thought was crucial. No one seems to question her role, but I asked people I interviewed for the reason. Maria Antonia Figueroa said that Celia had faced death many times in the underground and in the mountains, and she had huge intellectual credibility. They saw her, papers in hand, consulting with Fidel, watched her set up her own initiatives.

Underlying this revolutionary view of Celia, a simple fact remains: for every project she created, supplies were needed. Supplies equaled jobs. She created projects by the dozens to employ hundreds on each one of her seemingly small endeavors during the first years after victory, by setting up small businesses, whereas the jobs she created for women were stopgap measures put in place in the early months of the Revolution. Classically, there would be with one master craftsman in charge, a gifted artisan to spearhead the project. It might be a metalsmith, a woodcarver, a textile designer, ceramicist, leather worker, glassblower, stained-glass maker, cigar roller, baker, or an excellent yogurt maker. Then she'd establish an atelier to give them a place to work. This small place of production would be run by the master, who taught his employees how to craft specific products, how to meet demands, how to bring jobs to fruition. She also created a few businesses on whim: a bakery that made breadsticks, and another that made large crackers (Flávia said she was copying a type of cracker she used to buy in Brooklyn when she visited her Girona cousins there in 1948). Later, there would be much larger projects employing construction crews from the Department of Buildings and Construction, employed by one or two leading architects; and she moved on to set up larger units of manufacturing, such as a textile factory and a factory for making plastic shoes. One of Celia's factories made (or assembled) a small tractor, designed in Italy, so women farmers could work the land using more manageable, smaller equipment.

Quite early on, Celia created something akin to a permanent mission to liaise with the people of the Sierra Maestra, where she functioned as consul general. It was in an office separate from her own within the palace in Revolution Square, and was specifically designated to serve the citizens of the Sierra Maestra: farmers, bodega owners, housewives, teachers, mule-team owners, ranchers, and fishermen. Probably many were the two hundred-plus families that had been members of the Farmers' Militia and had helped them win the war. In the beginning, these men and women would arrive in Havana unannounced. I'm under the impression that she opened the office out of need. This group was quite apart from war widows who came to see Celia personally, usually women who had to find a way to survive. Celia soon realized that they needed basic education and opened a school, not far from Once, where they were taught to read, write, and know enough arithmetic to run a household. They were also taught to sew. When they graduated and were ready to return to the Sierra, they were given sewing machines so they could make clothes for themselves and their families, and generate income from sewing for other people as well.

Celia and Fidel were the only people many of these knew in Havana, and when they arrived at the bus station, they'd ask where they could find the two heroes. Now, Sierra arrivals could be directed to the newly opened Sierra Maestra office, where Carmen Vásquez, Celia's protégée from Pilón, would take care of them. Carmen described her job, and what happened on a typical

Luis Crespo and Celia speak with Antonio Nuñez Jiménez while Raúl Corrales, on the porch, with camera held ready to make a shot, keeps an eye on Fidel. They have returned to the *Comandancia* La Plata, the rebel army's headquarters during the war. They have convened here to sign the Agrarian Reform Law, on May 17, 1959. *(Courtesy of Oficina de Asuntos Históricos)*

day when one of the mountain families would arrive to ask for Celia and Fidel. She claims that Celia—and sometimes Fidel— made it a point to meet with them on the day of their arrival. The husband might have come to ask for a tractor, and while the initial meeting was taking place, the farmer would talk to Fidel, who enjoyed catching up on Sierra news. Meanwhile, Carmen would book them into a hotel. This was a procedure she followed on Celia's orders.

The couple could stay for whatever time they needed; these were never quick, turnaround trips. On Celia's orders, Carmen would automatically schedule a complete medical examination, because built into the visit would be complete physical recuperation. This could take between one and three months at no cost to these visitors. If, after an evaluation of their health, the doctors determined they needed surgery or extensive therapies, these were also scheduled. "Nothing was denied." They might be sent abroad, if that were necessary, and Carmen made all travel arrangements.

Automatically, on that first day of arrival, Carmen also scheduled facials, manicures, shampoo, and hairstyling, and trips to purchase clothes for the farmer's wife; there were similar appointments for the husband. Carmen says that these visitors (and there were several per week) were treated like friends. She'd arrange for them to go to the Once apartment early in their visit, so that Celia could catch up on Sierra news, because Celia was interested in all the marriages, births, and deaths that had occurred, plus current opinions that were circulating in those hills she'd lived in. It seems that none of these medical procedures or elaborate therapies was viewed by Celia as an obligation, or a perk. She believed in good health; that looking good was part of being well; and the happiness and personal dignity of the people from the Sierra was something she wanted from the Revolution. Carmen told me that Celia followed each recovery, every operation, and all the makeovers closely, taking an interest in every detail. Cronyism, favoritism, Evitaism—call it what you like—Celia had the power and resources to set up this office to take care of health, housing, jobs, and provide start-up loans to the veterans who had assisted the rebel army.

She attended to women affected by the war though her own office, which was also located in the palace. "For Mother's Day and Christmas, she'd send for things to give to all the mothers of Martyrs of the Revolution, like Frank País's mother. She attended to this personally. She'd sometimes send to Europe for presents to give to them on Mother's Day," my translator, Argelia Fernández, told me, because during those years, Argelia had been the wife of Cuba's ambassador to France. "One time, while I was in Paris, we were asked for eiderdown quilts. There would have been hundreds of these coverlets. Celia personally took care of this. It was always something really nice she wanted, something the women could really use. Nobody bragged about doing this. In fact, this isn't known. Only the ambassador and his wife knew about this, and security." Celia would send for presents from these countries to give to war widows and to the mothers who had lost their sons and daughters; and Argelia says that the job was usually placed in the hands of security, but she had elected to buy them herself because they were female things. Argelia thinks Celia was brought up Catholic and gave these presents "because it was consoling."

IN 1959 THE NEW GOVERNMENT began literacy programs, and Celia educated her staff like everyone else. "In 1959, Celia sent

In Santiago, on November 30, 1959, Celia and María Antonia Figueroa celebrate the third anniversary of Frank's Battle of Santiago. The living room of María Antonia's house, where they are pictured, has its walls decorated with portraits of Fidel and Chibás. *(Courtesy of Oficina de Asuntos Históricos)*

for people from Pilón and placed us in jobs that were needed here in Havana," said Elbia Fernández, Celia's old friend and younger cousin from Pilón whom she called "La Maestra" (The Teacher). "She sent for my brothers, one by one. They all worked in the sugar mill. . . . Celia told my father: 'Please tell La Maestra to come with her husband and child, and she can have a large house for all of you.'" Celia had already set up a schoolroom in one of the apartments at Once for the house employees, but she wanted Elbia to oversee the literacy program for her employees who worked at the palace. Elbia says that Celia already had teachers to instruct this staff, but she wanted her friend, La Maestra, to give up a very pleasant and worthy life teaching in Pilón, to move to Havana.

"It wasn't easy," says Elbia. "The students were all adults who had come from the country. The majority were from the Sierra. It was in the palace buildings, in the center building. I started out in the *Consejo de Estado*, and then took over the Central Committee." (This would have been the staff of the two highest offices of the government.) Celia wanted Elbia to prep her staff for what was called the "Battle of the Sixth Grade."

Everybody worked hard and worked long hours, like their bosses. The biggest problem was scheduling classes a variety of people could attend. Elbia and Celia came up with a solution: the same classes would be taught three times a day, and if one of the students missed one session, he or she could catch the next one. When Elbia arrived, Celia's staff was already literate, meaning they'd passed their literacy test a year earlier. But to get a sixth-grade diploma, they "were taught in three levels of achievement." When they had passed each level, they would be in sixth grade; and to reach sixth grade, they had to take tests that were given by the Ministry of Education. Elbia's job was to get them ready for these tests. She began by teaching all the subjects (in sets of three) in 45-minute increments; and at the end of this campaign, they'd pass the tests and be ready to move on to the "Battle for Ninth Grade."

Everybody had to attend the classes: cooks, waiters, chauffeurs, security—and Elbia says the staff attended enthusiastically but were always extremely tired. "There was a cook. She would sleep in class. Some were so tired that I would let them sleep. If he sleeps, he will revive, I thought. And I'll repeat the class. If you repeat, you learn more the second time. So the cook became literate and got his diploma." Celia felt that she must lead by example, and her employees must not fall behind, and was aware of her responsibility to the nation. The syllabus was put together by advisors in the Ministry of Education, and on Saturdays the instructors would go to special schools where they learned what to teach the following week. These classes lasted all day Saturday. "We would go in the morning, have lunch there, then would have an afternoon session," Elbia sighed. It had been a very hard job, six days a week, and she had missed Pilón.

33·
Turning Havana into Pilón

WHEN CELIA FIRST MOVED TO ONCE, most people from Oriente Province who'd gone into exile in Havana were headed home. In her own family, only Flávia and Rene stayed because they'd established a new dental clinic in Havana. Chela and Pedro went back to Manzanillo, and Silvia and her family returned to Santiago. Celia (and Fidel) started off in the ground-floor apartment at Once No.1007 in February, but whenever an apartment became available, Celia would take it and move close friends or family members in.

She started with her cousin Miriam Manduley and Miriam's husband, Pepito José Argibay, a commander; they took over the original ground-floor apartment as soon as Celia was able to move up to the first floor. On the floor above that, Lydia Castro, Fidel's sister, lived with a woman called Mima (who had been Raúl's nanny), or at least they lived there for a time. Orlando, Celia's younger brother who had been living in New York City, and his Puerto Rican wife, Aleida, also moved into an apartment on that floor (before he left her and their son, Gustavo, who was born in 1961 or '62). Celia hired the building's former janitor and moved him onto the roof.

There were four apartments on each floor. Celia started to contact the owners, carefully asking them if they wanted to move. If they did, she made sure they would find better apartments in other parts of town. "Celia didn't insist," Sergio Sánchez, Celia's nephew, pointed out. She found out what each person wanted and "if the owners of two-bedroom apartments preferred to have four bedrooms" in her conversation with them, she offered them more. "The word spread, and people left."

Next, Celia turned to the block; she moved people out of houses and replaced them with people she liked, people she could trust: in short, people from Pilón. Her guardian angel, Hector Llópiz, was one of the first. He'd returned from exile, and she urged him to move with his family to her street; then his sister Berta and her husband moved into the upstairs apartment of the same house, a stone's throw from Celia's front door. It took several years, and Sergio says it finally came down to the couple who lived in a "very pretty house" directly across the street from the entrance of Celia's apartment building. He described them as "a couple who were rich and unfavorable to the Revolution." By then, he says, security had increased whenever there were attempts on Fidel's life, so "Celia talked to them herself, and pointed out that with all the police cars in front of their house, they must be experiencing a complete loss of privacy. She asked if they wanted to leave the country and, if they did, she would help. If they didn't, and wanted to move, they could look for a house any place where they'd feel happy and comfortable. They left." But they stayed in Cuba, in a much grander house in a better location.

SECURITY WAS THE ISSUE. Their revolution couldn't survive without Fidel. "The Eisenhower administration had been contriving to overthrow Castro by force since March 1960. The CIA recruited groups of Cuban exiles in Miami and trained them in various parts of Central America, especially Guatemala," writes the Mexican historian Jorge Castaneda. Fidel survived because he was elusive, did not barricade himself in the classic manner—in a presidential palace with a tall fence surrounding it. Forever the guerrilla, he stayed on the move; yet many people on that block told me that he lived in Celia's apartment, arriving often in the middle of the night.

"Security here is relative," said a longtime resident of the neighborhood, Pedro Ugando, who lives in a building directly behind Celia's. He explained the reality of the post-victory situation. "This is what in Spanish we call a *zona helado,* a frozen zone. You can't just move into this neighborhood. Before people are given permission to move in, they are investigated. It is about two complete blocks. In the years 1960 to 1963, cars would drive by and machine-gun or shoot this area. It happened in other areas, too. . . . Some of the people whose houses and goods had been taken away from them were counterrevolutionary. Even though this is a frozen zone, they would come by in their cars and shoot. . . . I think that espionage started in '59, and we still have it." In the early years, the building was guarded, but not particularly heavily.

The security system at Once, in hindsight, barely existed. There was one policeman at night and two militia members. As it turned out, the militia members were schoolgirls who came from the Lydia Doce Militia. Although they'd been trained at a military school, they were volunteers. I interviewed Sonya Bedoya, who was fifteen when she protected Once. She'd been assigned to a police precinct where she'd go to receive her evening's assignment. The police would select two young women each day and put their names on the roster. The girls would check the bulletin board, then get into olive green pants and a gray jacket with an olive green stripe down the sleeve (uniforms designed by Celia and similar to the tunic she wore in the Sierra), a loaded "bullet belt" about two inches thick plus a magazine of ammunition that fit into a leather pouch. They'd be handed a Czech rifle, or at least that was always what Bedoya was allotted, and they'd go, with their policeman, to their assigned location, which wasn't always Once; sometimes they stood watch over convents.

The first time Sonya guarded Celia and Fidel's apartment house was toward the end of 1959. "I don't remember, but I think guard duty was six hours. We guarded the entrance to the building. I saw everyone who came and went in those days, Fidel included. The first time I saw Fidel was in the middle of the night. I had to wake up the other girl on duty, but the policeman and I were awake. Same as with everyone else, when you see an important person, you never tire of seeing him. He was younger then, straighter, seemed even taller. He said good evening warmly. Now he looks tired. Has too many things on his mind." Bedoya told me this in 2006, before Fidel underwent a couple of operations. Her account simply proves that, in the early years, Fidel counted on his bodyguards to protect him; but after the CIA-backed Bay of Pigs invasion, in 1961, state security took over. Now, some members of state security occupy the house.

FIDEL'S PERSONAL LIFE BEGAN playing itself out in a public drama: Naty Revelta, with whom he'd had an affair in the mid-'50s and fathered a child, was trying to reestablish a relationship and regain some of her former significance. Meanwhile, Dr. Vexel-Robertson moved to Havana and edged out the young Marita Lorenz, still living in the Havana Libre. Miffed, Lorenz took part in a conspiracy, under the influence and guidance of Frank Sturgis, who worked for the CIA. Most of these dramatic events were played out at the Havana Libre between early 1959 through 1960. In other words, his personal life became hectic. Longing for a simpler life, in 1960, Fidel and Celia rented (for a dollar a year) a large villa in Cojimar, a village outside Havana. They had to drive around the bay then (the tunnel under Havana Bay had not yet been constructed), via the eighteenth-century villages of Regla and Guanabacoa. The Cojimar property was on a hill, with woods and a stream. It was, in that aspect, reminiscent of the Sierra Maestra, as well as a romantic fishing village. From the hill, they could see the wharf area, where fishermen set out each day in small boats and returned to use the town's big set of scales to weigh their catch; the famous small marina where Hemingway kept his boat, the *Pilar*, and its pilot, Gregorio Fuentes, lived in the village. Hemingway sponsored the village's fishing contest in 1960, and it was won by Fidel, a highly competitive sportsman. According to village lore, he took this opportunity to tell Hemingway that he'd gotten some ideas on guerrilla warfare from reading *For Whom the Bell Tolls*. The weekends at Cojimar were pleasant.

Celia opened a house for boys in the village. Some came from the Sierra Maestra, a few were orphans, some were godchildren from among the dozens of children whose baptisms she and Fidel had witnessed, performed by Father Sardinas and other priests who came into the Sierra. All were scholarship students new to Havana. She and Fidel were trying to give these children a home, an education, and a sense of belonging. She furnished the house with her father's things: among them were his collection of canes

Celia opened a house for boys, many orphans from the Sierra Maestra, in the village of Cojímar. Some were godchildren from among the dozens of children whose baptisms she and Fidel had witnessed during the war in the mountains. Here she speaks to students of the Escuela Sierra. *(Courtesy of Oficina de Asuntos Históricos)*

and walking sticks that had decorated the porch in Pilón, and a few surviving pieces of his furniture.

Photographer Raúl Corrales, a Cojimar resident, speculates that she was starting a family—although when he told me this it sounded too abstract, too super-socialistic, but now I can see that this may have been what she was doing. Corrales, who worked with Celia for years, claims that the villa and the children were good for Fidel. It was a private, quiet place where he could get away and do some thinking; and there was a stream on the property that he liked to walk along, be close to nature. Corrales felt sure that Celia proposed this house in order to get Fidel away from the Habana Libre. It worked for a time. The house at Cojimar had to be abandoned because it was on the coast, and no matter how well guarded, it was vulnerable from gunboat attack. There was only one road in and out. They put in another road, but negatives mounted, and the weekend getaway no longer measured up, since Fidel's life, at this point, was clearly in peril.

COMMENTS MOUNTED, across the country, that Fidel should marry her. "Everyone thought he was going to marry her. If he didn't, it was only going to cause Celia to lose face," one woman explained. "This reached him, and it reached her. They talked it over and Fidel proposed they get married. Celia told him that it's only gossip. And if the essential feelings aren't between us, we shouldn't carry it out. She also told him: these people don't know what it is we have together." And then, my source—within the family, who asked that I maintain her anonymity—says that Celia explained her reasons: "She told him that she felt older now. When she was young, she'd had marriage on her mind, but now, she wasn't so interested. He understood what she was telling him."

From what I gather, she was reassuring and made it clear that they could keep what they had together, be as they had been in the Sierra Maestra here amid all the complexities of life in town, that is was all right to keep the status quo. But mainly this: he was free to come and go.

Celia was far too smart to accept an arrangement of the type she was being offered: a life filled with his present and past women. She would not have wanted to be put in the position of asking that age-old question: where were you last night? I know she believed in marriage, but not for marriage's sake. Long before this, she'd often comment to her friends that married women end up being subordinate. If Fidel stayed with her, at her urban command post, that sort of question need not come up. She may have been disappointed with this solution, but not jealous. She could see right through Fidel—and that's not very romantic. This solution was a defining moment: together, they would be partners and play out this moment in the history of their country.

IN 1960, CELIA FOUND her developer's legs. She'd work all day at the palace in Revolution Square and take up her design projects at night, working from home. Notorious for her late-night confabulations, she was no different from the men; all were workaholics, taking care of the nation by day, shunning sleep in favor of regenerative pet projects after dark. If you worked for Celia, you had to keep her hours. The best example of what this meant came from Maria Victoria Caignet and Gonzalo Cordova, Celia's interior design team, who told me that a man from the

Celia, smiling with pleasure, is being honored at the founding of the National Federation of Cuban Women, held August 23, 1960, in the union hall of La Central de Trabajadores de Cuba. With her are Fidel and Vilma Espín. *(Courtesy of Oficina de Asuntos Históricos)*

telephone company appeared at the door of their apartment announcing that he'd come to install a new line. This was extraordinary because AT&T had been banished from Cuba by then, and getting a new telephone was impossible. They had had no idea what was afoot. It remained a mystery until the phone rang in the small hours of the morning on their new line and Celia said, "Now you can't escape me, even in the dead of night." They were forewarned. She called them anytime, but usually between 2:00 and 4:00 a.m., when she had time to work on one of the architectural projects. "Celia was so nice about it. She offered such good excuses," Caignet said, laughing, "that we didn't really mind. You'd work from night into morning. It was like a party. It became contagious to work all hours." Over the years, working for Celia turned out to be a huge plus for anyone in the design field. Her projects were completed, buildings got constructed, good materials were used in the construction—no matter what crisis or stringent cutbacks were affecting the rest of the country. And her buildings were well maintained, even during the Special Period of the 1990s they were noticeable for their good repair. "Thanks to Fidel," Caignet commented.

AT THE VERY END OF 1959, Celia engaged the Caignet Cordova design team. Maria Victoria Caignet had just graduated from the Ecole des Arts Décoratifs in Paris, and Celia asked her to give Cuba a new image. It would start with the Revolution's first official Christmas gift, which Celia wanted to be natural and Cuban, hand-delivered to every embassy in Havana. They settled on a reed basket, woven in Cuba, packed with a bottle of rum, a small clay pot holding a mint plant, some limes, and a recipe for mojitos printed on a cocktail apron. During 1960, Celia planned, with Caignet and Cordova's help, most of the diplomatic receptions stressing the importance of simplicity—of ingredients and of materials. But there was more to it than the design element. "Each reception was a creative moment. A gift from Celia to Fidel," Caignet explained. She and Cordova had been put in charge of these events. From the earliest days of the Revolution, state receptions formed a major part of diplomacy between Fidel and the leaders of other countries because so many wanted to visit Cuba to meet Fidel. But, Caignet says, "nothing is more boring than a reception: same food, same waiters, same policemen, same guests. They are only interesting to the guest of honor." She stated, dispassionately, that a year into the Revolution Fidel had become impatient with receptions, as did the other Cubans who had to attend them. He complained so bitterly to Celia (who refused altogether to attend) that Celia and her design team took over all receptions from then on. They'd be a surprise, since she changed the theme for each, and as Caignet says, "It became more fun."

By the end of 1960, the large reception hall in the Palace of the Revolution had been completely refurbished with panels of native woods and planters filled with Sierra Maestra ferns. There was a rock bed brought from a mountain stream in the Sierra Maestra, and one particularly famous wall covered in bark. "She would fill that wall with white orchids and foreign visitors would marvel at this," Caignet said.

Celia and the designers planned every aspect of the official receptions there: the invitations, decorations, favors, menu, tablecloths, plates, flatware, and glasses. Everything was created by the design team, who say that if anything they did spoke to Celia of the past, or was even remotely *batistiano*, it was banished. The food was always local, delicious and very simple, and this aspect had been particularly refreshing to visitors used to the elaborate dishes of Spain. Cordova recalled that they had decided to serve tamales—"As we do in Cuba, in a clay pot"— for Brezhnev's visit—"He went nuts over it." Sometimes they moved these receptions around the city, and on one occasion Celia brought in Cuba's all-male syncopated swim team to entertain at a reception she held in one of the diplomatic houses, a house with a long balcony overlooking the pool. Verano, the fashion workshop she'd set up, was brought in to design their bathing costumes, and, at the last minute, she added an ankle bracelet so that when the swimmers kicked a leg in the air, visitors could see a little band of flowers.

"She wouldn't go to receptions. She made us stay to make sure nothing got changed. If we weren't attentive, someone would come out with a silver platter," Cordova explained while Caignet laughed. Silver platters had been banished by Celia and replaced by carved wood platters (or huge plantain leaves) in the new, simpler, more natural Cuba. She'd ordered waiters to wear guayaberas and pronounced bow ties and black jackets for waiters too hot for the climate, as well as being too formal, too Spanish, and positively un-Cuban.

One time Celia decided to barbecue lamb inside the large, high-ceilinged, Art Deco banquet room at the palace. It appealed to her to make a break with the usual presidential formality, and well ahead of the event she, Caignet, and Cordova started preparations for the upcoming reception. They got the metals workshop to assemble small oil drums, cut them in two, and mounted them on stands to make the barbecue grills. They placed one at the end of each of the long banquet tables, and did a test trial, cooking the meat in the huge enclosed room. Everything went to plan. On the night of the reception, Celia inspected her masterpiece, arriving at the banquet hall several minutes before the guests were due: the coals were hot, the lamb was cooking beautifully, and everything was perfect. She added a few guava leaves to each fire, to give flavor, and having done this, she went home.

The guava leaves had been a little damp, and the room began to fill with smoke as the guests arrived. "When Fidel walked in, you couldn't see anything. There was no way out for the smoke." Cordova and Caignet quickly located Fidel to explain what had happened. They made a few suggestions about what might be done, such as open the windows, which were high up on the wall, although they weren't sure if they'd open. As it turns out, "Fidel loved it." Another person who attended this event claims that Fidel walked around all night saying, "This is wonderful. I can't see a thing."

FIDEL CONTINUED TO WORK at least eighteen hours a day, then he'd meet friends and colleagues. In short, he didn't get much sleep, was busy and happy, but he deeply missed being in the Sierra. Sometimes, when he felt like that, Celia would bring a fisherman from Pilón to tell Fidel jokes.

34. 1960–1961

The United Nations

CELIA IGNORED THE POSSIBILITIES of personal danger and resolutely refused to have bodyguards. She drove her own car, and in that way she was like Frank. Later, this habit of going it alone took on a kind of symbolism. It is not unusual for Cubans to tell you that she was protected by the love of the people. Many believe that she was so well loved no one would touch her. Perhaps this even extended to a superstitious belief in her invulnerability, because in Cuba this is an aspect of Santeria that is strongly felt. The question is, did she count on such factors? I tend to think she just took off, was too busy to wait for anyone, by nature was too secretive and independent to share what she was up to. With a personal driver she would have to be forthcoming. Plus, she liked to do things her way. She never got much sleep. Close friends and her house staff would keep a tally, and if she went out after being awake more than 48 hours, they'd accompany her. Meaning, they'd just get into the car, apparently without her objecting too much.

Celia, however sophisticated, was a country woman and enjoyed doing things for herself. One woman I met at a senior citizens' center told me that she glanced out her living room window one day to see Celia in the street, inspecting a flat tire on her car. Fascinated, she'd watched as Celia opened the trunk and hauled out the jack, got down on her knees and levered up one side of the chassis. Celia was only a dozen blocks from Once and soon people recognized her and rushed to help. Although Celia was very cordial, she waved them off, saying, "I know how to change a tire." And nobody was going to contradict her. Mind you, this same woman was an avid reader of *Country Life*, and the Spanish magazine *Hola!*, and sent for publications covering the life of Britain's monarch, Elizabeth II. She'd telephone Miriam Manduley whenever these arrived, and they'd pore over the issue about a queen so close to their own age.

Around 1961, Celia ordered a small Italian jeep made of canvas and fiberglass and began driving it everywhere. She was getting things done and very happy with the inroads she was making, raring to go partly because she'd put on her artist's hat, and was able to wear it and still take care of her government duties. Secure in her role, she started creating new hotels to enhance tourism. She had a drawing table moved into Once, began working on ideas, finding sites; this is the period when, I think, she set up workshops to produce ceramic tiles and stained glass. She talked her ideas over with Mario Girona and his American wife, architect Dolly Gómez.

Whereas the old tourist industry focused on travelers from New York and Miami, promoting Cuba as a playground for gambling and prostitution, the new tourist industry turned away from the United States; tourists came from England, France, Italy, Lebanon, Africa, Norway, Finland, Russia, Australia, Argentina, Canada, and Mexico. The new tourist wanted to experience the Revolution. So Celia (aided by Fidel's carte blanche enthusiasm) generated hotel projects all over Cuba, choosing locations of natural beauty, where tourists could stay a month or two, and experience Fidel and Celia's idea of utopia. If you wanted to fish, swim, or cut sugar-cane, they found a place for you to stay for a month or two. She recruited artists to collaborate in these projects.

Still overseeing the development of the Guama resort in the Zapata Swamp, Celia asked sculptor Rita Longa to create a group of bronze, lifelike figures to dot the landscape there. She alerted Maria Victoria Caignet and Gonzalo Cordova that they'd be furnishing the rooms and the dining areas as well as designing plates and silverware. Out of this grew another industry, small but important: for a brief period in the early '60s, simple, cleanly designed furniture from her workshops was exported and marketed in France, Spain, and Denmark under the brand Emprova. Gonzalo Cordova explained that Celia rejected tourism as an influencing force and favored instead the creation of a new form, because she wanted to create a new architecture both modern and essentially Cuban. She sent her design team all over the world to redecorate Cuba's embassies with simple furniture, and to hang the walls with new paintings by Cuban artists.

One of the most positive aspects of these projects was that Celia started traveling around the country, getting out of Havana, conducting her own fact-finding tour on the state of the Revolution. She revisited old haunts: favorite fishing places, places where she'd loved to camp, beautiful locations to place hotels and to start up small industries in the eastern part of the island. She listened to people all over Cuba. She let them tell her how they were faring.

IN LATE SEPTEMBER 1960, Celia left her projects to represent Cuba at the United Nations. A large Cuban delegation traveled to New York to attend the General Assembly. They arrived the afternoon of Sunday, September 18, 1960, at 4:32 p.m., two hours late and in the rain. Within 24 hours, they'd changed hotels, ending up in Harlem, at the Hotel Theresa on 125th Street, where she and Fidel had a suite on the 9th floor; it was nearly empty of furniture, say her cousins, artist Julio Girona and his sister, Inez. And since there was no other place to put famous visitors, Fidel sat with them on one bed.

The Theresa's manager (Love B. Woods) struck a hard bargain: five suites of two rooms with a bath; thirty rooms without bath spread over the 7th, 8th, and 9th floors—half the original number of rooms for twice the cost of the hotel they'd moved from, the Shelburne. But the Cubans found warmth uptown in Harlem, and Love let them hang a Cuban flag outside his building. Things had been combative when they'd arrived at the Hotel Shelburne, on Lexington Avenue at 37th Street. They'd been greeted by about a thousand anti-Castro demonstrators held at bay by two hundred policemen. A fight broke out as soon as they arrived, and hand-lettered signs went up in windows through the neighborhood: "Fidel, Commie, Go Home!" Then the Shelburne's manager (Dan Grad) decided to collect an extra $10,000 as a cash deposit against possible damage. Fidel claimed they didn't have that kind of money. The next day, at 7:00 p.m., he, Celia, and six others piled into a black Oldsmobile and rode eight blocks to the United Nations Secretariat on First Avenue. The rest of the delegation (77 others) had to scramble for transport, while the police, totally in the dark about what was going on, radioed for help as they saw Cubans streaming out of the hotel. Police cars, sirens screaming, arrived from all directions; they escorted the rest of the delegation to the U.N. while two hotel station wagons, loaded with luggage, shuttled between the Shelburne and the Cuban mission, which, at the time, was located nearby at 155 East 44th Street.

Fidel explained to Secretary General Dag Hammarskjold that they had been prepared to put up $5,000 for their twenty suites, but the hotel had held out for the full $10,000, and he'd interpreted this as an invitation to leave. The State Department, acting in the interests of security, had confined the delegation to Manhattan and Fidel pointed out that it was not Cuba's fault that the U.N. was located in New York. Hammarskjold called William Zeckendorf, a New York real estate developer, who arranged for twenty suites plus 85 single rooms to be made available at the Hotel Commodore. This should have been a perfect solution, as the hotel was conveniently located on Lexington Avenue at 42nd Street, but Fidel was miffed and declined the offer. He said that Cubans should have "the right to choose the hotel we want." They went to Harlem (and paid more money than either the Shelburne or the Commodore would have charged), arriving a little after midnight.

On the following morning, Celia's three Girona cousins arrived with jugs of water from their apartment in Brooklyn. Then Celia went out to purchase a little refrigerator and a hotplate. She wanted to make sure that Fidel had safe food and drinking water. That morning, Malcolm X and African-American journalists came to Fidel's suite, and Fidel told them of his brush with "incredible inhospitality" at the Shelburne. The Gironas say Fidel kept insisting that he would have preferred to camp out in Central Park.

Throughout Monday, there was an impressive array of visitors: Soviet premier Nikita Khrushchev, Egypt's president Gamal Abdel Nasser, and India's prime minister Jawaharlal Nehru. All visited the 9th-floor suite and sat on the bed with Fidel. According to the *New York Times*, Khrushchev "swept out of his headquarters at the Soviet United Nations mission" (located on Park Avenue at 68th Street) and into a Cadillac Fleetwood. Reporters who had been camping out in front of the Soviet residence shouted, "Where are you going?" and the premier, leaning out the car's window, replied, "We Communists don't tell our secrets." When Khrushchev arrived around noon at the Theresa, it was surrounded by "thousands of spectators and hundreds of policemen." He spent twenty-two minutes in the suite on the 9th floor. Then, arm-in-arm with Fidel, he walked to his Fleetwood at the curb. That same afternoon, Khrushchev made a point of walking very slowly from the rear of the General Assembly to the front where he gave Fidel the now famous bear hug.

Tuesday night, September 21, the Afro-Cuban comandante Juan Almeida flew in from Havana. He'd been with Fidel when he attacked the Moncada on the 26th of July, 1953, and as a fellow prisoner on the Isle of Pines, aboard the *Granma* in December 1956, in Column 1 "José Martí," and a commander of the Third Front in Guantánamo during Batista's summer offensive in 1958. Fidel invited NAACP (National Association for the Advancement of Colored People) leaders to meet Almeida while he spoke with a supporter of Patrice Lumumba of the Congo. It was past midnight when police broke up the crowd of around three hundred people who had gathered in front of the Theresa. One carried a placard with a picture of Fidel and a hand-lettered message: "Man, like us cats dig Fidel the most. He know what's hip and bugs the squares."

On Wednesday the 22nd, President Dwight D. Eisenhower gave a lunch for the representatives of Latin American nations, but Cuba was not included. When Fidel was asked by reporters whether he cared to comment on being excluded, he looked embarrassed and said that it was better to say nothing. A few minutes later, he reconsidered this opportunity, and told reporters, "We are not sad. We are going to take it easy. We wish them a good appetite. I will be honored to lunch with the poor and humble people of Harlem. I belong to the poor, humble people." Uptown, he and Almeida lunched in the Theresa's dining room with a bellboy they'd serendipitously invited. They ate steak, drank beer, and took questions from the press. That night, the Cuban delegation was honored at a reception sponsored by the Fair Play for Cuba Committee. It, too, was held at the Theresa, and was thought by many to have been the best party in town. The two hundred guests included Langston Hughes, Allen Ginsberg, and Henri Cartier-Bresson. The next day, the Hotel Shelburne's management announced that it would return all the Cuban delegation's money, without deducting charges incurred during their brief stay there.

On the evening of September 23, the Russians hosted a party. The Cubans arrived late. Khrushchev, misdirected by one of his staff who mistook a fire truck coming down Park Avenue with a red light flashing for the Cubans, went down to the street entrance at 6:55 p.m., expecting to welcome them. Reporters, camped outside, were curious to see Khrushchev killing time in the doorway. Television crews turned on their lights, cameras rolled while recording a piece of Cold War ad-lib diplomacy: Asked what he thought of Eisenhower's speech, Khrushchev gave his opinion that it was "soft music without content." And, to their question of how long he planned to stay in the United States, Khrushchev responded: "I feel like staying, so I'm not going," then quipped, "I will stay here, but apparently I will not be granted citizenship." The Cubans finally arrived, but only after they'd kept their new and powerful ally waiting for thirty-eight minutes.

Monday, the 26th, would be Fidel's big day at the United Nations. He shocked the General Assembly by giving a speech that lasted for over four hours, spoke of U.S. aggression against Cuba, and warned the other underdeveloped nations to watch out for a similar fate. He observed that millionaire presidential nominee John F. Kennedy must have learned all he knew about guerrilla warfare from Hollywood films. He condemned the United Nations for assisting Joséph Mobutu's rise to power in Congo, and called for the return of Patrice Lumumba whom he termed the "rightful premier." Finally, Fidel defended socialism by saying, "If a person from outer space were to come to this Assembly, someone who had not even read the *Communist Manifesto* or had not read Karl Marx or the United Press, Associated Press cables or other publications of 'a monopolistic character' and was asked how the world were divided, how the world is distributed, and on a map of the world he were to see that the wealth of the world is divided among the monopolies of four or five countries, he would say that the world has been badly divided up. It has been exploited." This is a sentiment he still voices regularly.

"Fidel is talking too much," was Celia's comment, according to Julio Girona, who sat with her. That pretty much sums it up. She didn't particularly like the free-for-all atmosphere that had developed. Again, as in the Sierra, Fidel seemed to be following his own script. After ten days of pure drama, the Cuban delegation left on the 28th.

BACK IN HAVANA, the new government was confronting resistance. Every day, on her way to work Celia saw long lines of people at the Central Bus Station; and when she asked what was going on was told that they were trying to get tickets. There were no travel restrictions, no official reason why people couldn't travel to other parts of the island. She went about solving the issue in her own style: she contacted photographer Raúl Corrales and asked him to investigate the situation by taking pictures. He told her he would need a car and a driver.

That evening he and the driver went to the station. Corrales left the car but instructed the driver to "stay, but don't talk to me." His assignment had been to find out what would happen at midnight, when most cross-country buses rolled out of the terminal headed for all parts of the island. When Corrales took out his camera, he was detained by security and accused of being a foreigner because of the way he was dressed: "I had recently returned from Spain and owned a nylon shirt. No one else had these yet in Cuba." Corrales replied that he was not only Cuban, but a photographer on assignment (not mentioning Celia) "for one of the new government offices." Hearing that, they put him in a police car and took him to the nearest police station while his driver drove to Once to inform Celia.

Half an hour later, Celia arrived in her jeep at the police station, alone, wearing her military uniform with a pair of high-heeled shoes. Corrales laughingly commented that she knew how to make an entrance. She jumped out of the jeep and walked smartly into the police station, paused in the entrance to smile at everyone, then saw Corrales and said, casually: "Corrales, how are you? Are you waiting for someone?" With that, she swept into the commander's office.

Word traveled through the station the minute they saw her arrive, and the station chief was waiting; he asked what he could do for her. She explained that Corrales was photographing "transport" and she'd been in too much of a hurry to give him papers. "Do you mind giving him the necessary paperwork?" she asked. The station chief assured her that everything would be taken care of. She left, and Corrales went back to the bus station with a bunch of documents.

"The same man that caught me before, caught me again," Corrales continued, and this time security took him to the administrator of the bus terminal who asked Corrales what he thought he was doing. He answered he was taking pictures of the Central Bus Station and the long-distance buses. Corrales says: "People were sleeping on the floor. There were no tickets. The ticket windows were closed. If you wanted refreshments, there weren't any, not even in the bar. A few bottles of baby formula were available, but only about one per fifty persons. The situation was terrible." The administrator—a candidate for the "burnt up with prejudice and wishful thinking category" that one British diplomat used to describe a good many people in Cuba at that moment in history—looked at the police documents and said, "Don't you have another document? The police have nothing to do with this. I run this place. If you want to work here, you must have a document from the Ministry of Transportation. That is the only thing I will accept."

By this time it was about 3:00 a.m., but Celia was still up, waiting for Corrales. She listened to his account, told him to go home and get some sleep. In a few days she sent this message: "Go and take all the pictures you want" along with a letter signed by no less a person than the Minister of Transportation. That night he found the situation to be the same, but they had to let him take photographs. From that night on, he made a photo-documentary report for Celia. Soon they discovered what was going on, since some buses never pulled out of the station. "I was troubled because I realized that there was always a line of people for the Santa Clara and Oriente buses," Corrales told me and explained that this was a form of resistance. These two places symbolized the 26th of July Movement: Che's defeat of the Cuban army at Santa Clara, and Fidel's ability to defeat government forces in the mountains of Oriente Province. Both had assured the success of the Revolution for the 26th of July Movement. "It was terrible. They were telling the people that these buses were out of order. It was anarchy. I did my photo work showing that there were long lines, no buses, no toilets, no glasses, no refreshments."

Celia continued to call Corrales and ask for more photographs. "As soon as I started taking pictures, everything would work well, because buses would arrive from another station to pick up people. My camera had become an engine. I printed copies of my photos and Celia knew what to do with them." She showed them to people in high places and to the minister of transport. She gave them to the press. This was her process for implementing change. She was throwing light on the situation, putting it in high relief— the way late afternoon sunlight strikes the face of a building and brings up every detail—so that all the bad things would stand out brightly on the surface.

She and Che came up with some unorthodox solutions. "When Che was minister of industries, there was one point when cigarettes were bad, with pieces of stems in them . . . people called them 'firemen' because they kept going out." Sergio Sánchez had been explaining how Celia and Che schemed together. "At once, she set up a paper bag for people to put examples of the bad cigarettes in. Then she sent the bag to Che." Every once in a while you see a film clip of Che dealing with Cuban matches, which famously didn't light (for the same reason that the buses didn't leave the station, I suppose). He struck match after match in an appearance on television, making viewers aware that he was unable to light his cigar. And the problem eventually stopped.

CELIA RARELY TOOK VACATIONS, but sometimes—after a meeting—called for a military plane and would fly to Pilón, where she'd get into a boat still wearing high heels. She'd fish until dark, usually with an old friend who also liked to fish, Wilfredo Fernández Soriano (the "Teacher"'s brother). They'd fish for snapper. Celia preferred a very simple manner of fishing: she held a line, never a pole, and fished in the same way as Santiago, Hemingway's fisherman in *The Old Man and the Sea*. She would wait with the line in her hands until she felt a tug, then haul in her catch. After one of these trips, she'd fly back to Havana refreshed, and resume working.

35. 1961–1963
The Bay of Pigs Invasion

"IF YOU CAN'T STAND UP TO CASTRO, how can you stand up to Khrushchev?" John F. Kennedy aggressively challenged Richard Nixon during the final months leading up to the 1960 presidential elections. Kennedy blamed Eisenhower for tolerating Batista; and Nixon—Eisenhower's vice-president and Kennedy's opponent— for being weak. Finally, on October 6, Kennedy delivered his most famous challenge in Republican Cincinnati, Ohio. He labeled Nixon indifferent to a "communist menace 90 miles from our shores," and called for funding anti-Castro guerrillas. As it turned out, Eisenhower was already doing so.

By the end of October 1960, Eisenhower announced an economic embargo against Cuba on the eve of the election. Although Nixon lost, in early January, and with only a few days remaining in office, Eisenhower broke off diplomatic relations with Cuba. This was a very odd thing to do just days prior to Kennedy's inauguration. Very little was said about it at the time, although Senator Albert Gore Sr. of Tennessee did go on record calling it "inadvisable" to take such a step when there was about to be a change in administrations. On January 10, the *New York Times* reported jungle training camps in Guatemala. In other words, the planned invasion of Cuba was not a particularly well-kept secret, but was not discussed in Congress.

"BY THE TIME OF THE INVASION, we'd already made many laws; the United States had taken some measures against Cuba, such as declaring an embargo, the economic blockade, and we replied by nationalizing U.S. industries," Castro said as he discussed the cause of the 1961 invasion with Brazilian writer Frei Betto in 1985. The United States cut off our sugar quota, "and we nationalized some industries and all the sugar mills. We responded to its measures by taking measures of our own," referring to the Agrarian Reform Law that changed landholdings, and nationalized American assets worth $1 billion. Still, Fidel told Betto that though he'd been anticipating an invasion, they had been surprised by the attack on Cuba's air bases on April 15, 1961.

"I stayed up the whole night at the command post, because there were reports that an enemy force that had been detected just off the coast of Oriente Province was going to land." The command post was Celia's apartment on Once. "Whenever such situations arose, we divided up the regions," Fidel said, and he continued: "I stayed in Havana. . . . I was told of the possible landing; I stayed alert, and at dawn I saw some planes flying near the command post—which was a house here in Vedado."

Raúl had gone to Oriente; Juan Almeida to the central part of the island; Che was put in charge of defending the Pinar del Rio region west of Havana. And, just like the old days in the Sierra Maestra, Fidel sent Celia to the front while he stayed at command headquarters. It had worked before, why not again?

"The landing began that same night," Fidel told Betto, "at around midnight [between April 16 and 17]. They tried to destroy our Air Force so as to control the skies, but we still had more airplanes than pilots: eight planes and seven pilots. . . . At dawn, they were in the air, heading for the Bay of Pigs, as soon as we realized that that was where the main attack was being made."

Celia drove at breakneck speed to the Zapata Swamp. She went to the house attached to the Australia sugar mill. From there, she collected information and phoned Fidel. He took notes as she spoke, making notes of what she told him, with a few lines between points and below that a list of what he had to do:

"CELIA SAYS:

That she communicated with Australia Sugar Mill and
was able to confirm that the ship attacked Playa Giron
and another [ship] [attacked] Playa Larga.

That the militia [illegible] groups [are] with the people,
however, these need support and reinforcements. Given
at 03:29 on the 17th.

[That] South of Havana at Playa Rosario ships are
approaching the beach.

[That] I notify the School of Militia Cadres in Matanzas of
the mobilization. That the men [who are] there should
be prepared/ready to leave.

FIDEL:

Cojimar's Special Column is ready.

Alert the two Reserve Battalions.

[Send] One company to Playa Larga and another to
Aguada de Pasajeros from the forces at the Escuela de
Matanzas.

That the battalion from Australia [Sugar Mill] advance
toward la Playa.

FIDEL:

Company from Covadonga

Company at Cayo Ramona

[Send] Anti-tank battery to Covadonga and another to
Giron.

Move 120 Mortar on Giron.

[Send] Captain Fernández with troops from the School in
Matanzas toward Jovellanos.

Place to [put a] post in southern zone toward Pinar del Rio
is Cubanacan.

[Order] Universo [Sánchez to] move four anti-tank
batteries."

[The end of third page]

(This document was a gift from the Cuban Council of State's Office of Historical Affairs, a.k.a. "Celia's Archives," to George Washington University, in honor of a North American and Cuban conference held in March 2001 to discuss the Bay of Pigs, forty years after it occurred.)

FOR FOUR DAYS, from April 17 to April 21, a small army and a tiny air force (but, as Fidel noted, they still had seven planes), augmented by a large people's militia (armed by the USSR), waged a battle led by Fidel and his officers.

"The rebel army consisted of only 25,000 men," historian Jorge Castaneda writes. "Castro had no choice but to arm the population. He would never have done so had he not been certain of their loyalty and support. The resulting 200,000 militiamen played a central role in Cuba's victory. They allowed Castro to deploy lightly armed, mobile forces to all possible landing points, forming a huge early-warning network."

The CIA and White House plan called for "freedom fighters" recruited among the disenchanted Cuban exile community to land on a beach near the Escambray mountains. The Americans were sure that there was enough dissatisfaction among Castro's army and militia that dissidents would spontaneously join the invaders and oppose Castro's government. Not only did this fail to happen, but those reaching shore received no assistance from the offshore boats, and were bombarded by the rebel army. And the small but effective Cuban air force kept the rest from approaching the coast. The rebel army sank one of the boats; the fatal shot was fired from a tank on the beach. CIA troops who did land couldn't escape into the Escambray without confronting the Zapata Swamp. About 1,200 men were stranded and had to surrender. (Over the next twenty months, these men were held in prison in Havana until Cuba exchanged them for money, baby formula, and medicine.) Celia's workers on the hotel project at Guama could see and hear the battle. Caignet said it was like fireworks.

SOMETIME IN 1961, Fidel asked Celia a second time if she wanted to marry. They'd just been through the most harrowing experience since the war. Circumstance—that favorite *raison d'être* of José Martí followers—and victory over the Americans may have caused them to revisit their vows to stay as they were: in a partnership that many Cubans disapproved of or were bewitched by. Celia's solution was this: she had an additional floor constructed on the roof of the building at Once, an apartment for Fidel.

BY 1962, LACK OF SHOES, due to the American embargo, had become a national problem. Celia turned to supplying Cubans with footwear. First the government tried to reorganize the existing industry by closing down small cobbler shops and opening factories. Bad workmanship, a shortage of cowhides, and any number of other problems were the basis of bad production, and people complained bitterly about the product, accustomed as they were to American-made shoes. Shoes were rationed. Certificates to purchase them were mostly issued by the unions, but some were distributed by the Committees for the Defense of the Revolution, which existed in every neighborhood. These two groups, the unions in particular, discussed who needed shoes and who could wait for them. The CDRs took care of distribution to housewives and nonunion workers. Inevitably, people of revolutionary spirit were favored over the less politically inclined. This was a perfect situation for a dispute, and protests broke out everywhere. In this climate, Celia opened a factory in Havana to produce plastic shoes. She bought molds from Italy and gave priority to hiring women; and since the majority of the workers in this factory were women with children, hers was one of the first factories to set up a day-care center.

ALSO IN 1962, Fidel reminded Celia that it was time to assume responsibility for the child they'd named Eugenia and baptized in the cave near Altos de Naranjo, whose father, Pastor Palomares, wanted them to raise her and give her an education. Celia wrote a letter to the grandparents. She waited and heard nothing, then sent three telegrams, and these, too, went unanswered. Fidel sent a man to get the child.

"I felt very proud," Eugenia Palomares told me. "There was someone called El Morito who came on horseback. I came to Havana with a small box that held my three dresses and my only shoes." Celia arranged to have a woman meet them in Providencia, and bring Eugenia to Havana.

"When I arrived it was night. Celia was waiting. I didn't know her but my grandmother told me: when you get to Havana you'll meet your godmother who is a very thin woman, and your godfather is tall with a beard. You should ask for their blessings." Asking godparents for their blessings was a traditional courtesy in Cuba. "I said to Celia: Give me your blessing, Godmother," Eugenia recalls. "I hugged and kissed her. She did answer me, but not like my grandparents, who said: *Santica mija,* God bless you. Celia presented me to Ernestina, the cook, very affectionately, and to some other people I think were guards. They looked at me with pity. After all these years, I now realize her reason: my body was weak and my spine was curved from carrying wood and pails of water for my grandparents. I was very thin, but my belly was bloated from parasites. My grandparents only knew about herbs." On that first day, Eugenia felt that Celia had snubbed her greeting. This was followed by a sense of inferiority when she sensed how shocked they were at her appearance.

The next morning, she woke up feeling sad. "I missed my grandparents, their house, the mountains, everything. I had never seen electricity, a television, air conditioning, or a gas stove, since ours had been wood. Or seen floors. The floors in our house were of earth. Or walls. Ours had been made of planks and parts of the palm tree. Or a ceiling, since ours was made out of pieces of zinc and palm. I'd never heard this way of speaking, or known these kinds of people. All of it made me cry." Ana Irma Escalona took charge of the situation. "She combed my hair and showed me how to wash, because I'd never seen a bathroom."

ANA IRMA ESCALONA HAD COME to Havana in hopes of getting a scholarship, and Celia had asked her to stay at Once. Ana Irma, who worked for Angela Llopiz and did some courier work for Celia during the days she was hiding in the underground, took charge of all the apartments: Celia's public one, where everybody congregated around the kitchen and dining area, and Celia's private apartment that contained her bedroom and office. Celia asked her to be Fidel's housekeeper, too, taking care of the new apartment on the roof. Mainly, Ana Irma took care of his clothes, since he showed up every day to replace his uniform and put on a hand-laundered, carefully pressed one. These uniforms were hung in large closets in a separate dressing room created for him in one of the back apartments on the first floor. Ernestina González, Celia's cook, also became Fidel's cook.

ON EUGENIA'S FIRST MORNING at Once, as soon as she saw Celia, she ran and gave her a kiss. Again, she asked for "your blessing, Godmother," and Celia seemed to consider this, but chose instead to remain silent. But she hugged Eugenia, and kissed her, and asked her how she'd slept. Miffed, "I didn't answer her question," Eugenia says. Then Ernestina served breakfast, which included bread and butter, new to the little girl's palate; she was not consoled by food. Ernestina then handed her a glass of cold water from the refrigerator, which Eugenia set on the floor, in a corner, copying her grandmother, who used a glass of water as a talisman. Things improved later in the day when Celia presented her with a big doll. "It was my first toy. In the hills, dolls were made from rags." And sent her shopping for new clothes.

When Fidel arrived, Eugenia was with Celia, Ana Irma, and Ernestina in the kitchen. He came in and Celia introduced them, "Look Fidel, this is Palomares's little girl." Fidel sat down, pulled her onto his lap and asked, "How are your folks?" and Eugenia told him they were well. "How are your studies?" She replied, "Well." So far, two short answers. "Then he asked me if I knew how to cook. I answered yes, and he said, 'Well, tell me, what do you know how to cook?' I said, 'Mostly I know how to roast coffee.' Then and there, he asked me to tell him how I did this. I told him that my grandmother would stand me on a chair near the stove and I would move the coffee beans around inside the pot, and that it took a lot of time. When the beans got dark, and had a strong smell, we'd put in a little bit of brown sugar."

Fidel encouraged her to tell him what else she was able to do, so Eugenia explained how she'd help her grandmother when a pig was slaughtered. "Two or three of us would go to the river to wash the intestines. We'd come back and my grandmother would make blood sausages and we would braid the small intestine. All this seemed to interest him, so he continued to ask questions, especially about the seasonings."

On the following day, Celia sent her to see Dr. Álvarez Cambra, an orthopedist. Eugenia revealed, with his prompting, that she always carried pails of water from a well to her grandmother's house, walking on a very narrow path with a heavy pail in her right hand, and carried wood the same way. "I'd take wood to the river where my grandmother went to wash clothes twice a week." One of Eugenia's hips was higher than the other, which called for therapy. After that, Celia's nurse, Migdalia Novo, picked Eugenia up at 5:30 every morning, and they'd go to the gym at an orthopedic hospital. At 7:00 they ate a packed breakfast, and Migdalia would take her to school and show up again to bring Eugenia home, to Celia, at the end of the school day. "Celia gave me a kiss every day when I came home from school. She'd ask what I'd learned that day." But it was Fidel who could easily spend hours talking to her.

BY THE END OF 1963, Celia had nearly finished setting up her own parallel security system. She had been moving her old friends from Pilón into houses around her building on Once as they became available since she didn't fully trust state security. She was creating her own safety zone.

"Half of Pilón came to live on Once Street. *Gente de confiance.* Eventually, her Pilón friends lived on the street all the way from Paseo to 16th, or eight city blocks. You might say that she planted the street with people she could trust," Celia's nephew Sergio Sánchez told me, chuckling.

His parents had moved to Havana and occupied a house on 12th, but the back door opened onto the end of Once, and the kids in the family—Flávia's, Silvia's, Acacia's, and Griselda's children— often entered Celia's house via Silvia's, going in her front door and exiting out the back. They describe how Celia concentrated on landscaping in the '60s, always having trees planted. She put in lots of fruit trees, choosing large ones, so people couldn't see her building from the street. "There were three *nispero* [sapodilla] trees with small fruit, brown on the outside and light purple or red violet fruit. When they bloomed, Celia would put a net, a mosquito net, over them so the bats couldn't eat the fruit. They were big trees. This created a stir, and a lot of comment in Vedado, since these trees came up to the first floor." Raysa Bofill, Griselda's granddaughter, recalls Celia's garden, as do several of the children. There was a tangerine tree with lovely fruit that Celia wouldn't let them pick because "they're for Fidel."

When I visited Berta Llópiz, we sat on her balcony and could see Celia's building, but not clearly because the trees were in the way. Berta assured me that Celia planted trees of all kinds to camouflage the building, particularly from above, to keep it out of view of U.S. planes flying overhead. And since security guards block the street, Berta and I could not stroll over to inspect the building.

With Fidel living there, on a permanent but slightly ad hoc basis, state security moved into the two back apartments on the ground floor. Celia preferred her method to theirs, thought they called too much attention to the place, and in the first few years claimed everyone knew when Fidel was there from the number of cars outside. So she built a garage so Fidel could drive into the building—she did this by knocking down the next house and building an addition to the apartment building.

IN 1963, FIDEL STARTED TO PLAY basketball again. In high school, he'd been the star of his team, so he started using the court at the Ranchos Boyeros arena every day. This large, circular-shaped facility is located on the highway to the airport, and Celia thought it was too dangerous for Fidel to go there, but carefully refrained from mentioning this; instead, she lauded his exercise. She asked a well-known architect, Joaquin Galvan, to design a multistoried gymnasium with a basketball court and a bowling alley, and the huge, poured-concrete building was constructed near Once. (Later, she had a swimming pool complex built, facing 12th Street.) But, in many ways, the gym was a great success. Raúl Corrales saw Celia nearly every day then, and says, "Evenings, he would work with her. Afterward, he would play basketball, or bowl. He began to use this 'sports time' to discuss things with people. She would say, 'Come to my place tonight,' and people knew that they would have an opportunity to speak with Fidel." These appointments, surrounded by the camaraderie of sports, were casual and extended far into the night. It seems that everybody liked her solution.

In my lifetime, women in a similar position, that is, first Ladies, have redecorated rooms, but none to my knowledge have ordered major pieces of construction. But Cubans don't see this as presumptuous. She was a hero, and her war record afforded her "the right," as Cubans like to say, to make high-level decisions, particularly those that enhanced the safety of Fidel.

Celia organized a party to celebrate Fidel's 37th birthday on August 13, 1963. While she cuts the cake, and the President of Cuba, Osvaldo Dorticos, watches from behind her, someone has just placed a straw hat on Fidel's head. *(Courtesy of Oficina de Asuntos Históricos)*

CUBANS WERE NOW FIVE YEARS into the Revolution. Concerned people (not to be confused with conservative people) still thought their leading couple should have gotten married. This sentiment is still voiced by people from Oriente Province who think of Celia as their hometown girl. They continue to be displeased with Fidel. Celia, to them, was straight out of an adventure story: they'll tell you that they knew about her before they'd even heard of Fidel. She'd been their beauty queen, their Madonna (Sisters of Mary chairwoman), their benefactress (the King's Day toys), Angel of Mercy (nurse in her father's no-fee medical office), and when she turned into an outlaw (worked against Batista's government and escaped arrest) and became their own "Most Wanted Person" (after the landing), even the least risk-taking citizens had loved her and hidden her in their houses. People of Oriente prayed for her, celebrated her survival, watched her become a war hero, saw her take her rightful place in Havana. They followed her on television, would see her in parades or taking part in conferences. Fidel is great, they told me, but what is the matter with the guy? She risked her life for him. He should have married her. To this day, they want to see the fairy tale come to its proper conclusion, and feel gypped at the outcome. In Oriente, it is the people who love

Celia. The unresolved relationship is still a bone of contention, one without resolution.

FLÁVIA TOLD ME THIS: "There was *no amor*, like people say. It was a relationship that was neither romantic nor platonic." Celia would brush off questions by saying that she and Fidel were "work comrades." *No amor* is precisely the age-old recipe for good marriage. Affection and not romantic love is what it takes to make the long haul. If popular psychoanalysts, such as Ethel Spector Person or Stephen Mitchell, are right, romantic love, in most cultures, is considered to be too catalytic and confrontational for the day-in and day-out requirements of marriage. They write that society stays away from romantic love, this "act of the imagination" where the rules of engagement become inventive and passionate, set by only two people, the two that are involved (presumably blocking out all those other people, like in-laws, who want to be in on it). Yet both Person and Mitchell have found that cool and rational partnerships fall so far short of emotional expectations that, increasingly, people are willing to have a period of too much *amor* even if it usually doesn't last forever. Or, as Mitchell writes, it doesn't last forever because, out of fear of losing it, they essentially kill romance. Only the very brave and inventive make it last forever.

Brave and inventive—Fidel Castro and Celia Sánchez Manduley were that, and much more. I suspect they had exactly what it takes, and chose not to go public with it. They absolutely did not relinquish their loyalty to each other, or their day-to-day contact. They forged a bond to weather all storms. Maria Antonia Figueroa called it a life made up of "days of treason, days of deception, sometimes followed by days of glory and happiness."

I see it as an unbreakable friendship. They may have been taking a stab at being utopian, but I doubt it. Their highly private, dovetailed alliance started in the Sierra Maestra. Why would these two, of all people, think they had to account to anyone for their private lives? They were revolutionaries creating a new society, and as guerillas had been more than ready to lie about whatever must be protected. In the 1960s, what had to be protected, above all, was the Revolution, and that, it seems to me, is the tie that binds.

36. 1964

The Archives

IN 1964, CELIA ESTABLISHED the Office of Historical Affairs, officially founding the archive on May 4, simply by announcing it in a conversation with a group of people at her house. I don't know who these people were, but she informed them that she had decided to create an office that would function as an institution responsible for the documents. It would operate under the direction of the secretary of the presidency (herself). "In this manner, characteristically informal, and from her living room," historian Pedro Tabío Álvárez writes, "the *Oficina de Asuntos Historicos* was born."

Some of the material is transcribed, some are facsimiles; all the original materials were copied on microfilm and onto 35mm film, starting in 1964, by Raúl Corrales; the documents are organized by author and date: "It was the custom of Fidel and other guerrilla chiefs to note the date and hour of their writing," Tabío noted. Next, Celia hired a small staff (friends from the underground, like Elsa Castro) to visit soldiers, make interviews and record them, and she built up a photo collection.

The entire project was eventually adopted by the Council of State. This is the highest governmental body in Cuba, generally numbering 10 to 15 members. Not all those on the Council of State are politicians—some are scientists, farmers, writers. Today, her great trove of primary source materials serves as the country's

Celia never forgot the 26th of July Movement's debt to the people of the Sierra Maestra. Here she is in late 1963, waiting to board a plane to make one of her many trips to Santiago de Cuba. *(Courtesy of Oficina de Asuntos Históricos)*

official archive of the Revolution, and as its presidential library. Unofficially, it's called *Fondo de Celia*, Celia's Archives.

She was not a diarist, although she longed to record her days in the Sierra, and bought a diary for that purpose. According to Nydia Sarrabia, Celia started a diary on March 1, 1958, but other than the date, left the opening page empty; then, on March 6 she wrote, "Never did I think I'd write a diary. My life never seemed interesting enough to write trifles. The war and these circumstances oblige me to note things of interest to make sure that the history of Cuba is true. Raúl has recorded all the facts since the beginning of the Revolution." But in the end, she filled only the first few pages.

In the mountains, however, she began to make copies of Fidel's letters and started keeping her own notes; she began to develop the collection, starting with herself and Fidel first, then, within a month or two, requested materials from the other commanders. Some records, at her suggestion, were buried in mason jars, and these, according to the curator of Celia's documents, Nelsy Babiel, still turn up under farmers' plows in the Sierra Maestra spring.

37.

The Florida Story

CONSEQUENCES OF THE REVOLUTION persist in nearly every Cuban family. When the prisoners taken at the Bay of Pigs finally left Cuba in late December 1962, Celia's sister Chela and her husband, Pedro Álvarez, were on the same boat, emigrating to Florida. As with all Cuban families, their story is seen across the 90-mile divide.

The Álvarez family had returned to Cuba in 1959 to participate in the Revolution, and that is when the boys went to the Jesuit-run Belén school and stayed in Celia's apartment. The Álvarez family hoped—at least for a time—they could live within the Revolution. Celia must have hoped that Pedro could help the 26th of July Movement government by heading up the Rice Institute. But as seen from the Cuban side of the divide, the Álvarez family was not "mentally prepared" for what was taking place, and left. And in this, Celia's extended family mirrors nearly every Cuban family at that time, many of which are divided into two parts: those who stayed, and those who decided to go. The typical Cuban family may not have such dramatic characters, nor assassination as a plot, but it would be hard to find a family with 100 percent of its members remaining in Cuba.

Celia's sister Flávia, from her penthouse overlooking the Malecón, told me the following in 1999: "Pedro Álvarez was a millionaire, the owner of a rice mill in Manzanillo. . . . And when the Revolution triumphed, Fidel proposed to make him the head of the Rice Institute of Cuba. But he didn't accept because they were already talking about Communists, and it was like a four-letter word. He was afraid, but kept working until his business was nationalized."

"We lived in the Focsa Building, in Havana, in a large apartment on the twenty-third floor," Chela explained from her nice though modest house in suburban Miami, and "were asked if we wanted to trade the apartment in exchange for coming here. We came. We didn't have to pay. Three of our children, our sons, were already here. As soon as they closed the Colegio de Belén, our sons came. Our daughter stayed in Havana with us."

"All of the family, including Celia, advised Chela to go," Flávia confirmed. "Her children had left. Only her husband and one child remained. The boys had left Cuba. It was not a time like now, when they could come and go. Then, it was a matter of forever. . . . They wanted to leave because the priests had advised them. . . . You know the position of the Church in those days." The boys had been in an evacuation of children to Miami, now known as Operation Peter Pan, which took place between 1960 and 1962. A Roman Catholic priest in Miami, aided by the U.S. waiver of visas for children under sixteen and fueled by CIA-planted rumors that all Cuban children would be sent to the Soviet Union for their education, flew 14,000 Cuban children to Florida. Although their children had gone ahead of them to Miami, Flávia assured me, "It was very hard for Chela and Pedro to leave the country and go to live there."

A realist, Celia never held out much hope for Pedro as a revolutionary. Flávia says that Celia simply said to Chela, "You can stay here, but your children are there, and you will be separated. So you had better go to be with them." Flávia continued: "They went in the boat that came to pick up the Giron [Bay of Pigs] prisoners. Celia arranged to have them taken with the mercenaries. When they arrived in Miami, their son was already in a training camp of the CIA."

"WE WENT ON THE PLAYA GIRON exchange ship," Pedro Álvarez, in Miami, said, confirming what had been reported by his sister-in-law. "When I took the luggage, when I got onto the ship, I said nothing will harm us again. Then, one of my sons was a patriot, in favor of the [counter-] revolution."

WHEN THEY ARRIVED IN MIAMI, Flávia continued, "Pedro and Chela went in search of him because they were shocked at what he'd done. They arranged to take him out of that camp." The young man's name was Guillermo (he was also referred to as William) and joined a paramilitary group when he was eighteen years old. He'd been recruited and trained by a Florida-based terrorist group that carried out missions in Cuba.

IN MIAMI, PEDRO SPOKE ABOUT the group, confirmed that it was sponsored by the CIA, and said his son had been attracted to them. "They had infiltrated before. They had been on these missions. They'd done this stuff before. The people who infiltrated Cuba openly talked about it." Pedro and Chela brought Guillermo home and thought that that would be the end of it.

"AFTER THAT, HE STARTED to work in a parking lot," Flávia said, to fill in some of the story. "The only one in the family who wrote to him was me. There was no regular mail between the two countries, so if I knew someone was going to Mexico, I'd send him letters. Celia knew. When I got Chela's mail, Celia would ask, 'What did she say?' and I would go over to Once and show Celia the letter. Fidel appreciated their attitude. He appreciated that they didn't make any statement to the press when they arrived." Another member of the family commented dryly, "Fidel behaved elegantly because Pedro left four million dollars in the bank."

The family thought that Guillermo had broken ties with the CIA, but one day, in May 1966, he casually mentioned that he was going fishing and, instead, went on a mission to Cuba, where he was killed. The operation's lone survivor, named Tony Cuesta, identified the others, including Celia's nephew.

GUILLERMO'S PARENTS are understandably filled with anguish, although four decades have passed since his death. Chela lamented sadly, "People said: 'Don't take these young boys.' But Tony Cuesta went to a party and told them: 'We have a mission.' And Guillermo went." Pedro was fatalistic: "If they hadn't killed him that day, he would have gone back [to Cuba]. . . . He was very tough, since the day he was born. He wasn't afraid of anything or anybody."

In Havana, I spoke to his uncle, Comandante Delio Gómez Ochoa, who confirmed all the parts of the story. "I knew the boy William—Guillermo. I knew all the children. In 1961, when I came back to Cuba, I met them." (Ochoa led a column in the Sierra Maestra, became Fidel's liaison in Havana during the last months of the war. In 1960, he went on a mission to overthrow General Trujillo in the Dominican Republic. When he returned, he married, and eventually divorced, Celia's youngest sister, Acacia.)

Ochoa is retired from the army now, and we spoke at his house in Playa, which is not far from the sea. "The landing was close by. It was an operation set up by the CIA in order to attack the president's house; the president was Dorticos. He lived near the Chateau Miramar. . . . There was a large area between 5th Avenue and the beach, where the Hotel Havana has been constructed, on the other side of 5th Avenue. All of that area was known then as El Monte Bareto. It wasn't a mountain. There were a lot of trees and a lot of growth that extended from the other side of 5th Avenue all the way to the coast.

"They came in a very fast boat. We didn't have boats with that speed. They landed. Those who remained on the boat were discovered by the Cuban coast guard. A militia unit nearby were the ones that encountered them."

The small fast boat from Miami landed on the beach with enough time to set up missiles before the Cuban militia attacked them. Some members of the party went into the Monte Bareto woods, but Guillermo got back into the boat. By that time, Cuban units—Ochoa said these were small boats with radios—closed in, and they exchanged fire; then two other units of the Cuban coast guard intercepted the boat in which Guillermo was alone, at the wheel. When the coast guard arrived, they ordered the boat to halt, but it didn't. "So the coast guard started shooting, and one of the shots hit the gasoline tank of the boat, and it exploded. That is how the action ended."

"He was blown to pieces," is Flávia's version. "Pedrito, his father, called his cousin to . . . request [that] the government give them the remains." There were none. Flávia says that Celia could do nothing, although she tried. "She told the cousin to go to the general staff of the navy, to be officially informed. They told her that they had not been able to find anything at all because the boat had carried a huge amount of explosives."

Tony Cuesta, hit by a grenade, survived. Ochoa recalls, "He lost one arm and one eye, and was in prison for a long time here in Cuba, [and] when he was captured, talked about it. . . . For about four or five days they looked for the remains of the boat, and they could find nothing, and felt that the Gulf Stream took it out. They even sent divers to look for it. They traced the exact spot and sent divers down, but didn't find anything. The navy divers searched for days."

Another relative, who had work in the Ministry of Foreign Relations, told me that it is generally assumed that Guillermo had been recruited because he knew Celia's apartment on Calle Once. He'd also come to Cuba to participate in one of the CIA's attempts to kill Fidel.

Guillermo's older brother, Jorge Álvarez, lives in Miami and supplied an important detail no one else mentioned: "I spent two weeks with Celia in Havana when I was twelve. My father sent me to Havana with her, asked her to get me into the boarding school Belén. While I was in boarding school, Guillermo and I spent a lot of weekends with her. We slept there once a week for a period of six or eight months." When he went to Miami, Guillermo would have been fourteen. It would be unusual for a fourteen-year-old not to mention that Fidel Castro lived in his aunt's apartment, and even stranger for a CIA agent to ignore this information.

The family was shocked by Guillermo's death. For a time, no one spoke about it. Still grieving, Pedro Álvarez said to me in 2000, "And there is another thing: when they killed our son, we knew that all of them [in Cuba] were crying, but no one bothered to send us a cablegram. They were afraid of what would happen to them there. No one sent an expression of grief. This child was one of Celia's favorites. She didn't even call."

BACK IN HAVANA, I confronted Flávia with Pedro's assertion. "We didn't call Chela because we didn't know what we could say to her," she lamented. "In the first moments, I was heartbroken. It happened in the midst of a general mobilization that was happening here in

Cuba. . . . Every time Kennedy made a speech, there was a general mobilization to get prepared. Years later, the telephone rang. Rene [Flávia's husband] answered it. He said it was Chela . . . that her voice was trembling. I said, 'You know we all love you, as always, and we know that you feel the same way about us.' We talked about many things but we did not speak about Guillermo."

"MY BROTHER WAS KILLED IN 1966," Jorge Álvarez Sánchez told me, "and for ten years we lost connections with Cuba. Then they started calling back and forth, and writing. Flávia is the one that started that scenario."

"THEY WERE VERY NICE CHILDREN," Ochoa added softly. "They had the same personality of the mother, because the father was not someone you could speak to. Even while we were up in the Sierra Maestra, the boys' father, who lived in the Manzanillo area—a rice grower—was an enemy of our procedures before the triumph of the Revolution. . . . Like all the other rice growers, he had to pay a tax, but Celia had to pressure him."

"FIDEL DIDN'T OFFER MY FATHER the job at the Rice Institute," Jorge Álvarez clarified. "Celia is the one who told my mother to have him go see Fidel. It was in the first two weeks that he was in Havana that she wanted my father to meet with Fidel. But my father didn't like what he saw. He is a very straight person. My father sees things in black and white. Gray is not his color." Pedro Álvarez, according to his son, would have been unwilling to serve in the Castro government—not even as an advisor on rice production.

Jorge is the child who returned, the first in the family to take a step toward reconciliation. He began to tell me his own story. "I am an engineer. In 1979 I was working in Libya, and one of the guys I worked with, an Italian, was going to Cuba. I gave him Flávia's telephone number, which I'd never forgotten." They were each on their way home, and stopped in Italy. The other engineer urged Jorge to come along with him to Cuba, and so Jorge placed a call to Flávia.

"In 1979, one of Guillermo's brothers, Jorge, called from Italy." Flávia recalls this moment with a fresh delight, as if it were yesterday. "He was on his way home and wanted to come to Cuba."

Jorge filled in more details: "Celia sent me a visa. I didn't have a Cuban passport. The consulate [in Italy] stamped it in my American passport. And she paid for all my expenses."

"I got very excited anticipating Jorge's trip," Flávia continued. "He stayed at the Riviera Hotel. I went there to see him and, from there, I called Celia, who told Jorge that she had asked a friend to get some cassava from Manzanillo and that she was going to bring roast beef. The dinner was at my house, with all the typical Manzanillo food. Kiki [their oldest brother, Manuel Enrique] came with his wife and children. Orlando was still married then. Silvia and our cousin Nene came with her two girls. Celia was already ill."

FLÁVIA FORGOT TO MENTION that Julio César, Griselda's son, who had played with Jorge when they were children, also came. Jorge said they'd been delighted to meet again, and that he had loved meeting Julio César's children, Raysa and Ariel. Jorge says he enjoyed the trip—"They treated me well, and they looked happy"—and claims he asked Celia, "Are you still taking care of your child?"—referring to Fidel. She didn't answer. He admits that Celia was very kind to him, and says that she ate nothing and left the party early. Celia could not have been particularly happy with his question, but on the other hand, she probably took it for what it was: Jorge was speaking for Miami.

Everyone concurs that the families had been separated by Guillermo's death, but it was Manuel's memory that held them together. "My grandfather was a beautiful person," Jorge said.

CHELA AND PEDRO WERE NOT PREPARED for the new government, even though it was run, in part, by Celia. "They did a lot of horrible things to us," Chela remembers. "We went to Vedado. We still had our house in Manzanillo. They took the house in Manzanillo and converted it into a military garrison. Celia didn't do anything to avert that." Pedro immediately softened his wife's remark by saying, "I know she was sorry about the way we were treated, but she didn't do anything for us. We think she didn't do anything because she thought that everybody was going to be equal. Everything was going to be good. This property was going to be given out equally." To this Chela quickly added: "I love her a lot, but I am still resentful. We left everything there. And all of us who came here without a penny—we all had had maids."

While Julio César was trying to sort out the chronology of an event, he said—in clearly a slip of the tongue—that the date in question took place "after we lost Celia to the Revolution." Many relatives, like the Gironas, regret that they didn't spend more time with her, and say that she seemed to be too busy for them to interfere. She was busy, no doubt about that, but Fidel was possessive. If Celia was with her friends and Fidel arrived, they left. Inez Girona recalled one particular occasion when she and a group of friends were at Celia's and Fidel came in. He'd said, loudly, to Celia: "Who are these people?" although he knew all of them. They left. How many members of the family felt that they had lost her, I asked Pedro. "She always loved us. We didn't lose her to the Revolution," Pedro said. But, he went on, "if somebody had said to Celia, 'Someone has to die. One of your sisters or Fidel,' it would have been one of her sisters."

Taking into account all the people who were close to Celia and were affected by the role she played in the Revolution—and this included her seven siblings, their spouses and children, her numerous cousins and their families, and if you add in her friend, Fidel, the biggest target of them all—it is amazing that all these people (around forty, I calculate) survived the Revolution and the counterrevolution, too. So far, they've died only of natural causes, with the one exception: Chela and Pedro's son, Guillermo.

38. HAVANA, 1965–1970

The Household and the Coppelia Ice Cream Parlor

IN HAVANA, CELIA'S DUTIES were overtly governmental, since she held several ministerial posts as secretary to Fidel Castro on the Council of State and the Council of Ministers, the two branches that lead the country. In 1965, she was elected to the Central Committee of the Cuban Communist Party. As a member of the Central Committee, she had come to wield considerable— one might think complete—political power. Yet the most frequent reply when I asked people about it was that she was not political: her real power was her ability to help people. Exactly what she did on the Central Committee, I do not know, and I was advised by Pedro Álvarez Tabío that I'd never get access to documents held by the party. But she did gain extensive power and, by 1978, was a member of the Politburo.

In 1966, Fidel increased the household by bringing home two more children. He had serendipitously discovered Teresa Lamoru Preval and her brother on a trip to Oriente Province. He was on his way to give a speech, and his driver stopped to help a truck that was stalled on the road.

"I was eight years old and going to a place in Mor County that was far away. My uncle's wife had just given birth and I was going to my uncle's home to help out with the new baby. My uncle was the manager of a grocery store in La Melba, and the truck was full of goods for his store. Fidel came by with his caravan of vehicles, stopped and tried to help us. He asked what he could do. They couldn't fix the truck. Finally, he said he'd take us to town. My uncle told him that he had to stay with the truck, because it was loaded, but to take me, Teresita."

Fidel struck up a conversation straightaway: asked what grade she was in school, how she helped around the house, about members of her family, whether she could cook and what she cooked, and how she helped her mother clean house. "The conversation lasted until we reached town. When we got to my uncle's house, Fidel asked me if I wanted to come to Havana to study. I said yes, but I told him that my brother, who was older, also wanted to study. I asked if I my brother could come too, and Fidel said yes. He said that anyone in the family—any of the children—could come. But the others were too young."

Two issues were at work here, one relating to the Revolution on a grand scale, the other highly personal. The first is the enthusiasm felt in Cuba, at that moment, about giving children an education. The government—Fidel, Celia, Minister of Education Armando Hart, and others—had decided to bring children to the capital and educate them there. By 1963, there were 70,000 scholarship students in Havana and the other main cities, the majority the children of farmers. By 1966, educating rural children in Havana was the norm, and an honor for those involved. Second, Fidel was probably thinking about Eugenia, who was very lonely living in the Once house filled with adults.

There were plenty of nieces and nephews running in and out of Celia's apartment in those days, but never once did they mention Eugenia in all the times I interviewed them. Eugenia was giving Fidel and Celia some trouble, was acting out, and admits now that she was very rebellious, would misbehave, and Celia would say, "I am going to tell Fidel." Likely he thought that other children, closer to Eugenia's age, would be a solution.

Fidel continued to his destination, but he sent one of his men to the Lamoru household to carry his invitation to take Teresa and her brother to Havana and discuss it with their mother. "My mother cried a lot. Everybody had been surprised. All afternoon the house was filled with all of our neighbors. Some urged my mother to let us come to Havana; others said the opposite." Teresa and her brother were excited at the prospect. Finally, that evening they got into the jeep and met Fidel at the hall where he'd given his speech. It was late at night, and they traveled with him to Holguín, where a plane was waiting to take them to Varadero. They landed just before dawn. Fidel, the children, and his entourage, spent a night in a hotel, and from there he telephoned Celia to tell her that he was bringing two children to live at Once.

"We arrived in Havana in the afternoon. Celia was there and he introduced us, told her our names." It was August and extremely hot. Teresa says Celia was wearing Bermuda shorts, a sleeveless blouse, and espadrilles, that she had her hair pinned up and wore no makeup. Teresa recalls that she was "very loving," and talked to both of them. "Then she left us with Ernestina and Ana Irma, and went to talk to Fidel."

Teresa is such a self-confident adult that I suspect Fidel saw a spunky, outgoing, well grounded child and concluded she would be good company for Eugenia. Eugenia says she was wildly happy when the other children moved in. Teresa's brother's name was Fidel, and he was around nine years old; Celia called him Fidelito, and "I became Teresita," she says. Celia's relatives think it was entirely Fidel's idea to bring children to live at Once, and Celia went along with it. This seems likely; after all, Fidel, not Celia, was always the one who could spend hours talking to children. His bringing in children, and coming to visit them, was part of how Fidel domesticated the household Celia was creating.

The first day, Ana Irma taught the children how to make their beds, and even though they were fairly young, Fidel insisted that Ernestina must teach them how to cook. Each child was given a permanent household task. Fidelito was introduced to Robert, who cleaned floors and carried out various janitorial tasks, and was taught how to polish Fidel's boots. Ana Irma sat the two little girls down and demonstrated how to pick lint off Fidel's socks.

NEXT, CELIA AND FIDEL turned to a somewhat unlikely project, though it is one that makes perfect sense in the context of a house full of children. "Again, I was summoned to her apartment," Mario Girona said. "Fidel was there. Celia said, 'We are going to make an ice-cream factory. We have lots of flavors and we want to sell the ice cream in a special place.' " The building of the Coppelia Ice Cream Parlor was driven by the desire to transform a run-down park into a respectable location. The leadership wanted to construct it in time for an important international conference soon to take place, which Girona recalls as happening in the National Radio and Television Institute's Yara Theater, located in the heart of Vedado on the corner of L and 23rd. At the time, the Yara was considered the city's best piece of modern architecture. Girona thinks that the project may have been sparked by the fact that the Russian delegation would be attending the conference and staying at the Hotel Havana Libre diagonally across the street from the site.

"It was a Monday. I asked Celia about capacity. She told me that their ice-cream parlor would be for one thousand people. I want to make sure you understand the shock of hearing such a thing. Up to this time, an ice-cream parlor was a small place with a counter, a few tables and chairs, with a capacity for maybe forty people. A thousand people! So I asked her, 'At one time?' and she nodded and said, 'Next Monday, I want to see your ideas.' "

The location they'd picked had been a city park, covering more than a full city block. It had once been the site of the Reina Mercedes Hospital, demolished years before. The grounds, though still lovely, had deteriorated. By 1966, the park consisted of a few ramshackle concession stands of a down-at-the-heel beer garden with drinking and dancing. Everything about the place was unkempt, derelict, and slightly dangerous. Girona called it "a problem spot on an important artery." Soon the new ice-cream parlor would transform this park.

On the appointed Monday, Mario Girona met Celia at the Ministry of Construction. "I made a presentation of drawings. There were some photographs of the site and I showed some sketches. Celia said, 'I think it's wonderful. Fidel will probably never say no to what I like.' "

The story goes that Fidel had found, or perhaps confiscated, the recipes for thirty-seven flavors (the numbers in this story vary) and sent technicians to Canada to learn the science of manufacturing them. He wanted a very good product; he wanted to make the best ice cream in the world. And for this ice cream to be produced in the world's biggest ice-cream parlor, served to, in his opinion, the world's greatest people.

"We only had six months to make the Coppelia. Six months for everything: the drawings, the structurals, the equipment. I put together a strategy. I picked the best engineers, and, to gain time, we needed to make prefabricated elements—elements that could be repeated and made on the site. It was going to be a roof—a dome—on columns. All the columns would be prefabricated; each with a 'holding' for the upper floor. The beams could be made on the site. We covered the roof with asphalt. Everything was from Cuba."

THIS TIME, IT WAS CELIA who decided to bring another child into the household, a boy whose mother had been killed in an automobile accident. Celia waited about a month and then sent someone to Santiago to pick him up; he was almost seven years old.

Antonio (Tony) Luis García Reyes had already met Celia. "I met Celia in Santiago. My mother's job was to take care of visitors' houses for the party. Celia stayed in one of these houses, spent four or five days. I was very small." The father consented to Tony's going to the capital. But he and the other children, Teresa and Eugenia, assume that Celia initiated this adoption by speaking with his uncle, Jorge Risquet, a member of the Central Committee.

During the week, the children boarded at the José Martí School in Santa Maria del Mar. Tony explained their life as schoolchildren: "On Sunday afternoon a bus picked us up in the Parque Central across from the Hotel Inglaterra. We took the 27 bus from Once to Parque Central. No cars drove us. There were no privileges. Saturday morning we were sent home. We'd go back to the scholarship school on Sunday afternoon, from September to June." The children were forbidden to tell anyone who they lived with or to reveal their home address. Tony continued: "When the school year was over, you could go home—to your parents' home. But I preferred staying here, because Celia would send us to the beach at Varadero. She paid for this from her own money. Sometimes we'd go for fifteen or twenty days, the other kids and I, Fidelito, Maria Eugenia, and Teresita, the four of us from the house in Once."

THE COPPELIA ICE CREAM PARLOR remains one of Celia and Fidel's greatest projects. The block enclosing it is covered in trees and large bushes, and all paths lead inward, winding gently through a dense landscape of lush vegetation to converge at a two-storied, circular ice-cream palace. This building, even during the Special Period of austerity in the early '90s, was kept freshly painted a dazzling, spun-sugar white. The rooms are open to the air. At the core of the building is a dome, and this section has an upper floor decorated with red and blue "jewels" as Cubans sometimes affectionately call the panes in stained-glass windows. These sparkle because the sun hits them directly above the trees. On the ground floor, Girona put in very long counters, with stools, to accommodate several hundred guests; there, you are hidden from the outer world.

The Coppelia project forged ahead. Girona worried that they wouldn't make their deadline. He says they were still tearing down the old concession stands on opening day, as they inaugurated the new one. "We finished for the June event. Celia came." Characteristically, she kept a low profile.

THE CHILDREN DID GO HOME to their families, but Celia also presented them with an option: she could bring their parents to Havana instead. Eugenia liked to go home. She claims that since Fidel always asked about her grandparents, she'd developed the habit of staying in contact with them in order to have a ready reply for Fidel. The first time she went back to Oriente, Celia sent gifts to her grandparents: a sewing machine with lots of fabric, thread, and needles for Eugenia's grandmother, a saddle for her grandfather. "Celia sent a battery-run radio, which was very large for the house. Of course I took along a suitcase with all my new clothing." One of the security guards took Eugenia to the airport, and asked the stewardess to care for her. She was met in Manzanillo by party members and driven to Providencia. From there, she went by mule cart. "I was a new girl. I was thin, still crooked, all hair. They called me La Niña, everyone wanted to see me. I was like the mascot of the town. People came from all the nearby places: Santa Dominga, Minas del Frio, all the campesinos came to see La Niña. They brought me letters for Celia."

FILM DIRECTOR TOMÁS GUTIERREZ ALEA told me that Coppelia was created to represent the utopian aspects of the Revolution, that it was supposed to be a place where the new members of society who were supporting the Revolution—young, old, black, white, urban, rural, rich, poor, gay, straight—could congregate. The architectural setting acted as a kind of social arbitrator, he explained, which was why he made Coppelia the setting of his Oscar-nominated film *Strawberry and Chocolate*, where two antagonists meet to bury their differences. As presented in the film Coppelia entirely fulfills its mission. In Havana, it has long been the place where you go on your first date; it is jokingly called a schoolgirl's Tropicana; it's where you take your mother on her birthday, where you meet up with your friends. Since the Coppelia opened, on June 4, 1966, it has served up to 35,000 people daily.

ON THAT FIRST TRIP HOME, Eugenia began giving her clothes away. "When I got back, Celia was waiting for me and opened the suitcase. She asked about my clothing, and commented, 'You are going to have to go around with one hand in front and the other in back.'" Her suitcase was filled with letters, and Celia answered all the letters, solved all the problems. "One had a problem with his farm; another needed a wheelchair; others needed operations." On the next vacation, Celia explained that personal things shouldn't be given away. "You can give people presents, but not personal items. Those are not to be given away. Also, don't bring letters. You are not a courier, and she gave me an address so they could write directly to the palace."

THE NAME COPPELIA was derived from the ballet of that name, which the National Ballet of Cuba was particularly famous for performing. The accountant on the project, Roberto Fernández, told me Celia designed plaid skirts for the waitresses (the ballet is set in an alpine forest) and selected slender young women who resembled ballerinas to work there. But the Coppelia Ice Cream Parlor was a wildly successful venue from the very start, and the svelte young waitresses couldn't physically cope with the job of carrying several thousand scoops of ice cream on a daily basis. Artist Rita Longa designed Coppelia's first sign: a ballerina with fat legs in fishnet stockings looking like a sugar cone, a frothy tutu as the ice cream, outlined in neon.

Coppelia did make very good ice cream, which was entered in international food fairs and sent abroad as diplomatic gifts. A member of the foreign ministry told me that pint cartons, packed in dry ice, accompanied diplomats everywhere; anyone traveling to Chile in a certain era took a container of *coco glace* for Salvador Allende. Right after Coppelia opened, Fidel sent three flavors to Ho Chi Minh.

Time stops when you eat ice cream; sometimes memory takes over. One wonders how many times Fidel recalled the ice-cream birthday cake Celia served him in the Sierra Maestra. This ice-cream factory kept inventing new flavors, and reached a total of about sixty by 1980. It has always been a successful enterprise. And it is the place that pleases as much as the ice cream.

COPPELIA HAD ONLY JUST OPENED when Mario Girona got another call from Celia, asking him once again to come to her apartment. He found her alone, because this project was a secret. Fidel had a shack outside Havana, where he went to clear his head, and the only thing in it was a camp bed. Celia decided to fix the place up, covertly. She wanted it to be a surprise. According to the Cuban journalist Soledad Cruz, "She tried to smooth him out"— she viewed part of her role as sanding off Fidel's rough edges. She wanted to make the presidential retreat—perhaps in a rare concession to public opinion, but certainly out of fondness for Fidel—acceptably presidential.

"It was a very rustic place. I designed a bathroom. We put in a bar." Girona kept it simple, and says it was a very small bar, more like a stand-alone cabinet. When the work was finished, Girona contacted Fidel and they drove to the place together. "And when Fidel saw it, he hated it. He threw the bar out the door. 'Who did this?' he wanted to know." But, as usual, Fidel changed his mind when he heard it had been Celia's idea. Mario went into the weeds to retrieve the bar and haul it back inside. "He was never critical of anything she did." When they got back to Havana, Mario telephoned Celia, who'd been waiting for Fidel's reaction. In the end, the battle of upgrading the shack had been settled relatively easily. Fidel liked to be taken care of, and Mario says Celia explained that she only wanted him to be comfortable.

Years later, Celia telephoned Mario Girona and Dolly Gómez, Girona's wife and architectural partner, about another clandestine project. She wanted to reconstruct Fidel's ancestral home, the house his father built in Biran, Oriente Province, which had been destroyed by fire. The architects traveled to the site and easily found the foundations. Although the house had been made of wood, enough had survived for them to take measurements. They set about collecting photographs from others in the Castro Ruz family, relying primarily on Fidel's siblings Ramon and Juanita. They recorded family members' recollections of the place, and spoke with neighbors. The early photographs provided them with details and scale, and soon the architects worked up a plan. They gave the blueprint to Celia, and she took it to Fidel. He was pleased. She reasoned that he could take visiting dignitaries there, as nearly all expressed a desire to visit the Sierra Maestra. He gave his consent, and construction began. The result is a large plantation house, set on high posts that rise above ground-floor stables, and surrounded on all four sides by verandahs. The president now had a homestead. Celia Girona told me that Celia felt Fidel needed to have a tangible connection to his emotional past, which rebuilding his family home gave him.

THE YEAR 1966 WAS A SUCCESSFUL ONE for projects. Celia capped it with the Cohiba cigar factory, El Laguito, which she established to produce Fidel's favorite cigar, the *lancero* he'd been enjoying since 1959. "I found a man who rolled a good cigar," Fidel explained at the thirtieth anniversary party for Cohiba at the Tropicana nightclub in 1996. "It was slender but long, and made of good leaf. He dressed his cigar in a pale [tobacco leaf] wrapper." One of the trademarks of the Cohiba cigar is its blondness, compared to the dark, sweet cigars of the past: the new cigar was pretty to look at, seemingly mild but deceptively strong. The Cohiba's inner leaves are given an extra stage of fermentation and are, compared with those of standard cigars, more powerful.

Celia had overseen the production of Fidel's cigars from the beginning, and those for other leaders. (Che's were rolled in the Cabaña fortress.) She did this for reasons of security. Gradually, however, her products took on a new role. Whenever Fidel's entourage traveled abroad, they handed out Celia's cigars. Later, she sent them abroad, in hand-carved boxes produced in her wood workshop, and soon they had become widely appreciated state gifts.

She set up the small cigar factory in a vacated mansion in a rich suburban area. This splendid villa, set in a large garden, has all the departments of a regular cigar factory. The bundles of tobacco are aged there, in a small former guest house located in the garden, at the end of a long, palm-lined path; leaf selection takes place in a cabin, a place that may have been used for cooking, or storage; rolling takes place inside the villa proper, amid some of the original pieces of furniture.

Celia's secondary reason for opening the factory was to give work to as many women as she possibly could. Under her direction, all the rollers in this factory were women (and continued to be until the early 1990s when, for the sake of equality, a few men were admitted to the rolling room). El Laguito takes its name from a section of Havana that was the most glamorous part of town in the old days. She was breaking real ground in this endeavor by placing the factory in this district, and by giving some of the tobacco industry's very special jobs exclusively to women. In the 1950s, women everywhere had been elbowed out of the work force as good jobs in factories were reserved for men. Women had always been part of the cigar industry, however: they helped with the fermentation of the leaves, but rarely got the best jobs rolling cigars. At El Laguito, women did everything (except for one role in management, held by Eduardo Rivero, who had created the cigar). At the time of the thirtieth anniversary, Emilia Tamayo González was named director and the first female chief executive of any Cuban tobacco factory. By then, she'd been at El Laguito for twenty of its thirty years.

The success of the Cohiba brand lies in the selection of the leaves, of the specific farms where the leaves are grown, and in the extra fermentation. Fidel glamorously promoted the *lancero*, but by 1968, they produced two more shapes (*vitolas*) and had *lanceros, especiales*, and *panatelas*. After production of these was perfected, *robustos, esplendidos*, and *esquisitos* were added. The members of the new government were paying homage to certain growers of excellent tobacco who, historically, had been short-changed. Cohiba's trademark pale outer leaf, the wrapper, has been exclusively grown by a family of tobacco growers on the privately owned Robaina farm in San Luis, Pinar del Rio Province. This family has produced tobacco since 1846. "I come from a long line of tobacco growers," Alejandro Robaina told me. "My grandfather was an excellent grower and my father, Maruto Robaina, was the best in the country." Yet, year after year the old Spanish buyers would tell him that his leaf was not quite up to par that year in order to lower the price. Cohiba uses Alejandro Robaina's pale "shade tobacco," and it has brought Fidel much needed income for his government. When I visited Robaina at his family's farm, "Fidel spent over thirty minutes here," he told me jubilantly.

In many ways, Cohiba is the biggest project of them all. Celia's business cards in the 1960s were engraved on very thin pieces of cedar, the kind used to separate the rows of cigars in a box of export habanos. And she encouraged a line of clothing (produced in a fashion workshop named Verano, which also produced sugar-sack dresses worn with "Cuba" belt buckles) made of the gauzy fabric used in the fields to cover high-grade wrapper tobacco.

CELIA LOVED ARTISTS. And at the beginning of 1968, Danish abstract artist Asger Jorn painted murals in her office at the Archives. Jorn had come to Cuba to participate in an exhibition at the invitation of Wilfredo Lam, whom he'd met in Paris in 1946 when they were young unknown artists and Jorn worked for Fernand Leger and Le Corbusier. Their friendship deepened in Italy, where they shared a ceramics studio in Abisola.

After the exhibition was over, Jorn wanted to stay on and do something more for revolutionary Cuba, and just how sincerely he meant this can be illustrated by the fact that just a few years earlier, in 1964, Jorn was given a prestigious Guggenheim award for $2,500 but refused it. Only recently has his telegram to Harry F. Guggenheim become public. It read: "Go to hell bastard. Refuse prize. Never asked for it. Against all decency mix artist against his will in your publicity. I want public confirmation not to have participated in your ridiculous game."

Jorn contacted Celia at the suggestion of Carlos Franqui, who was in Paris. He found a sympathetic home at the Office of Historical Affairs; it seems likely that he painted Celia's office first, then moved on to the walls in the large room on the ground floor (formerly it was a bank), hallway, stairwell, and mezzanine. Late one night Celia jokingly painted a little mural of her own. Using cans of paints he'd left on the floor, she drew a scene from the Sierra Maestra, with a tank and some palm trees, expecting him to paint over it. But he didn't.

IN THE FIRST EIGHT YEARS of the Revolution, Celia authored at least three truly great projects: Coppelia, Cohiba, and the archives. In the last of these, she was betrayed by one of her carefully selected staff members, a man she'd appointed director, who copied the archive's contents and left the country in the late 1960s. Carlos Franqui—almost always referred to by her family and colleagues as "a traitor to Celia"—went abroad on a project at Celia's behest and took, without her knowledge, photographs he'd made of documents she was preparing to publish in a book. This was to have been the archives' first publication of primary correspondence and other documents from the war. What exactly Carlos Franqui did remains subject to debate, but one thing is clear—he was not a "whistle blower," stealing material and divulging it to set a record straight. He simply wanted to scoop the archives, and get the glory for bringing these materials to public view.

Franqui had been in the Havana underground, and was sent during the war to the Sierra Maestra for safety. He was the editor of the newspaper *Revolución*, the organ of the 26th of July Movement, published in the first months of 1959, after they'd gained power. He was dismissed, but not for anything personal. In a media revamp, he emerged with a less favorable position, and complained about it. I did not interview Franqui before his death, but I know that Fidel rarely entertained objections—unless you'd been there at the beginning with him, at Moncada or on the *Granma*. Celia had given Franqui a job in the new office she'd set up, where they were seriously cataloguing the Sierra Maestra material. The office was located in a bank one block from Once. Franqui worked there, for her, before he went abroad. She was so confident of his return, although he kept extending his stay, that for two years she made sure he received a salary from her office, and sent money for his child's operation. He began publishing the material in Mexico, Spain, and in the United States. Since she'd

Cuban artist Wilfredo Lam, left, and Chilean painter Roberto Matta, center, raise their glasses in a toast with Celia and others, at a 1967 reception held in the Palace of the Revolution. *(Courtesy of Oficina de Asuntos Históricos)*

been preparing this material for publication herself, she naturally took this personally. From what I was told, she reacted in a quiet, refusal-to-discuss, heartbroken manner.

I came upon the Franqui conundrum inadvertently, through asking one innocent question: "People are shaped by their successes, but even more so by their losses. What were Celia's greatest disappointments?" It was one question from a very small set that I asked every person I interviewed. Better than 90 percent of the answers had been just a name: Carlos Franqui. Writer Miguel Barnet simply comments, "Franqui is a fake. He re-created material." Later, after I'd been given access to the archives, and to original documents, I began to see what Barnet meant by this somewhat enigmatic statement. A Franqui text I'd stored in my laptop differed significantly from the text in the original document. Mostly, it was conceptual content that was altered. One obvious example is *Doce,* Franqui's early book about the "twelve" survivors of the *Granma* when he, better than anybody else, knew there had been sixteen (immediate survivors; or twenty-one, depending on how you count them). But Franqui evidently preferred a biblical metaphor; no doubt it sold better.

Julia Sweig, Senior Fellow at the Council on Foreign Relations, in Washington, researched documents in the archives in the *Oficina de Asuntos Historicos*, Office of Historical Affairs, in preparation for her doctoral dissertation. She hits the nail on the head regarding Franqui: "Because of my extensive access to the OAH collections, I had the opportunity to compare many of the original documents with the version published in the 1976 and 1980 collections and with those housed in Princeton University Library's Carlos Franqui Collection, which contains the photostatic copies of the material that Franqui photographed. I found in many cases that the published documents omit substantively significant portions of the text in the original documents, but without the standard use of ellipses to indicate where text has been left out. In other cases, the published version of the document is misdated."

I knew Franqui's material well before I was permitted to use the archives, and have had the luxury of making my own comparisons. Other historians have not always had that privilege, since the archives have not been readily open to scholars—and likely will remain, as is the case with most archives, closed to the general public.

Franqui's books leave most of us, desperate as we are to figure out what went on among those crazy revolutionaries, in a state of confusion. I pointed out to Barnet that Franqui is usually quoted as saying he left Cuba because the Castro government had turned Communist. "I met Franqui in Europe. He was there two years before he defected. He was the pro-Soviet one," Barnet said, and laughed. "Later, he told everyone the opposite."

When I was finally given permission to use these documents, one of the first questions I asked the director of the OHA, Pedro Álvarez Tabío, was about the material Franqui had been publishing for decades. He explained that the documents were never in jeopardy, but their publication is considered a theft—which, under international copyright standards, it undoubtedly was. Tabío also showed me a carbon copy of Celia's book, never published.

While plenty of other people defected, or at least left the country, Franqui falls into a special category: the corrosiveness of the books he produced, filled with discrepancies in narratives, usually failed to explain their shared history, and Cuba's, fully. Most Cubans I questioned see Franqui as a manipulator of friends, and of facts. The latter is unforgivable since it concerns their own history. "He's not a good writer. He isn't even a good journalist. He is an opportunist," Barnet summed up Franqui's faults. Then he added softly, "He was a friend of Celia's."

Photographer Lee Lockwood, whom I consider a reliable source, told me that sometime in the early 1970s (so not quite a decade after Franqui left the country), when he was in Cuba photographing Fidel, they were in a house outside Havana, and Franqui was there, at the same location, visiting Celia. Who knows what was said at that meeting. Was it reconciliation?

The problem lay very close to her heart, Celia's nephew, Silvia's son Sergio, suggested. "Every night Carlos Franqui came to Once, jacket thrown over his shoulders, when he was the director of the OHA. He had the combination to the vault. He took the Sierra documents."

"Copies of them," I corrected. But then I wondered, do I really know that?

39. The 1970s

The Kids, Lenin Park

IN THE ELEVENTH YEAR of the Revolution, Fidel decreed that the country would bring in its greatest sugarcane harvest ever: the goal was 10 million tons. "Fidel would cut a lot of cane," Tony laughed, recalling those days at Once. "He would get home at whatever hour, all full of red soil, and his boots covered in mud. We didn't have an elevator then. He'd go up the stairs, and Roberto would boil. He'd just cleaned the stairs. Now he had Fidel's boots to clean — and he would make them beautiful. And Fidel would put the boots on and leave, and five or six hours later, it would happen all over again. Roberto would roll his eyes and blow through his teeth. This would happen day after day, over and over. It wasn't only Fidel. It was all his personal guards who walked upstairs with him."

Everybody cut cane. Celia cut cane. She wore her old Sierra Maestra tunic with its wide belt, heavy gloves, and wielded a machete. There are many photographs of her in the cane fields, and not one with a smile on her face. The country cut 8.5 million tons, indeed the largest harvest in Cuban history.

THE SAME YEAR, construction began on Lenin Park, and Celia was in charge of this exceptional project. Its purpose was quite explicit: to protect a huge tract of land that sits above the city's aquifer. There are three parks that protect the aquifer, and this section would make that protection complete. They needed to expropriate the land and get rid of a highly toxic textile factory discharging dyes directly into a stream. First, Celia shut down the factory and had it removed. Lenin Park was a huge undertaking, and the costs were spread through different ministries. She got it off the ground by using her power as a member of the Central Committee. Completing it required volunteer work from many different institutes and schools. Every member of Celia's extensive family can tell you about doing volunteer work there.

IN 1970, CELIA TURNED FIFTY, and did so with a house full of teenagers to contend with. Besides the basic four (Eugenia, Teresa, Fidelito, Tony), there were three brothers named Luis, Ezekiel, and Jesus, who were scholarship students in the Cojimar house. Fidel had invited a fourth boy, Ramon Fuentes, whom the kids called Escambray, to join this group.

"What happened to Escambray was similar to my brother and me," Teresa explained. "During one of Fidel's visits to that area, he met a family and they talked. Fidel liked the boy a lot, and wanted to know what he wanted to be when he grew up. Escambray told Fidel that he wanted to work in aviation. Fidel talked to the family, as he'd talked to my family." He was one of thousands of farm children who came to the city to study. Few returned to the countryside, even though the government was building universities everywhere outside Havana, with the assumption that children would further their education in their own provinces and become leaders.

"When Ezekiel had a fever," says Teresa, "he came to Once to be cared for." Ezekiel was the youngest of all the children, and Celia kept her eye on him. "He stayed there, from then on. Luis, Ez, Jesus, and Escambray would spend the weekend in the house. Or go on Saturday or Sunday. It reached a point that Celia said, don't go back there, stay here. This is when she built an extension on the Once house." There were extra bedrooms with bunk beds. The three brothers appealed to Celia to let their sister come to Havana. Ondina Menendez Sánchez joined them (and still lives at Once), with lots of medical problems. She'd come to the right place: she had an operation on her legs after she arrived, one of many, and she was fifteen. In addition there was a boy named

Celia relaxes at her favorite beach hotel in Santa Maria del Mar. She sits in an aluminum chair, tape recorder in her lap, gold watch—a gift from the women of Manzanillo in 1959—on her wrist, her ever-present cigarette between her fingers. She is smiling, no doubt at antics by the teenagers she and Fidel were bringing up, outside the frame: Eugenia, Teresa, Fidelito, and Tony. *(Courtesy of Oficina de Asuntos Históricos)*

Arcimedes from Ecuador who stayed there briefly, joined by his two brothers. Today Jesus and Fidelito are dead; Escambray is a career officer in the military. When I thought I was going to meet him, he had to get permission to give an interview to a foreigner, which wasn't granted. And I never managed to speak with Ezekiel. Teresa would set the interview up, and he'd equivocate.

Eugenia recalls: "Usually, there were around eleven on the weekends." They'd arrive home from school, settle into their rooms, go to see Ernestina in the kitchen. "We would take coffee up to Celia on the second floor, where all the offices were, where she kept her papers. We would take coffee up to her and she would take time to ask about school. She'd ask us what Ernestina was cooking. No matter how hard she was working, when we came she'd put it aside and talk to us." When they were there during school breaks, longer than the usual weekend, Tony says Celia would spread signs around that said things like: Don't make any noise, I'm working. She had a folder for signs.

On Saturday, they'd all share a midday meal. "There was plenty of food, because food came from the palace. In the beginning, Celia and Fidel were on ration cards. Four of us children were on [them as well]. Carmen Vásquez went to the store to pick up the groceries. We had a normal quota. Celia took the cigarette quota for everybody. Ernestina was on the card, too." Ernestina cooked special Oriente dishes; Celia sometimes made desserts. "Ernestina had the touch," Tony remembers. "I learned a lot from Ernestina. She cooked very well. Fidel wanted us to learn how to cook. Anyone interested would learn from her. She knew, by feeling, how much salt to use. She would just throw things in and it was delicious."

Celia joined everybody for the Saturday meal. She'd serve herself, as everyone did, and sit on a step that separated the kitchen from the dining area. "I, Eugenia, would sit on the step to imitate Celia. I would rush to sit on the step. The boys sat at the table. Ernestina liked to eat standing up. Celia had a little stool she used as a table. Then she'd eat from a bowl." Just as she had done in the Sierra Maestra.

Then they'd go out. "We would go to parties at other places," Tony described how it had been. "At friends' houses, friends we'd made at school. In Cuba, on Saturdays, kids meet in their friends' houses. All you need is cold water and music to party. All you really need is music. We'd dance and tell jokes every Saturday." Then they'd come back to Once. "Most people knew we lived at Once. . . . We were treated like everyone else because people were trying to be equal." At Once, they were filled with self-importance. "You couldn't get bored," Eugenia says. "There were three phones at least in the house. The white phone was the guards'. It rang when Fidel was coming over. '*Viene la gente*' was the message. We even started picking it up. We knew to leave the room if the phone rang and she started talking to someone other than family, and we never picked up a document to read it. There were three phones: black, green, and white. We'd answer them and call to her, 'You have someone on the green phone,' we'd tell her."

For supper, they'd have eggs, bread, and any leftovers. "We had small suppers. The ration only covered one meal. Celia hardly ever ate at night." She told the girls bedtime stories—she told them about Clodomira, about her life with her family among the orchards of their farm, and about her days with Column 1 in the mountains. Celia told them about Clodo's notebook with the squiggles, and how she'd traveled to see Flávia, and about going to the hospital with letters for her father.

At some point, Celia decided to give the children lessons in table manners: she set the table and explained the uses for each piece of flatware, and demonstrated how to place a napkin in their laps. Then she sent them to a really good restaurant, and quizzed them when they got home.

On Sunday mornings, everybody lined up at the sink. Celia made them wash their clothes. Celia taught by example and lined up, too, as did the boys. "She brought us up to be independent," Tony reported. "When I was small, I washed my clothes. We had to. When we were very small, Ana Irma did it. By the time we were ten, we washed our own clothes. At school we'd wash our socks." If they didn't, he told me, they were grounded, and couldn't go to parties, movies, parks, baseball games. Teresa added that the same thing happened if they didn't make their beds, or acted out in some unacceptable way. When this happened, Celia would ask that the child write a letter, addressed to her, describing what he or she had done, and why. Then she'd read through, correcting spelling and grammar, before handing the letter back for the child to make a clean copy.

Celia's family, the Sánchezes, congregated on Sunday evenings after the kids had gone back to school. "They were younger than us, by at least five years," says Silvia's son Sergio. Sunday supper at Celia's had been a tradition long before Eugenia and the other children arrived. Clever, the Jamaican gardener from Pilón (now buried in the Sánchez plot in Colón Cemetery) who had tended Celia's garden and carried around her cupcakes to sell at people's back doors so she'd have pocket money, came early on these Sundays to see the adopted children and stayed to see the Sánchezes and watch TV. Celia stocked up on aguardiente and cigars, which he'd finish off completely in the course of the long day. He sat on one of the two rocking chairs she'd kept from the house in Pilón and then be joined by Miguel Ugando, Ernestina's ex-husband, who sat in the other rocking chair. Allegedly, Ugando came to visit his son with Ernestina, Pedro, but the kids think he came to see Ernestina, although they were divorced. Miguel and Cleever spent the afternoon watching baseball on television. Late in the afternoon and early evening, the Sánchezes would arrive. Everyone got the same treatment. "She was so informal," Raysa Bofill, Griselda's granddaughter, recalls. "She had banquettes, but she never used them. We would eat on the floor, which was red, burnt-red tiles from the original apartment. She didn't make changes if she didn't need to. She didn't have time for keeping house."

Alicia Otazo, Flávia's daughter, remembers going there every Sunday. "Celia had sofas. Her house had wainscoting that was polished and varnished wood, and wood on the ceiling, too, like a typical cottage. And a ceiling fan in an old style. The sofas were upholstered in vinyl. Two sofas in a corner, with a two-tiered table between them where she put her papers. . . . She would always sit on the sofa that faced out, next to the table, and there were always fresh flowers in a vase. If mariposas were in season, it would be those. The walls were painted white."

Raysa found a couple of snapshots to show me. Everything was as described except for the banquettes, which were handsomely covered in very wide, black and white vertical stripes.

Eduardo Sánchez came to Once every day. "At Once, sometimes she would say to me, 'Stay for lunch.' She would sit on her step and I would sit on the banquette. She would tell whoever was serving food, 'Give him a lot. He's big,' and feed me pieces from her fork. 'Here, try this,' she would say to me."

Eduardo began to work for Celia in 1968, and worked for her for two years before actually meeting her. Rarely do people hire someone without meeting them, and certainly not Celia, who wanted to know everything about her staff: their health, their dreams, their expectations. So that piece of information sent up an alert in my mind. Eduardo explained that one of the rebel army commanders told Celia about him. "I was from Camaguey, from the city of Ciego de Avila. I had a hair salon there." Celia told the comandante, "Send him, we need creative people." She directed the Council of State to send a letter requesting Eduardo's presence in Havana.

This corresponded with a period in Cuba in which male homosexuals were being hounded and persecuted. Celia would have hated this. I went to the OHA office to see Nelsy Babiel, who was hired by Celia and is now the director of her materials in the archives. She told me that Eduardo was one of several homosexuals Celia protected by creating jobs for them. As the atmosphere surrounding them became more dangerous, she kept a watchful eye over several men in the 1970s by asking them to stop by her house every day. "It was the only way she knew how to protect them," Nelsy said.

"One day, it was January 18th, my birthday, I went to the archives and saw her at a distance, through a glass pane," Eduardo told me. The archives is housed in a 1950s bank with a fair number of glass partitions. He happened to speak to Celia's sister Acacia and said, "Today, I've had the loveliest birthday present, because I've just seen Celia from afar. A week later, I went back. Acacia called me over, and behind one of the columns was Celia. I met her face to face."

I interviewed Mariela Castro, the director of the Cuban National Center for Sex Education. "Celia didn't know how, but she found a means to protect homosexuals." She went on to say that Celia did not have an institution to work with, and she wasn't in a position to make legislation. All she could do was protect them. "Institutions were being created to develop the country, the party, the government; to defend ourselves, and to learn to survive in our sovereignty. At the time, nobody worried about the rights of homosexuals. . . . Nobody's creative imagination would have led to this institution, not at the time."

Eduardo continued: "One time I was at Once, and Fidel came in with Pepin Naranjo. Fidel put his hand out to get something and touched me. I flinched. I felt like a mouse under an elephant's foot, and I told Celia: 'I don't know where Fidel ends and God begins.' She answered, 'For heaven's sake, don't tell him that.'"

In 1968, Eduardo began to work in one of Celia's workshops and in 1970 began restoring furniture for Las Ruinas, an exclusive restaurant being built in Lenin Park. Celia made the architectural design of Las Ruinas very modern but used groups of antique chairs restored by Eduardo and other teams in her many workshops to decorate it; she also used antique pieces of stained glass.

LENIN PARK OPENED IN 1972, a far cry from the old Spanish parks that were so much a part of Celia's life in Manzanillo, but not unlike the rolling fields outside Pilón. She was neither working quickly nor taking the easy way: she was behind the epic task of planting 80,000 mature trees, each with an extensive root system. And it was her idea to import birds from the not-too-distant province of Pinar del Rio, only to have most of them fly back home. She worked with many architects, but gave a start to a young architect, Juan Tosca, who helped her lay the foundations for a wonderful urban park where no buildings could be taller than the vegetation. She commissioned works of art from Portocarrero, and supplied his paints and rum while he worked on the project. On opening day, Celia made sure everybody who lived in Once was there as well as nieces and nephews. She introduced them to everything the park had to offer, sent the kids on hikes and trail rides. Eugenia fell off a horse.

The park reflects Celia's good taste and practical nature, but just as much her eccentricities. Critics immediately point out that there are no paths. "People will make paths where they want paths," she told her project manager, Lucy Villegas. Here, people walk wherever they want (although not always conveniently). Leaves are allowed to lie where they fall from the trees. When she discovered gardeners raking them up, she told them to let them fall and see the patterns they made on the ground. Celia disliked the topiaries in other Havana parks, because topiary took up too much time, and was unnatural. She would likely have labeled it unCuban.

Today, Lenin Park is a swath of gently rolling hills and open spaces, a refuge from the city center. The park lies on the southwestern edge of Havana, but along well-established roads linking the capital to the ancient tobacco fields that stretch from Havana Province to Pinar del Rio. Slightly to the west lies José Martí International Airport and its newest terminal, No. 3, which opened in 1998 and was designed by Mario Girona (his last project before his death) and Dolly Gómez. Lenin Park's eastern boundaries touch on La Mantilla, home of Detective Lt. Mario Conde and his creator, the writer Leonardo Padura. Today Lenin Park has sixty or so restaurants, numerous food stands, art galleries, a narrow-gauge railroad, a rodeo, baseball diamonds, swimming pools, fields and wooded areas, a bust of Lenin in white marble, a garden that is a gift from Japan, an amusement park that is a fairly recent gift from China, and at least a million visitors a year.

40.

Life at Once

THE CHILDREN LOVED SPENDING HOLIDAY time at Once, especially the week-long school holiday to commemorate the Bay of Pigs victory, Semana de Girón, which was celebrated every year. They didn't go on vacation "like everybody else," according to Tony. Celia would take them to work in the fields. "Volunteer work. We'd clean cane fields. The people who worked in her office did this, too. It was in the countryside outside Havana. We'd go in the morning and come back home."

It was those stay-at-home, stay-in-Havana vacations that gave Celia time with the children. She taught them how to cook. She made sure they knew how to debone a chicken or a turkey, which they all learned how to do, and were surprised to hear that she'd learned the secrets at Macy's, where she had taken cooking classes during her long stay in New York City in 1948. She taught them traditional Oriente recipes, like corn pudding made with the milk squeezed from the kernels and stirred constantly over a low flame. She made sure they all knew how to dance, and taught the girls how to use makeup. "We all had boyfriends and girlfriends," Eugenia explained.

Tony elaborated on Celia's approach to their social lives. "If anyone had a girlfriend or boyfriend, Celia would talk to us. She wanted to know who they were, where they lived, if they were

Pilón, 1972. Celia continued to return to Pilón to fish with Gustavo Navea Torres. She has a tape recorder in her lap and is wearing a T-shirt she designed sporting Mella's, Camilo's, and Che's portraits. The fisherman was a storyteller. Sometimes, when Fidel was overworked, she'd bring Navea Torres to Havana to tell Fidel jokes. *(Courtesy of Oficina de Asuntos Históricos)*

revolutionaries, and what their parents did for a living. She asked us to find out this information." When Eugenia met a boy on the Isle of Youth (formerly the Isle of Pines) on a school outing, she related, "I told Celia that I had a boyfriend, and she asked where he lived. I told her San Francisco de Paula." Celia told Eugenia to bring him to Once. "Celia was lovely. We were very young. Twelve years old. We went steady for two years. He'd given me a ring and Celia gave me a gold ring to give to the boy."

She continued: "I lost interest in my boyfriend and fell in love with somebody else. I didn't know how to break it off, so I asked Celia. She said, 'You have to be sincere, be frank, tell him that you like him, but that you don't love him anymore. Tell him the truth. Ask for the ring back. Give him back yours.' Celia didn't know it was because I'd fallen for someone else. Celia wouldn't have liked that."

"We asked her if we could go to Oriente with our boyfriends," Teresa said. The girls were around fifteen at the time. "Celia told us, 'I don't think it's the correct thing to do, but I'm going to talk it over with Fidel.'" (When Celia was fifteen, she and her girlfriends would walk in their favorite park in Manzanillo and invite boys to the beach. She surely recalled those happy trips to the Sánchez farm with her boyfriend, Sadurni, but also how they had traveled there with a chaperone.) A few days later, after she'd spoken to Fidel, Celia gave Eugenia and Teresa the answer. "She said, 'If the boys want to visit you while you're there, you could leave first and they can visit you.' And when Fidel heard this he said, no, 'It sounds too much like a honeymoon.' So, the boys didn't go. We were like a normal household."

But it wasn't a normal household. For one thing, the children didn't give reciprocal parties, because Teresa told me that "at Santa Maria del Mar, we'd met Olivia, the niece of Commander Calixto García. We asked if we could bring her home and she came, but after she left, Celia explained why we couldn't bring people into the house. She gave us examples, told us stories of people she thought she could trust: ambassadors, ministers, important people she'd trusted, who had attacked them. 'We have to be very careful. We have to take care of Fidel.' After that, we never asked to bring guests again."

Eugenia finally got up the courage to tell Celia that she was going steady with someone Celia didn't know about. "Is he a militant?" meaning: Is he a party member? Celia wanted to know where he lived and what he looked like. "Ask him for a photo and bring it to me." Eugenia's boyfriend was on the judo team, "He was strong, elegant, a mulatto, and wearing a swimming suit in the picture I showed her. She didn't like him from the photo." Yet Eugenia says that Celia admitted she might get a better impression from meeting him in person. "I brought him to the house. He was completely frightened. His hands were trembling." Meeting Victor, Celia sent Eugenia off to make coffee and asked about his job, about sports. When Eugenia brought out a plate of pastries with the coffee, he declined both, and Celia teased him by saying, "You're so overweight." He was extremely body conscious. Celia gave him a little tour of the kitchen, and then Eugenia's room ("It was always neat. It had to be. Celia demanded this"). Then Celia asked about their plans for the rest of the day, and they told her they were going to the movies. She asked Victor to bring Eugenia home early.

"I felt things had gone well. When I got back that night, Celia was waiting for me and told me that she did not like him. And she listed the reasons. She'd had him investigated! She had all the information on him. He lived in Luyano. He had a son with a woman. His parents were divorced. There had been problems of violence between them." Celia told Eugenia: "This man won't be good for you."

Even though Victor had not informed Eugenia of any of these facts, she was eighteen and resisted taking advice from Celia. "I told her I was in love. I told her I was going to go steady with him. Celia told me he couldn't come to Once." This was in 1975, and the relationship continued for a couple of years. "Celia knew. I thought she didn't know, or was just being discreet."

One day in 1977, Eugenia was leaving the apartment as Fidel was coming in. He said, "Where are you going all dressed up?" and Eugenia says she couldn't lie to him. "I answered, 'I'm going to see my boyfriend.' And Fidel said, 'Are you still going steady with him? Where's he taking you?' and I told him to Restaurant 1830. Fidel said, 'He's taking you there? It's so expensive.' The restaurant was a lie. Instead we went to the tower next to it, and sat outside at the café."

Fidel talked to Celia. "She's in love with him, let her go steady," and mentioned that Eugenia looked very good, and seemed to be happy. This exchange was reported to Eugenia later that night by Migdalia, the nurse, who had listened to Fidel and Celia's conversation. Celia agreed, but said, "I don't want him here." So, on that basis, the relationship continued.

TERESA GAVE A FULLER PICTURE of those years: "We all had boyfriends and girlfriends, but with Ezekiel, Celia really suffered. He was the youngest, and he started an affair with a woman named Orquidia he met at Varadero, on the beach," where Celia sent them for a summer holiday every year for a couple of weeks. "His relationship with Celia was wonderful [because] the rest of us children would accept whatever she said, but he'd argue back." At this point in our conversation, Teresa and Eugenia conferred, and decided that Orquidia had been between eighteen and twenty years older than Ezekiel. Teresa continued: "She looked good, physically. And there was a big drama about this relationship, which lasted quite a while—all of it followed closely by Celia, of course, who would talk to me every day to find out how it was going." In about four or five years, Ezekiel fell in love with somebody else. After that, he got married. But his new wife was nervous, and went into the hospital just before their wedding. Teresa shook her head, "His love stories were terrible."

Tony went AWOL over love. "I had a big problem with Celia," Tony told me. "When I was doing my military service in the navy, in the *Marina de Guerra*, I left without permission. I was in love with a girl, with blue eyes. Head over heels. I was crazy to see her. I was stationed at Mariel, the 2746 military unit. We were on lookout for submarines. I was a radio telegrapher. When I left my post, Celia was shocked. She found out about it, and when I got home, she was waiting for me."

Tony was about sixteen when he committed this dereliction of duty. He went home to Once several days later. "When she saw me she said, 'Sit down in the living room, I have to talk to you. I know what's going on, so don't lie to me.' So I answered yes, I'm AWOL. I'm in love. And she said, 'Don't move from here. Tomorrow, early, they are going to pick you up and take you back to the unit.'" Celia held the rank of major; she was, and always would be, a comandante, so Tony was really putting her to a test. His godmother was still, mentally no less than technically, a soldier. I doubt she gave much weight to his declaration of love, or his style of declaring it, since Cubans are much given to jumping off the cliff in matters of love. "In the morning they picked me up. When I got up, she was waiting for me, and she said,'You have made a very big mistake and you are going to pay for it.' When I got to my unit, the chief told me I'd be put in prison for six days. I had been there for only three days when they took me out to a military judge, who talked to me, and took down my statement, my testimony, from which I was to be judged. The judge said that Celia had called to ask about me, and she'd asked if six days were the normal sentence for what I'd done. They told her no. So Celia said, 'Then apply the normal sentence.' It was eight months."

He was sentenced to eight months, not in prison but in his unit without leave. By this time, he said, he was near the end of his three-year military duty. "Altogether, I spent three years and eight months. They asked me if I wanted to go to Angola. I went. I don't want to brag, but I was good on the radio. Good at my job."

IN 1974, CELIA WENT BACK TO SCHOOL. The six children were grown, although they still lived at home; Tony and Fidelito were in the military but still came to Once whenever they could get passes. She wanted to study Marxist philosophy at the Nico Lopez School, a four-year course leading to a university degree. Comandante Delio Gómez Ochoa was also studying there. He'd married her sister Acacia, and lived in the neighborhood, on Linea and 10th. He was studying economics. Every Saturday afternoon they would go to hear two lectures, covering various issues, delivered between 2:00 and 6:00. They taped the lectures and listened to them again later in the week, when they completed the study assignments. Celia set up a classroom in one of the empty back apartments where she met with her study group of five women, which met every night during the academic year. Delio met with a separate group, mostly at the Once schoolroom. Through the rest of the '70s, Celia studied the Marxists and took exams.

AFTER FIFTEEN YEARS OF ANTI-COLONIAL STRUGGLE, Portugal, having just overthrown its dictator, withdrew from its African colonies. Cuba came to the aid of Angola's MPLA government led by Agostinho Neto, which faced domestic and foreign opposition, including from South Africa and Zimbabwe. Cuba sent 480 specialists—one of them being Tony.

Tony was living in Luanda with his uncle, Jorge Risquet Valdes. "A car came to tell me that Fidel wanted to see me. . . . I went to see Fidel, who was in a visitor's house [for foreign dignitaries] in Luanda. He hugged me. I had long hair at the time, and Fidel asked me if I'd left my barber behind in Cuba. 'Is this an Afro you're wearing?'" Tony has blue eyes with a sharp, but playful gaze—he looks a bit like Frank País.

In March 1977 Fidel made a somewhat jubilant victory tour, accompanied by Celia, of several African nations. (Staff and friends say that Celia didn't like traveling then, so I think it likely she wanted to visit Tony.)

"When Celia got to Angola, she sent for me. She was in a neighborhood called Fotungo de Belas. Celia liked to mix with

In March 1977, Celia accompanied Fidel to Angola, where she visited Tony, serving in the Cuban navy and living in Luanda. She is seated here between two Angolan women. *(Courtesy of Oficina de Asuntos Históricos)*

people, wherever she was, but it was the most godforsaken place. When I went to see her, she asked me, 'Do you know this place well?' and I told her, 'Like the palm of my hand.' So she said, 'Let's go for a walk.'" And they had walked around in this barbed-wire-encircled community, largely empty yet still dangerous, a place where people were ambushed. "She couldn't go around there. It was forbidden."

The next day, she showed up at his unit to take him out."She came by and said 'Let's go.' We got into a car and left fast, without anybody seeing her. We reached a *kimbo*, a poor part of town, and she stopped the car. She got out. She greeted everybody. She ate oranges. It was at night, after eight or nine. I was around nineteen at the time. She was alone. [There was a curfew.] It was not allowed. The people were very poor, without schooling." Celia took Tony back to his post and dropped him off, but kept an eye on him as her driver left. "When I got back to the unit, I was dressed down. But she saw what was happening. She overheard the officer," who was shouting at Tony because he'd disappeared. "So she came back, identified me—singled me out. And then she said to the officer, 'This is the end of this discussion.' She was saying this to the military! She was giving orders to a commanding officer! But nothing more was said about it."

Clearly, Celia wasn't above pulling rank and, aside from the fact that she was always impatient with bureaucracy, as she gained more and more power, she became explicit about it. She could be counted among a rare breed: a recusant. But in this instance, she acts like a mother—a Cuban mother who is visiting her son in Angola, off the battlefield, making sure she would see her son. She didn't see any reason for him to get flak about it.

A COUPLE OF MONTHS LATER, Celia was in the emergency room. "One day she went into the room that was a storeroom with all Fidel's clothes. The air conditioning was up high. Suddenly, she couldn't breathe. They took her to the emergency room at Calixto García Hospital. They called Flávia and asked her to come immediately." Alicia Otazo, Flávia's daughter, and I spoke in a small conference room adjoining her office as dean of the School of Biology at the University of Havana, in December 2006.

Flávia had explained what happened when I talked to her in 1999. "Celia called me. She said, 'I'm on my way to Calixto García. Something is happening to me. I can't breathe. The air is missing from my system.' When I arrived, she was already there; they'd taken an x-ray and had processed it. There was a tumor in one lung. The x-rays disappeared, but I saw it, and Celia saw it, too. . . . We wanted to see what the x-ray showed. The next day, when I got to Celia's home, I found Dr. Selman, a very special doctor, Fidel's, one of the most important doctors in Cuba. She sat down with us, Acacia and me, and told us that Dr. Selman told her that she ought to be operated on that day, if she were willing."

"They took out one of her lungs," Alicia explained. "After the operation, they told her that they had removed the lung because there were nodals with aspergillus fungi. This is a fungus that can be found in moist places."

STORIES CIRCULATE THAT CELIA'S LUNGS were contaminated by a fungus carried through letters from Africa. And Celia herself sparked this, because she told Flávia, "My house has to be cleaned up, and I must protect myself. I open up all the mail that comes from everywhere." The doctor had mentioned this contamination from an African source as possibility, according to Flávia. "They cleaned up the house," Flávia continued. "They painted. Everything was ready in a month or so, and she was allowed to go back to the house . . . She started constructing a hotel she was interested in."

I thought this story about the mail so bizarre that I wanted to speak to a doctor about it, and a friend invited me to meet Dr. Isolina Pacheco who confirmed the story regarding this diagnosis.

Alicia, speaking in 2006, stated the situation explicitly: "The doctors didn't mention that they saw the spot on her lung. This led to everything else. We later found out that once they saw the x-ray, they knew she had cancer, but didn't mention it. We all knew afterward. They didn't inform her it was cancer. They just said they would operate. Two authorities were present. . . . It was a complete lie. She had no radiation therapy, no drugs, no chemotherapy. They worked out the lie so well that the plaster was removed from the whole building, closet doors were taken off, windows enlarged for greater ventilation. Miriam Manduley was moved out of her apartment while this was done. They tested. It was all a montage." But there is one mitigating factor that surfaced in this discussion. A few moments later, Alicia, with real sadness, admitted: "She was aware, I feel, that she'd not been told the truth."

Flávia died in 2003. I looked again at my 1999 interview with her. She'd said: "Her clinical history was kept somewhere, it was updated, but it was kept confidential. She knew where it was. Celia had a feeling that she hadn't been told the truth. But the whole family believed the story of the fungus."

Migdalia Novo, Celia's private nurse, was present at the operation. She came to the Office of Historical Affairs for an interview in 2007. When I asked her about the fungus and whether it had been the source of Celia's health problems, she answered, "No." She continued: "When she was operated on, in Cuba, we weren't accustomed to be told, to your face, the diagnosis. It was difficult to explain to her what she had. Her internist, in a meeting with the surgeon and another internist, decided to tell her a little white lie. They told her it was a fungus named aspergillus. A fungus she never had. Her bedroom in the apartment was humid, and this fungus originates in humid places—like caves. The internist said to me: 'We need your cooperation once again. You are going to the apartment. You are going to take samples. We are going to inform her that the aspergillus fungus exists there.' We told her that this aspergillus is what she had, but it was a white lie." I asked if Cuban doctors today tell their patients if it is cancer. She replied, "Now, yes. My husband suffered from heart problems and they spoke of it openly. It was just this particular illness." I interjected, "You mean cancer? But Celia hated to be lied to." To that, Migdalia replied: "That is true. But in my years as a nurse, you can help the patient psychologically. They won't feel anguish. What hit Celia strongly, and what she felt most, was that she had so much still to accomplish. So, if there is a person you are treating, and you state this [honest diagnosis], you have to be careful. She knew what she had. When speaking with certain people, she would say: I know what my diagnosis is. Celia never actually believed she had this fungus." Novo was repeating an age-old argument and a view commonly held into the 1970s.

"Wasn't she angry with her doctors?" I asked Novo. She replied, "She would call certain people and tell them that she had been lied to."

"Good for her," I replied.

Not to be silenced by my comments, Novo continued quietly, "Yes. She didn't want to be lied to. She was a doctor's daughter. The illness was in the family."

She could live with that knowledge, was fully aware that her father and uncle had died of cancer, and that she was dying. But being lied to? She must have made a mental compromise. To my best knowledge, her surgeon, Dr. Eugenio Selman, and internist, Cuco Rodríguez de la Vega, Fidel's doctors, were still alive in 2012.

What part did Fidel play? The family children, Sergio and Pepin Sánchez and Raysa Bofill, think Fidel made decisions for Celia because that is what she wanted.

Two World Meetings and a Wedding

THOUGH SHE WAS ILL, Celia took on one last significant project: overseeing the design and construction of a convention center to host a summit conference of the Non-Aligned Movement (NAM) to be held in Havana in September of 1979. Fidel had been named the president of that organization and Cuba would be the host of its big gathering.

The Convention Palace in Havana is a large white building that sits on the edge of a woods in Cubanacan, and was inaugurated in late August 1979. Sixty heads of state and several thousand delegates attended the conference, including Yugoslavia's Marshal Tito, Palestine's Yasser Arafat, and Vietnam's Pham Van Dong. They walked a red carpet into the building to be greeted by the Cuban head of government. Fidel was at the pinnacle of his power and had come a long way since Celia had helped him host dignitaries of non-aligned nations at the Hotel Theresa in 1962.

For this conference, Celia had prepared—still insisting on doing most things herself—houses for the guests, converting confiscated residences in Laganilla and Cubanacan: refurbishing the carpets and furniture, hanging Cuban art on the walls. She had started in May 1979, and readied 132 protocol houses throughout the summer. In one, she became so ill that she could not leave, and had to go to bed there. Flávia chose this incident to illustrate the beginning of the end of Celia's life. "This was something she never did. Not in a room that was unfamiliar to her, not at an embassy house. And she asked that nobody call her, because she was feeling so ill."

Celia was not quite sixty years old. Pictures taken in 1979 show that her face was lined, the skin somewhat slack, but her eyes still glittered, and her gaze remained serene. In the mid-1970s, Celia had had a face-lift (psychoanalysis and plastic surgery are part of Cuba's idea of mental health), and several photographs show Celia with taut skin, long loose hair, wearing dozens of Mexican necklaces over a drawstring-gathered peasant blouse. Although completely uncharacteristic of the way she usually looked, these images reflect this one last willful attempt to look her best.

Between May and September, she developed a cough (although some people make a point of saying she didn't cough) and was attending Saturday classes at the Nico Lopez School. It was her final year of study. Two students in her class say that she not only coughed, but had started smoking Cuba's cheapest, harshest cigarettes. The evolving clinical history, not surprisingly, showed that her lymph nodes were inflamed.

BACK FROM ANGOLA, Tony decided to get married. He didn't want to disturb Celia and made all the arrangements. "I just told her one day that I was going to get married." In Cuba, the state provides the wedding ceremony, pays for a few nights in a hotel, and provides a cake and refreshments for a reception. He set the date, booked a room in the Havana Libre Hotel himself. He stressed to Celia that he'd taken care of everything, and Celia said, "I am going to help you." And he assured her that he had money. "It's not about money," she replied. "I'm going to help in other ways."

She asked the lawyer at the Palace of the Revolution to perform the ceremony, found a place nearby, on 12th and 17th, hired a photographer, and had a special wedding cake delivered. "She had a suit made for me, a wonderful suit, and a dress for my wife. She had Cuco [the dressmaker, head of the Verano workshop] make it." The wedding took place around nine at night. Celia attended. "The party lasted until five in the morning. When I was leaving for the hotel, she came over and asked me where I was going and I told her the Habana Libre, for my assigned honeymoon. And she said, 'No. No. Go to the Marazul. I'm giving you a present of 15 days there, at the beach. I've already paid for it. Go."

IN SEPTEMBER, SHE TRAVELED to New York to attend a meeting of the General Assembly of the United Nations and to give a party at the Cuban Mission, hosted by Fidel. She brought all the staff she needed; in fact, she brought everything, even salt and water. This reflected the level of paranoia—or vigilance—to which U.S. aggression against the Revolution had driven the Cubans. The Cordova-Caignet team was called upon to plan and produce the party. Maria Victoria Caignet says that giving government receptions had become routine by then, and as usual, they gave the party an entirely Cuban theme. Everything was Cuban, from the dinnerware to the menu. Caignet led me to shelves and cupboards in her apartment to show me a sample of each item. Glasses— sets for cocktails, wine, beer and water, from the glass-blowing workshop. They used Cuban sand, which makes the glass come out green, and blown the glasses into wooden molds. Most were straight-sided goblets with a little pedestal.

Platters and serving dishes were kiln-fired from red clay, a vibrant, fiery shade found in tobacco fields. Serving platters, carved from the most precious woods of the Sierra Maestra, had been fitted out with simple rope handles. Buffet plates, eight inches in diameter, were made of all kinds of wood, some light, some dark. Serving spoons were wood, carved in one of Celia's workshops. Mats, woven from fine grasses in Taino Indian tradition, and napkins cut from colorful textiles that had been woven, printed, and dyed in Cuba. All the food was imported from eastern Cuba, and from Oriente came an indigenous flatbread made by pounding cassava root. Meat and fish and vegetables were packed in ice, and transported to New York.

The meal started with rum cocktails. "There was a small bar, but mostly the cocktails were passed on trays, metal trays we also took along. We took rum, we took everything: cigars, even the salt. The only things we bought were flowers and plants. We took wine, Socialist in origin. The wine was from Chile." Evidently exported before the military coup of 1973. "The silverware was metal, made in Europe. We always bought it from Sweden or Denmark." They took cooks from the palace, and waiters. "They wore white

In September 1979, Celia traveled to New York to attend a meeting of the General Assembly of the United Nations and to organize a party at the Cuban Mission, hosted by Fidel. She brought all the staff she needed; in fact, she brought everything, even salt and drinking water. This was not mere scrupulous attention to detail, but a reflection of the level of paranoia—or vigilance—to which U.S. aggression against the Revolution had driven the Cuban government. *(Courtesy of Oficina de Asuntos Históricos)*

guayaberas. There were eight or ten of these men." And lots of security, Caignet says, in addition to the NYPD. "Three to four hundred people attended: Africans, Europeans, independents. Not so many Latin Americans [were friends of Cuba] at that time."

After the meal, coffee was passed around. "We had a special tray with little holes in the bottom, because for cups we used *guiras,* which come from a tree. *Guira* is the same shell used to make maracas. We used very little ones cut in two, the outside is polished, with some simple designs cut in them—filled with black, sweetened coffee."

Celia attended the arduous General Assembly meetings. Back home, the Cuban people seemed to know that she was dying—not officially, but by a very efficient grapevine that exists in the eastern section of the country, where everyone was particularly fond of Celia Sánchez. Marisela Reiners, a Spanish professor at the University of Havana, grew up in Santiago and described her parents' concern. They took turns sitting in front of the television

Celia chose Santiago as the place to make her last public appearance. She traveled there November 30, 1979, for the anniversary of Frank's great uprising, and pinned medals on the old combatants, knowing they wanted to see her one last time. *(Courtesy of Oficina de Asuntos Históricos)*

throughout the entire United Nations meeting (Cuba broadcast the sessions gavel-to-gavel) just to catch a glimpse of Celia and assess the state of her health. Her appearance, during that week, was widely discussed throughout Santiago, Manzanillo, Media Luna, Campechuela, Pilón, and Bayamo.

CELIA CHOSE SANTIAGO as the place to make her last public appearance. She traveled there November 30, for the anniversary of Frank's great battle, and pinned medals on the old combatants, knowing they wanted to see her one more time.

At the Nico Lopez School, she very nearly finished her coursework, but was unable to attend classes in December, or take exams, and had two subjects pending. She didn't graduate, but except for those two exams, she'd completed her degree. Ochoa suggested to the director that they waive those last exams and award her a diploma. "But it was never done. She was already in very poor health."

In December, she still managed to spur on a new project that had been several years in the making. She'd noticed that Cubans were not eating enough vegetables, and decided to grow more varieties in Cuba. Seeds were purchased from Holland and other countries, and planted in fields not far from the palace. Organic gardens there still actively produce vegetables, rimmed by herbs and flowers—cosmos and marigolds—to attract insects. A form of this garden has been duplicated behind nearly every school, military post, and police station since Celia's death.

IN RESEARCHING THIS BOOK I listened to stories and was given countless examples of Celia's making decisions for Fidel. Suppliers of these accounts ranged from soldiers to architects to staff members and family, including the adopted children. Tony recalled that Fidel would be resting, and somebody would come with a problem, and Celia would tell them how to solve it. "Are you sure that's what I'm supposed to do?" the person would ask, and Tony claims that she'd say, "Yes. Do it just as I've told you." And they'd better do it that way, Tony added, because she and Fidel discussed everything.

It had been this way since the Sierra Maestra. Their interchangeability certainly started there, when Fidel would tell her to please go down the mountain and dig trenches or brief the men what to do while he dealt with planning a battle. Now, in Havana, he'd tell her: Celia, I need some sleep, take care of everything. At her death, this exchange of roles took some by surprise. It is just that some people forgot that it was the way the two of them dealt with life.

At the end of her life, it came as a surprise to many that Fidel took care of everything that was hers. "They felt they had the right to this close relationship," Raysa Bofill said of Fidel and Celia. "The fact is that he could make decisions for her. They would discuss things between themselves, and that was that." Nobody else was privy to what they were thinking. And that is how it played out at the end. "At her death, we knew nothing. Fidel kept her illness from us," Alicia Otazo stated bitterly.

As Christmas approached, Celia concerned herself with everyone's annual holiday. She wanted Flávia to take her daughters to Guama. She didn't really want to go, but Flávia and Griselda went to the resort, and the girls planned to join them there. Alicia and Elena went to Once to see Celia on December 22. "She was in a room at the back of the house. You entered it from one of the halls. She had an intravenous tube in her clavicle and she had on a sports suit of light wool she liked very much. She had two of these, one blue and one green, and was wearing the green one that day, I think. My mother and Griselda were in Guama only because Celia wanted them to go, so the two of us were alone when we went to see Celia at Once." Celia encouraged the girls to leave for Guama the following day. "Raúl came in. We were surprised by this. Raúl leaned down to give her a kiss. She looked up at him and said, 'Be careful, you'll catch something.' I will remember this forever. The last time I heard her voice," Alicia said. "My sister and I were embarrassed to stay there any longer, with Raúl in the room. We thought they needed to say something privately. We left out of respect for them." It would be Celia's bitter humor that stuck with Alicia.

On that day, or the next, Eugenia went to see Celia. "We knew she was ill, but not terminal, so I said, 'Godmother, I am going to marry Victor.'" This is the same Victor that Celia had rejected as a bad husband for Eugenia. Celia replied, "If you are going to marry Victor, then let him find a house for you because I'm not going to find you one." Eugenia had never actually been to Victor's apartment, but knew he had one. Celia asked her when the wedding was going to take place, and "I gave her the date. I told her the 29th of December, 1979." That was a week away. "So you've picked the date," was all Celia could answer.

Eugenia feels sure that, by mentioning the house, or lack of one, Celia still thought she could forestall the marriage. During the following week, Ernestina started to make Eugenia's wedding arrangements, and Eugenia recalls going to Once every day. "Celia had switched bedrooms, and her room was next to mine. I was studying at the teachers' college in Guines, but came home every day." Celia discussed Eugenia's wedding plans with Fidel, although Eugenia says, "Fidel came and I told him. He also asked me if I had a place to live. I said yes. He said, 'Be sure to send me an invitation. I'll come.'"

During that week, Celia was very unwell. She would try to get up, but soon go back to bed. Eugenia saw how ill she was and was filled with remorse; she decided to postpone her wedding. "I told Fidel, and he advised me not to. He said, 'The invitations have been sent out. What are you going to tell people? What can be the reason to postpone your wedding? The enemy can't know that she is sick.'" (I asked if he meant the CIA, and she confirmed that it did.) "Fidel told me: You must go ahead and get married. This is the only thing I have to give you." And he pulled a few hundred dollars from his pocket and handed it to her. Then he went in to see Celia while his bodyguard, Pepin Naranjo, followed Eugenia into the kitchen, asked her, "Where are you going to live?" Pepin soon rejoined Fidel in Celia's room, and Eugenia pressed her ear to the door.

Eugenia continued: "They had all been speaking softly, but I wanted to know what they were saying, and tried to hear. I couldn't, but found out from Migdalia what happened. Celia asked Fidel why he'd given me money because she was going to give me a week at the Marazul Hotel as a wedding gift. Fidel had replied: 'Don't worry; she can spend it on whatever she wants.' Then Fidel said that he wanted me to spend my honeymoon at the Hotel Riviera, and it sounded like an afterthought."

Sometime that week, Celia recovered a little. She was able to move around. She met with some of her friends, talked to the Nico Lopez students who got together in the back apartment schoolroom. She read, went over some papers while reclining on the living room couch. Then she had a relapse and decided to go to the hospital. She switched on a lamp that lit the balcony. This was a signal, only done when there was an emergency, alerting the guards outside that they should bring a car to the door. She walked downstairs, told them to take her to Calixto García Hospital. An x-ray was taken and read before she was transferred to the small clinic within the palace, but soon she felt well enough to return to Once. After that, a member of the family stayed in her bedroom at all times, and Celia's sisters returned to Havana. It was during this time that Celia asked Eugenia to tell her all her wedding plans. Eugenia says that she felt miserable, but described them, and "Celia told me that she'd didn't want to see me in a veil. I'd like you to wear your hair loose, held by some combs, and put flowers in your hair. And wear a white dress." Then they set about finding a design that they liked, and sent for Cuco. "All this was happening within a week," Eugenia reminded me.

ON THE AFTERNOON OF THE WEDDING, Fidel came to tell Eugenia he couldn't attend. He had to be somewhere at eight. "I was packing my suitcase. I cried a lot. I felt terrible. Fidel tried to console me. 'How can you be crying now? Are you afraid of the man? You've been going steady for four years.' And I said, 'I'm crying because my godmother is so ill.' And he told me not to worry, and to remember that the enemy cannot find out that she is ill."

The ceremony took place at 8:30 p.m., only a few doors away. It was photographed by Raúl Corrales, at Celia's request. Everybody waited hoping Fidel would come, but he didn't, so they all continued on to a city park nearby, between 8th and 10th on the Malecón, for a buffet supper arranged by Ernestina, and attended by Eugenia and Victor's colleagues and school friends. Eugenia took her wedding bouquet and placed it at the foot of José Antonio Mella's statue, across from the steps of the university (Eugenia's idea, not one of Celia's). After the reception in the park, they went, by Fidel's arrangement, to a formal sit-down dinner, held at a diplomat's house, where two or three more photographers were present.

At 4:00 a.m., the couple was ready to leave. "In spite of all the attention I received," Eugenia admits, "I was a very independent person and I had asked my boyfriend to find a hotel for us. We chose the Capri. When we finished signing our papers, which were witnessed by Ana Irma before all the people of the immediate family, Victor and I received an order from the commander in chief." Fidel had learned about the last-minute switch to the Capri, and had their luggage removed from the Capri and sent to the Riviera. She didn't realize that Fidel picked the Riviera because it was so much closer to Once. "I wanted to go see Celia, so she could see me in my wedding dress, but Dr. Selman said no. It would be too emotional. So we left for the Riviera. Our luggage was there waiting for us."

During the following week, Eugenia went to visit Celia every day. Ernestina and Ana Irma had filled her in on the wedding details. "She knew everything about the wedding. She told me that I had looked just the way she wanted, with my hair loose, with combs. She knew that Victor had worn a blue tee-shirt under his jacket. She'd liked that. . . . I couldn't keep from crying. Celia just looked at me and said, 'How long is it going to take for us to get the photos?'"

On her honeymoon, Eugenia was studying for an exam and attending classes every day; she became ill. "Looking back, it was probably from tension." And disappointment: Victor's apartment was a basement room next to a garage. "Like a janitor's room. Cars parked outside the door. It was horrible." I asked if she thought Celia had known where the apartment was. Eugenia thought a moment or two and said, "Celia would have known. She knew everything." There was no running water; Eugenia had to draw water in a pail and carry it to the apartment. Eugenia hadn't come very far from the days of her childhood, when she'd carried water in the Sierra Maestra.

ON JANUARY 4, 1980, Celia went to the clinic in the palace, where she died on January 11. Alicia Otazo remembers: "Two guards took her. When they were carrying her out—she was taken in a chair—she told Flávia to remember to bring her slippers. These were pink chenille slippers she'd put aside for the hospital." During her final week there, she ordered her loyal photographer, Raúl Corrales, to take pictures of the plants in the new garden nearby. He told me that she wanted photographs of plants growing. It had been difficult, but he had done the best he could to carry out this poignant request. He'd photograph the young seedlings, spend hours developing the negatives and making prints. He did this every night that week and would take prints to her in the morning, then leave and start all over again—until she died. Celia kept busy with at least one other project during that final week. She selected marble to be installed in some of the floors at the Convention Palace, and ordered some new landscaping. That is how she died: watching plants grow, adding finishing touches to her country's newest piece of architecture.

ALL THE FAMILY MEMBERS were with her except the children. In Celia's delirium, she called out the names of Flávia's daughters and of Sergio, Silvia's son, who was in Angola. On January 6, the doctors decreased the sedation so she could speak to the family. "We saw her for a moment. She couldn't speak well," Alicia says. Not everyone could fit into the room, so they went in two groups:

her brothers and sisters, her cousin Miriam Manduley, Ernestina and Ana Irma, and Flávia's daughters. "It was a Friday, and she died the following Friday."

A day or two later, everyone assembled at Once. Fidel had asked them to be there, Alicia says, to tell the family the truth. "He said it was his responsibility that none of us knew that she was dying of cancer. Our feelings were very strong, because no one could understand what was the matter with her. A close person is in denial. We couldn't think that she would die."

SINCE THAT TIME, Fidel has pained them all by not speaking publicly about Celia after her death, keeping her memory for himself. "Fidel was a jealous widow," Alicia remarks. "He was a possessive husband. He compartmentalized all her illness for himself. He kept the family from knowing until three days before her death."

THE ARCHIVES HOLD THE CONTENTS of the tiny purse Celia carried to the hospital. It is a leather envelope with a zipper, and held the essentials of her existence: two cigarette lighters, four pens (gifts of friends), a vial of pills (with label obscured), an emery board, and a slender white plastic hairbrush.

42. JANUARY 11, 1980

The Country Is in Mourning

ON JANUARY 11, 1980, the newspaper *Juventud Rebelde* printed a 12:30 p.m. edition. Its headline: THE COUNTRY IS IN MOURNING. "At 11:50 a.m. today *la compañera* Celia Sánchez Manduley, member of the Central Committee of the Communist Party of Cuba, Deputy to the National Assembly, and Secretary to the Council of State, passed away."

The Council of State had declared that flags would fly at half-mast from 4:00 p.m. of that day, the 11th, until 6:00 p.m. on January 12. The casket would be placed at the base of the José Martí monument in the Plaza of the Revolution at 8:00 p.m., the paper announced, "where workers and all people are welcome to visit. Tomorrow, at 3:00 p.m., it will be moved to the Pantheon of the Revolutionary Armed Forces." Another headline read: "She lived for the Revolution, she lived and will live on in the Revolution."

The next day, January 12, 1980, *Granma*, the official paper of the Communist Party, printed its masthead in black ink instead of the usual red ink.

ALL THROUGH THE NIGHT OF THE 11TH, people arrived from all parts of Cuba and filed past the casket at the foot of the Martí statue in Revolution Square. The newspaper carried a picture of a line so long that it winds in a huge oval. On the front page, along with the headline "Celia Sánchez Is Dead" is a picture of her, in her uniform, taken on Pico Turquino. "The country is in mourning. She was one of the daughters most steadfast and loyal, a tireless fighter, a heroine of the Cuban Revolution," and telegrams, on the inside pages, were printed that had been sent by people from Manzanillo, Pinar del Rio, and "heroic Santiago." Messages continued to be printed throughout the week, along with editorials about her and poems. One poem described her as "a violet among the grasses." This wildflower image would be the theme of Armando Hart's funeral oration. He called her Cuba's most authentic native flower. He did not assign a species, but the orchid and the mariposa are usually coupled with her image.

Partnership with a wildflower, especially the mariposa, in Cuba's collective memory, suits her well. Brought up in the philosophy of José Martí, Celia is still the embodiment of his particular form of Cuban patriotism; and she is referred to as *martíana*. She was true to herself, and to her country. She was a tireless worker who toiled until the day she died, a Catholic, a revolutionary, a communist, a tenaciously loyal friend.

HER BODY LAY IN STATE for nineteen hours while special groups traveled from Manzanillo, Santiago, and the Isle of Youth to participate in the funeral. *Juventud Rebelde* reported that during those nineteen hours millions of people had walked past the casket to honor "a revolutionary woman."

Eduardo Sánchez, the young hairdresser she'd brought to Havana, went to see her body reluctantly because "I felt it couldn't be true. I hadn't done her makeup or anything. I was so upset, I couldn't eat or bathe or anything." But he had gone, and when Celia's sisters saw him, they'd lowered the velvet rope and asked him to stay with the family who were in an adjoining room, and with Fidel. They all sat in rocking chairs throughout the night. "When you see any man cry, it is very impressive, but to see Fidel Castro cry. . . . I was on the other side of the coffin and Fidel was facing me. He was very red, like a pomegranate. And tears flowed down both sides of his face. I saw everyone who passed: priests, beggars, night people, from every sector of the population. Military—even members of the military would embrace the coffin. They didn't leave the plaza. The people stayed. Everything was quiet, and when the cortège left at three, it was a sea of humanity that you saw there. It was a human wave."

TV channels were scheduled to carry a documentary film at 2:00 p.m. of the interview Celia made with Santiago Álvarez, describing her arrest at the La Rosa bar in Campechuela, and her escape into the *marabu*. And funeral coverage began at 3:00 p.m.

At 2:30, the cortège began to move from Revolution Square. The vanguard carried a huge straw wreath covered with hundreds of orchids with the words, on a satin ribbon, "For Celia from Fidel." (In 2000 I attended a commemorative service on the 11th of January marking the 20th anniversary of her death. Old combatants carried in a huge round wreath of orchids, but the banner on the wreath read "Council of State," which amounts to the same thing since Fidel was president, but was less intimate.) Her funeral procession was made up of five groups, and reflected the new revolutionary Cuba. In the vanguard were members of the Central Committee of the Communist Party, ministers of state, followed by chiefs of other state organizations. Next were ex-soldiers and collaborators of the rebel army, and this group contained many of her women couriers, members of the underground, men and women from Manzanillo, Campechuela, Pilón, and from the Sierra Maestra.

The last three groups, those closest to the coffin, began with members of the rebel army—Faustino Perez was among this group. There were survivors of the *Granma* and of combat in the Sierra Maestra. The penultimate group was entirely political, and Jorge Risquet was in this group. It was followed by the honor guard, composed of Fidel, his brother Raúl, Juan Almeida, and Ramiro Valdes, leaders of the 26th of July Movement and the rebel army. Celia's old friend from Media Luna and member of her Farmers' Militia, Guillermo García, walked there, as did Carlos Rafael Rodríguez, leader of the Communist Party. The honor guard also included the former president of Cuba, Osvaldo Dorticos; the 26th of July Movement's national director, Armando Hart; Sergio del Valle and Pedro Miret, for whom she'd stolen those maps for Fidel of the Cuban coastline; and her colleagues in the Politburo.

The honor guard and the casket were the last to leave the square. At 3:00 p.m., the procession moved out to the wide empty streets skirting Nuevo Vedado; it went past her new garden and turned in the direction of the sea, of the archives, of Once, but stopped short of these to pass directly in front of her stained-glass workshop before entering the gates of Colón Cemetery. At 3:43 the casket was placed on the marble floor of the FAR (*Forces Armadas Revolucionarios*) monument in Colon Cemetery, as the "26th of July March" was played at a slow and mournful cadence. At 3:52, the body of Celia Sánchez Manduley was sealed in tomb No. 43, next to the tomb that holds Haydée Santamaria. Armando Hart began his eloquent and heartrending speech, in which he called Celia Fidel's "alter ego"—his trusted *compañera*, his second self.

EUGENIA ALSO STOOD INSIDE the monument along with members of the family, and with Fidel. They gathered around Celia's coffin. To her amazement, she saw tears fall from Fidel's lowered head and splash on the floor. There were no sobs, just huge tears falling to the stone floor in an outpouring of grief. She was shocked. "Nobody dared look at him."

Eduardo Sánchez recalls this: "The nightmare started when she died. I felt so bad that I went home and made a big thermos of coffee. I asked a friend to take me out of there. We'd visit people, and I'd ask them to replenish the coffee. I walked the Malecon, crying, and saying I didn't want to go home. Then I drowned all that in work. I kept the storeroom at Verano better than I ever had, did my best work ever, and did it in honor of Celia."

IN 1982, TWO YEARS AFTER CELIA'S DEATH, Fidel contacted Dolly Gómez and Mario Giróna to ask them to design an orchid garden in her honor.

That year, Teresa Lamoru Preval got married. "My brother and I stayed at Once after Celia's death because we were the only unmarried ones. He got married in 1980, and I in 1982." Fidel made all the arrangements for their two weddings, just as Celia would have done. "I got married in Ana Irma's house. Cuco, Celia's tailor, who made all our clothes, made my wedding dress. I had him make my daughter's *quinceanera* dress."

After two years of living in her husband's apartment, Eugenia asked Fidel if he would help her find a place to live. She felt that Celia would not have wanted her to live in that miserable room with no running water forever. "She wanted me to live a normal life, didn't want to punish me. Celia solved everyone's problems, and she would have gotten around to solving mine, too." Fidel replied with a note. He wrote: "First thing, don't pick a mansion. And above all, put the house in your name, not your husband's." But Eugenia says, "I didn't understand it was good advice. I was still in school. My husband was working. He had to pay the rent." So she informed Fidel of her opinion on the matter, and he didn't budge from those conditions. Only then did Eugenia grasp that the check she got every month, part of a scholarship to continue her education, could be the basis of budgeting; she could put the lease in her own name and pay rent to the state, from her monthly student's stipend. "My husband was very upset. He couldn't understand it. So I would just say, 'These are Fidel's orders.'" She and Victor divorced not long after that, and Eugenia raised her two sons in that apartment, of which she is now the owner.

IN 1996, FLÁVIA WENT TO MIAMI. "I woke up one night and my father was on my mind. I was reminded of the unification he taught us to practice, and that I hadn't seen Chela for thirty-three years. Only she, Silvia, and myself were still alive then. And I decided I would go and see her. Chela was eighty and her husband eighty-four."

Flávia spent about a month in Miami and the trip went as well as can be expected, considering the fact that no one had changed their politics. According to Pedro, "One day she told me, 'I am a Fidelista, a Raúlista, and an Internationalista.' I didn't know what to say."

Although Flávia enjoyed being with her sister, she saw no point in staying in Miami. What Miami had to offer was not enough. She missed Cuba. "I've complied with all my duties of the Revolution," she declared. Then she tried to explain what she'd meant by this: "I am not a militant member of the party. I believe in God. I believe in the spirit of my father. And I can die and say that I was there at the beginning [of the Revolution]." Then, laughing, she added, "I will never step out of Cuba again."

IN HAVANA, CELIA'S LEGACY is in her buildings and projects, such as Coppelia, the Cohiba cigar factory El Laguito, the archives, Lenin Park, vegetable gardens, and in the people who grew up in the capital, brought there for an education, and who stayed to go on to lead successful lives, and never looked back. If Celia has a successor, he is the historian of the city of Havana, Eusebio Leal, whom she encouraged personally. He has created large projects funded by the state, sanctioned by Fidel, projects that enhance the city, generate income, create jobs, and celebrate Cuba.

The painter Asger Jorn died in 1973, and the Danish government decided it was important to preserve the large group of murals he made in the Office of Historical Affairs in 1968. Three years, from 2006 to 2009, were spent restoring them, including the scene painted by Celia.

In the years following Celia's death, special medals and commemorative stamps were issued with her image; her portrait is the watermark on several pieces of the country's currency; a Spanish ballet was named for her; her name is on schools, hospitals, and various community centers, from Cuba to Zimbabwe. In recent years, the house in Media Luna where she was born was declared a national monument. The house in Pilón, badly damaged by the 2011 hurricane, is in the process of restoration. Wood to rebuild the house is being seasoned.

In Manzanillo, her image dominates Revolution Plaza in an extravagant tableau, mostly made of shining steel, of the landing of the *Granma*, a powerful reminder of her role in the Revolution. Yet there is another monument, located on the upper end of Caridad Street. This old thoroughfare, once a steep, two-way street, has been converted into a wide set of steps paved in dark red terracotta. Cross streets intersect it, functioning as wide landings, as the steps climb upward. On each landing, the buildings are covered in murals made of ceramic tiles that glitter in the sunlight. At the bottom, the murals feature palm trees against a clear blue sky, but as you climb higher, the murals are of fields of sunflowers. Cubans place sunflowers on the altar of the Caridad del Cobre Virgin, and this mural casts Celia Sánchez in the same manner. White doves hover and swarm in a field of sunflowers. At the top of this strange picture, Celia's head, sculpted in terracotta, emerges. It is as if she's wearing a dress, stiff and enormous, like the jeweled dress worn by the Caridad Virgin. The monument is two-sided and faces the Sierra Maestra in the east, the sea, and Havana to the west. In a tradition I find fitting both in its beauty and its irony, people of Manzanillo commonly use the monument as a marriage altar.

Acknowledgments

A few close friends gave me good advice and generously shared their expertise: film-editors Thom Noble and Antonia von Drimmelen; television producer Lucy Scott; Cuba expert Sandra Levinson; fellow writer Corey Sabourin; historian Anne Hayes; graphic designer Lawrence Wolfson; architect Gabriel Feld and psychoanalyst Nellie Thompson, who assisted me in many different ways.

In the book world, I have been loyally supported by literary agents Charlotte Sheedy and Meredith Kaffel; and senior editor at Rizzoli, David Morton who have provided encouragement to me personally every step of the way. As the project expanded, they were joined by Jess Taylor, a master at storytelling. At Monthly Review, I'd particularly like to thank John Simon for his enthusiasm for the book. Michael Yates, Martin Paddio, and Scott Borchert have gracefully guided the manuscript to publication.

In Cuba, I am grateful to the many people who shared their knowledge of Celia Sánchez and the Cuban Revolution mentioned throughout the book; I want to single out Nelsy Babiel, curator of Celia's papers at the Office of Historical Affairs, and my translator, Argelia Fernández, for their constant help and encouragement. But a handful, early on, paved the way. I'm especially grateful to Bruno Rodríguez, Lizette Vila, and the late Pedro Alvarez Tabío for their assistance in gaining access to the historic documents.

Writings about
Celia Sánchez Manduley

BOOKS AND ARTICLES

Editorial. "A Celia." *Granma*, 11 enero 1986, 1.

Acosta, Teófilo. En Zimbabwe: escuela "Celia Sánchez Manduley." *Granma*, 18 junio 1981, 5.

Aguirre Gamboa, Fidel. *Celia, heroína de la revolución cubana.* La Habana: Editora Política,   1985.

Alarcon Marino, Roberto. *Historia de Media Luna.* La Habana: Editorial de Ciencias Sociales, 2005.

Álvarez Tabío, Pedro. "Celia. Cabal imagen del pueblo." *Bohemia* 77/2 (11 enero 1985): 2.

——. "Todo importa después." *Bohemia* 76/18 (4 mayo 1984): 54–59.

——. *Celia: ensayo para una biografía.* La Habana: Oficina de Publicaciones del Consejo de Estado, 2003.

Benítez, Augusto E. "En recuerdo de Celia. Museo histórico de Pilón." *Bohemia* 80/2 (9 enero 1987): 61–62.

Bequer Cespedes, Adelaida. *Celia: la flor más autóctona de la Revolución.* La Habana: Editorial de Ciencias Sociales, 1999.

"Biografía. Celia Sánchez Manduley." *Militante Comunista* (enero 1986): 96.

Castillo, Bernal, Andrés. "Como una madre para los combatientes rebeldes. Celia: la primera mujer guerrillera." *Juventude Rebelde,* (18 marzo 1982): 2.

——. "Conoció a Fidel en febrero de 1957." *Trabajadores* (18 febrero 1987): 4.

Editorial. "Celia: la mas autóctona flor de la Revolución." *Granma,* 10 enero 1981, 1.

Editorial. "Celia." *Granma,* 12 enero 1986, 1.

Editorial. "Celia, en el recuerdo eterno." *Trabajadores,* 11 enero 1982, 3.

Chirino, Lilan. "Celia, aquella muchacha excepcional." *Juventude Rebelde,* (10 enero 1985): 6.

Espín, Vilma, with Nayda Sango. "Habla de Haydée y Celia." *Bohemia* 73/10): (6 marzo 1981): 36–39.

Fresnillo, Estrella. "Celia vive." *Juventude Rebelde,* (11 enero 1981): 8.

Guerra, Wendy. *Nunca fui Primera Dama.* Barcelona: Bruguera, 2008.

Hart Dávalos, Armando. "Discurso en el sepelio de la compañera Celia Sánchez Manduley, 12 enero 1980." *Granma,* 13 enero 1980, 4.

——. *La más autóctona flor de la Revolución.* La Habana: De la Cultura Ediciones, 1990.

Oficina de Publicaciones del Consejo de Estado. *La epopeya del Granma.* La Habana: Oficina de Publicaciones del Consejo de Estado, 1986.

Oficina de Publicaciones del Consejo de Estado. *La fibra mas intima y querida de la revolución: palabras y escritos con motive del vigésimo aniversario de la desaparición física de Celia Sánchez. 10–11 de enero del 2000.* La Habana: Oficina de Publicaciones del Consejo de Estado, 2000.

Lechuga, Lilian. "El padre de Celia." *Bohemia* 75/40 (7 octubre 1983): 84–89.

National Security Archive. "Bay of Pigs: 40 Years After, Index of Declassified Cuban Documents." George Washington University, February 15, 2005, www.gwu.edu/~nsarchiv/bayofpigs/cuba.html.

Oliva, Milagros. "Celia: comunista, constructora, soñadora." *Mujeres* 24/1) (enero 1984): 8–9.

Pena, Jacinto E. *Celia en la clandestinidad.* Bayamo: José Joaquín Palma, 1990.

Rodríguez Menéndez, Roberto. *Una muchacha llamada Celia.* La Habana: Editorial Pueblo y Educación: Pablo de la Torriente, 1996.

Sarabia, Nydia. *Manuel Sánchez Silveira: médico rural.* La Habana: Ministerio de Salud Pública, 1971.

Sarabia, Nydia. "Celia palma y clavellina." *Revolución y Cultura* (119) (junio 1982): 7–13.

Oficina de Publicaciones del Consejo de Estado. "Testimonios: Celia habla acerca del recibimiento de la expedición del *Granma*." in *Cinco Palmas.* La Habana: Boletín de las Oficinas de Asuntos Históricos y de Publicaciones del Consejo de Estado. Vol. 1 (May 1, 1994): 42–58.

Thomas-Woodward, Tiffany A. *Myth, Mother, Mujer: Celia Sánchez Manduley, a Cuban Revolutionary.* Albuquerque: University of New Mexico, 1999.

Waldo López, González, and Maria Del Carmen. "Para Celia." *Muchacha,* enero 1984, 42–43.

FILMS

Álvarez, Santiago, dir. *Celia.* Filmed interview, November 3, 1976. Havana: Instituto Cubano del Arte y la Industria Cinematográficos, 953 II-A, R2.

Celia: leyenda y presencia. Documentary directed by Pedro Álvarez Tabío. 27 min., Tele-Rebelde, 11 enero 1985. Available at http://www.cubainformacion.tv.

Galiano, Carlos. "Celia: imagen del pueblo." *Granma Resumen Semanal.* (3 febrero 1980): 5. (He refers to the 1976 film by Santiago Álvarez.)

"La Plata." *Celia, fuego y canto.* Pedro Álvarez Tabío, prod., and Haydée Tabraue Garí, dir. La Habana: Televisión Cubana, 2000.

LITERATURE AND POETRY

Alonso, Dora. "Se lo ceñiste, Celia, a los valientes." *Revolución y Cultura* 122 (octubre 1982): 29.

Garzón Céspedes, Francisco. "Las fotos de sus manos." *Revolución y Cultura* 122 (octubre 1982): 25.

Editorial. "Photograph of Celia Sánchez Manduley." *Hoy,* 26 febrero 1959, 2.

Barnet, Miguel. "Celia: amó lo bello porque lo bello era lo justo." *Revolución y Cultura*122 (octubre 1982): 29.

Caignet, Maria Victoria y Gonzalo Córdova. "Un sentido de la cubanía muy particular." *Revolución y Cultura* 122 (octubre 1982): 32.

García Valdés, Manuel. "A Celia Sánchez Manduley: envíos poéticos." *Mujeres* 20/7 (junio 1980): 46–47.

Hart Dávalos, Armando. "Celia." *Biblioteca Nacional, Revista* 71/1 (enero–abril 1980): 5–20; *Bohemia* 72/3 (18 enero 1980): 58–62; *Verde Olivo* 21/3 (20 enero 1980): 8–13.

Hernández García, Edenia. "A la flor de la Revolución." *Mujeres* 20/7 (junio 1980): 46–47.

Leyva, Audecelia. "A Celia Sánchez Manduley." *Yumurí* (Matanzas) 5/24 (15 junio 1980): 2.

Morales Cano, Onofre. "A nuestra Celia Sánchez 'capitana del pueblo.'" *Yumurí* (Matanzas) 5/24 (15 junio 1980): 2.

Morejón, Nancy. "Celia." *Revolución y Cultura* 122 (octubre 1982): 27.

Orta Ruiz, Jesús. "Poema a Celia Sánchez: 'Pido permiso a la muerte.'" *Granma Campesino* 23 (enero 1980): 18; *Trabajadores* (12 enero 1980): 6.

Pineda Barnet, Enrique. "Celia. Poema." *Gaceta de Cuba* 187 (julio 1980): 11.

Ramírez, Luisa. "A Celia." *Con la guardia en alto* 19/4 (abril 1980): 33.

Rivero Suárez, Aleida. "Celia de todos los días." *Granma Campesino* 23 (enero 1980): 18.

Robinson Calvet, Nancy. "Y aquí en el corazón del pueblo." *Granma Campesino* 23 (enero 1980): 18.

Serrano Coello, Carmen. "Poesías a Celia." *Maguana* (Baracoa) 3/8–9 (abril–septiembre 1980): 23.

Vidal, Rafael. "Celia Sánchez." *Yumurí* (Matanzas) 5/24 (15 junio 1980): 2.

Select Bibliography/Further Reading

BOOKS AND ARTICLES

Acosta, Heberto Norman. *La palabra empeñada*. La Habana: Oficina de Publicaciones del Consejo de Estado, 2006.

"Address of His Excellency Dr. Fidel Castro of the Government of Cuba, and Chairman before the 34th Session of the General Assembly." *New York Times*. 14 Oct. 1979: 66.

Aguilar, Luis E. *Cuba 1933: Prologue to Revolution*. Ithaca, NY: Cornell University Press, 1972.

Ameringer, Charles D. *The Cuban Democratic Experience: The Auténtico Years, 1944–1952*. Gainesville: University Press of Florida, 2000.

Anderson, Jon Lee. *Che Guevara: A Revolutionary Life*. New York: Grove Press, 1997.

Argote-Freyre, Frank. *Fulgencio Batista*. New Brunswick, NJ: Rutgers University Press, 2006.

Babun, Teo. *The Cuban Revolution: Years of Promise*. Gainesville: University Press of Florida, 2005.

Baez, Luis. *Secretos de generales*. Barcelona: Losada, 1997.

Bardach, Ann L. *Cuba Confidential: Love and Vengeance in Miami and Havana*. New York: Random House, 2002.

Bayo, Alberto. *One Hundred and Fifty Questions Asked of a Guerrilla Fighter*. New York: U.S. Joint Publications Research Service, 1959.

Beals, Carlton. *The Crime of Cuba*. Philadelphia: J. B. Lippincott, 1933.

Blight, James G., Bruce J. Allyn, and David A. Welch. *Cuba on the Brink: Castro, the Missile Crisis, and the Soviet Collapse*. New York: Pantheon Books, 1993.

Bonachea, Rolando E., and Nelson P. Valdés. *Revolutionary Struggle, 1947–1958*. Cambridge, MA: MIT Press, 1972.

Bonachea, Ramon L. *The Cuban Insurrection, 1952–1959*. New Brunswick, NJ: Transaction Books, 1974.

Bornot, Thelma, and Enzo Infante Uribazo. *De Tuxpan a La Plata*. La Habana: Editorial Orbe, 1979.

Brenner, Philip. *The Cuba Reader: The Making of a Revolutionary Society*. New York: Grove Press, 1989.

Burri, René. *René Burri: Cuba y Cuba*. Milan: Federico Motta Editore, 1994.

Cabrera, Lydia. *El Monte*. La Habana: Ediciones C.R., 1954.

Casal, Lourdes. *Women, War, and Revolution*. Edited by Carol Berkin and Clara M. Lovett. New York: Holmes & Meier, 1980.

Castenada, Jorge. *Compañero: The Life and Death of Che Guevara*. New York: Knopf, 1997.

"Castro Costs New York $170,000 in Two Days." *New York Times*. 13 Oct. 1979: 5.

Castro, Fidel, and Frei Betto. *Fidel Castro Talks on Revolution and Religion with Frei Betto*. New York: Simon and Schuster, 1987.

"Castro Says He Felt Safe in New York." *New York Times*. 16 Oct. 1979: B6.

Castro Speech Database. Latin American Network Information Center, University of Texas at Austin, http://www.lanic.utexas.edu/la/cb/cuba/castro.html.

"Castro Visit All but Stops Activity in Usually Bustling Midtown Area." *New York Times*. 12 Oct. 1979: A1, B3.

Cedeño, Pineda R., and Michel D. Suárez. *Son de la Loma: los dioses de la música cantan en Santiago de Cuba*. La Habana: Andante, 2002.

Chomsky, Aviva, Barry Carr, and Pamela M. Smorkaloff. *The Cuba Reader: History, Culture, Politics*. Durham, NC: Duke University Press, 2003.

Coltman, Leycester. *The Real Fidel Castro*. New Haven: Yale University Press, 2003.

Corrales, Raúl. *Playa Girón*. La Habana: Editorial Letras Cubanas, 1981.

Coyle, Beverly, and Alan Filreis, eds. *Secretaries of the Moon: The Letters of Wallace Stevens & José Rodríguez Feo*. Durham, NC: Duke University Press, 1986.

Cuban Revolution Collection. (MS 650), Manuscripts and Archives, Yale University Library, New Haven.

Cuza, Malé B., Pamela Carmell, and Malé B. Cuza. *Women on the Front Lines*. Greensboro, NC: Unicorn Press, 1987.

Desnoes, Edmundo. *Punto De Vista*. La Habana: Instituto del Libro, 1967.

Desnoes, Edmundo, and William Luis. *Los Dispositivos en la flor: Cuba, literatura desde la Revolución*. Hanover, NH: Ediciones del Norte, 1981.

Depestre Catony, Leonardo, and Eladio Blanco Cabrera. *Cuando el país llama: epistolario*. La Habana: Editora Política, 1990.

Diaz Roque, José. *Eduardo Chibás: el gran cívico*. Cienfuegos, Cuba: Ediciones Mecenas, 2005.

Dieterich, Heinz, Paco Ignacio Taibol II, Pedro Álvarez Tabío, Ernesto Guevara, and Raúl Castro Ruz. *Diarios de guerra: Raúl Castro y Che Guevara*. Madrid: La Fábrica, 2006.

Domínguez, Jorge I. *To Make a World Safe for Revolution: Cuba's Foreign Policy*. Cambridge, MA: Harvard University Press, 1989.

Dorschner, John, and Roberto Fabricio. *The Winds of December*. New York: Coward, McCann & Geoghegan, 1980.

Dosal, Paul J. *Comandante Che: Guerrilla Soldier, Commander and Strategist, 1956–1967*. University Park: Pennsylvania State University Press, 2003.

English, T. J. *Havana Nocturne: How the Mob Owned Cuba and Then Lost It to the Revolution*. New York: William Morrow, 2008.

Escalante, Font F. *Executive Action: 634 Ways to Kill Fidel Castro*. Melbourne: Ocean Press, 2006.

Espinosa, Belkis, and Jorge L. Llópiz. *Cine Cubano: 30 Años En Revolución*. La Habana: Centro de Promoción y Estudio del Cine "Saúl Yelín," 1989.

"Excerpts from Castro's Speech before General Assembly at U.N." *New York Times*. 13 Oct. 1979: 5

Falagán, Benítez I., and González D. G. Orozco. *El Órgano Oriental: Señor De La Música Molida*. Bayamo, Granma: Editorial Orto, 2004.

Fernández, Revuelta A. *Castro's Daughter: An Exile's Memoir of Cuba*. New York: St. Martín's Press, 1998.

Fernández, Robaina T. *El Negro En Cuba, 1902–1958: Apuntes Para La Historia De La Lucha Contra La Discriminación Racial*. La Habana: Editorial de Ciencias Sociales, 1994.

"Few Reminders of the Gaudy Past If You Go . . . " *New York Times*. 21 Oct. 1979: XX23.

Fitzgerald, Frank T. *The Cuban Revolution in Crisis: From Managing Socialism to Managing Survival*. New York: Monthly Review Press, 1994.

Frankel, Max. "Castro Arrives in Subdued Mood." *New York Times*. 19 Sept. 1960: 1.

Frankel, Max. "Castro Can't Find Lodging Here; One Hotel Cancels Reservation." *New York Times*. 16 Sept. 1960: 1.

Frankel, Max. "Castro Flies Home with Praise for Khrushchev and U.S. People." *New York Times*. 29 Sept. 1960: 15.

Frankel, Max. "Castro Plays Fan to Soviet Premier." *New York Times*. 24 Sept. 1960: 3.

Frankel, Max. "Castro Remains out of Spotlight." *New York Times*. 25 Sept. 1960: 36.

Frankel, Max. "Cuban Delegations Pleased by Attentions from Russia." *New York Times*. 21 Sept. 1960: 17.

Frankel, Max. "Cuban in Harlem." *New York Times*. 20 Sept. 1960: 1.

Frankel, Max. "Cuban Is Cautious on Issues at U.N." *New York Times*. 23 Sept. 1960: 17.

Frankel, Max. "Diplomats Study His Ties to Soviet." *New York Times*. 22 Sept. 1960: 14.

Frankel, Max. "Hotel Will Admit Castro and Aides." *New York Times*. 18 Sept. 1960: 1.

Frankel, Max. "Journey of Inquiry in Castro's Cuba." *New York Times*. 22 Jan. 1961: 8.

Frankel, Max. "Winds up His Stay Visiting Leaders." *New York Times*. 28 Sept. 1960: 19.

Franqui, Carlos. *Family Portrait with Fidel: A Memoir*. New York: Random House, 1984.

Frometa Suarez, Sergio. *La Lucha Clandestina de Movimiento 26 de Julio en Jaguaní*. Bayamo, Granma: Ediciones Bayamo, 2004.

Gadea, Hilda. *Ernesto: A Memoir of Che Guevara*. Garden City, NY: Doubleday, 1972.

Gálvez, William. *Frank: Entre El Sol Y La Montaña*. La Habana: Unión de Escritores y Artistas de Cuba, 1991.

Geldof, Lynn. *Cubans: Voices of Change*. New York: St. Martín's Press, 1991.

George, Edward. *The Cuban Intervention in Angola, 1965–1991: From Che Guevara to Cuito Cuanavale*. London: Frank Cass, 2005.

Geyer, Georgie A. *Guerrilla Prince: The Untold Story of Fidel Castro*. Boston: Little, Brown, 1991.

Gilly, Adolf. *Inside the Cuban Revolution*. New York: Monthly Review Press, 1964.

Gimbel, Wendy. *Havana Dreams: A Story of Cuba*. New York: Knopf, 1998.

Girona, Julio. *Memorias, memorias, memorias sin título*. La Habana: Editorial Letras Cubanas, 1994.

Gleijeses, Piero. *Shattered Hope: The Guatemalan Revolution and the United States, 1944–1954*. Princeton, NJ: Princeton University Press, 1991.

———. *Conflicting Missions: Havana, Washington, and Africa, 1959–1976*. Chapel Hill: University of North Carolina Press, 2002.

Gómez Carballo, Armando. "Un vikingo en La Habana: Asger Jorn en la Oficina de Asuntos Históricos del Consejo de Estado." *Boletín*. La Habana: Oficina de Asuntos Históricos del Consejo de Estado, 2012.

González-Lanuza Rodríguez, Gaspar. *Clandestinos: héroes vivos y muertos*. La Habana: Editorial de Ciencias Sociales, 2007.

Gosse, Van. *Where the Boys Are: Cuba, Cold War America and the Making of a New Left*. New York: Verso, 1993.

Gott, Richard. *Cuba: A New History*. New Haven: Yale University Press, 2004.

Greer, Germaine. "Women and Power in Cuba." *The Madwoman's Underclothes: Essays and Occasional Writings*. New York: Atlantic Monthly Press, 1987.

Griffiths, John, and Peter Griffiths. *Cuba: The Second Decade*. London: Writers and Readers Publishing Cooperative, 1979.

Guevara, Ernesto. *Episodes of the Revolutionary War*. New York: International Publishers, 1968.

———. *Reminiscences of the Cuban Revolutionary War*. New York: Monthly Review Press; distributed by Grove Press, 1968.

Guillermoprieto, Alma, and Esther Allen. *Dancing with Cuba: A Memoir of the Revolution*. New York: Pantheon Books, 2004.

Haberman, Clyde, and Albin Krebs. "Of Irony and Castro." *New York Times*. 15 Oct. 1979: B8.

Hart Dávalos, Armando. *Aldabonazo: Inside the Cuban Revolutionary Underground, 1952–58, A Participant's Account*. New York: Pathfinder, 2004.

Hart, Richard. *The Cuban Way*. London: Caribbean Labour Solidarity, 1978.

Higgins, Trumbull. *The Perfect Failure: Kennedy, Eisenhower, and the CIA at the Bay of Pigs*. New York: W. W. Norton, 1987.

Instituto de literatura y Lingüística de la academia de Ciencias de Cuba (Institute of Literature and Linguistics of the Cuban Academy of Sciences). *Diccionario De La Literatura Cubana.* La Habana: Editorial Letras Cubanas, 1980.

Kaplan, Fred M. *1959: The Year Everything Changed.* Hoboken, NJ: J. Wiley & Sons, 2009.

Karol, K. S. *Guerrillas in Power: The Course of the Cuban Revolution.* New York: Hill & Wang, 1970.

Kornbluh, Peter. *Bay of Pigs Declassified: The Secret CIA Report on the Invasion of Cuba.* New York: New Press, 1998.

Laemlein, Tom. *U.S. Small Arms in World War II: A Photographic History of the Weapons in Action.* Oxford: Osprey Publishing, 2011.

Lekachman, Robert. "Strange Alliances." *New York Times.* 21 Oct. 1979: E21.

Leon, Brother, and Brother Alain. *Flora de Cuba.* La Habana: Cultural, 1954.

Lewis, Flora. "Today's Havana: Few Reminders of a Gaudy Past." *New York Times.* 21 Oct. 1979: XX1, 22.

Lewis, Oscar, Ruth M. Lewis, and Susan M. Rigdon. *Living the Revolution: An Oral History of Contemporary Cuba.* Urbana: University of Illinois Press, 1977.

Lockwood, Lee. *Castro's Cuba, Cuba's Fidel: An American Journalist's Inside Look at Today's Cuba in Text and Pictures.* Boulder: Westview, 1990.

Loomis, John A. *Revolution of Forms: Cuba's Forgotten Art Schools.* New York: Princeton Architectural Press, 2011.

Macauly, Neill. *A Rebel in Cuba: An American's Memoir.* Chicago: Quadrangle Books, 1970.

Malaparte, Curzio, and Sylvia Saunders. *Coup d'état: The Technique of Revolution.* New York: E.P. Dutton, 1932.

Marel García, Gladys. *Insurrection and Revolution, Armed Struggle in Cuba, 1952–1959.* Boulder, CO: Lynne Rienner, 1998.

Martín, Zequeira M. E. *Guía De Arquitectura: La Habana Colonial (1519–1898).* La Habana/Sevilla: Consorcio obras públicas y transportes, 1993.

Matthews, Herbert L. *The Cuban Story.* New York: George Braziller, 1961.

Matthews, Herbert L. "Batista Holds Foes Block Earlier Vote." *New York Times.* 7 Jun. 1957: 1.

Matthews, Herbert L. "Castro Rebels Gain in Face of Offensive by the Cuban army." *New York Times.* 9 Jun. 1957: 1.

Matthews, Herbert L. "Cuba is Still Smoldering under Batista Regime." *New York Times.* 17 Mar. 1957: 6.

Matthews, Herbert. "Cuban Rebel Is Visited in Hideout." *New York Times.* 24 Feb. 1957: 1.

Matthews, Herbert L. "Latin America Racked by Political Tensions." *New York Times.* 12 May 1957: 3.

Matthews, Herbert L. "New Chapter in Galindez Case." *New York Times*. 24 Mar. 1957: 192.

Matthews, Herbert L. "Old Order in Cuba Is Threatened by Forces of an Internal Revolt." *New York Times*. 26 Feb. 1957: 13.

Matthews, Herbert L. "Populace in Revolt in Santiago de Cuba." *New York Times*. 10 Jun. 1957: 1.

Matthews, Herbert L. "Power Transfer Pondered in Cuba." *New York Times*. 17 Jun. 1957: 3.

Matthews, Herbert L. "Rebel Strength Gaining in Cuba: But Batista Has the Upper Hand." *New York Times*. 25 Feb. 1957: 1.

Matthews, Herbert L. "Situation in Cuba found Worsening; Batista Foes Gain." *New York Times*. 16 Jun. 1957: 1.

Matthews, Herbert L. "The Shadow Falls on Cuba's Batista." *New York Times*. 11 Aug. 1957: 170.

Matthews, Herbert L. "West Cuban City Opposes Batista." *New York Times*. 14 Jun. 1957: 8.

McCook, Henry C. *The Martial Graves of Our Fallen Heroes in Santiago de Cuba*. Philadelphia: G. W. Jacobs, 1899.

McDonough, Tom. "The Many Lives of Asger Jorn." *Art in America*. (July 2002): 56–61.

Menéndez Tomassevich, Raúl, and José A. Gárciga Blanco. *Rebeldía*. La Habana: Letras Cubanas, 2005.

Meneses, Enrique. *Fidel Castro*. New York: Taplinger Publishing, 1966.

Mitchell, Stephen A. *Can Love Last?: The Fate of Romance over Time*. New York: W.W. Norton, 2002.

Monroy, Juan Antonio. *Frank País: Un líder evangélico en la revolución cubana*. La Habana: Editorial Caminos, 2007.

Montejo, Estéban, and Miguel Barnet. *The Autobiography of a Runaway Slave*. New York: Pantheon Books, 1968.

Moore, Carlos. *Pichón: a Memoir*. Chicago: Lawrence Hill Books, 2008.

Narvaez, Alfonso A. "Juanita Castro Comes to Town to Portray Brother as a Tyrant." *New York Times*. 13 Oct. 1979: 4.

Narvaez, Alfonso A. "Security around Cubans Restricts even Protectors." *New York Times*. 14 Oct. 1979: 20.

Nossiter, Bernard D. "Castro, at U.N., Asks Rich Nations to Give $300 Billion to Help Poor." *New York Times*. 13 Oct. 1979: 1, 5.

Oltuski, Enrique. *Vida Clandestina: My Life in the Cuban Revolution*. San Francisco: Wiley, 2002.

Orozco, González D. G. *Azúcar y Dependencia En Manzanillo: 1899–1952*. Manzanillo, Granma, Cuba: Editorial Orto, 2006.

——. *Después De Dos Ríos: Presencia y Recepción Martíana En Manzanillo*. Manzanillo, Granma, Cuba: Editorial Orto, 2004.

——. *Manzanillo En Los 50: Rebeldía y Revolución*. Manzanillo, Granma, Cuba: Editorial Orto, 2004.

Pacheco, Judas M., Ernesto Ramos Latour, and Belarmino Castilla Mas. *Daniel, comandante del llano y de la Sierra: biografía*. La Habana: Editora Política, 2003.

Padura, Leonardo, and John M. Kirk. *La Cultura yla Revolución Cubana: Conversaciones en La Habana*. San Juan, P.R: Editorial Plaza Mayor, 2002.

"Palabras ante la muerte de Frank País" (Testimonies) in 13 documents. La Habana: Organización Nacional de Bibliotecas Ambulantes y Populares, 1959.

Pérez, Louis A., and Rebecca J. Scott. *The Archives of Cuba: Los Archivos De Cuba*. Pittsburgh: University of Pittsburgh Press, 2003.

Pérez, Louis A. *Cuba: Between Reform and Revolution*. New York: Oxford University Press, 1988.

Pérez Sarduy, Pedro, and Jean Stubbs. *Afrocuba: An Anthology of Cuban Writing on Race, Politics and Culture*. Melbourne, Aus.: Ocean Press, 1993.

Pérez-Stable, Marifeli. *The Cuban Revolution: Origins, Course, and Legacy*. New York: Oxford University Press, 1993.

Person, Ethel S. *Dreams of Love and Fateful Encounters: The Power of Romantic Passion*. New York: W. W. Norton, 1988.

Phillips, R. Hart. *Cuba, Island of Paradox*. New York: McDowell, Obolensky, 1962.

———. *The Cuban Dilemma*. New York: Ivan Obolensky, 1962.

Portuondo, Yolanda. *La clandestina tuvo un nombre—David*. La Habana: Editoria Política, 1988.

Quirk, Robert. *Fidel Castro*. New York: W. W. Norton, 1993.

Ramonet, Ignacio, Fidel Castro, and Andrew Hurley. *Fidel Castro: My Life,A Spoken Autobiography*. New York: Scribner, 2008.

Randall, Margaret, and Judy Janda. *Women in Cuba, Twenty Years Later*. New York: Smyrna Press, 1981.

Reid-Henry, Simon. *Fidel and Che: A Revolutionary Friendship*. New York: Walker, 2009.

Rodríguez Salgado, Ramón. *Vergüenza contra dinero*. La Habana: Editora Política, 2007.

Rodríguez Téllez, E. *Un Guerrillero Del Primer Refuerzo*. La Habana: Ediciones Verde Olivo, 1998.

Ruiz, Ramón E. *Cuba: The Making of a Revolution*. Amherst: University of Massachusetts Press, 1968.

Salas, Osvaldo, and Roberto Salas. *Fidel's Cuba: A Revolution in Pictures*. New York: Thunder's Mouth Press, 1998.

Schellhardt, Timothy D. "President Is Hopeful that Interest Rates Have Peaked, Concedes Peril to Housing." *Wall Street Journal*. 17 Oct. 1979: 2.

Schumacher, Edward. "2 Congressmen Visit Castro and Report He Favors U.S. Ties." *New York Times*. 14 Oct. 1979: 1, 20.

Schumacher, Edward. "3,000 March Protesting Castro's Visit, 500 Backing It." *New York Times*. 13 Oct. 1979: 4.

Schumacher, Edward. "Castro Abruptly Leaves City under Tight Security." *New York Times*. 15 Oct. 1979: A3.

Schumacher, Edward. "Security Is Intense as Castro Arrives for Speech at U.N." *New York Times*. 11 Oct. 1979: A3.

"Share the Wealth, Castro Tells U.N." *New York Times*. 14 Oct. 1979: E1.

Skierka, Volker. *Fidel Castro: A Biography*. Cambridge/Malden, MA: Polity Press, 2004.

Smith, Earl E. T. *The Fourth Floor: An Account of the Castro Communist Revolution*. New York: Random House, 1962.

Smith, Wayne S. *The Closest of Enemies: A Personal and Diplomatic Account of U.S.-Cuban Relations since 1957*. New York: W. W. Norton, 1987.

Smith, Wayne, James W. Porges, and Michael Reagan. *Portrait of Cuba*. Atlanta: Turner Publishing, 1991.

Stout, Nancy. *Habanos: The Story of the Havana Cigar*. New York: Rizzoli, 1997.

Stout, Nancy, and Jorge Rigau. *Havana/La Habana*. New York: Rizzoli, 1994.

Stryker, Deena. *When the Revolution Was Young: Living in Cuba and Talking to Its Leaders, December 1963 to June 1964*. Raleigh, NC: Beaufort, 2004.

Stubbs, Jean, Lila Haines, and Meic F. Haines. *Cuba*. Santa Barbara, CA: Clio Press, 1996.

Sublette, Ned. *Cuba and Its Music: From the First Drums to the Mambo*. Chicago: Chicago Press Review, 2004.

Suchlicki, Jaime. *Cuba: From Columbus to Castro*. New York: Scribner, 1974.

———. *University Students and Revolution in Cuba, 1920–1968*. Coral Gables, FL: University of Miami Press, 1969.

Sweig, Julia. *Cuba: What Everyone Needs to Know*. Oxford: Oxford University Press, 2009.

. *Inside the Cuban Revolution. Fidel Castro and the Urban Underground*. Cambridge, MA.: Harvard University Press, 2002.

Symmes, Patrick. *The Boys from Dolores: Fidel Castro's Schoolmates from Revolution to Exile*. New York: Pantheon Books, 2007.

Szulc, Tad. *Fidel: A Critical Portrait*. New York: William Morrow, 1986.

Taber, Robert. *M-26: The Biography of a Revolution*. New York: Lyle Stuart, 1961.

_____. *The War of the Flea: A Study of Guerrilla Warfare Theory and Practice*. New York: Lyle Stuart, 1965.

"The Man from Havana." *New York Times*. 13 Oct. 1979: 18.

Thomas, Hugh. *Cuba: The Pursuit of Freedom*. New York: Harper & Row, 1998.

Torres, María A. *The Lost Apple: Operation Pedro Pan, Cuban Children in the U.S., and the Promise of a Better Future*. Boston: Beacon Press, 2003.

"U.S. Analysts Say Cuba is Keeping Forces Abroad." *New York Times*. 21 Oct. 1979: 5.

Valdés, Nelson P., and Edwin Lieuwen. *The Cuban Revolution: A Research-Study Guide (1959–1969)*. Albuquerque: University of New Mexico Press, 1971.

Velázquez Fuentes, Francis. *Josué*. Santiago: Ediciones Santiago, 2009.
Whitney, Craig R. "In Moscow, Uncertainty on U.S. Policy." New York
    Times. 12 Oct. 1979. A3.

FILM AND TELEVISION

CBS News. "Rebels of the Sierra Maestra," *CBS News Special Report*,
    May 19, 1957. Don Hewitt and Leslie Midgley, editors, Wendell
    Hoffman, camera, and Robert Taber, reporter. Located at the
    Paley Center for Media, New York.
Lyman, Will, Stephanie Tepper, and William Cran. *Frontline: The Last
    Communist*. Alexandria, VA: PBS Video, 1992.
Splinter, Romano, dir., *November 30th*, FAR (Revolutionary Armed
    Forces) training film with documentary footage and interviews,
    1981. Located in FAR Archives.

AUTHOR'S INTERVIEWS/CORRESPONDENCE

Acuna Núñez, Maritza. Author's interview, Media Luna, 23 April 1999.
Álvarez Sánchez, Jorge. Author's interview, Miami, 4 July 2000.
Álvarez Tabío, Pedro. Author's interviews, Havana, 1 February 2000; 14
    May 2000; 17 May 2000; correspondence, 24–25 August 2002.
Álpizar López, Michael. Author's interview, Havana, 15 April 1998.
Aragón, Dr. Isolina. Author's interview, Havana, January 2000.
Áreas, Alberto. Author's interview, New York, 10 November 1999.
Babiel Gutiérrez, Nelsy. Author's interviews, Havana, 29 May 2000; 19
    December 2006; 8 January 2007; 11 January 2007.
Barnet, Miguel. Author's interviews, Havana, 20 January 2000; 3
    February 2000; 8 January 2007.
Bedoya, Sonya. Author's interview, Havana, 8 January 2007.
Bofill, Julio César. Author's interviews, Havana, 29 August 1999; 1
    September 1999.
Bofill, Raysa. Author's interviews, Havana, 28 December 2000; 8
    January 2000.
Bofill, Raysa, and Ariel Bofill. Author's interview, Havana, 28 August
    1999.
Caignet, Maria Victoria, and Gonzalo Cordova. Author's interview,
    Havana, 14 March 2000.
Castellanas, Nene. Author's phone interview, Havana, 24 March 2008.
Castro, Elsa, and Carmen Vásquez. Author's interview, Havana, 27
    August 1999.
Castro, Elsa. Author's interviews, Havana, 4 February 2000; 26
    February 2000; 22 March 2008; 25 March 2008.
Castro, Mariela. Author's interview, Havana, 9 January 2007.
Corrales, Raúl. Author's interviews, Cojimar, 11 March 1996;26 February
    1997; 8 March 1998; 5 September 1999; 22 March 2000.

Coyula, Mario. Author's interview, Havana, 17 March 2008.
Cruz, Soledad. Author's interview, Havana, 22 December 2005.
De la Rosa, Oscar. Author's interview, Havana, 5 March 1998.
Escalona, Dermidio (Comandante). Author's interview, Havana, 7 March 2000.
Escalona Ramírez, Ana Irma. Author's interviews, Havana, 9 February 2000; 1 April 2000; 5 May 2000; 4 July 2000.
Fernández, Eliseo. Author's interview, Campechuela, 23 April 1999.
Fernández, Pablo Armando. Author's interview, Havana, 10 April 2000.
Fernández, Roberto. Author's interview, Havana, 24 February 2000.
Fernández Gonzalvo, Argelia. Author's interview, Havana, 24 March 2008.
Fernández Soriano, Elbia. Author's interview, Havana, 18 December 2006.
Figueroa, Maria Antonia. Author's interviews, Havana, 9 March 2000; 18 May 2000; 18 June 2000.
García Reyes, Antonio Luis. Author's interview, Havana, 4 January 2007.
García Sosa, Elicier Ángel. Author's interview, Campechuela. 23 April 1999.
Girona, Inez. Author's interview, Havana, 20 January 2000.
Girona, Inez, and Celia Girona. Author's interview, Havana, 9 April 1998.
Girona, Inez, and Julio Girona. Author's interview, Havana, 5 February 2000.
Girona, Celia. Author's interviews, Havana, 5 February 2000; 9 February 2000.
Girona, Julio. Author's interviews, Havana, 30 January 2000; 13 February 2000.
Girona, Mario, and Dolly Gómez. Author's interviews, Havana, 8 April 1998; 15 May 2000.
Gómez Ochoa, Delio (Comandante). Author's interviews, Havana, 3 March 2000; 24 March 2000; 25 March 2000; 10 April 2000.
González Arzuaga, Ernestina, and Pedro Ugando. Author's interview, Havana, 16 February 2000.
Guerra Matos, Felipe. Author's interviews, Havana, 9 March 2000; 3 April 2000; 3 May 2000; 5 May 2000; 3 June 2000; 4 July 2000; (phone) 24 March 2008.
Hernández Garcini, Otto. Author's interview, Havana, 3 January 2006.
Iglesias, Carlos "Nicaragua." Author's interview, Havana, 7 June 2000; phone interview, Havana, 24 March 2008.
Lamarou, Teresa. Author's interviews, Havana, 2 January 2007; 8 January 2007.
Larramendi Rhodes, Dalina. Author's interview, Havana, 1 September 1999.
Larramendi Rhodes, Marilena. Author's interview, Havana, 19 August 1999.
Llópiz, Berta. Author's interview, Havana, 11 June 2000.
Longa, Rita. Author's interview, Havana, 11 April 1998.

Martín, Marilena. Author's interview, Havana, 11 March 1996.
Martínez, Ricardo. Author's interview, Havana, 12 March 2000.
McManus, Jane, and Bill Brent. Author's interview, Havana, January
    2000.
Montero, Elsa. Author's interview, Havana, 29 May 2000.
Novo, Migdalia. Author's interview, Havana, 8 January 2007.
Orozco González, Delio. Author's interview, Manzanillo, 19 April 1999.
Otazo Sánchez, Alicia. Author's interviews, Havana, 21 December
    2006; 28 December 2006; 24 March 2008.
Pacheco, René. Author's interviews, Havana, 14 January 2000; 20 April
    2000.
Palomares, Eugenia. Author's interviews, Havana, 29 December 2005;
    27 December 2006; 2 January 2007.
Pantaleón Fundora, Juan. Author's interview, Havana, 24 March 2000.
Puebla, Tete. Author's interview, Havana, 8 January 2007.
Quevado Pérez, José. Author's interview, Havana, 1 April 2000.
Ramos, Pablo. Author's interview, Havana, 3 September 1999.
Reiners, Gerardo, and Marisela Reiners. Author's interview, Havana, 18
    February 2000.
Reiners, Marisela. Author's interview, Havana, 27 February 2000.
Robaina, Tomás. Author's interview, Havana, 20 March 2008.
Rodríguez Téllez, Eloy. Author's interview, Havana, 17 March 2008.
Rojas, Marta. Author's interview, Havana, 27 December 2006.
Sánchez, Eduardo. Author's interview, Havana, 2 January 2007.
Sánchez Manduley, Chela, and Pedro Álvarez. Author's interview,
    Miami, 7 July 2000.
Sánchez Manduley, Flávia. Author's interviews, Havana, 12 April
    1998; 30 August 1999; 1 September 1999; 6 September 1999;
    7 September 1999; 5 May 2000; 28 May 2000; 4 June 2000;
    correspondence, 18 October 2000.
Sánchez, Sergio. Author's phone interview, Havana, 26 May 2000.
Sánchez, Sergio, and Pepín Sánchez. Author's interview, Havana, 21
    December 2006.
Sarabia, Nydia. Author's interview, Havana, 18 June 2000.
Vásquez Ocaña, Carmen. Author's interviews, Havana, 18 January
    2000; 8 February 2000; 9 February 2000.
Vilias, Lisette. Author's interview, Havana, 10 January 2000.
Villegas Oria, Lucila. Author's interview, Havana, 11 January 2007.

SELECTED DOCUMENTS IN THE
OFFICE OF HISTORICAL AFFAIRS ARCHIVES

Acosta Ferrales, Clodomira, and Lydia Doce [Biographical Materials].
    Comisión de Historia, Regional Guanabacoa, 1970.
Asensio Duque de Heredia, Oscar. *Frank and 30th of November*,
    Testimony [n.d.].
Castro, Fidel. Letter to Celia Sánchez, 15 June 1957.

——. Letter to Celia Sánchez, July 1957.

——. Letter to Celia Sánchez, 1 August 1957.

——. Letter to Celia Sánchez. 11 August 1957.

——. Letter to Celia Sánchez. 14 August 1957.

Fajardo, Manuel. Testimony regarding landing of the *Granma* [n.d].

Frank: Testimonies about Frank. Enzo Infante, Luis Clerge, Gloria Cuadras, María Antonia Figueroa, René Ramos Latour. File of documents.

Guevara, Ernesto (Che). *Lydia* [n.d].

Mendoza Reboredo, Jorge Enrique. Obituary, *Granma*, 26 February 1994, p. 1.

País, Frank. Letter to Fidel Castro, 5 July 1957. *Presencia de Lidia Doce*. Booklet, 1974.

Sánchez, Celia. Letter to Arturo Duque Estrada [n.d.].

——. Letter to Elsa Casto, Manzanillo [n.d.].

——. Letter to Noelia [n.d.].

——. Letter to Dr. Manuel Sánchez Silveira, 19 September 1955.

——. Letter to nieces Alicia and Elena Otazo Sánchez, 10 May 1956.

——. Letter to Fidel Castro, 7 July 1957.

——. Letter to Fidel Castro, 9 July 1957.

——. Letter to Fidel Castro, 11 July 1957.

——. Letter to Fidel Castro, 16 July 1957.

——. Letter to Frank País, incomplete, n.d., ca. 16 July 1957.

——. Letter to Haydée Santamaria, 31 July 1957.

——. Letter to Haydée Santamaria, 2 August 1957.

——. Letter to Dr. Manuel Sánchez Silviera, 5 September 1957.

——. Letter to Fidel Castro, October 1957.

Index

Page numbers in italics refer to photos, maps, and their captions.